AMERICAN HARVEST

Also by Marie Mutsuki Mockett

Picking Bones from Ash

Where the Dead Pause, and the Japanese Say Goodbye

★ ★ ★ ★ ★ ★ ★ ★ ★ ★ ★ ★ ★ ★ ★ ★ ★ ★ ★ ★

AMERICAN HARVEST

★ ★ ★ ★ ★ ★ ★ ★ ★ ★ ★ ★ ★ ★ ★ ★ ★ ★ ★ ★

GOD, COUNTRY, AND FARMING
IN THE HEARTLAND

MARIE MUTSUKI MOCKETT

Graywolf Press

Photographs on pages 3, 7, 129, 285, and 377 copyright © Sumaya Agha. Photograph of *Joy in the City* by Bernie Wilke on page 365 reproduced with the permission of the artist; photograph by Juston Wolgemuth.

This publication is made possible, in part, by the voters of Minnesota through a Minnesota State Arts Board Operating Support grant, thanks to a legislative appropriation from the arts and cultural heritage fund. Significant support has also been provided by the National Endowment for the Arts, Target, the McKnight Foundation, the Lannan Foundation, the Amazon Literary Partnership, and other generous contributions from foundations, corporations, and individuals. To these organizations and individuals we offer our heartfelt thanks.

This book is made possible through a partnership with the College of Saint Benedict, and honors the legacy of S. Mariella Gable, a distinguished teacher at the College. Support has been provided by the Manitou Fund as part of the Warner Reading Program.

Note to Reader: Certain conversations have been reconstructed to the best of the author's abilities and certain names have been changed. In some cases, incidents have been compressed to accommodate the narrative flow.

Published by Graywolf Press
250 Third Avenue North, Suite 600
Minneapolis, Minnesota 55401

www.graywolfpress.org

Published in the United States of America

ISBN 978-1-64445-017-8

2 4 6 8 9 7 5 3 1
First Graywolf Printing, 2020

Library of Congress Control Number: 2019933485

Jacket design: Kyle G. Hunter

Jacket photo © Sumaya Agha

For my father

We love because it's the only true adventure . . .

—NIKKI GIOVANNI

AMERICAN HARVEST

★ ★ ★ ★

PROLOGUE

★ ★ ★ ★

THIS IS THE LAND OF PRIMARY COLORS: red combine, blue sky, yellow wheat. Under the earth, pancaked layers of sediment conceal elusive minerals coveted by men, and the strewn, jigsaw bones of monsters awaiting reassembly. Untouched, the surface is a prairie, a tough lattice of grasses and shrubs that frame the darting meadowlarks and snakes who work together with the ants to survive dry days. There is little moisture, though winters can bring three feet of snow; rain will bring only half that. The Oglala Sioux, the Comanche, the Kiowa, and other Native Americans who once lived on this land by themselves hunted for buffalo and foraged for berries, nuts, and wild potatoes. But Europeans supplanted those potatoes for wheat. The buffalo have dwindled. The Indians who live here no longer predominate. Now the land is dotted with windmills and farms, though the coyotes still sing in the evening, and you can train your eyes to spot the thin caramel-colored frames of the antelope camouflaged by kicked-up dust smearing the spaces between the clusters of hardy yucca.

The primary colors give way to gradations of scarlet, pink, and lemon in the early morning when the sun peers over the horizon. At sunset, the sky often employs a darker palette, particularly if the light is bruised by a storm or smoke from a wildfire. You can sit on top of a cylindrical, fifteen-foot-high steel grain bin and watch the sun go from one end of the horizon to the other. Your view might be impeded by clouds, or "weather," by which is meant rain and that old enemy hail. You can do this and feel just how tiny a passenger you are on the sphere that is your home as you whirl around and around the sun. You can feel the vastness of the sky, the inch-by-inch eternity of a day.

You might see a storm. Or rather: you would feel it first. Sitting there on the grain bin, there is a cool exhalation on your face. And though the temperature fluctuates during the day, this cold breath is an intruder. It lets you know that Something Else has entered the prairie. Sometimes the storms stay far away, and you can watch them as a man observes a game of football; they are *out there*, crawling on wispy gray legs across the prairie. Sometimes the sky slices and sputters with lightning, and you can watch that from a safe distance, too, though you shouldn't forget to look behind you. Things come up from behind sometimes.

The rain might come toward you at a great velocity, generally growing first in the west. Clouds gather and heave, vapor massing. If you see this great gray, inky thing racing toward you, and if you are near shelter, scurry off the grain bin and into someplace dry, even if you are just getting into your pickup truck. Because you will want to be inside before the hail or the lightning commits its annihilation of the crop.

When it isn't raining, you feel a quiet and persistent sentience. All around you, things are growing. Wheat seeds sprout and climb toward the sun, a fraction of an inch a day. This is a thing to consider. As you sit on the grain bin that is your perch, for miles and miles around you, plants are reaching. Sunflowers turn their shaggy manes toward the sun, and in the summer, their black kernels swell and grow fat. Things aspire, reach, ripen. You might even hear the crack of the hard seed shell when the first thirsty tongue of the plant slides out, looking for wet dirt. Maybe you hear the mass exhalation of thousands of kernels of wheat as they fatten into the little balloons that will become seeds. This world is alive and busy. It requires that you pay attention.

The smallest elements are in perpetual motion, always creating or decaying, directed by some invisible force. Perhaps this is why it is easy here to feel that God exists, and that he inspires awe.

We focus on the plants—maybe because we eat them. But our story really starts with the soil. Without the soil there is nothing in which to grow the wheat, nothing to hold the moisture, and nothing to hold the tractors and trucks and bins.

This is the story of the land and the people who own it and how they learn over and over again who owns what and how best to coax things out of the land, and how planting and harvesting teach them what to believe, or how they try to take what they believe and plant it in the land.

★ ★ ★ ★

PART ONE

★ ★ ★ ★

ONE

I AM FROM THE COASTS: seventeen years in California, four years of college in New York City, more years of ping-ponging between the East and West Coasts (Cambridge, the South Bay, back to New York City, and San Francisco). I have routinely flown over the rest of the country. When I look out of the windows of an airplane, I can see them down there: the flyover states, otherwise known as "the heartland."

Let's take seven. Texas, Oklahoma, Kansas, Colorado, Nebraska, Wyoming, and Idaho. When you fly over—if you do—do you see the checkerboard of monoculture fields, the eerie circular green shapes formed by robotic sprinklers, and the small towns connected by twists of interstate? What do you think?

I know what I am supposed to think—mall towns, white, ignorant, superstitious—but I don't think these things.

Perhaps my resistance comes from the accident of my birth. My parents represent two countries previously at war: my father, America, and my mother, Japan. They overcame in one generation the enmity of their parents and governments to have me. I would like to believe reconciliation is this simple. I'd like to believe that even if chaos lingers in the structure of our cells, our hearts need not be solely shaped by the experiences of our parents.

There is also my family's farm, which is located in two of the seven states I mentioned—Nebraska and Colorado—though the majority is in Nebraska, in the southwest corner of the Panhandle. Our family, the Mocketts, has owned this farm—which once exceeded seven thousand acres—for over one hundred years, and while most settlers who were homesteaders have sold their land and moved to the city, my family is part of an odd minority that held on to their land and continues to farm it. We did this even though we, too, had all relocated to urban centers: my father near San Francisco, my uncle in Seattle, and my aunt in Denver. My father and his two siblings each owned a third of the farm, and we were joint landlords, returning to Nebraska every so often to check on the crops.

As a child, I went to Nebraska every summer for harvest. After I became an adult, my father always asked me to go with him, but I mostly didn't, because I was busy in the city. Then one year, when I was between jobs, I flew from New York to California, got into my father's car, and we drove the twelve hundred miles from my parents' house to the center of the country. We did this in about twenty-three hours, because that is how he liked to do it: no motel stops. That was how his father did things, and all the men in the family going back for generations did the same; you drove—buggy or car—until you got to wherever you were going.

We drove straight to a field of wheat. Only now does it occur to me to wonder how he knew which field to go to. It was 2004, a time before Siri and Alexa had the answers to everything. My father must have made a call at a pay phone when we stopped for gas hours before. He must have reached someone who knew what the rough plan for the day was going to be. And then he must have guessed where the crew would be and driven out to the field, and there we were.

It had been ten years since I'd last been to harvest, and while things were mostly the same, the equipment had gotten bigger. I stood in a field while my father took his canteen and went off to talk to a truck driver to find out the latest protein reading. A little while later, Eric, who cut our wheat each summer, drove up in his pickup truck and stopped beside me. I don't know where he came from; he must have been over the hill and then driven over to see who had churned up dust. Eric rolled down the window and fixed me with a tolerant look. He did not smile. He even seemed to scowl. "Well," he said. "You said that you'd be back."

"Yes." I didn't know what else to say.

"Ten years. Took you long enough."

I felt silly standing there in my city jeans and my sneakers already filled with burrs; my father had on boots. The sun was strong on my face; Eric had on a baseball cap. I thought he looked a lot like Kevin Costner.

Eric glanced out at the country with a squint of interest, as though he had suddenly spotted an antelope. But he hadn't. He was just squinting. "You'll want your water," he finally said. "Gets so dry out here you won't notice."

"Yes. Thank you." I had already forgotten about water. My father had made sure both the canteen and the thermos were full before we went to the field; he was always reminding me to drink plenty of water, but I had left the thermos in the car.

For a moment I thought Eric might say something else. But then, without making any more eye contact, he rolled up his window and drove away, leaving me standing there in the stubble.

It rained a little while later and my father came back to me. "Nothing to do but go to town," he said gently. He nodded at the sky. "Looks like it will be here for a while." And so we took the lonely stretch of highway back into Kimball, Nebraska, where my father grew up and where his parents had been born, and where his grandparents had been homesteaders.

We did not have a house in town anymore; my grandmother had sold it to the town pharmacist when she moved into an assisted living facility in Denver. The house had been the biggest brick building in Kimball, built in 1921 to accommodate a banker. It had French doors and a majestic maple staircase, and my grandmother had filled her home with objects collected from her travels around the world, first undertaken on steamships and later by plane. But all that was gone. Now when we visited Kimball, we stayed in "the bunkhouse," a windowless three-room wooden shelter erected inside an aluminum Quonset hut that stood across the street from the Union Pacific Railroad tracks. The bunkhouse had been built in anticipation of the loss of the family home. It came with a kitchen unit and a bathroom and shower, sleeping quarters and a lounging area, all of which were kept cool with a powerful air conditioning unit. And this is where my father and I went now.

My uncle, then around sixty-five, and my cousin Paul, forty, were already inside the bunkhouse, seated on reclining armchairs rescued from my grandmother's house. "Hello!" my uncle greeted me. His eyes sparkled with a dynamic mix of intelligence and mischief. He had a slight hunch, resulting, I suppose, from years of looking through microscopes and at lab reports.

"Hello," I said. I was nervous around my uncle because I knew my father was uneasy around him too. I was more comfortable around Paul, who was ten years older than me and worked as a computer engineer.

We were all seated in the armchairs, waiting for the fields to dry.

When I had told my friends in New York that I was heading to the farm, nearly all of them had been curious. How big was the farm? What did we raise? And, nearly all of them asked, was my farm organic? Whole Foods had recently opened in New York City, and we urbanites had been learning to shop its choice meats and produce. So I asked the men: "Is our farm organic?"

There was a long pause as the men chewed and swallowed cashew nuts. Someone had brought a large container of cashews from Costco, and it was sitting on the tool bench in the main room. When Eric came to visit not long after, he would eat a handful, and after he left, the men would say that it was good we had cashews because Eric liked them.

"No," my uncle said.

"Why not?"

He looked amused, and his voice, when he answered, was shot through with mock wonder. "Why don't we farm organic? Or why does anyone farm organic?" He was a scientist and he liked questions, though there was sometimes the implication that not all questions should be asked. *"What is organic?"* In fact, my question might be downright useless.

But I didn't think it was useless. I felt a flutter of panic. It was my responsibility now to keep my question alive, as if I were a nurse in the NICU of premature questions.

"Most of my friends in New York ask me right away if we farm organic."

"No one farms organic." We were in Nebraska, which was not the same as New York at all.

"Why?"

We were a family that prided itself on curiosity. When my grandmother was alive, she read books, magazines, and newspapers (the *New Yorker* was a favorite) and sent us all articles to read. If a book particularly impressed her—*The Fatal Shore* by Robert Hughes comes to mind—she shared her copy with each of her children, and they discussed their reading experience with her either in person or during a Sunday phone conversation.

The star of our family was my uncle, the particle physicist. Stories about him were legion. My grandparents met as children in Nebraska, but left home in the twenties, meeting again later as adults, and starting their own family in California. But in 1947, when my father was nine and my uncle twelve, the family moved back to Nebraska to care for the farm and aging family. By high school my uncle was so irritated by the inferiority of his new teachers that he simply took over the physics class and taught it himself. He was also elected student body president. In retaliation for all this confidence, his science teacher gave him a C, and my grandmother, armed with copious evidence, marched to the principal's office and made sure the grade was overturned so her talented, if somewhat precocious and arrogant, son could go to the best college. He went to Reed College, in Oregon, then to MIT, and eventually worked at the Stanford Linear Accelerator Center. Absolute faith—joy, even—in the power of reason persists in the family.

Once, when my uncle called my father, he said: "In a decade we will completely understand the nature of matter."

"*I* don't think it will be *quite* that easy," my father said to me after hanging up.

Another time, when I was an adult, I watched my uncle and my cousin Paul inspect a wheat field damaged by hail. They plucked a few heads of grain and counted the number of kernels missing. From this they deduced the average number of kernels missing per plant, then the number of stalks in a square foot, then the acreage, and then they began to try to predetermine how much insurance they were owed. Along the way they bickered and conceded and recalculated as necessary. This kind of thing counted as *fun* in my family. I watched with repressed horror. I understood what they were doing, but this level of granularity was not how my brain wanted to spend its time.

I tried. Once, when I was reading Stephen Hawking's *A Brief History of Time*, I'd asked my uncle how a particle could be in two places at once. He had snapped at me that this was not at all the point of quantum mechanics. "We can't predict the *location* of a particle, because observation appears to change what's being observed."

"So the particle is in two places at once?" I asked again.

"That's *not* what I said." His bark had been so filled with venom that I had stopped discussing the book with him, lest the soft tissue that was my stupidity be even more perilously on display. (I would remain confused about the concept of quantum mechanics until I saw a nice five-minute YouTube video posted online by Dr. Quantum, which succinctly illustrates the concept via an animated version of the double slit experiment. I recommend it.)

But back to that afternoon in the Quonset with my uncle, cousin, and father.

"Okay," I said. I told them that my question was a kind of red herring appetizer. Here was the main course. "Why are our farmers and harvesters, who are conservative Christians, okay with GMOs, while people in the city, who believe in evolution, are obsessed with organic food?"

Now the quality of my question was not rejected outright. Instead, the men looked amused, as though the question were a new toy. We began the dissection.

My uncle peered over his glasses. "Our farmers are Christian and the people in the city are atheists. You are sure?"

I said I did not know for sure, but the Knowellses, who farmed our land, appeared to be some sort of Christian; the women all wore skirts and no makeup.

"Aren't they Mennonites?" my cousin Paul asked.

"I don't know exactly what they are," my uncle said.

"Didn't you ever ask?" I was surprised.

"That would be rude." Despite being the most rational member of our family, my uncle observed the social rules instilled in him by my grandmother.

"I'm sure they are Christian," I said. "I never hear them swear."

"Eric doesn't swear either," said my father.

"Is Eric Mennonite?"

"Something else. He told me once. I forget," my father said. "It wasn't important to me. He's Eric."

"Good man," said Paul.

"Very bright," my father added.

"Very bright. Eats a lot of cashews," said my uncle. His real name was Paul, and he was named after his father, Paul, and he also named his son Paul. This was a lot of Pauls. My father thought it was stupid to have so many Pauls in the family and that it was a sign of needing, blindly, to cling to tradition when forging out on one's own would be the sensible thing to do. My father thought the presence of so many Pauls had to do with a lack of ingenuity, which he told me is what *our* family had, because we were creative. We were artists.

For many years, though, I didn't know we were artists. I thought we were the black sheep of the family. My father didn't have a steady job while I was growing up, loved art, and married a Japanese woman long before it was common for a white man to end up with an Asian woman. I saw us not as interesting and unusual but as odd, even though my worldly, globe-trotting grandmother unfairly favored me because my mother was not white and I was mixed and would be raised with two languages.

But to me it looked as if my uncle Paul had done things correctly. He went to the best schools and had four children and saved all his money and was adored by his peers and married a woman from New England who was blond. He was on the opposite side of the political spectrum from my father, who did not like parties or labels, but voted liberal. My uncle was a steadfast Republican, and never forgave Bill Clinton for killing the Super Collider, which was going to be built in Texas; instead, my uncle went to CERN, in Switzerland, to help build instruments that could detect muons for study. Together, my father and uncle perfectly mirrored the rules of birth order: the older brother, conservative, and the younger, liberal.

But there was also this third path—the farm. In this world, my father and his brother were aligned and agreed on attitudes like "Eric is very bright." They weren't pandering when they said this; I had heard it often. I also had no idea what it was that made Eric very bright in their eyes, as Eric neither went to the very best schools, nor seemed to have much interest in J. M. W. Turner's ability to capture the atmospheric and elusive mutability of light and air that foreshadowed the rise of Cy Twombly. It was somewhere in here—the farm—that my father and uncle were bound together. The land bound us all.

"How do you know your friends are atheists?" my uncle asked me now.

"Most people I know don't believe in God in any conventional sense. They don't believe God controls the world. Do you?" I asked.

He didn't answer. His mind was chewing on the other parts of my question, and my cousin Paul was beaming. Paul liked the question. Beside me, my father was also turning the question over in his mind. As they did, he enjoyed deciding if a question was a good one or not. But he was a gentle person, and his impulse, like mine, was to try to make the question the best question it could be.

"You mean," my dad said, "that while the Christians believe that God created everything, they like GMOs. Well, Marie. They are farmers."

"The GMOs have helped us," my cousin said.

"I don't know why people in the city want organic," my father said. "I don't even think they know what organic is."

"It's a fad," said my uncle.

"But people like it," I said.

"I don't think they know what it is," my father repeated.

"I don't even know how we would raise organic," said my uncle.

"There is no reason to be organic," my father said.

"All food has been modified. There is no *natural*," my uncle said.

"People worry about pesticides . . . ," I began.

"We have never used pesticides and we don't farm organically. You are confusing things."

"You think," said my cousin in his summarizing voice, "that the Christians don't mind playing with genetic material, even though they believe God created everything and some of them don't like stem cells, and your atheist friends like the idea of food in which the genetic material hasn't been modified, even though they don't believe in God, and even though all food has been modified."

"Right," I said. "So if we don't believe in God, and we think everything can be explained by evolution and genes, why does it matter if we alter the DNA?"

"Ah."

They were all quiet. It was a good question. It was based on some assumptions, but it was an intriguing question. Finally, my uncle patted me on the shoulder. "You'll spend a long time with this one."

At the end of harvest that year, my father and I took the slow road back to California. He liked meandering drives home and a gradual reentry to city life. He bought me a pair of Hopi bear paw earrings in Colorado and a pawned turquoise bracelet in Utah. In Nevada we took Highway 50, "the Loneliest Road in America." We listened to music— Jussi Björling and Robert Merrill singing "The Pearl Fishers"—and we discussed "Marie's question," coming to no clearer conclusion than we had in the Quonset. Sometimes we were silent. That was the last time we went to the farm together.

Before he died, my father said: "If I die, you should trust the Knowellses. And you should trust Eric." He said this to me because he knew that if he died, the farm would come to me, and I would need help. Eric would know all the ways in which I did not know how to do anything, which is to say that I can't drive tractors or operate machinery and, most of all, that I do not know how to fix things that break, because I was raised in the city and not on the farm. Eric fixes everything.

Even though I had met Eric in my twenties, it wasn't until after my father's death, when I was thirty-seven, that I got to know him well. One summer in Nebraska during harvest, after my father died, I was in the pickup with Eric on our way back to town from the wheat fields, when we saw a party of four in a minivan by the side of the road. A pudgy and pasty middle-aged man was bent over the fender. When he straightened, he was frowning and his shoulders were slouched. He did not—as would Eric—move to find a set of tools inside his car, or begin tinkering or unscrewing bolts. He did nothing to suggest he had even the vaguest idea how to fix the minivan.

"Michigan plates. Road trip. I think they're a Mormon family," said Eric to no one in particular. He pulled over.

When Eric got out of the pickup, he walked slowly, hands in pockets. We—his hired help, his son Juston, and I—followed behind. It is a farmer thing to walk and then stand with hands in pockets. The slow walk is reflexive and has the effect of scaring as few people as possible. I have often wondered if it's a holdover from the days when most farmers raised animals and had to make sure the colts and calves would not be startled by men coming into the paddock.

The man with the car trouble was an automotive engineer. Later, at the trailers, the crew would point out that the automotive engineer couldn't fix his own car. "That's called irony," Eric's son Juston would explain.

There was a Brigham Young University bumper sticker on the rear window of the minivan. Eric was right. They were Mormons. He dropped to one knee and examined the bumper of the minivan. He pulled a pair of pliers out of the leather pouch strapped to his waist. He never went anywhere without his pliers—except onto an airplane. All the boys had pliers. Eric and the Mormon conferred under the car with the pliers, and their voices were muffled. Then their heads came back out.

"Your fender's loose and it's bangin' the tire. I can fix that for you so it holds till you get home," Eric said. In situations like this, his face is mostly expressionless. He doesn't smile extra hard to convey friendliness, which is what I would do—what many of my city friends would do. With Eric, it is the opposite. His default face for strangers is a kind of blankness. He smiles in private. Were we all like this one hundred years ago? Did we all smile in private, and not at the bank tellers, waiters, and taxi drivers?

All the same, the Michigan Mormon automotive engineer regarded him quizzically at first, and then it was as though an understanding overtook him. There passed between them an unspoken exchange I could not read. It had something to do with the way Eric said he could fix the problem, and with the two of them being men. I don't know how else to put it. It all happened so quickly. Then I wondered if there was some secret Christian body language that told them that the car could be fixed and Eric was to be trusted. I thought about the stories of history, about a man meeting another man in the desert and drawing an arcing line in the sand and the other man mirroring the line so the two lines made a fish, establishing that they were both Christians. Nothing like that happened here; we were standing on asphalt. I thought all this before I learned that many people do not consider Mormons to be Christians.

The people in the minivan followed us to the trailer park where Eric was staying. We parked beside the service truck, which was named Lily. Then, with the aid of various bolts and drills, Eric and his crew fixed the minivan and sent the people on their way back to Michigan. Eric does this kind of thing without thinking. At least that's how it looks to me. Much later he would tell me: "I don't help everyone. Just sometimes God leads me to do it."

Eric grew up in Lancaster County, Pennsylvania; his parents were descended from German immigrants, and were farmers. His ancestors were Anabaptist, a branch of Christianity whose most familiar adherents are the Amish and Mennonites. The term "Anabaptist" means "to baptize again," and was originally an insult leveled by Catholics and Lutherans. A motivating factor among Anabaptists in the fifteenth century in Europe was to act in response to the Catholics who baptized infants. Since a baby hardly knows he is being baptized, let alone why, the Anabaptists argued that baptism ought to take place in adulthood, when one is conscious of one's actions; the earliest members were thus "rebaptized."

We usually refer to the people in Europe who reacted against the Catholic version of Christianity as "Protestants." But while Protestants, like Catholics, were comfortable both managing churches and influencing the governments of countries, the Anabaptists were not. Eric's forefathers never ran a country or a kingdom, and have also long practiced nonresistance and nonviolence. This made them easy targets of prejudice, persecution, and, on occasion, murder.

Past generations of Eric's Anabaptist relatives would have dressed "plain," which means the men would have worn black suits, and the women dresses, no makeup, and bonnets on their heads. (I have heard more-modern residents of Lancaster County refer to Old Order Anabaptists as "bonnet people," as a quick way to explain where on the scale of old-fashionedness a family lies.) Eric might have stayed in Pennsylvania, farming corn, soybeans, and wheat, as his parents had, were it not for an article he saw as a child in *National Geographic*.

In 1972, the journalist Noel Grove penned a story in the magazine, replete with stunning color photos, about the "custom harvesters" who trek across the middle of America to cut the country's wheat. Here were men in jeans and checkered shirts, covered with dust and sweat as they commandeered behemoth machines and traversed the interstate highway system to remove the wheat from fields through a combination of skills requiring nothing short of primal masculine mastery. They were as strong, tough, and smart as the blades in their combines. Speak to most harvesters of Eric's generation and their eyes will glow as they remember that photojournalistic essay and how it ignited in them a desire to follow the same path, which would take them to the interior of the country. Speak to men who live in farm towns and who watched the harvest crews come and go every year, but who themselves never made it out on the road, and they will all say with deep yearning: "I always wanted to do that."

At nineteen, Eric went on his first harvest trek as a hired hand for an established custom harvester. Years later, when the original harvester retired, Eric took over his boss's route, and continued to build and expand his business until it became the reliable machine it is today. There are currently about 450 members of US Custom Harvesters, Inc., the umbrella organization to which most US custom harvesters, including Eric, belong. No official data exists on the percentage of US acres cut by custom crews, though Eric says he remembers once hearing that 50 percent of all US wheat is cut by teams like his. The US Custom Harvesters organization does figure that the average cost to cut one thousand acres of wheat with a custom crew is about $35,000, while the cost of a combine alone can set a farmer back more than $250,000, and this sum does not account for the cost of fuel or a wheat truck. It is cheaper for most farmers to hire a crew for cutting.

Prior to World War II, farmers cut their own wheat with machines pulled either by draught horse or tractor. The older machines used a rotating sickle—like a lawn mower—which cut off the heads of stalks of wheat and either tied them into sheaves, via a machine called a "binder," or cut the wheat close to the heads, via something called a "header," which sent the cut grain up a conveyer belt and into a wagon pulled alongside by horses or mules. In both cases, the bundles or cut heads were threshed by a separate machine, which removed the grain from the chaff. While farmers owned their own cutting equipment, they didn't always own their own threshers; enterprising larger farmers invested in that machinery to harvest their own crops and, for a fee, let smaller famers who could not afford to purchase the equipment take turns threshing their crops. Sometimes the threshers became migrants, moving from town to town. Variations on this system persisted from the settling of the heartland, in the 1870s, to the 1920s.

The combine harvester "combined" the jobs of the headers, binders, and threshers into one machine. The first patented version was manufactured in Michigan in the 1830s by Hiram Moore, but farmers, always a thrifty bunch, were reluctant to invest money in new equipment, no matter how practical. World War I changed things. Hired hands were sent to war, and the labor-intensive binders, threshers, and headers suffered a loss of attention. The all-in-one combine came to the rescue. The price of grain went up, giving farmers more capital, and the combine was put into production, with sales increasing throughout the twenties. By the thirties, use of the combine had spread across the Great Plains.

World War II changed everything again. The government required greater output from farmers to meet wartime demands, and harvesting was seen as a patriotic duty. Meanwhile, the draft removed hired help from farms. These forces converged to send a new wave of pioneers across the prairie: the custom harvesters, who would haul their gear over state lines to help reap the wheat of shorthanded farmers. Though there were years of expansion and contraction after the war, custom harvesting, once seen as a stopgap measure during wartime, continued to evolve, with the new interstate highway system eventually making the transportation of equipment easier.

Routes across state lines were established by men who handed down their itineraries to their sons, and harvesting became a family business. By the time I was born, our farm in Nebraska had used custom harvesters for decades. In California, my father would get a call from Ray Knowells—the man who planted and looked after our crop in our absence—that the wheat was ripe. My father would immediately pack his sedan, and we would get in and drive the twenty-three hours to Nebraska. Upon arrival, we looked forward to seeing a man named Harvey—the first Texan I'd ever met. He would travel to our farm and remove his hat when he spoke to us. I'd listen to him talk with an inflected drawl and wonder what angled and whorled place he could have come from that had twisted his voice into such a corkscrew.

It was on one of his annual treks, in the early 1990s, that Eric first met my father in Nebraska. Harvey from Texas had long retired, and our replacement crew had broken down somewhere in Colorado, so my father had gone off in search of new help and found Eric looking for work by the grain elevators. By the end of the summer, he had decided to ask Eric back; the men had worked well together. No grain had been spilled, no neighbor's field had been cut by accident, and no tempers had flared. Eric and my father became friends.

Over the nine years since my father died, Eric and I have talked a lot about farming. I have visited his farm in Pennsylvania and seen him on our farm during harvest. I have also gotten to know his wife, Emily, and his sons, Winston and Juston. When Eric's older son, Winston, got married, I attended the wedding and the reception, held in a barn. I have also gone to Eric's church. Once, Eric asked me if any of my friends go to church.

"No," I said.

"What about your friends who are people of color? Or from other countries?"

"They don't either."

"Why? They could find a community."

"A lot of them don't feel welcome," I said.

"Church is for everyone. Jesus loved everyone."

He said this with such genuine, heartfelt feeling, I wasn't entirely sure how to counter it. Is it really possible for everyone to love everyone? Can we all just gather and decide that we are all the same and that Jesus loves us, and that we will love one another as he did, and that's all there is to it? History seems more complicated than this, and I said so to Eric. He didn't say much in reply.

Sometime after my father died, I asked Eric my organic-versus-GMOs question and he answered the first part of this question definitively: we should trust the science of farming.

"The science is good," he said. "I trust it."

Addressing creationism versus evolution was trickier because here we were discussing God. Everything I had been taught in school inclined me toward respecting the beliefs of every individual. But I knew a deeper set of rules lay beneath that simple pledge to be tolerant. The unspoken dictum sounded like this: If a person wants to adhere to the misguided notion that man walked at the same time as the dinosaurs, well, that's fine. But obviously no one who believes that Adam and the T. rex fought over the same pool of lava is going to end up with the intellectual tools necessary to, say, come up with the iPhone. Steve Jobs wasn't a creationist. And for a while, this was part of my problem with all of the "Eric is very bright" comments my family made. If he believed in creationism, how bright could he be?

It turned out that Eric liked questions, and the harder the better. He wasn't the kind of person who answered a question glibly and then hoped you didn't bring it up again. Instead, he would return to my questions over and over. If I asked him why we planted mostly wheat in Nebraska, he would tell me that the climate and moisture there suited wheat. But then he would also take me to see a cornfield in Pennsylvania, so I could compare its soil to the soil in Nebraska. After that, he would never stop asking me to look at the soil of the farms we visited. If I asked him if his church condoned cloning, he would say it did in some circumstances, and then take me to meet different dairy farmers in Lancaster County, so I could ask them directly about cloned cows (answer: a "good milker" is something you might want to clone). At some point, Eric figured if he was going to answer my questions completely, he needed to understand me.

He came to the city. He said his main goal in coming to New York, other than to see me, was a field trip to Whole Foods, which he had never experienced. And so we found ourselves one afternoon taking the escalator down to the basement of the Time Warner Center and entering the resplendence of organic produce, free-range poultry, and antibiotic-free meat and cheese that is "America's Healthiest Grocery Store."

He and Emily had worn red windbreakers on their visit so I wouldn't lose them in a crowd, but they needn't have bothered. There stood Eric, a bulwark of calm, permanence, and stillness amid the quietly aggressive shopping maneuvers of trim women in Lululemon athletic gear and men in J.Crew jackets.

What would Eric, who has harvested literally billions of tons of wheat with his combine crews, make of the shoppers grabbing bags full of quinoa and Hudson Valley–grown apples?

Eric waded through the store with his thumbs tucked into his belt loops. He moved half as fast as everyone else. I watched him examine carrots, pumpkins, and squash with patience and purpose. If a subterranean disaster had befallen us, he could have held up the building on his shoulders, Atlas-like. Together, we navigated sunflower oil, bulgur, and dairy products, and he occasionally offered up a comment or asked a question in his low, measured cadence.

After twenty minutes, grim determination had taken over Eric's face. "Marie," he said, slow and deliberate. "This thing about organic. I want you to understand. It is *marketing*. Do not fall for it. You know what farming is and how it works. Do not fall for these labels."

We went to dinner that night at Per Se, owned and run by celebrity chef Thomas Keller, because I explained that dining out was one of the major ways New Yorkers understand food. On the menu that evening were doughnuts dipped in chocolate. I tried to explain the various ways these doughnuts were to be interpreted: as an American delight, a high-end take on a low-class food, a stab at irony. "Irony is important in the city," I said.

I watched Eric finish his glass of wine—one of only three times I have seen him drink alcohol. And then he quietly commented: "This question about organics and evolution, Marie. It's really a question about . . . the divide." That's what he said. "It's not just about God and science. Not really."

Any number of things can happen to your mind if you drive across

the country every year for thirty years. Eric had patiently studied the
details of his repeated trips, like a monk reading and rereading the
Bible. I imagined him squinting at these details until they coalesced,
and what he saw, he likes to tell me, was "the divide." He thought I
was seeing it too. And because I saw the divide, at dinner that night he
suggested that perhaps one day I would do his harvesting route with
him. "That's the best way to understand the country." My question, he
seemed to imply, couldn't be answered by a sentence or a conversation;
it required a journey.

My own family had always expressed the wish to one day do the
entire harvest route. My cousin Paul had gone partway with one of our
former harvest crews, but had never done the entire thing. "That would
be interesting," I said.

Eric told me he wanted to share his America because he feared how
little we have come to understand each other. The divide between city
and country, once just a crack in the dirt, was now a chasm into which
objects, people, grace, and love all fell and disappeared.

I knew better than to grab at the invitation right away; Eric's people
don't grab. Also, I wasn't ready. When I saw him, Eric would occasionally bring up the idea that I might go on harvest. As the political tensions in the United States grew increasingly grave, he seemed to be
thinking about the possibility more and more.

"If you come with us, you'll meet farmers," he promised me one
summer in Nebraska. "You'll meet hunters. You'll meet some racists,"
he conceded. It was clear the invitation had moved from a vague idea to
something he had imagined more concretely.

"Will I be in danger?"

He smiled. "No. 'Course, I'll protect you if you are. But you won't
be. You'll meet closeted Democrats. Guys who will make George Bush
make sense. Lots of Christians. I want you to see the Tetons and the
wheat in Idaho. I want you to see the sunsets there. I want you to know
this America."

He didn't say it, but I knew that God had spoken to him to share all
this with me.

And then I also thought, How hard could it be to go on the road with
him? It might be like traveling to a foreign country and learning another language and hearing how to see as locals do. I am good at this.
As a child in Japan, I was a little alarmed when so many of the adults

I encountered would confide in me with statements like "We want you to understand our culture." They wanted me to learn to look for frogs in rice paddies, or to appreciate half-wilted cherry blossoms over those in full bloom. They did this, I now know, because my face was often the first outsider's face they had ever seen, and certainly I was the first foreigner with whom they could converse in their language after the war. It had felt like a weird pressure at the time, but it has happened so often, I have come to think of it as normal. How hard could it be to go on the road with Eric, through the middle of America, which is, after all, my own country, and try to learn something about it?

Maybe then I would know what I think about them, the flyover states. And so began my journey to see the heartland.

TWO

ERIC'S ANNUAL ROUTE always starts in Texas because that is where American wheat first ripens. The crew will follow the wheat belt north as it continues to mature; the wheat ripens at a rate of about twenty miles a day. Over the years, Eric has built up relationships with farmers who own land in each of the seven states, and they all work on the assumption that he is coming to cut their crops. Each year the arrangements are made on a handshake; there are no paper contracts.

For harvest this year, Eric is traveling with Emily and Juston. His older son, Winston, usually accompanies him, too, but his wife is expecting a new child, and he will stay home in Pennsylvania with her. Two other family members are with the harvest crew: Bradford and Bethany, who are brother and sister, are Eric's nephew and niece. Bradford is twenty-two and Bethany will turn twenty while on the road. The others are young men from the community back home. Competition to get into Eric's crew is fierce, and most of these boys will have called a year in advance for an interview and a chance to participate. Rain or shine, they will be paid a daily flat fee, and will be fed, housed, and given a chance to see the United States. This year there is Luther, the oldest at twenty-five; Michael, who is twenty-two; Samuel, who is also twenty-two; and Amos, who is twenty-three. This is the first year that a woman has been part of the group; Bethany and I will share a trailer that Eric purchased.

A few days before I arrive, Eric drove 1,400 miles with his crew, from Lancaster, Pennsylvania, to Hydro, Oklahoma, where a friend and fellow harvester, Dwayne, lives. The combines and tractors were all ferried on the backs of flatbeds hauled by semitrucks. Eric dissuaded me from making this drive, and asked me instead to fly to the Will Rogers World Airport in Oklahoma City, where I pick up a rental car, a "small SUV" that still feels larger than anything I'm used to. I drive through a heavy rainstorm, and after it passes, I see a rainbow in my rearview mirror.

Eric has given me directions. I thought that when I asked for a land-mark, he would direct me to something like a McDonald's in town, but he does not choose a place whose logo juts obtrusively out of the land. His instructions imply a faith in my powers of observation. He has told me to "look for a bridge where there's work being done," and that once I see the bridge, I will see two combines. Along the way, I pass signs for Halliburton, Hobby Lobby, and Trump-Pence. And then I turn off the interstate, and there is the bridge with yellow tape and there are the combines set up on trailers, attached to two semitrucks. The rigs are parked on a farmer's gravel lot, by an unused barn. The rain has now completely passed and the combines gleam in the sun, a glossy, confi-dent red against the green-and-gold landscape.

Each combine costs anywhere from about $250,000 to $350,000. With its hydraulic lift and changeable header, a combine is about as close to a Transformer as you will find in the real world. Each one weighs nearly thirty thousand pounds, which means it must be care-fully placed on the back of a semitruck to be hauled across the country. All the different pieces of harvesting equipment are a bit like pieces of a puzzle, with space at a premium. To accommodate three combines, four headers, a tractor, three grain hoppers, and a grain cart, all of which must be loaded onto four semitrucks, Eric has devised different ways to transport each configuration. One truck has a combine and a hopper behind it, and another has a combine with a hopper and two headers fitted inside; the header is the knife of the combine and the part that cuts the wheat. This particular hauling method requires that the combine face forward, and when I arrive, Juston is wrapping the front windshield with a thick plastic sheet for protection. "One rock," Eric says, "and that glass shatters into a million pieces. And it's miser-able cutting without a windshield."

It is decided that Juston will drive me into the camp where the trailer houses are. This will happen a lot over the course of the spring and summer: the men will do the driving. There are practical reasons for how and why this happens: I often do not know where I am going, and the men do. Juston also jokes to me that I am about eight years old in farm years. The age is not chosen arbitrarily: ten is about when kids start to drive tractors, and I cannot truly drive a tractor.

Juston chats happily. "It's been a while since I've driven a passenger car," he says. "It feels so small." There is something about the way he confidently zips along these country roads that makes me feel as though, in his capable hands, the SUV has shrunk to the size of a roller coaster car.

Juston attends a Christian university in Pennsylvania, where he is majoring in English. He is tall, good-looking, and a little bit brooding, with a fuzzy beard, mustache, and blond hair of an indeterminate texture and length because he keeps it hidden under a Wheeler Brothers Grain cap at almost all times. Juston's smiles are slow to form, and always feel genuine because they are so hard-won. He has an inward quality, and by his own admission needs time to himself to recharge after being out in the world.

There is a hole in his ear where he wears an earring when he isn't on harvest, and we occasionally joke that his true identity is as a hipster. But this is merely a joke, because he is no hipster. He's the son of a farmer who never went to college, which makes Juston a bridge between worlds. He likes language and the analysis of ideas in a way I find comforting and familiar, while his fellow farmers often tease him about his "college talk."

Now we are driving onto Dwayne's property. A bonfire is burning slabs of wood and tree branches. "That's how we get rid of trash in the country," Juston says. There are some men—boys, really—working on a truck in the lot, and they stare as we park. They are slim and fit and they all wear jeans and boots. They are a version of the boys I have seen year after year in Nebraska who come to cut our wheat. All are white, and they avert their gazes; farm boys are shy.

Juston has explained to them that I am a writer. "I hope you don't mind," he says, chuckling. "I told them you were from San Francisco. And one of them asked, 'You mean, like, she's a Democrat?'"

"Oh my God," I say. Then I remind myself I need to stop saying "Oh my God" this summer. "I mean, Oh my . . ."

". . . word."

"Oh my word," I say.

"I told 'em . . . I said . . . 'It's not like she's the only Democrat!'" Juston laughs with glee.

After he parks the car, I move my things into my trailer and then go to see Emily, who has been waiting to greet me by the door of her trailer. She says that it is time for dinner. Emily has cooked dinner for both crews—Eric's men and Dwayne's men—because Dwayne's wife, Carrie, has been busy with her girls, one of whom is graduating from high school. Even though Emily has prepared everything in her trailer, we will be eating in Dwayne's house. "We use houses when we can," Emily explains.

Dinner is a large affair—so many people at the table. On the menu that night: a chicken casserole, Waldorf salad, and chocolate éclairs for dessert. There will always be dessert.

There is no alcohol and will be no alcohol all summer. The crews often come from families that have Old World habits, which involve saving water and avoiding baths, and so, in addition to the no-alcohol rule, Eric and Emily insist that their crew must shower.

Emily shoos me into the area where the adults are sitting. Dwayne has an idiosyncratic accent I have never heard before, and Juston explains to me that he sounds like he is from southern Oklahoma. Carrie is a sort of superefficient and terrifyingly talented woman from Oklahoma City, and her accent seems more typically Southern. Carrie is good at everything. Her house is spotless. There is always enough soap. She makes the best brownies (from scratch), and her daughters are well dressed and have good manners and do everything well at 4-H, and one has earned a scholarship to college.

The conversation takes off when the men start to compare their combines. Eric uses something called Case International Harvesters, which are red, while Dwayne uses Gleaners, which are silver. The defenders of the Gleaner claim it cuts a clean sample, by which they mean it doesn't crack the grain.

"Does it?" I ask.

"Well." Dwayne tosses his head. "Yes!" He leans into the phrasing of his answer as though to indicate that there is a hidden layer of meaning behind what he says and perhaps even behind my question. I feel terribly out of place.

And then, exhausted, I go to the trailer and change into my pajamas, climb into my bunk, and fall asleep.

In the morning, we caravan to Texas.

The entire procession of vehicles—all seven configurations—is tightly secured on flatbeds and trailers, and each assembly now noses out of the parking lot by the anonymous farmer's barn and heads out for the start of the great American wheat harvest. The longest configuration is so long, Luther is unable to make the right-hand turn to get onto the freeway, and swerves left into town, where he will do a series of turns until the truck is facing the right way.

Emily rides with me so I don't get lost. We pause on top of a slight crest to catch a view of the trucks proceeding one by one. "When harvest begins," Emily says to me, "they start out as boys, but go home as men."

We drive and drive. After we cross the Red River Valley, the earth bleeds red, as though we have punctured the country, which is only now releasing her deepest secrets for us.

I admire the way the mesquite stands silhouetted starkly against the sky, and how its distinct black lines are echoed in the carved and arched shapes of the wrought iron signs and brands hanging outside the entrance to every ranch we pass. Each cemetery has its own clear sign also fashioned of metal and framed against the blue heavens. Pioneer names etched into marble leap out of tombstones and declare the dead. This is a landscape absent of extraneous communication, by which I mean advertising. Words seem to matter more, and to be used more sparingly as a result.

I spot unfamiliar birds and vegetation. There are succulent cacti with golden flowers, now in full bloom. I wonder if the yellow rose of Texas is this yellow cactus, but when I look up the term, I learn that a yellow rose is a yellow girl, meaning a biracial girl. I wonder if I qualify.

The scissor-tailed flycatcher is featured on the license plate of Oklahoma—it is the official state bird—but I see it all over Texas, fluttering from telephone wires to bushes and over to barbed wire fences, dragging along an impractically long tail, forked like a rattlesnake's tongue. It is as if someone took a sensible bird and added to it a repressed desire for whimsy, embodied in the guise of this unnaturally long tail. The flycatcher has a white head, and hints of peach that might be tangerine under its black wings. Every bird is different: some are darker, some smaller, some more gray than black. But intelligent caviar eyes stare out of each bird's slightly pyramid-shaped head, and I start to think that the scissor-tailed flycatcher is a key to understanding Texas, a state that appears so rough-and-tumble, but that has room for something so charming.

"Turtle!" Emily points. "They say when there is a turtle and a snake on the road, it means there will be rain."

I am disappointed not to have seen a turtle. There are no turtles in the wild where I live.

A moment later I see a snake. "Snake!" I say.

"Let's don't tell Eric," Emily says, a little somberly.

We are 1,476 feet above sea level and on the High Plains, an arid stretch of the North American continent that, though flat, is elevated due to the upthrust of the Rocky Mountains to the west, the same way a tent pole yanks up canvas to transform flat fabric into an A. This is partly why the plains farther west—closer to the mountains—are higher than the plains to the east. In farming terms, this western land is used for "dryland" farming, which is another way of saying the crops are not irrigated by a sprinkler system but depend on the grace of rain clouds releasing moisture.

We are in Crowell, Texas, the "wild hog capital of the world," about two hundred miles northwest of Fort Worth, and eighty miles west of Archer City, which cinephiles know as the setting for the film version of Larry McMurtry's *The Last Picture Show*. Small, dusty, and ramshackle Thalia (population 193), eleven miles due east of Crowell, was retroactively named after the fictional town of Thalia featured in McMurtry's books.

Crowell is also the county seat, though you might not immediately pick up on its status. Begin, first, with the population, which was 840 in 2016, and 1,016 in 2006. Populations are often on the decline in the towns where we will stay. Texas is a football state, to which the popularity of the show *Friday Night Lights* attests, and this means each Texas town is supposed to have its own team. But Crowell's population is so small, it cannot field the twelve players needed. Crowell has compensated for this deficiency by coming up with a six-person football team, something small towns in Texas do; they call it "six-man football." In 2014, the Crowell Wildcats won the six-man football state championship. This fact is repeated to me often.

There is a square in the center of town. I have seen many town squares—in Brussels, Sonoma, New York City. There is a dignity to a square in the middle of a town, and my first impression is that Crowell is hardly holding on to its own. The buildings are slightly dilapidated. In the middle of the square is an ochre brick building, which in places reveals its original rust color; has the sun bleached the bricks? War memorials pop up around the town hall with the names of all the local veterans. Emily tells me the town hall is where we will go if there is a tornado.

In every town, Eric has an arrangement with either an RV park or a farmer who can house us in a spare lot. In Crowell, we stay in an RV park, a gravel-covered area with allotted campsites for large vehicles. Each campsite comes with its own picnic table and firepit. We can also hook up electricity, water, and sewage. The combines and trucks are parked south of town by the grain elevator.

We are the first ones here for harvest. There are no other combines or crews, and Eric is proud to be first. It means he is ready. It used to be that dozens of harvesters came to town. There was so much custom work that the town's excitement was palpable in a sign that read "Welcome Harvesters!" This year there is no sign.

Over the course of thirty years of custom harvesting, Eric has watched such towns die one by one. It is a point he makes to me repeatedly. Eric and Emily observe as we drive along that a movie theater was built here and the drive-in theater went away; a Walmart came and people moved here for jobs; the Walmart went to the town next door and the town died. With all these changes, the people—especially the young people—have fled, though the fields in the Great Plains have remained.

Farmland is disappearing in the United States. From 1982 to 2007, more than 23 million acres of agricultural land were converted to developments, with Texas, California, and Florida leading the list of states shedding arable land. Fields located closest to urban centers are vanishing the fastest, as they offer the most convenient land for new malls, offices, and housing. Also, these fields are often the most productive, and people tend to settle down in a location where they can make food.

Everyone needs to eat.

Juston takes me into town to buy boots and a hat. Farmers wear baseball caps. This is because they are often in pickups and other vehicles for long stretches of time, requiring them to lean back against a headrest, and the wide brim of a cowboy hat gets in the way. All the same, I get a cowboy hat because I am concerned about the sun. In his later years, my father had noncancerous growths removed from his head, and Eric has been by told by doctors to wear a wide-brimmed hat and to cover his ears.

The shop is cramped, with the feel of a secondhand store crammed with mismatched merchandise. There are racks of one-off utilitarian shirts, pants, and shoes. There are artifacts from the past, abandoned farming gear haphazardly attached to the walls: scythes, knives, horseshoes, and objects I don't recognize. Eric would. There are old suspenders with silver buckles for sale in a glass case. There is an odd assortment of uncategorized books. The newest item—just in!—is jewelry made in Mexico.

On a wooden sign on the wall is this ditty: "Feeling tired, worn-out and abused, this is the place. Join us. Get amused! By all means sit and tell us something new! Have a cup of coffee from us to you!" Below this are numerous photographs of customers in the shop and in town. I am told that if I come early in the morning, around 8:30, I can sit with the old-timers and talk about the way the town used to be.

The majority of goods a human might need are here in the general store. There are a limited number of cowboy boots and field boots; the crew wears field boots. Try as I might, I can't get anyone to clearly explain the distinctions between the two kinds of boots. It's as if we are talking about the difference between jazz and other forms of music: you know it when you see it. To my layman's eye, it seems the cowboy boot is stylized, often with a heel and an angled if not a downright pointed toe. A field boot has a lower heel, often a lower shaft, and is made to be slipped on and off easily. But there are exceptions.

There are few options in my size. There are few options for women at all. But Juston and I find a pair of men's boots in a size seven. They are caramel and black and handmade in Mexico. If I wear two pairs of socks, my feet fit inside.

"Truth is, you want 'em loose," Juston says.

In Oklahoma City we will visit a proper Western shop, Juston says. This will have to do for now.

Juston and I have quickly established an easy rapport. For years, it seemed, he was a small, shy child, driving his father's tractor during wheat harvest and barely able to make eye contact or muster a hello. At one point, Eric and Emily told me proudly that Juston wanted to be a pastor. I had run into him every now and then at his home, and more recently at Winston's wedding.

Then one day, perhaps a year ago, Juston picked me up from the train station when I came to Pennsylvania to visit his family. The young boy was now a man. And he seemed to be angry about something. I feared he resented having to drive me from the Amtrak station in Philadelphia all the way to Lancaster County. He was so tense, I finally asked: "Are you . . . upset about something?"

"I'm afraid my people will ruin this election."

There was a lot here to unpack. "Your people?" I asked. "You mean . . . white people?"

"You don't know?" he asked, smiling as if he felt both surprised and a little sorry for me. Then he took what I have come to call a "Wolgemuth pause." Wolgemuth is his family's last name. As his father does, Juston thinks before he speaks—though he talks a lot more than Eric. "We are evangelical Christians, Marie."

"You are? You're sure?" I didn't even definitively know what an evangelical Christian was.

He was quiet again, as though running my question through a data-processing bank to reconfirm. Then he nodded. "Yes. Technically, we are evangelicals. Yes."

And then our conversations began.

He revealed to me that he felt as if he was raised in a *Star Trek*–worthy simulator, by which he meant a conservative groupthink strain of Christianity. Since that trip, he has been sharing his most profound thoughts with me, and his most intellectually capacious school papers about God.

Beyond the obvious differences in our backgrounds—I am forty-six and he is twenty-two—I was surprised by how quickly I felt a kinship with him. We have kept up a correspondence, and we talk about God as the thing that anchors all of Juston's beliefs and doubts.

Among the major religions, I'm most familiar with Buddhism, and I had originally thought that since Juston was supposedly going to be a pastor, I could, with his help, increase my understanding of Christianity. I thought Juston would be like a terrarium: I would be on the outside watching God waddle around inside of him and, thus observed, God would make some sense to me at last. But this is apparently not what God had in mind. God had in mind that a conservative

Christian would question whether God even exists, and then decide to talk to me about it and try to determine what, if anything, is real, and I would go into the terrarium and be asked to waddle around too.

On a rainy day when there is nothing to do, Juston and I go to the Red River Valley Museum in Vernon.

We walk through a series of rooms dedicated to Texas history, then enter a hall furnished with more than 130 species of animals. The early part of the exhibit features taxidermied animals from North America, and I briefly feel like a child again, relearning the names of the creatures of the woods: fox, squirrel, deer. Juston squats and stares the wolf in the eye. I do the same. He says he did this often as a child and it used to terrify him. When I look at the wolf straight on, I try to imagine what it would have been like to be an early American settler, faced with a predator intent on eating my property. Would I have shot it?

When we move over to the Africa section, I can't keep all the gazelles straight. There are so many species. Dozens of heads hang on the beige fabric walls, as though an encyclopedic herd is pressing in from all sides and pausing, midstride, in the nightmare that is this killing room. The dead animals are called "trophies." At this point, I don't yet know that, down the road, I will go hunting and watch a pig die and delight in handling guns myself. At this point, my brain just trots neatly down its anti-gun, anti-hunting path of scorn. I would never travel to kill, as did William A. Bond, after whom this room was named. I would travel for art and maybe for food. Definitely for love.

Then Juston says: "Marie. This room is important to me because this is where I decided evolution is probably right and creationism is probably wrong."

The admission—the first I've ever heard of its kind—takes me by surprise. I wait for him to say more.

"Like with the deer. You have your curled antlers and the flat ones and then the totally impractical ones that just stick out. Why would God make a mistake with antlers? God would just make the perfect deer, perfectly suited for the environment. He's God. So something other than God has to be behind all these gazelles. It has to be evolution. Not that I'm a materialist. Did you read my paper?"

"Yes!" I say brightly.

"And?"

Here is a snippet from his paper.

The true question is intention; Genesis one does not intend to be cosmologically correct, and to draw modern science out of it misunderstands its objective. In this way, understanding Genesis [1] as scientifically inaccurate is not a liberal idea that disregards Scripture. Instead, it views Scripture as authoritative, interpreting Scripture with its true intention in mind. Consequently, the Bible, and especially Genesis [1], can remain God's authoritative Word, but it should not overrule modern understandings of science.

Juston is tracing a line of thinking I have never pursued, and though I recognize certain signposts—it's in English, Genesis is scientifically inaccurate, Western science wasn't around at the time of the writing of the Bible—he adopts attitudes and needs that I have never had. What assumptions is Juston challenging? What does Genesis mean? What is this conversation actually about?

"I don't completely understand everything you are saying in it," I tell him, and I can tell he is frustrated with me. But it is also the truth.

One way this story could play out would be for us to rejoice that Juston might now join the ranks of those of us from liberal states and liberal cities. I could teach *him* about our ways so he will be more fluent. But something about this scenario does not feel right. I know when I meet someone from "my world" and can assume we share the same language, the same tastes, the same jokes. This happens when I meet someone from, say, Australia who has seen similar television shows, read some of the same books, and perhaps eaten at the same chain restaurants. That is not what this feels like. The closest experience I have to this current feeling is when I meet someone from another country, and though they wear distressed jeans and are able to recount dramatic moments from *Friends*, I don't know for sure that they listen to the national anthem with skepticism. They are not—and he is not—from my world. I cannot make assumptions.

We are not in a terrarium. Juston has not made landfall with me on an island of liberal blue. Instead, it feels as if we have both taken a long and treacherous journey and come upon a preordained trail—like a footpath on the Continental Divide, or between two tectonic plates—and now that we are here, it's as though it is expected that we can both walk side by side and speak the same language. What did he see on his way over? And then I wonder, If I go all the way back to the place where Juston started, to God, will I really find nothing but the simulator? If that is all there is, how did Juston even get out of it? How did he know to try?

On the outskirts of most functioning farm towns, there is a miraculous thing called the grain elevator, which is usually located by a railroad. Harvested wheat is unloaded there. The grain is then lifted out of the tub into which it was dumped and, via a series of tubes, moved into large bins, where all the farmers' wheat is pooled together cooperatively. Farmers are people who cooperate. The Union Pacific will rumble through from time to time, and purchased wheat—often traded in Kansas City—will go off by railcar to the docks in Seattle and beyond. This was always exciting for me as a child—to see the train stop at our town elevator in Nebraska and receive a load of wheat.

There are eight different kinds of wheat recognized by the US Department of Agriculture, generally categorized by when they were planted (spring or fall/winter), how hard they are (soft or hard), and their color (red or white). Winter wheat, which is planted in the fall, accounts for about 75 percent of wheat produced in the United States. Most of what we will cut on our trip will be hard red winter wheat, though there will also be spring wheat and soft white wheat. Historically, half of US wheat production has been exported to feed people in other countries; top customers have been Japan, the Philippines, and Mexico, or places that want wheat and flour in their diet and either do not grow it or grow it in limited quantities. China has also become a top importer of US wheat. In all these countries, wheat is not necessarily a part of the traditional diet, but as populations modernize, they want to eat the foods that they see modern people eating, which include bread, pizza, and pasta, not to mention hamburgers with buns. And flour-based foods are a good source of calories for people who might otherwise not get enough to eat.

The US is always competing with other wheat-producing countries—notably Russia. Exports fluctuate due to trade wars, tariffs, and even gluts in the market. When this happens, farmers may try to grow something else on their soil, if they can, so as to avoid selling their crop at a rock-bottom price. They are also often limited by what they will be able to sell to a buyer, or middleman.

Not all farm towns have a location to receive a niche product like organic wheat; if a farm grows organically, it will need to have a purchaser, which may be hundreds of miles away. And even then, if the organic buyer or mill experiences a glut, it may turn away the crop or lower the purchase price, reducing what should have been a premium good to animal feed. Nearly every farmer I've spoken to has an anecdote precisely like this.

My cousin Paul, who lives in Seattle, likes to tell me that he occasionally sits in his car by the shipyard, at Terminal 86, the grain port, which receives wheat via one of the many branches of the Union Pacific Railroad, or via the Burlington Northern Santa Fe Railway. The wheat is unloaded there into large shipping containers and then departs to other countries. Paul likes sometimes to imagine that it is our own wheat, off on a tanker, journeying across the quiet seas to feed someone in China.

In Crowell, the grain bins and elevator are located to the south of town, and nearby there is a wide dirt-and-gravel parking lot that is empty now, but that in a week or so will host all the equipment for all the other harvesters who will roll into town. This is where our crew has left the machinery. Once the trailer houses are set up, the boys—and Bethany—go off to prepare the gear. The stretching of metallic limbs and the rolling down off of platforms and the hydraulic lifts in action make the equipment look like lunar rovers slowly unfolding and preparing to explore unknown terrain.

Transported on the backs of semitrucks, combines cross the country on the interstate system at seventy miles an hour. But on their own, combines lumber down county and country roads at a pace of about fifteen miles an hour; it can take them some time to reach the field they will cut. They are rarely driven out to a field on a semitruck, because once cutting starts, the semitruck is pulling a grain hopper and is waiting to receive a full load of wheat by the edge of the field, which it will take to the elevator.

The technology that gave the combine its name has remained the same since 1834, though combines have become more efficient with the introduction of diesel-fueled engines and the aforementioned hydraulics. The earliest models also did not have air-conditioned cabins.

The driver endured dust and noise, and many older farmers, like my father and uncle, were hard of hearing after a lifetime of exposure to the cacophony of so many moving metal parts. The newest combines are connected to computers and GPS locators, which track a plethora of information. If, for example, after years of cutting, you notice how one patch of ground in the land yields peculiarly thin wheat, you might fertilize that patch more heavily, and the computer can remember the exact coordinates for you and relay this information to a tractor, also outfitted with a computer and connected to a fertilizing unit.

The computer can also remember the contours of a piece of property. I like to joke with Eric that pretty soon a farmer will just sit in his truck and let the combine harvest on its own, much the way a child at the beach can drive a toy dune buggy by remote control.

Then there is the grain cart system, a revolutionary addition to harvesting popularized in the midnineties. While the combine cuts the grain, a tractor pulls up alongside it with something that resembles a metal bucket on wheels attached. The combine can continue cutting while simultaneously dumping a load of wheat into the grain cart. Once the cart if full, the tractor will go separately to a waiting semitruck and unload the grain into the back of the semi's hopper. A semitruck cannot go over as diverse terrain, as a tractor can, and thus must remain parked in a part of the field—or on a road—where there is enough firm ground to support its weight; no one wants a truck loaded with grain immobilized in a field.

When I was a child, the tractor and grain cart system did not exist, and combines needed to trek out to the grain trucks to unload, resulting in hours of lost cutting time. Since harvesters are always battling time and the elements, an hour isn't something anyone can afford to lose.

All these pieces—the hoppers, tractor, combines, and their headers—are unpacked and lined up in rows. It is a trademark of Eric's crew that his vehicles are always neatly parked. More than once, a new farmer will approach Eric and say something like "I been watching you for a few years, wondering if maybe we can work together." The "watching" generally begins with the parking.

If the day ends before we have finished cutting, which can and does happen often, the equipment is left in the field, parked tidily. But it isn't enough to park the equipment neatly in a row; the space used for parking must be considered carefully, so a truck can get in and out

and a combine can turn around. I will spend the entire summer trying to guess where I should park a pickup so as to most efficiently use
space and to avoid being asked to move to a less disruptive position. It
will make me feel good when a passing stranger says: "You park like a
farmer's wife."

The men unload and line up the trucks and the combines, communicating mostly through hand gestures—*back up, stop, back up, stop.* I am
reminded of the silent form of communication that is dance. The best
dancers know that our bodies talk. "We project . . . beauty through our
bodies . . . love, happiness, heartbreak, elation," says the great American
ballet dancer David Hallberg in an ad for the jeweler Tiffany. I sense
in all the hand motions of Eric's crew a set of meanings beyond mere
directions. I cannot yet name what this meaning is, other than, at this
point, to call it "teamwork."

Before the crew is hired, they will all have acquired a commercial
driver's license (CDL), which enables them to drive a truck. I had offered to get one so I could drive a truck, too, but no one took me up on
it. The boys can all drive tractors; most of their fathers were farmers,
and they have inherited all the nuances of farming body language—
hands in pockets, standing completely still, caution around large equipment. Their bodies sense edges and danger with a radar-like sensitivity
that I don't have; conversely, they know when to get in the middle of a
mechanical contraption to fix it. This is because they have been raised
to want to fix things and ferret out where something might be broken.
They look at problems and their minds figure out quickly how to re-
attach, weld, mend, or otherwise rewire. Such skills—once known to
most men, including my father—are becoming obsolete, and are being
transferred into the bodies of fewer and fewer boys. Families lose their
farms, or move to towns or cities where the skills aren't needed and so
don't develop. My father lamented, for example, that I wasn't good at
driving stick shift. "We just grew up differently," he would say, sighing.
At the same time, I am a girl, and, in general, women aren't taught the
same skills as men; in these traditional communities, women tend to
have a different role that requires different abilities.

The men know their skills are not widespread. There is the oft-
repeated story about the rest stop on Interstate 80 in Wyoming where a
crew was eating lunch when they saw an egregiously large RV stop for
fuel. "Real big thing," Eric says. "Got the satellite dishes. Everything."

While the driver was pumping fuel, semitrucks arrived and parked nearby, shortening the space through which the RV could drive out. For what felt like half an hour, the boys watched the RV back up, pull forward, back up, pull forward, and they narrated to one another the mistakes and overcorrections the poor driver was making. When they tell the story, it's mostly through gesture. They point here, now there, now here, and turn their heads back and forth, and the cumulative motion demonstrates the distress of the driver unaccustomed to navigating both space and a vehicle of this size.

Finally, Eric said: "Shall I put him out of his misery?" According to Juston, Eric went over to the RV and, in his hands-in-pockets way, offered to drive the RV out of the gas station. He was respectful, so as to not embarrass the man who couldn't drive his own vehicle. Once dislodged, the RV continued its journey, and not long after, the crew continued its interstate caravan to Idaho.

One of the combines will not start. It was driven onto the flatbed back in Pennsylvania, but now that we are in Texas, the engine will not turn over. The batteries are new; it cannot be the batteries. The combine is thirteen feet high and its interior is a labyrinth of wires, gears, and other parts.

"Let me take a look inside," says Luther. He opens the compartment where the engine lives. And this is when we all learn that Luther's head houses a vast and invisible map where parts move and intersect with wires all at the same time, and that Luther can consult the map and follow the instructions and find a destination. When he emerges from the inside of the combine, he is holding a piece of cable. "Needs a new relay switch." His voice is dry, as if he could use a lozenge, and he has a slight drawl.

Eric folds his arms and nods, beaming. Luther has potentially saved the crew hundreds of dollars.

A relay switch is a kind of an electrical lever; turn it on or off and electricity will flow and different parts of the combine will move. Luther has determined that one of the relay switches that sends electricity from the battery to the combine has failed and needs to be replaced. Or, as they say in Lancaster County, "needs replaced."

"You could be a combine mechanic," Eric says, beaming, delighted to have discovered a treasure.

Luther smiles back at him, then goes over to Lily, the service truck, to rummage around for a replacement switch. He finds it, and a short time later, the combine starts up.

Luther has confided in me that his dream is to get a job working for a real farmer. As a young man, Luther used to entertain himself by taking apart engines and reconstructing them, learning how all the parts work. Luther wants to be able to use his mechanical side while also working the land. He is from a Mennonite farming family, but—and this is an attitude I often hear among boys who work for Eric—his family "farms cows," which means Luther grew up on a dairy farm. He does not want to work with animals; he wants to work with crops. Animals, the boys often tell me, smell.

The boys are happy huddled around the combine. They are happy with machinery, happy climbing things, happy driving and working. I haven't seen anyone lose their temper.

Before dinner, Bethany says something intriguing to me in the trailer. She says that she likes to be able to see the solution: she does not want to be a part of a process but wants to see the result of her work. "It is," she says, "a very Lancaster County way to be."

And then I think that if all we need—if the goal of farming—is to find a solution to a problem, then it hardly matters if you are a man or a woman.

At dinner Eric is restless. By seven the sun is speeding toward the horizon and he wants to go for a drive. Evening light is short and magical and we should see it before it fades. But we don't go out until Eric has had his dessert—cherry cobbler that night. It is a favorite, and so good that Eric has an extra helping. Then a few of us pile into a pickup with Eric.

It is so red here in Texas—there is even a park called Copper Breaks State Park, where the earth coalesces into ruddy forms resembling statues. I feel as if I am inside a hollow and glowing chamber.

We continue out into the remaining light. I think of how right now the wheat is ripening across the land at a rate of about twenty miles per day. The settlers crossed the prairie at ten to twenty miles per day and then stopped to rest. Does the ripening stop, too, when the sun sets? At the end of the day, the sun hangs over the west like a lantern beckoning us onward. If we followed the lantern, we could leave this red earthen chamber of a heart. But we won't catch the sun. We will have to stop and wait for it to circle around again.

We stop and climb over a fence. Eric hops over easily and is sucked into a field. Samuel stops to wait for Bethany; determination shows in her body and in her expression. She wants to demonstrate that she can do what the boys can do and she climbs over without complaint. Samuel helps me, too, and I am humbled. Crossing a barbed wire fence like this is one of the earliest memories I have of my father teaching me the physical vocabulary of farm. He stepped on the lower strip of barbed wire and pulled up the top strip so I could climb through the space in between. But I was a child then. When I was an adult, he taught me to climb over the wire by supporting myself on the wide pole to which the wire was attached. These days, fences are not anchored to wooden poles but to metal stakes, and they are much harder to grab for balance than the pole.

Eric is long gone. He has charged into the center of the field. I don't have on boots; I am wearing sneakers. My feet snag brambles. I stop on the edge of the field like a child who can't yet swim in deep water. Tomorrow, I tell myself, I will remember to wear my boots; I hadn't worn them for fear of looking pretentious, as if I was wearing a costume. But the boots are absolutely necessary. Even so, from here on the edge of the field, I can see that the crop is terrible. Weeds have won the battle for water and choked out the wheat.

"What happened?" I ask Eric when he returns.

"I figure that the farmer did not kill the weeds."

"Is he organic?" I mean it as a joke, but no one laughs or answers.

Eric thinks the farmer let cattle graze on the growing wheat in an effort to get more money off the land. The wheat grew back—a little—and so did the weeds. It is terrible "dirty" wheat and may not be worth cutting. We all go back into the pickup to look at another field, and this time, I don't climb the fence.

It is dusk and the country is crawling with creatures. I think I am good at seeing animals, but Eric is better. He sees the roadrunners and the turkeys before I do. I spot what I think is a . . . dog. Is it a dog?

"Coyote," says Eric and I am thrilled.

Then I have doubt. I am a person who often doubts. "How do we know it is a coyote and not a dog?"

"Dog won't run like that," Eric says.

"He was wild?"

There is something knowing in the way he nods. Yes, he says, this is the beauty of a wild thing. Of wild things. We are not in a park set up for tourists, but in a wild place, where wild things behave as they were meant to.

I want more than anything to see a live armadillo. I have seen two dead ones on the side of the road. I am hopeful one will come out at night.

There is a tall tale the farmers tell, of an armadillo who had just died and the harvest crew who picked him up in Texas and kept his carcass in their freezer, and carried him all the way to North Dakota, following the wheat as it ripened, twenty miles a day. Once in North Dakota, they put the armadillo on the highway, where he thawed and was discovered by locals, who, amazed that such a creature lived unknown in their environment, put the story in the paper: the armadillo who had lived and died incognito in North Dakota.

"I saw a jackalope," Bethany volunteers. She's joking, of course.

"We can find a dead one and take it to Idaho," I suggest. Everyone laughs.

That night, right before I fall asleep, I hear a coyote singing. Another one answers. I drift off listening to them sing to each other, the way the cowboys say they do, and it's as if time hasn't passed, or maybe as if I've gone back in time and the coyotes are singing under the stars and the land is vast and unfenced and a wild thing can run and run forever.

We begin each day with breakfast. The time is determined the night before and we set the alarms on our phones accordingly. I tend to rise early, and if I haven't showered the night before in the trailer, I do in the morning. The boys take off their boots before entering Eric and Emily's trailer. I will learn to tell if I'm late, early, or on time for every meal by how many boots are assembled on the wooden crates at the foot of the steps to the trailer. Farmers are always getting muddy and always take off their shoes at a doorway.

Emily reads from the Bible. She uses the New Living Translation, a version of the Bible first translated in 1996 from the original Greek and Hebrew. Her voice, though a pretty soprano, is plain and unadorned. Prettiness was one thing the Protestants and Anabaptists rebelled against when they left the Catholic Church: too much self-conscious red velvet and gold embroidery. For me, there is always something in the Protestant and Anabaptist version of Christianity that is slightly self-effacing, as though it refuses to embellish what is naturally pretty. Emily begins with the Psalms.

"Oh, the joys of those who do not follow the advice of the wicked, or stand around with sinners, or join in with mockers. But they delight in the law of the LORD, meditating on it day and night. They are like trees planted along the riverbank, bearing fruit each season. Their leaves never wither, and they prosper in all they do. But not the wicked! They are like worthless chaff, scattered by the wind."

The Bible is so full of seeds and wheat.

After Emily reads, Eric prays. His prayers always mirror whatever it is we need that day—patience to endure downtime, or gratitude for safety. Eric once told me that he learned long ago not to pray for God to alter the weather; this is not the role of prayer, because if it stops raining just for us, then someone else will suffer. But he can and does ask for God to give us courage, strength, and patience.

Breakfast is often absent much conversation. But today, midway through, Eric says: "Let's prepare for transport." He pauses. "Let's say eight o'clock." The crew starts chewing their cereal again with renewed gusto.

There is a moment after breakfast when Juston pulls Eric aside. I will see this periodically during the summer. Juston occasionally gives feedback to his father when he finds Eric to have been too gruff or unclear.

Eric is telling us that we need to prepare the equipment for full transport from the elevator parking lot to a field. The headers of two combines will ride out on a flatbed trailer, which will be pulled by a pickup. The third combine is a new model; the header is made so its wheels can be rotated and then pulled behind the combine to the field without a trailer. The idea behind this design is to eliminate the extra flatbed trailer altogether.

Luther and Bradford, those computer-age farmers, wear Bluetooth headsets, and they look at ease, fusing technology, machinery, and silence. They are ready to work.

We are cutting for a farmer named Tommy, and he is waiting for us in the lot by the elevator after breakfast. He has his own pickup and will drive it out to the field. He is in his fifties, farms along with his brother and son, and one day will own the entire farm. He takes his hat off when he meets me, and talks haltingly about the poor harvest the year before, and how he had put some of his crops into canola, and how, after an entire year of waiting, the wheat this year does not look so good. He asks me where I am from. I explain my diverse origins, and he nods.

"How do you feel about what's going on in the world?" he asks.

"I worry," I say simply.

Tommy nods and then mentions how he wishes Donald Trump would stop his tweeting. "It don't seem necessary," he says.

Bradford climbs into the cabin of one of the red Case combines and Juston gets into another. Samuel takes a semitruck, Luther the pickup pulling the headers, and Bethany the tractor. We are short a driver, so one combine will be left behind.

There is so much excitement around cutting the first field of the year, but the crew is quiet and focused. The maneuvering of a combine must be done with care; if it falls over, a strong cable is needed to pull it back up. Eric drives another pickup truck to the field, and I ride with him. Our caravan is slow on these dirt roads. Once the combines are in the field, Bradford approaches the flatbed trailer attached to the pickup and picks up one of the twelve-ton headers with the combine's claws. Then he rolls out into the field of wheat and begins to cut, shred, and bin grain at seven miles per hour. Hydraulics, that wondrous modern discovery that we usually take for granted, has, in a matter of minutes, attached blades to the combine and thus transformed the lumbering and ineffectual cabin into a super locust, capable of stripping a crop in a matter of hours.

Waiting for the combine to cut a test patch is always tense. On the one hand, there is the temptation to just cut the entire field on a hunch that it is ripe. But if the grain is too wet or not ripe enough, the wheat will be wasted, or fined at the elevator, or will need to be put through a machine called a "dryer," which is pretty much what it sounds like: a mammoth metal structure, a kind of popcorn popper the size of a pickup truck, that tosses around 500 to 1,500 bushels of wheat while simultaneously passing hot air across the kernels. But not everyone is lucky enough to own a dryer, let alone pay for the energy to run one, and we do not have one in Texas.

Bradford cuts a swath of wheat. Over the CB radio, he reports that his sensors measure a moisture reading of 12 percent.

"I still want an official reading," Tommy says.

Then the combine returns to edge of the field where the grain cart is waiting. The combine swings around a giraffe-like neck from its back, and the giraffe neck spits a waterfall of amber grain into the cart. Eric climbs up into the cart with a metal coffee can in his hand, and a moment later jumps back out. With the alacrity of an emergency technician delivering a severed limb to the ER, Eric speeds off. We sit and watch the sail of dust behind him grow ever smaller; not much moves out in the country, so you notice anything that does.

On average, there are forty bushels per acre of wheat cut in the United States. Farmers would put it like this: "The average is forty bushel wheat." We will not make that here. Dryland wheat—grown in fields that, like this one, are not irrigated—generally makes closer to twenty-eight bushels per acre, and this is a vast improvement from my childhood, when yields were often in the teens. One bushel of wheat is made up of approximately a billion kernels and weighs about sixty pounds. When milled into flour, a bushel can make about ninety loaves of whole wheat bread; if you take out the husks of the kernels and mill the grain into white flour, you can make about forty-two loaves of white bread. Alternatively, a bushel of wheat turned to white flour can make forty-two pounds of white pasta. If you are the sort of person who enjoys math, as my extended family does, you can calculate just how much bread or pasta a two-thousand-acre farm can make. Or I can give you the shortcut statistic that the entire state of Kansas produces enough wheat to bake 36 billion loaves of bread, which could feed everyone in the world for two weeks.

We wait for Eric. People sit in the shade, or inside the cabins of trucks, or, as my family always says, they "visit." Perhaps half an hour later, there is a call on the CB radio in the semi. Samuel answers it.

"It's Eric," Samuel calls to us from the window of the truck. "He says we can cut."

Harvest has begun.

I make a mistake on the first day. I leave my water jug in the pickup because it is heavy and I don't want to carry it everywhere. Not long after, someone—probably Eric—drives off with the pickup to go look at other fields, and I am separated from my water. It is hot. It doesn't take me long to get dehydrated, and then I have to ask for a drink of someone else's water. I swear to myself that I will never make this mistake again. But I will. Of course, no one else does.

That day I also make one ineffectual attempt to drive the tractor. Bethany takes me out. She drives around the field once, explaining what she is doing. Eric had taken me out once before, in Pennsylvania, and then it had seemed easy enough. I just needed to pay attention to the terrain, the speed, the clutch.

"Okay, now you try," Bethany says and slides over.

So I get in the driver's seat. It ought to be easy and I ought to drive the tractor around. But my mind does something strange. It fills with questions. How fast should I go? Should I or should I not brake? How close should I get to the truck? And there is just the *feeling* of the tractor in my hands. I can't feel how wide it is. I know that much of maneuvering the tractor will entail driving up beside the truck or a moving combine, and I don't have that intuitive spatial sense that everyone else seems to have. I'm not even convinced I can quickly develop it in the same way that, say, I've managed to successfully commandeer a couple of rental vans after a lifetime of owning only small passenger cars.

I drive with little confidence.

Beside me, Bethany laughs lightly, as if she's embarrassed for me. I think she has probably never seen a grown woman so incapable with a tractor.

Without much further discussion, it's decided I will be a "ride along," which means I won't operate anything, but will sit next to the crew as they drive. I would have needed convincing that I could actually drive the tractor, and they don't indulge me. Juston tries to make me feel better. He repeats that in farm years I am about eight years old, which is how old he was the first time he drove a tractor. He says that even now, even though he has his CDL, driving anything large makes him nervous. Everyone understands. Most people don't drive trucks.

I can, however, drive the pickup. There is always a shortage of drivers when the men are operating equipment; Luther has ridden back to town with Samuel to get another wheat truck, and the pickup is unattended. I am delighted when I am asked to move it with the combines as we switch fields. I am told to leave the keys in the pickup. We will leave our keys in all the vehicles all summer. This is so anyone can drive and move anything as needed; there is no fear of car theft.

The roads are all unpaved and I have to remember them without the aid of GPS. I have to be a bumblebee. I always have to know which way is north, and remember landmarks for mental maps, so I can trace the roads in my head and reverse course when necessary. My father taught me to do this, and I have to recall the lessons so I can speak with the people I am spending all my time with now. The crew does this quickly. They pick out the same landmarks, as though special trees and abandoned vehicles, or "where we saw that coyote," are somehow marked in neon. Occasionally we do see a coyote. When we do, Bradford takes a shot with his assault rifle. "I'm going to take a shot," he announces over the radio.

Often I drive the pickup behind Juston. We go everywhere on dirt roads. On one dirt road there is a broken-down and abandoned car and we manage to pass the headers of the combines just over it so the car—and the combine—does not sustain any damage. There are power lines, fences, trees, and all manner of obstacles, and it is as though the men are threading the eyes of giant needles.

The crew splits up at one point—two combines, the grain cart, and a truck go to one field, and a combine and wheat truck go to another. Bethany, Bradford, Amos, and Samuel are often together, while Eric, Juston, and Luther make up a second team. When we are working hard, which we are for a few days, Emily drives the lunches and the dinners out to the fields. She calls Eric over the radio to learn our location and precisely where she should park and which way the pickup should face to avoid the wind blowing chaff into the food, and because she's a farmer's wife, she, too, dusts off the mental maps she has stored in her mind all year, and follows them. One time I'm entrusted with driving dinner out to Bradford; he is working clear across a rough field lined by terraces, which are raised areas meant to make a sloped field comprise as many flat segments as possible. I try to decide if I should drive at an angle or straight over the terraces. Again my head fills with questions that stop me from just moving.

I've heard Bradford admonish others to drive their combines and the tractor at an angle over the ridges. Does he mean all vehicles should do this, or just the combines? Will I look reflexively too careful if I drive the pickup at an angle? Will I look like a sissy? Am I asking too many questions? I drive straight over.

"Marie," I hear Bradford's voice say. "Drive at an angle."

I've overthought the instructions. I am always overthinking instructions. I am supposed to do what I'm told and not assume that there is an extra layer of invisible meaning over everything.

One day I am by myself, driving through the mesquite, when a tiny rainbow jewel of a bird darts in front of me and I stop and watch as the thing flutters to my right. All my life I have wanted to see a painted bunting. It is iridescent green, with an indigo head and a scarlet chest. Like the scissor-tailed flycatcher, the painted bunting seems like a completely impractical bird for this tough environment. It disappears before I can take a photo. I want everyone to see what I have seen. I ask everyone if in all their years of coming to Texas they have ever seen a painted bunting, and they haven't. I keep asking, while Eric is measuring protein and moisture levels, and I start to feel like the painted bunting myself—extraneous and unnecessary. Everyone is patient about the fact that I have no discernible skills, about the way I exclaim how beautiful it is in the evening when the light is streaming through the cheat grass by the side of the road, so it glows like crystal fog. "It's still weeds, Marie," Eric says.

Eric is often busy giving a ride to farmer Tommy, and I am shy about asking Bradford and the others for a ride after driving over the ridge incorrectly, so I wait in the air-conditioned combine cabin with Juston. He tells me he will spend most of his time that summer "driving truck." He likes truck. He's not sure he really fits in here with the other farmers, but he also likes to be in the country. It calms him. He says he knows that his mind will quiet after a summer on harvest, and that mine will be too. The lack of excessive conversation will slow my mind down. He knows we have the same kind of hyperactive brains and that the country will soothe us both. When we aren't together, he says, he listens to podcasts like *BadChristian* and *The Liturgists*, which have been part of his healing.

"I didn't know there were podcasts for people like you . . . people who . . ." I don't want to say *in recovery* from Christianity, as if he has a form of addiction.

"There's a lot of us." He pauses for a long time. "It starts with hell," he finally says.

"I don't understand what that means."

Juston says he started questioning his world while on mission in Germany, which was supposed to be part of his training to become a pastor. Refugees were coming into Germany from Syria, and terror had clearly sculpted their faces. Juston began to wonder: How could an all-loving God send people to hell? And if we are saved as a people, as the Bible said, then aren't we saved? At what point and how does God decide that someone is going to go to hell? And at the same time, he wanted to believe in God. And so began a period of struggle.

"Did you always doubt?" I ask.

"I'll play you a recording of me preaching sometime," he says. "I sound so sure. I sound like I believe. But even then I was doubting."

"What did you do about the doubt?"

"I read books. Rob Bell." He explains, briefly, that Rob Bell is a pastor who has written on the subject of hell and Jesus, and has become influential to Juston and in certain Christian circles. "There's a lot of evangelicals who don't like Rob Bell because, basically, he says hell doesn't exist. But I like him. If you want to understand what I'm talking about, you could start there."

And then it rains.

Outside there is thunder and lightning. I hadn't even noticed it was going to rain. I ought to have noticed. My father started every day by looking at the weather. He ended every day with the weather too.

My conversation with Juston comes to a complete stop. Over the radio I hear a few urgent phrases. The grain in the back of the combines will get wet; there is no cover. We need to unload into a truck that has a tarp. The boys—and Bethany—all strong hands and biceps, furiously crank handles to spread the tarp over the grain. One combine is stuck with a flat tire and we leave it; Juston moves his to higher ground. Then there is a scramble into trucks, and we drive back morosely to the trailer houses.

In the trailer, I download a weather app to my phone.

In the morning, the sky is blue; storms can pass swiftly on the plains, and the hot temperatures and aridity can quickly dry a wet crop. We just need to wait till the wheat is dry again. "I don't think there was any hail," Eric says. He has checked the weather map. What he means is that the rain was a setback but it did not destroy the harvest.

In the meantime, we have to see about the combine with the flat tire, which we learn has been punctured by a deer antler. Eric says that deer antlers are often found on the periphery of fields; deer lose them as they jump over fences. Lily the service truck is like a mobile hospital for equipment, and all summer I will see the multiple ways she can be employed. Today Eric drives her out to the abandoned combine while Luther follows in a pickup and hooks up an air pump from Lily to the flattened tire. Then I drive the pickup behind Eric as he slowly wheels the combine to the mechanic in town and Luther takes Lily back to the trailers. The shop has a coatrack made of deer antlers. I will see deer antlers everywhere in Texas: as table settings, chandeliers, and always as coatracks.

The mechanic deflates the tire, and puts the entire rig up on a block. He struggles to get the tire off, so Eric goes over and hits it once with his fist, at which point it pops off. Then the mechanic is able to begin the patch on the puncture.

Once the combine is fixed, we look at the fields again. They are still wet. And so we pass the time.

Spirits fall.

"It's always like this in Texas," Juston moans. "It always rains."

"Oh, Juston," says Emily. "We're just getting started."

At dinner, Eric says there is a rodeo nearby, but it is not a typical rodeo. It is a ranch rodeo. He asks who would like to go, since there won't be any work for a while. There is an entrance fee of twenty-five dollars. Because of this, not everyone will elect to attend. Eric is not going to pay for the boys. But they can use the pickups to drive to Abilene, where the rodeo will be. And so we go.

The region now known as Texas was originally inhabited by multiple Native American tribes; perhaps the best known are the Comanche and the Kiowa, who hunted buffalo and antelope and lived off the land.

Then the Spanish came to Mexico and Texas (though at the time, no one thought of Mexico and Texas in those terms, as the land was all part of Spain), in the sixteenth century, and brought with them cattle to graze on the "open range." Cattle from Mexico drifted up north to Texas and interbred with cattle that had drifted east from California.

In 1821, Mexico won its independence from Spain, and the Mexican government encouraged Anglos to settle Texas, to help clear away the Indians. But, of course, too many visitors can have unintended consequences, and in the first four decades of the nineteenth century, a tug-of-war ensued between Mexico and the United States over who would claim this land. Meanwhile, Native Americans fought on both sides. In the end, in 1845, Texas was admitted as a state, though not without considerable debate over the issue of slavery. Abolitionists did not want another slave state to enter the Union; until 1844, the number of slave and free states had been equal, but if Texas permitted slavery, it would tip the precarious balance. The Compromise of 1850 resolved these tensions for a time through a variety of actions: California entered the Union as a free state. The war with Mexico formally ended with a monetary settlement of $15 million. As humans continued to figure out their national boundaries, the cattle interbred, and the hardy longhorn was born: these cows were tough and resistant to disease, and they wandered the plains of Texas, eating and multiplying.

Once the Civil War was over, men and some women turned their attention to the lost herds of cattle roaming around Texas. The Texas ranches, some of which had been on life support during the Civil War, were reestablished, and hardy, individualistic men appeared on the plains to drive the wild cattle north and across the open range to the railroad, where they could be shipped east to a population hungry for meat. It is against this backdrop—the 1870s—that Larry McMurtry's epic novel *Lonesome Dove* is set. While in Texas, I am often asked by Eric and by Texans if I have seen the miniseries or read the book or both (I have). The open range and the great cattle drives ended around 1890, but as any Texan will tell you, the spirit of those times remains. It is easy to find traces of it in the ranches and in the people who made them.

Rounding up cattle requires particular skills. A cowboy is a man of the land and not the city, and in this way a cowboy is a version of Eric. A cowboy has to be able to fix things, move quickly, improvise, and read the terrain and other people's movements. For Eric and for the harvesters, the cowboy is not an exotic once-a-year sight on a dude ranch, but a familiar cousin with whom they share a dialect.

Real-life cowboy Teddy Blue Abbott said: "In character their like never was or will be again. They were intensely loyal to the outfit they were working for and would fight to the death for it. Living that kind of a life, they were bound to be wild and brave . . . In fact there was only two things the old-time cowpuncher was afraid of, a decent woman and being set afoot."

A cattle drive prized similar skills as a harvest run, down to avoiding women.

Harvest has many rules, including mandatory showering and zero tolerance for alcohol or smoking. In addition to this, dating is not allowed. This is the first Wolgemuth harvest with a girl on the harvesting team. And while a man may call and text his girlfriend during off hours—Eric supports and is certainly enthusiastic about his crews' relationships—anything involving sexual tension or chemistry would be distracting, and distraction is dangerous around heavy equipment.

Throughout the summer, my city friends will ask me about Bethany. She is as capable of the work as any of the men. My friends in the city project onto her all their feminist ideals, and this makes me incredibly nervous. Bethany is a gifted harvester, and on occasion speaks of her desire to do what the boys do. But hers is not the insistent language of feminism. She has no well-thought-out agenda, or a desire to insist on equal pay for equal work, or anything approaching such a conscious declaration of selfhood and equality. When she talks about her ideal life, she often mentions as a role model my friend Caroline in Nebraska, who helps her husband, Caleb, with nearly every farming activity. Bethany simply likes to farm.

Men and women are not the same, I am told over and over. "Anyone who works with farm animals, like cattle, knows that," the crew tells me. Women are diverting. Beautiful women are the worst. The West was won and the wheat is cut by men pushing through and working, and women appearing when needed. When they appear at other times, there is always the danger of distraction.

Eric likes that my first rodeo will be a "ranch rodeo" and not just a regular rodeo, which he says is more like a show. In the latter, professional rodeo riders go from town to town riding bulls and horses for the crowd's delight, not unlike a professional football team. A ranch rodeo is made up of teams of horse and bull riders, who are men who work on ranches. The names of the ranches are legendary in Texas and across the Great Plains states: Guitar, Green Land & Cattle Company, Stuart. They are the oldest and largest ranches, and are part of the legacy of how the West was settled. Among the ranches represented is Pitchfork, with which Eric is affiliated, because, on occasion, he cuts their wheat.

The first thing I notice at the rodeo is the smell of animals. Then we enter the slow conveyer belt of fashion, of men in cowboy boots accompanied by their women, circling the exterior ring of the arena. Nothing has prepared me for this, not even the one time I changed planes at the Dallas Fort Worth airport. There are suspenders, and more than once I hear the clatter of spurs. Men carry lassos in neon colors. Nearly every man is in a hat. I order the most foul fried chicken and fries I will ever eat. Around me is a sea of cowboy hats flexing on top of heads. I wonder, as I listen to the voices curl and flex, too, if they know how their drawl is reflected in the curvature of their flaxen hat brims.

Inside the arena, I see men sitting on thin railings. Some wear chaps and cock their hips from side to side to loosen up, as dancers do. In my mind's eye, I see the choreography of Agnes de Mille's famous ballet *Rodeo*. Lanky, wiry bodies are silhouetted against the light—they rest on a fence, on a horse, on a rail. The cowboy twitches; he readies his reflexes. He is not a patient farmer.

Before the rodeo begins, the emcee reads a poem in tribute to the cowboy. "Cowboys are tough," he says, and then goes on to remind us that we are here to celebrate "our heritage," to be thankful we can gather in a place like this arena and pray together. The grand procession includes buggies, and the teams of ranch hands ride together in their uniformed shirts and on the horses they will ride throughout the competition. And while there might have been a woman or two among them, everyone I see is white.

Girls carrying banners and riding ponies move in formation. And then the rodeo starts, with a series of men riding horses that buck. How quickly the men go into the classic bucking-bronco pose, one arm in the air, the other clutching the reins, and how beautifully nearly all of them fall, the controlled fall of a cowboy who has been thrown from his horse, who knows it is time to dismount, and who gives up the horse in lieu of clinging to time, because to do so would be to jeopardize his own body.

There are more events—I come to think of them as Olympic trials involving man and horse—including one where calves need to be separated from other calves, and each cowboy is allowed only one successful throw of his lasso. The technique seems to involve throwing a lasso over the head of the calf, and another around his foot. As soon as the calf is secured in these two places, one or two men leap down from their horses and do whatever is required—brand the cow, milk the cow, or lasso the cow. I can't explain how a lasso gets on the hind foot of a cow until Bethany explains to me that the rope falls down in a circle at the cow's feet, like a trap, waiting for the foot to step inside and be snared. Her eyes are shining when she tells me. She has a horse back home. It is her dream to be on a ranch, on a farm, on a horse. All she wants, she says, is to be a farmer's wife.

Samuel drives us back that night, a full two hours from Abilene to our camp. The darkness has clamped down hard on the land, and I think of all the aphorisms of night—how it falls like a cloak, how it drapes over the land, how it is immovable. The darkness is enormous and feels permanent.

Juston recounts a time when he was a child driving a grain cart in the dark. The lights on the tractor could illuminate a good distance, but then there was the cavern of darkness ahead, and the young Juston feared he would be forever separated from his family and not find his way back. I can see how, in a small child's mind, the imagination couldn't win against the persuasive power of the dark.

"That will change," Eric says, "once they put in the windmills." And against the night sky, in the distance, there are the slow and deliberate winking red lights of the windmills that stand on the land, and take motion from the air to power the things that people need.

THREE

IT TAKES A FEW DAYS FOR THE FIELDS TO DRY, and time seems to drag. At night, the crew disappears, and I don't know where they go, only that Bradford seems to be in charge. At dinner, they all wait for Bradford to finish eating, and when he's ready, he lifts his hand just slightly and all the boys, except for Juston, scramble away.

"Thanks for supper," Bradford will say.

"Thanks for supper," the others will echo as they funnel out the door.

"Uh-unh. Yep. You bet." Emily acknowledges each person individually.

Before I can climb out of my seat and move around the table—I am often wedged into a far corner—they are gone. Usually Juston retreats to the armchair in his parents' trailer to watch some television. Sometimes Eric will go look at the fields and I will look, too, but mostly I go to my own trailer and read.

Sunday rolls around. We have been here a week. On Sundays, Emily does not make breakfast but offers a packaged treat. Today she has sweet rolls from Costco. The crew files in and takes sweet rolls and eats them before we go to church. They are all, even Bethany, dressed in clean and bright blue jeans, with polished boots and pressed long-sleeved checkered shirts. We pile into two pickups and drive a good twenty miles. "Western Trails Cowboy Church" declare the iron letters hanging over the entry gate above a long driveway leading to a sprawling wooden complex that looks like a ranch house. The parking lot is already full of pickup trucks; there are few passenger cars.

Eric does not work on Sundays. Once upon a time, this was not unusual for harvest crews, for whom family, faith, and harvesting were tightly bound. Now harvesting is a business, and there are many custom cutters who will work on Sundays. Eric's day of rest used to give my father some pause. What if rain was forecast for Monday, and Sunday was needed to get the grain out of the field? And yet he conceded that the rule had never truly posed a problem.

"Cowboy church" sounds as romantic to me as any other notion about Texas I have held, though I am not clear what it means. No one can tell me exactly. I get half answers about the Baptist church and non-denominational churches, but for me, all of Christianity is such a blur of Jesus and hell and God that the minute differences mean about as much as thread counts and the source of pima cotton for luxury sheets in a five-star hotel. I don't, I think, know *how* to talk about church.

Inside the church, over the doorway to the sanctuary, are two Stetson hats and a metal crown made of thorns. One of the cowboy hats is clean and the other is dirty. Juston reads the iconography immediately. He explains that two thieves were executed with Jesus; one recognized Jesus and entered heaven with him, while the other was a sinner who went to hell. This is another way of saying *All are welcome here*. Taken another way, I suppose it also means *You might go to hell*. I will soon start to notice groups of three crosses everywhere in the countryside.

Cowboy church feels like an extension of the rodeo. The interior smells of wood and sawdust, and there are men in cowboy hats and young boys in spurs; the latter will be blessed during the service for placing in the regional rodeo. We are greeted by an older man who remembers Eric. "You're back," he says, overjoyed, gripping Eric's hand in a manly shake.

The harvesters are asked to stand up and introduce themselves and say who they are and where they are from. One by one, our young men stand. But we are not the only crew. The Deiberts, who were in a documentary with Eric called *The Great American Wheat Harvest*, are also here with all their men. The documentary makes the point that qualified harvest crewmates are now so hard to find that some custom harvest bosses must hire young men from countries overseas, including Australia, Scotland, Ireland, and South Africa. If a crew works the entirety of the wheat belt, a young man will be gone from May until October, traveling from Texas to Montana. This is a long time to live in a trailer and be so far from home, particularly since so many American youths go back to college in September. Most of the Deiberts' crew is either from Britain or from a former British colony, including two boys from Zimbabwe. All are white.

That day in cowboy church, a musical missionary group from the Midwest takes to the stage for forty-five minutes. The Hinkle Family goes from nursing home to nursing home playing music for old folks.

It is, Juston whispers, Christian music. Most of the songs are in three-quarter time, and arranged to get us to sway in our seats. There are a couple of polkas. There is a guitar, an accordion, and two singers.

A highlight of the performance is an original song, which begins with the preamble "We hear so much about endangered species—the redwood tree, the spotted owl, I do not see the Christian family." The song goes on and there is a verse about a graveyard in which tombstones bear names like "Peace," and "Absolute morality."

I don't remember what the pastor says. He rambles and I watch Eric and Emily and think there must be something they are seeing and hearing that I am not. There must be something their bodies remember in being here that makes this service familiar and comforting, which it is not to me. I've never understood how simply saying that Christ died for my sins could answer any existential question I might have, and I certainly feel suspicious of any God who would kill off his only son for me. Those who send young boys on suicide missions say something similar. It all feels like emotional blackmail. What brings Eric back here every year?

Afterward, Eric tells me he wishes I could have met the original cowboy church pastor, who was the kind of person who knew everyone. Even the drinkers and the people in jail. "I think Jesus was like this," he says.

"Supposedly he was, wasn't he?" I say.

Eric nods. "Jesus must have been an *incredible* person! I mean, I would love to have met him. He was *perfect*."

This is not the first time I have heard Eric praise Jesus's perfection. He speaks of Jesus with an awe that I find embarrassing. Stoic, squinty Eric gets so worked up about Jesus. His emotions about Jesus are like those creatures in a tide pool that inflate and flower into an iridescent spiral of tissue before clamping back down into something hard and tough and you wonder if the tide has merely shown you a mirage. What was it about this guy tacked to a cross that would, after more than two thousand years, make a grown man like Eric so wide-eyed? I read some of the parables in a mandatory Great Books college class. I didn't leave the Gospels filled with wonder. I don't feel wonder now in cowboy church either. In my attempt to understand "the country," I am not succeeding.

Then Eric wants to play what I have privately started to think of as the "country mouse and city mouse" game. The game usually starts with a question that is prefaced in one of two ways: "Why do liberals . . . ?" or "Why do city people . . . ?" This time, Eric asks: "So what would city people have thought about that song about the Christian family being in peril like the spotted owl? I mean, that's something, right? They go around playing for nursing homes. For old people."

I agree that it would have been a surprise for them to hear the juxtaposition. Out in the country, I can see why the Christian family might seem to be endangered. This is, after all, the same weekend that the *New York Times* published an article on open marriages, and how traditional ideas about family and marriage feel constricting these days. I doubt that the Hinkle Family would approve of polyamory. At the same time, I don't know of a secular group that makes it their life's work to go around playing music in nursing homes for old people.

There is something so completely trusting about the way Eric believes in the Christian family. He takes it for granted that it is a good thing. How do I explain that in my world the Christian family is seen as limiting, and judgmental of women, gays, minorities, and all manner of "others"?

"Do they think we are arrogant?" he asks.

I'm not sure what he means.

"Like we're better than everyone else?"

My mind does a slow calculation. I realize he is wondering if people in the city think that somehow Christians think they are better than non-Christians for not being gay and not having sex before marriage. The truth is so much worse that I don't want to tell him. I think of the Richard Dawkins quote: "The God of the Old Testament is arguably the most unpleasant character in all fiction: jealous and proud of it; a petty, unjust, unforgiving control-freak; a vindictive, bloodthirsty ethnic cleanser; a misogynistic, homophobic, racist, infanticidal, genocidal, filicidal, pestilential, megalomaniacal, sadomasochistic, capriciously malevolent bully." Or "More generally . . . one of the truly bad effects of religion is that it teaches us that it is a virtue to be satisfied with not understanding."

"They don't think you are self-righteous. They think you are . . . stupid."

"Because of evolution."

"Partly."

"And?"

"Because of your attitudes toward gays and lesbians."

"You have lots of gay friends."

"Yes," I say.

"Why do you think that is?"

Why do I think that is. "I'm a writer. I have a lot of creative friends, and gay people often come to the cities. Often they work in creative fields."

The crew is listening, standing around us in a casual semicircle. They don't make eye contact, but I can see their naked attention. *Marie knows lots of gay people.*

He says: "If I think back, there was a gay farmer who I cut for."

Samuel is incredulous. "Was there?"

"Yes. In Texas. But mostly, there aren't any gays on the farms."

"Like I said, they go to the cities," I say.

We get into the pickup trucks to go to lunch; there is a Mexican place in Vernon that returning crew members like Samuel and Juston want to visit. Along the way, the crew shifts the conversation over to the subject of Bethany's future gun, and my mind drifts back to church and my failure to understand almost everything about it.

I think of how quickly I have in the past leaped to the conclusion that stupidity accounts for our differences. Despite the legislation Obama passed for the working class and the poor, still the one quote conservatives and Fox News trot out is this: "They get bitter, they cling to guns or religion or antipathy toward people who aren't like them or anti-immigrant sentiment or anti-trade sentiment as a way to explain their frustrations." That's it. The flyover states summed up. Eric and Juston and all the others too. The defense against this statement is usually something about defending a "way of life," which to liberal ears sounds exactly like what Southern plantation owners said about slavery. And there we go. But I have promised myself—and Eric—that I will resist going down this well-trod path.

What does "Jesus died for your sins" actually mean? It can't mean just that because he died, I have to believe in him. *Or else.*

Sometimes white people confide in me: "You know, the truth is I can't tell a lot of Asian people apart." One response to a statement like this is to charge them with racism. The other, which I tend to agree with, is to assume that the white person is telling me the truth. They quite literally *cannot* see, because they do not know how, because they did not learn and because they did not try to or need to. I know this because I have been told by people in Japan: "I do not mean to be rude, but I cannot always tell white people apart."

I think maybe it is like this about Jesus. Maybe my brain short-circuits to the "stupid" assessment because I have never tried another neural pathway.

While I am thinking, I see a strange shape in a wheat field. Dark, pointed ears, like those of a German shepherd, stick up out of the heads of wheat. Before I have time to ask if anyone else saw whatever the thing was, it has receded and I wonder if I saw anything at all.

Dwayne has arrived with his crew. We call them "the Sisters." This is because Eric's crew is known as the Wolgemuth Brothers, and to distinguish the "Brothers" from Dwayne's crew, we call them "Sisters." To make the issue of gender equitable, Dwayne's service truck has a masculine name, Charlie, as a counterpoint to our Lily. Sometimes the Brothers and the Sisters will work together, and sometimes we will be separate.

Dwayne's crew parks their equipment down by the bins. They bring their trailers to the RV park in the lot next to ours. Other crews are also starting to arrive. Because Dwayne's wife has not yet come—her two girls are still finishing up school—we all eat together in Eric and Emily's trailer, which is another way of saying that Emily is now cooking for nineteen. I offer to help. Really, I do. But she doesn't seem to want my help. I tell myself I have a child and I know how it is. A woman knows her own kitchen, and someone walking in is likely to slow down a process rather than speed it up. All the same, the disparity concerns me, all the more so when I sit down for dinner and Emily stands. She seems accustomed to standing. I feel lazy, eating her food, and sitting, and not helping. It's as if I am not only the wrong gender but have regressed and am not even an adult.

That night there are large dishes on the table filled with corn, chili and beans, fluffy biscuits, butter, and a marshmallow salad. There is always dessert. Eric is in good spirits. He likes having all the boys around. He is the big boss and he tosses out questions good-naturedly to see how they will be answered.

"Who here farms organic?" Eric asks. "Your chickens, Samuel. Organic."

Samuel is a Mennonite. His parents—bonnet people—now run a boutique dairy farm–sitting service. When Amish and Mennonite farmers who run dairies want to go on vacation for a week or so, they call Samuel's parents to take care of the cows. There are many kinds of dairies—some with modern equipment and some without—and Samuel's parents can handle all permutations. His parents also raise organic, free-range chickens.

Samuel is at once lanky and muscular, with buff arms and an expressive face with hooded eyes that flutter when he is animated, and a wide, rubbery mouth that stretches into a broad smile. He switches from manly to goofy in an instant. He is what we would call "cute," and he is unaware that in my world people would value his physical beauty over his ability to drive and fix things and be trustworthy. In fact none of the boys seem to have any sense of how one goes about getting sex, or overtly flaunting sexual appeal. They are all, it has been repeated to me, virgins, and will remain so until marriage. There is simply a lack of the aggressive crackle that comes from eye contact with boys who are or will soon be sexually active and are encouraged to be so.

Bethany, however, has noticed Samuel. Her cheeks flush around him and she listens intently to his jokes and makes sure to laugh.

"It's really just you get the label," Samuel says of the chickens. His voice is low and musical and belies his boyish looks. "You open the door so the chickens can go out. But they don't go out. They stay in where the food is. But they have the option to go out, which makes PETA happy. It's silly."

"Really?" I ask.

"Really."

No one disagrees about the chickens and PETA. This exchange is one I have heard countless times when Eric has taken me to visit the family-run chicken and egg farmers in Pennsylvania who participate in a larger cooperative organization that pools their products; the concern for the happiness of chickens is a city thing. *As if*, the farmers always say to me, they would ever farm with the intent to degrade the quality of the very thing that makes them money.

"Who here made it to high school?" Eric asks.

Most of the boys raise their hands, and Eric asks where everyone went. The majority attended public schools, except for Luther, who attended a private Mennonite high school.

"Georgie. You didn't raise your hand."

"Homeschooled," Georgie says and some of the boys giggle.

"You go to high school?"

"No, sir." He tells us how last summer he worked with the Mennonite Disaster Service to rebuild houses that had been burned by the wildfires in Central California.

"Eighth grade," Eric declares. "Who else was homeschooled?"

Samuel reluctantly raises his hand.

"Home*schooling*!" Juston proclaims this the way some people might declare "Tahoe!" or "Cannes!," as though those in the know will hear the term and it will immediately conjure up a host of associated meanings and images and outfits.

"Are all your churches nonresistant?" Eric presses on.

They nod.

"If you take up arms, you cannot be part of the church?"

They nod again.

"What exactly does that mean?" I ask.

"It means," Eric says slowly, "they would let a cop attend, but he could not be a member."

The boys nod.

"Would you want to bear arms?" Eric asks.

"Might want to," Samuel says.

Some of the Sisters nod in silent agreement.

"But you can hunt?" I ask.

Eric nods. Then he adds: "You should all watch that movie. *The Patriot*. I have it here. Someday, when there's rain and it's slow."

"Colonial times?" someone asks.

"Yes," Eric answers.

Later, outside in the parking lot, Eric tells me: "Pay attention to Georgie's accent. That's how you know he's Old Order and that he speaks Pennsylvania Dutch."

I try to rewind the tape in my head. There is something unusual about the way Georgie speaks. He does have a lilt. Actually, Eric has a version of it, too, but I don't tell him this. Certainly Georgie's is more pronounced.

"My grandmother's family was from Lancaster County," I say to Eric.

"That's right."

"Before they came to Nebraska." I tell him I don't know to which denomination my great-grandfather belonged. I have sometimes wondered if some lingering trace of influence from the Lancaster County side of the family can be found in me. I don't know much about the Anabaptists except for their history of being persecuted and that they emphasize reconciliation. I know the latter only because it is something Juston told me.

Some evenings it seems as though the sky is a lid pressing down the light to the west and sending it away from us. As dark ink spreads across the eastern horizon, my heart feels crushed, as though it, too, is being drained of light. Then I feel a direct link between the vastness of space and my tiny human soul—a connection I feel palpably for an hour or two at dusk, when the sky is in opposition with itself: indigo here and red there. My blood wants to follow the red path of the sun. I want to bleed westward and my body wants to go there too. Eric almost always wants to use the last bit of sunlight to look at the fields. The light is calling us all to do something. I go with him when I can.

The crew continues their evening activities separately, without saying where they are going. Bethany doesn't tell me either when I ask. She shrugs. "Oh, we just drive around." But she's a terrible liar and I see she doesn't want to disclose to me where they have been, but that she is also uncomfortable keeping everything a secret. She seems to be unsure of what all my questions are trying to get at. Juston does not seem to care; he is happy to have time to either read a book or sit and watch television in his parents' trailer, or, if invited, go out with his father. I don't find this so strange; he has already told me he doesn't feel as proficient at farming as the rest of the crew and that he needs time to read and be alone with his thoughts. I, too, can be a loner and so don't find his solitude strange. At sundown, I, too, often lie in the trailer and read, unless I'm invited to take a look at the land.

And then, one evening after dinner, as I am reading Mari Sandoz, Eric bangs on my trailer door. I open it and he is wearing shorts and he says to me, a little wildly: "Want to go shoot pigs?"

"Yes," I say immediately.

"Meet by the pickup in ten minutes."

When I go out, I see Juston and ask if he is going to go hunting with us. "No." He smiles at me in a sort of big-brotherly way. "I don't really like the noise. But you should go." Then he heads into his parents' trailer.

Not long after, Eric comes out of the same trailer, carrying his cell phone and his gun and smiling widely. He is delighted. The boys are in the back of the pickup, holding a gun apiece. They are carrying a shotgun, a rifle, or an AR. Only Bethany doesn't own a gun, though Samuel is helping her research her first purchase. Bethany and Bradford climb aboard the truck and we roar off into the wild.

Pigs—what I was calling wild boars—are pests. It is explained to me that a wild boar is only a male, and so to correctly refer to the animals we are hunting I am to say "pig," though I have since heard people refer to them as "hogs." In my romanticizing way, I ask if we are going to do anything with the pig once we kill it. I am thinking we might cut it up and eat it the way the Ingalls family does in *Little House on the Prairie*. No, I am told. We will leave the pig in the fields and the other pigs will eat it instead.

I can feel Eric's frustration with my question, though I can also tell he understands that I simply don't comprehend why we are killing pigs, which, in my world, are as smart as dogs and feature in books like *Charlotte's Web*. "They are destructive," Eric says simply.

Eric has arranged with Jerry Bob Daniel that we will be on his property killing pigs. Jerry Bob owns the Circle Bar Ranch, which is affiliated with Pitchfork Ranch, which placed second overall at the ranch rodeo, and won the calf-branding category.

This is what the crew has been doing at night. This is also why Juston has not gone with them; he is not a fan of guns. Because there are concerns about one of the Sisters handling a gun—no one will say who—they have been keeping their nighttime activities secret.

Most of the boys ride not in the pickup cab but outside on the cargo bed, where they stand upright, brace themselves as Eric drives, and look for pigs. Luther has excellent balance and seems to stand completely still no matter how bumpy the dirt road, scanning the horizon with a pair of binoculars, a small, natural smile settled on his pressed lips. Samuel has all the gear. He has an AR and another set of binoculars and a scope. I wonder exactly how to spot a pig. I tell them about the strange animal I saw over the weekend with ears like a German shepherd. Could that have been a pig?

"Might have," Eric says. "But pigs usually travel in packs."

I ask Samuel why he has the assault rifle and he shrugs. "It's lighter. More compact and efficient."

"There," Eric shouts. I hadn't seen a thing. In the distance, off to the left perhaps ten yards or so, there is a smear of brown in the wheat. Eric barrels down the dirt road so we will be perpendicular to the pigs, who are feasting on the grain.

Eric stops the truck. "Cover your ears," he orders.

I am scared but excited. I cover my ears. Then, a powerful burst of energy and sound. A shell lands on the dash. There are more shots. Even inside the pickup I can feel just from the sound and from the thrust overhead that the bullet is more powerful than I am, and I understand that it can kill a man quickly. Off in the wheat field, the pigs are running for cover in the mesquite.

"Won't be the first time they've been shot at," Eric says.

We are done shooting now, and it is time to climb over the barbed wire fence to see if we have killed a pig. The boys are fairly sure we have not, but we need to check. Despite my new boots, I need Samuel's hand to make it over the fence, though Bethany has adjusted to the environment and clambers over easily. She is so tall, like her brother. These two giants are able to leap fences, but all my sit-ups and free weights and downloaded exercise routines straight out of Tracy Anderson's loft in Tribeca don't seem to help me much. We trudge through the field.

"Do you see?" Eric says to me. The wheat field has been trampled. Perhaps 50 percent of the stalks are bent low to the ground.

"It's worse than hail damage," I say.

"Can be." He nods.

I have seen so many signs in Japan warning me to be careful of the wild boar; I myself am born in the year of the boar and so feel somewhat protective of these animals.

When I talk to city people about farming, I often end up drawing on the analogy of gardening. Plenty of people don't think twice about killing gophers. Most gardeners understand that rabbits and deer, while adorable, are a nuisance to plants and roots, and to roses in particular.

Farming is full of tensions like this, though on a much larger scale. Fences do not keep out animals other than cattle. And so: open season on pig.

We have not killed a pig. All the pigs have escaped. So we go back over the fence and into the truck and farther out on the plains. We see many more pigs that evening. Now some of the boys are scouting with binoculars, and when they see a pig, they pound the roof of the truck and shout. If Eric sees pigs, he pounds the roof from the inside and shouts. At one point there must be thirty pigs and piglets foraging and grazing amid a herd of cattle. Eric is nervous. We may not kill the cows, as each is worth thousands of dollars. He does not want us to shoot into the herd of cattle, and this is difficult to resist, since so many piglets are mixed in with the cows, and piglets would be easy to kill. Killing piglets would be satisfying.

The evening drifts. We hop another fence and go into the wild. The beauty of the plains astonishes me. Pockets of mustard-colored daisies host a colony of so many bees, their numbers seem to belie the rumor that the bees are dying. We go up a small rise and a cloud of white butterflies exhales into the air, making way for us.

The plains of Texas are dotted with recessed areas the Mexicans called playas. In years when the rain is plentiful, the playas accumulate water and play host to killdeer, ducks, and other waterfowl. The playas are an ephemeral but constant source of life, and the vegetation dips down around them, expanding or contracting as their thirst for water is quenched.

We pass a deer blind, a camouflage-patterned rectangular structure raised on stilts and tall enough for one man. From here, a hunter can sit for a time and wait for a deer to come close enough for him to kill it easily. Our method that evening is much less methodical. We follow nature on and on into the wild. I can feel the rhythm of it, how easily raw nature can suck a man indefinitely toward the horizon, and our pace builds like a piece of music; we walk with increasing obsession, like Ravel's "Bolero."

We come upon a break where a sentry of pylons marches straight across our path. The pylons are tall, like emotionless robots, spindly, hard, and silhouetted figures projected against the canvas of a much larger sky. It is an interruption of nature by the world of man.

Bradford turns around. He speaks without embellishment. "Let's go back," he says in his soft but confident voice, a born leader. The others turn around immediately and follow him. This time Bradford finds a gate, which he swings open so we can all walk out, and I'm grateful not to have to climb anything.

The mood is a little bit low. We have seen hogs but killed none. It is getting dark and the sun is sinking into the horizon. The interplay of space and clouds and sun here in Texas means that the actual point of sunset can be spectacular, and tonight is one of those nights with a red orb—a UFO of a sun—plunging down through a strange pear-shaped cloud toward the horizon. We amble home. Then, from above, the pounding on the roof on the truck. Wild pig to the right. We look, and there they are, a small herd of pigs eating grain. Eric brakes.

Everything happens in silence except for the gunshot. I cover my ears. Brace myself. Then, bang. A moment later, the boys fly off the back of the truck, along with Bethany. They stride out into the field ahead of me, swallowed up by the wheat. I am lagging as usual, struggling with the barbed wire. I hear another gunshot. I look at Eric and he has what I call his inner smile, the smile he makes unconsciously when he understands something that someone has done and approves of it.

"That means they got it," I say.

"It's dead." The second shot was from a pistol; the pig was put out of its misery.

It is dead when I get there only a minute later. Completely lifeless, and surrounded by blood. I expect to feel something—pity or disgust or sadness. But I don't. It is as though a switch has flipped inside of me, and the pig has gone from being a wild animal I might have pitied to a grain-eating pest who has now been stopped. It is this easy to change my mind about something. It is this easy to place something I might have worried about—the life of a pig—into a compartment of my brain unreachable by my heart.

We leave the pig in the field, though Eric lets the farmer know we have killed one. It will be eaten, I am assured. Other pigs and buzzards will do the work of disposing of the carcass.

On the way home, we stop by the Circle Bar hunting lodge. A small group of structures make up the central part of the ranch; the buildings are from the town where Jerry Bob grew up. As a wealthy rancher, he is now preserving his childhood home, preventing the town from becoming a ghost village. The hunting lodge was once a church but has been redecorated in the style of the Southwest, with antler chandeliers and tartan-covered furniture, paintings of the Republican presidents, and the trophy heads of dead animals.

Most of the crew is lounging in the old hunting lodge and watching a rodeo on a large-screen television. Juston, who did not go hunting, is playing poker with some of the Sisters. His fingers are interlaced with a hand of cards. He is intent on winning. Occasionally he looks up and grins at me, but mostly he and the others are lost in their world of car talk, chips, and inside jokes. It feels civilized and strange, and he and the poker players look so far away. I think about my cat, Angus, and how at night it would take him an hour or so to settle down after coming home from hunting mice. I feel this way, too, and I fidget and finally browse through some books on Texas sitting on a shelf, and then it is fully night and time to go home.

We are in the wheat belt, the parts of Kansas, Oklahoma, Texas, Nebraska, and Colorado where wheat is the dominant crop. To the east is the corn belt, and to the southeast, the historical cotton belt. In the corn belt, corn is often grown on alternating years with soybeans and occasionally with wheat; rotating crops is healthy for soil. In general, land that grows corn is more valuable and thus more expensive than land that grows wheat, which is the cheapest of all these cash crops. Not all farm ground is exactly the same.

If you cut a slice of farmland as you would a cake, and you pull the slice out on a spatula, you would see layers. The grass and crops and roots are the frosting. They are embedded in the topsoil, which means the top two to seven inches of dirt, the most densely packed with microbes and nutrients and which feeds the newly planted crops. Beneath the topsoil is a layer of dirt called subsoil, which also contains decomposing matter, but which is much less rich with organic substances.

A seed planted in warm and wet soil will sprout, first by sending out roots to anchor itself in the topsoil. Then the seed will germinate a green part above the ground, poking up the first shoot, like a periscope, and unfurling its leaves to collect the sunshine. And then the plant grows using four basic ingredients: sunshine, air, water, and nutrients. In the process of growing, a plant, like a human embryo, must make its body out of what looks like nothing. Its cellular process takes basic building blocks and, following the programming encoded in its DNA, begins to make more leaves and then makes those leaves bigger, and then makes its stalk taller, and then perhaps adds even more leaves. The building blocks out of which this matter is created lie in the soil, and the most basic elements are nitrogen, phosphorus, and potassium. Light provides energy for this process through photosynthesis.

Most gardeners know that synthetic fertilizer can replenish soil that loses nutrients too quickly. But fertilizer cannot provide everything a plant needs. Healthy topsoil also has dozens of microbes that can't be replicated in a lab. Healthy topsoil contains bacteria, fungi, and microbes. You know you have healthy soil because it feels healthy; it's almost spongy. Agronomists like to say that this kind of soil has great "aggregate stability"; the combined microbes keep it nutritious and stable. Good aggregate stability means the soil is less likely to break down when tilled, when swept by wind, or when farmed.

If you have a garden, then you are probably familiar with the process of pulling weeds out of the soil to give your carrots or gladioli the best chance to grow. Farming involves a similar process, but if your farm is 1,500 acres, it is hardly practical to rely on human hands to prune your crop; you need machines.

Traditionally, weeds were controlled by the plow. In the fall or spring, before planting, a plow was dragged through the earth, beating up the soil and disturbing and displacing the roots and the bodies of the weeds so they died. Shortly after, crops were planted.

Plowing was a technique brought over from Europe to the United States, and it initially worked well on the plains. Then the plow failed. In *The Great Plains in Transition*, Carl Frederick Kraenzel writes repeatedly of "humid area values." In a humid state like Pennsylvania, a farmer can plow (or till) his field to get rid of weeds, and when the topsoil is exposed to the air, the humidity will help keep the soil from turning to powder as quickly as it does on the Great Plains. There is so much more precipitation in Lancaster, Pennsylvania, than in Kimball, Nebraska, where my family farm is; the former gets around forty-three inches of water a year and the latter seventeen inches.

On the Great Plains, once that precious topsoil faced the air, it often desiccated. Without enough moisture and nutrients to help it congeal, the topsoil blew away. It blew when the farmer was tilling, it blew after tilling, and it blew when it did not rain. What was left was subsoil. When the dust blew, it carried away the small bit of moisture in the top layer of sediment, and the sediment blew into nearby waterways, which ran into larger waterways, until big rivers like the Mississippi and the Missouri were choked with dirt, and the muddy pollution, in turn, choked the lungs of fish and killed them. The problems were multiple. The most well-known large-scale incidents of such blowing were dust storms in the thirties, which gave rise to the term "Dust Bowl" and coincided with the popularization of the combine harvester. By the sixties, when farmers were replacing lost nutrients via synthetic fertilizers, the topsoil was carrying chemicals when it blew, and the fertilizer landed in the waterways and fed the algae, which ballooned, so the once mostly clear waters were thick like pea soup, and began killing the fish, who could not breathe.

Nitrogen fertilizer is one of the key changes in agriculture that people point to when they talk about the Green Revolution. This was a period in the fifties and sixties when synthetic fertilizers, pesticides, machinery, and new strains of crops all worked together to increase agricultural output worldwide. Fertilizer use exploded after World War II, when domestic factories that had been used to produce nitrogen explosives switched over to making nitrogen fertilizer. The wheat that the fertilizer was feeding had changed, too, which contributed to greater output.

Until the twenties, much of the wheat on the wheat belt was related to the Turkey Red varietal brought over in the trunks and bags of Russian Mennonites fleeing czarist Russia. Today, this wheat is scarcely grown at all, though it has seen a revival in the niche market of heritage grains that re-create wheat originally grown on the prairie by American pioneers. Turkey Red is taller but less fruitful than the wheat I have seen with Eric. Because it is tall, Turkey Red's canopy creates so much shade that weeds have a hard time growing and competing for the sun. This is helpful.

But tall plants also take up moisture; the available water goes into making the stalk tall and there is less moisture for kernels to form. The height also means that the wheat is easily destabilized by wind or a light rain shower; the original Turkey Red wheat often fell down laughing drunk, and then it was hard to harvest and on occasion could not be harvested at all.

By the mid-twentieth century, scientists had bred new varietals of wheat that were shorter, and were sometimes referred to as "dwarf wheat." In 1935, the Japanese scientist Gonjiro Inazuka took a short wheat native to Japan, called Daruma, and crossbred it with an American wheat called Fultz. The resulting strain—Fultz-Daruma—was further bred with Turkey Red to produce something called Norin 10. This new wheat was only two feet high instead of four, making it hardy. Norin 10 could prop itself back up after a light rain. It utilized moisture more efficiently, so more grain was produced and more bushels per acre could be reaped from the land.

During the American occupation of Japan after the war, Norin 10 was discovered by the American biologist Cecil Salmon, who sent a sample to agronomists in the United States, who quickly recognized the potential benefits of this shorter wheat plant. Eventually, samples of Norin 10 found their way into the hands of the Nobel Prize–winning scientist Norman Borlaug, often called the father of the Green Revolution.

Borlaug, who was born in Iowa, had received a doctorate in plant pathology and genetics in 1942 from the University of Minnesota. He took a position at the Cooperative Wheat Research and Production Program in Mexico, which was funded partly by the Rockefeller Foundation and the Mexican government. Borlaug's goal was to combat world hunger by utilizing the many disciplines of science—genetics, soil science, agronomy, and others—to develop high-yield strains of wheat. Borlaug took Salmon's Norin 10 and crossbred it with other varietals in Mexico, eventually developing the precursors to the wheat that covers many of the fields I visit with Eric and his crew. Mexico, which had been importing wheat, now became a grower of surplus grain it could export. Famers around the world, including my family, saw this and wanted to grow the same kind of wheat.

Some say that in this transition from taller wheat to shorter wheat the makeup of the protein was changed, which in turn has caused gluten intolerance. Certainly the "heritage" grains do taste different from the newer ones, and you can increasingly find bakeries in places like San Francisco or Boulder, Colorado, that bake with these older varietals. But for farms, which are always in a financially precarious position, high yields are the best assurance for financial success and continuing the harvest life cycle. As a result, the older, taller grains have mostly been replaced by newer ones.

So the wheat was shorter and the yields higher. But still the dust blew, and the fertilizer with it. Something had to be done about the dust.

What if we did not plow? someone asked. What if the stubble from the harvested crop was left in the soil? This, after all, was what had happened on the prairie when the buffalo dominated it. The buffalo ate the grass, then moved on to another part of the plains, and the stubble that was left behind was sufficient to anchor the soil so a new crop of prairie grass could grow. If farmers could replicate this protective cycle, then perhaps the topsoil would not blow away quite so much. In that case, a farmer would need to plant the next crop directly into the old stubble. Credit for this idea is usually given to Edward H. Faulkner, who, in his 1943 book *Plowman's Folly*, first proposed not tilling the land before planting the field.

The problem, though, was that the short wheat, while losing less moisture, also couldn't produce a canopy to choke out the weeds; as it grew, the weeds got the moisture and nutrients first. But what if there was a way to kill the weeds that didn't involve plowing? What if a chemical could be sprayed onto the weeds and if in the window between the weeds dying and the seeds sprouting the new crop could grow?

This is, in fact, precisely what happened during what farmers often refer to as the "no-till revolution." In 2000, the price of Roundup, the chemical herbicide glyphosate made by the corporation Monsanto, dropped from as much as forty-four dollars a gallon to eight or nine dollars a gallon, making it somewhat affordable for the average farmer. This reduction in price forever changed farming.

Most plants use a specific enzyme to bind to the nutrients I listed above, and to metabolize these nutrients into amino acids, which plants need to grow. Glyphosate is a small synthetic molecule that binds to that specific enzyme and stops it from making amino acids. And without those amino acids, the plant dies. Glyphosate binds to an enzyme found in only plants and not in humans. To spread glyphosate effectively, it is mixed with water and something called a surfactant, which helps the glyphosate adhere to the leaves and plants on which it is sprayed; the idea is to enable the farmer to use as little spray as possible, but to make the spray targeted. The concoction—Roundup—and its low price meant farmers had new options not only for weed control but for planting.

I remember my father in the nineties passionately insisting to farmers in Nebraska that modern machinery could indeed punch through the stubble on the ground to plant seeds. He would get on the phone and argue that there was no reason to plow a field after harvest. "Just kill the weeds," he would say. "And then a year later, plant the new crop directly into the untilled ground using a hardy planter." We were the first in our county in Nebraska to practice this method of farming.

Sometimes when I visit the family farm in Nebraska, I see an old-timer tilling the ground; tradition is hard to give up. But slowly, field by field, farmers have switched over to no-till, if only to stop the top-soil from blowing away, gathering along fence lines, and burying the wooden and metal stakes under heaps of accumulated powdery earth. No-till makes it possible for a farmer to spend less money on fuel. In one report, the USDA estimates that "farmers practicing continuous conventional till use just over six gallons of diesel fuel per acre each year. Continuous no-till requires less than two gallons per acre. Across the country, that difference leads to nearly 282 million gallons of die-sel fuel saved annually." In 2016, the agronomist Jayson Lusk penned an op-ed in the *New York Times* praising the developments of mod-ern farming, noting that no-till had helped reduce soil erosion in the United States by at least 40 percent; the Soil Science Society of America agrees with this statistic.

No-till does not get much coverage in the mainstream media. I have my suspicions as to why: it's not an easy story to summarize, because it involves understanding an entire system of agriculture, and also it isn't a terribly sexy headline. In the past twenty years, I remember only one article in the *New York Times* about no-till, from 2015, titled "Farmers Put Down the Plow for More Productive Soil." In this piece, journalist Erica Goode cites most of the information I've covered above, noting that "government surveys suggest that the use of no-tillage farming has grown sharply over the last decade, accounting for about 35 percent of cropland in the United States." Goode covers the benefits of no-till, how it has stopped erosion and the seeping of fertilizer into water-ways. Only at the end does she slip in that no-till is partly facilitated by Roundup killing off the weeds that grow between harvests, and by the planting of a crop directly into stubble of an untilled field.

To people in the city, Roundup, as devised by Monsanto—the same company that created Agent Orange—is a horror, a Frankenstein chemical engineered to kill us all while making the corporation rich. Current coverage of Monsanto and Roundup in mainstream media re-flects this, and not without reason. A 2018 lawsuit in San Francisco awarded $289 billion to a man dying of non-Hodgkin's lymphona, which he claimed was brought about by two accidental and complete immersions in Roundup, though Monsanto has appealed and claims there is no scientific evidence to back the claim that Roundup is carcinogenic. But more lawsuits have already been filed.

At the same time, in November of 2017, the *Journal of the National Cancer Institute* conducted a wide-reaching study of forty-five thousand farmers and agricultural workers who use and are more widely exposed to Roundup than the average consumer or gardener, and found that there was no increase in the occurrence of cancer, except for a small uptick in the occurrence of a non-Hodgkin's lymphoma, the exact form of cancer for which the court in San Francisco ordered Monsanto to pay damages. Henry Salzberg, Bloomberg Distinguished Professor of computational biology and genomics at Johns Hopkins University, penned a comprehensive piece for *Forbes* magazine on glyphosate, determining that "the evidence that it causes any type of cancer is very weak."

But I also wonder about the scientific studies. Tobacco companies once insisted that science proved there was nothing carcinogenic in tobacco smoke, and this turned out to be untrue. People, I know, can bend the results of their studies to suit their aims. Are the farmers I know biased to accept Roundup because of the myriad benefits it has provided? Did my family defend Roundup for this reason too?

Or do I feel nervous about Roundup because I'm not a farmer for whom Roundup has so transformed my working life? Instead, I'm in a place where I can disassociate from Roundup's efficacy, and so I have the luxury of feeling skeptical.

Can we measure the tradeoff between soil erosion, pollution of waterways, and glyphosate's effects on the soil? If the very soil on which we depend is threatened, then so many of the other issues over which we fight will quickly become extraneous. Other times, I ask myself why I'm willing to tolerate cell phone use, but I worry about eating conventional carrots. And other times—many other times—I will simply pay extra for a bag of vegetables labeled "organic."

We wait for the field to dry, and then try to cut a little bit. But the rain comes upon us at night. In the morning—the same thing. I decide to go into Vernon to get my nails done. I have found a nail salon in town run by Vietnamese. I am delighted at the thought of meeting Asians in the middle of the plains. All summer long, the only Asians I will see will be manicurists like this, located in larger towns and cities, and they will run either beauty parlors or restaurants.

I chat with them happily in the nail salon, explaining who I am and where I'm from. I am a curiosity. Why is an Asian person getting her nails done in Vernon, and traveling with farmers?

I'm always explaining myself wherever I go. I am accustomed to it. In Japan I go through permutations of this exercise, explaining why I'm here at this temple/factory/school, and after about twenty minutes of conversation, I am usually asked: "Wait. Why do you speak Japanese?" Because my features never quite blend into any setting, I am often asked to account for my presence. It is always like this in the United States, even in California. One of the great joys of living in New York City was the fact that everyone was from somewhere else, and we exchanged the stories of our origins as equals; I felt at home precisely because everyone had an unusual background.

While I am a puzzle to the nail salon workers, I realize that they aren't a puzzle to me, as the harvesters are. "You came after the war?" I ask.

"Yes," they say.

"You have children?"

"Yes!" All this—the nail salons with the assortment of gel colors and creams and massages—is always for the children. Then we have the conversation I always have in these situations. They want to know that it is possible that their children might speak their language, while being American at the same time. I assure them that this is possible.

"It's usually up to the mother, though," I say.

"Always the mother," they agree.

I ask if they can recommend a Vietnamese restaurant to me, and they laugh.

"My mother's house!"

"My wife!"

"No restaurant?" I ask. They shake their heads.

Then my phone rings. It is Eric, letting me know that a tornado warning has been issued and that I should not leave town until it is over. About five minutes later, Juston calls to tell me the same thing. He is with his mother on his way to the Walmart in Vernon.

"Tornado?" someone else says. A white woman. "Oh. That's why it's so still outside." This has not occurred to me. While the manicurist works on my nails on one hand, I download radar with the other. I had been following the weather rather than the radar. Now I look for a storm. To the southwest there is a big, fat blob with bright pink in the middle.

I get another call from Juston, who asks me where I am. He urges me to go to the courthouse in town to ride out the storm. As I am about to leave, one of the patrons says to me: "Just go to the hospital. It's across the street." Then I get a text from Juston letting me know that he and his mother are outside. When I meet them, Juston is carrying the laptop. Of course, the computer is the one thing that must be saved if everything else is going to be destroyed. I don't have my computer. At least we are still at the start of this adventure, I think, and I don't have many notes yet.

We go to the hospital. No one is in the lobby or by the desk. I go outside. It is completely silent. Not a single car roars by and not one bird is singing. A few minutes later, Emily comes to get me.

"The evacuation area is inside," she says gently but firmly. "You really need to come in."

We go through a few sets of swinging metal doors and then are in an inner corridor—a square on the inside of the hospital. The nurses bring in chairs. People are sitting, or lying in wheeled, green vinyl armchairs that look as though they came straight out of the seventies. So, too, do the battered green oxygen tanks. I think of all the times I have read news stories about New Orleans or the tsunami in Japan and how people in hospitals worked to try to keep patients safe and healthy. And here I am, a complete stranger sheltering in a hospital. The staff offers me water. The nurses go around and around in laps, checking blood pressure, checking temperatures, checking medicated drip bags. There are a couple of male doctors who are brown- and black-skinned, and we give one another "the nod." We see one another.

We have no windows. We have only the sirens, which go off intermittently, extending the duration of the warning. We have texts coming in from people on the outside, and tidbits of gossip are whispered and shared. The school is on lockdown. Family members are entering the building. Other people are seeking safety in other shelters. We wait.

Later, Eric shows me a video of the tornado. It is a strange cloud, bulging down, drawn by an invisible force. It is like a vaporous entity trying to grow an udder. But as weirdly animallike as the cloud is, the ground is even more strange and alarming. This is where the dust and debris fly, as if the wind on the ground is recklessly striving to make contact with the cloud above. You can see the cloud straining to take a shape, and opposing the shape too. It is as though earth and sky are trying to come into contact, but know they are not supposed to. A tainted kind of love.

Eric says he watched it for a long time, drawn into a trance by nature. And then, abruptly, he said to the crew members with him: "Everyone get in the pickup." He drove west; west is usually the direction away from storms.

When I drive back to the trailers after the evacuation warning has ended, I cannot tell at first that a tornado has come through. Everything looks the same. Then I see a tree tossed on its side, a felled giant. Bethany shows me pictures of golf ball–sized hail. The fields I pass look like lace; the wheat has been shredded by the storm. The roads are lined with red water and mud. Windshields on cars have become a fragile lattice of glass barely clinging to the frame, especially if the driver did not stop and drive west, but accelerated into the storm out of panic.

Ah, I think. The turtle and the snake have been in contact and the weather has come at last.

FOUR

IN THE MORNING, Eric and I go to look at the fields. I ask him, as I always do, to tell me what he sees. He reads the pig prints in the ground and shows me where the hogs have burrowed. Some of the tracks are fresh. He wades farther out into the wheat and I follow.

"Is it about half?" I ask.

"Fifty percent loss." He picks stalks so I can see how the hail has hammered the wheat and sent the granules flying; they lie strewn all over the ground. In the quick heat, the hail has melted, and there is nothing left to demonstrate for certain that the storm has killed the wheat, but Eric cannot think of anything else that would scatter grain like this. It is as if we are at a crime scene, reading the forensic evidence.

"Does it upset you?" I ask.

"Nothing to do but accept it," he says, standing upright now and staring down at the field. His fingers are looped in his belt buckles. "I'd feel worse if it had been ripe enough to cut. But that wheat wasn't ripe yet. Couldn't have cut it anyway."

Back in the pickup truck, we see a herd of wild pigs trotting through the neighboring field. Through the open window, I can hear them grunting. Despite our machines, our guns, our rubber tires on the dirt road, and our efficiency, I feel we are still very small and helpless against the combined forces of the pigs and the weather. For all that my life in the city has sometimes felt overly controlled by technology, there is no amalgamation of man-made inventions that could have inoculated us against the near-complete destruction of this crop. We happen to pass a herd of cattle being unloaded onto a wheat field we had hoped to cut. We have not been told this expressly, but we assume that the wheat is considered such a loss that the farmer has decided to use it to feed cattle instead.

We stop going to look at fields, because the roads are too muddy to look any further. It was one thing when the fields were merely wet, but now many are lost completely and it is not at all clear what we should do.

We kill time.

In the beginning, Bradford still finds canola to cut, and he lays it down in rows so it can dry. I say "lay down," because this is what the canola header does: it cuts the stalk, then lays it down in rows behind the combine, rather than spreading it around as it spreads wheat chaff. Later, a combine with a special header goes through and picks up the rows, and the machine separates the tiny black seeds from the rest of the stalk. The seeds are collected into a bin, then transported to another facility, where they will ultimately be pressed and their oil extracted. After the storm, there are places where the canola remains. But soon there is no more canola to pick up. There isn't even anything that is broken that needs to be fixed. Or, that needs fixed.

Most of the time, Bethany goes out hunting with the crew, but occasionally she is excluded, and I try, when this happens, to get her to open up. I ask her about Samuel. But though she blushes, she is vague in discussing their relationship other than to say they are good friends and to agree that he is cute.

One day I find her sitting perturbed in the trailer; the boys have left her behind again.

"They won't tell me what they are doing," she says sorrowfully. "But I did hear one of the Sisters say that it involves Samuel stripping to his underwear, taking a photo with the drone, and getting a milkshake."

I laugh. The boys are always betting each other milkshakes.

Bethany smiles at me then, still sorry to have been left behind, but liking for the moment that she can share the image of Samuel and his milkshake. It is so nice to have this minute with her, but it also feels fragile. I have been so sure that just by spending time together, the crew and I will be able to overcome our differences. But here in the girls' trailer, I am starting to fear we may have little in common except for being girls. I'm not a good girly-girl, and neither is she, but both of us are nontraditional girls in completely different ways. The subtle cues that women employ to join in sisterhood are not working for us.

The next morning, Bethany notices that something is wrong with the sewer in our trailer. It is not draining. The Wolgemuths are unabashed in their concentration. Bethany's brow furrows, and her lips part as she calculates what to do. There is a spare piece of cardboard by the trash—my trash—and Bethany folds it in thirds lengthwise, turning it into a plunger. She attacks the backflow. Then she goes out of the trailer and comes back "with some chemical" and begins to flush the toilet and plunge it again. In time, she's able to dislodge the waste.

I had wanted to help her, but she had good-naturedly solved the problem on her own. In her ability to solve this problem, I can see shades of how my father sometimes wanted me to be—a girl who could use a plunger and fix plumbing without squeamishness. I'm not quite that girl.

Later that evening, I hear about another rodeo, this time in Vernon. Of course I want to go. I want to see and do as much as I can in this country. Only Georgie and Bethany go with me, and they took a lot of cajoling. No one else wants to pay another entry fee; they would rather go hunting. I offer to drive. I will pay the entry fee. And so Georgie and Bethany set out with me. And though I'm happy for the company, I'm aware, too, that I pressed to have it. It is as if they are entertaining me—an eccentric older relative from out of town, which I basically am—when they would prefer to play with friends.

It rained in Vernon, too, and when I try to park, I am directed into a muddy field beyond a large barn.

"Oh boy!" Georgie says. "Does this thing have four-wheel drive?"

I feel at one point as though the car has temporarily bottomed out, and is floating in a pool of mud. The car will not go farther. People walking to the rodeo stop and look at me, then keep moving; they have all arrived in pickup trucks. Georgie laughs and says he would not have driven the way I did, through a puddle, and I protest that I had not aimed for a puddle. It is just so muddy everywhere. Then the kids patiently tell me to back up and to turn, their eyes scanning for a part of the field where I will not sink.

Vernon is a fairly large town for this type of farming and ranching country: ten thousand people. It is home to the Walmart we frequent for extra jeans and groceries. It is also home to this rodeo, the Santa Rosa Roundup, first held in 1946 by E. Paul Waggoner, scion of what was once the largest ranch in all of Texas.

The Palomino Club is from Vernon too. The beautiful Palomino horses have glossy blond manes and tails, and light brown bodies; they are the Cheryl Tiegs of horses. As men in blue shirts guide their horses in a single line, then break that line into two, and then form concentric circles, and then a star, the announcer says some words that strike me so precisely, I write them down. "This country needs heroes and manly men no matter what you see. The cowboy never went out of style. See how they pivot through the mud. Be proud, Texas! They're you."

The crowd cheers in agreement.

When we leave, Georgie and Bethany spot an elderly woman trying to cross a puddle. Bethany, without thinking, goes over and gives the woman her arm so she can join her family on the other side of the puddle. There follows a slight battle of wills between Bethany and Georgie as to who will drive my car out of the mud. Georgie thinks he ought to because he is a man, and Bethany thinks she ought to because she is older than Georgie. I hand the keys to Bethany.

Georgie chortles. "You girls sure? You might get stuck in the mud! You might bottom out!"

Bethany's expression is one of rare annoyance as she relegates Georgie to the back seat, then takes the driver's seat while I sit next to her. Though it is getting dark, Bethany's eyes scan the muddy field looking for any tract of road that will not cause us to sink and get stuck. After an excruciating five minutes of navigating sinkholes, we are on pavement.

Bethany drives past field after field drenched with water; parts of the road are covered with water too.

"If this were Pennsylvania," she says almost primly, "this road would be closed."

It gets dark quickly, but the sunset lingers on the horizon's low clouds. It is darkly beautiful and I say so repeatedly.

As she drives, Bethany snatches looks at the scenery, while Georgie continues to chortle in the back seat. Bethany's face is set firmly in Wolgemuth determination; she will navigate the wet roads safely and get us home. But her face softens for a moment. "Do all people who look at the landscape think it is pretty?" she asks me.

"What do you mean?"

"When I was in South America on mission, I thought the scenery was gorgeous and I said so. But the people there just told me it was their home. You've traveled more than I have. I just wondered if people in other places know when something is beautiful."

It is such an interesting question that I don't try to answer right away. I want to stay here in this moment when she is asking me for an opinion. Finally I say that I think that in order to know that land is beautiful and unique, you have to have a religious or an artistic eye. Without that, I say, maybe the landscape doesn't give one a sense of awe.

"That makes sense," she says, nodding.

I think about her question for a long time even after the conversation has moved on.

Eric has called his farmers in Oklahoma to see if by chance the crops there are ripe, but those fields are many days away from being ready, and anyway, the farmers here in Texas are still hoping we will take care of their wheat. We cannot leave, and there is no telling how long it will take for the fields to dry and be ready to cut again.

We are running out of activities, and so we go to the Red River Valley Museum. We look at a map of the most famous of the cattle drives: the Chisholm Trail and the Great Western Cattle Trail. The cattle drives covered the ground at about twenty miles a day—the same pace at which wheat is said to ripen. The Chisholm Trail moved north, through Fort Worth, about 150 miles east of where we are. But the Great Western Cattle Trail ran almost right through Vernon; the old ghost town, Doan's Crossing, north of us, had a general store right on the Red River, which served as a landmark for the cowboys. Between 1866 and 1890, the years of the cattle drives, 6 million heads of cattle passed through this region.

Bethany says: "Harvest is the closest thing now to the cattle drives."

"No more *Mayflower* or Chisholm Trail," Eric agrees. "PETA would have our hide if we tried to do something like the cattle drives now."

The town of Quanah, just north of Crowell, is named for Quanah Parker, a Comanche chief, and the museum devotes considerable energy to his story. His mother was Cynthia Ann Parker, a white woman, which makes Quanah racially mixed, like me. I look at his photos. I am good, I think, at recognizing mixed faces. I am good at seeing a Caucasian nose set in a brown face, or picking apart the epicanthic fold on eyes, or seeing how the planes of a face slope or lie flat. I do not take in the general effect of a person's face; I study the details of faces. I do this, I know, partly because I long for someone to see me in kind and to know that I am a person with a history, a mixed heritage, and not just a general exotic blur. I study his face. I can't tell that his mother was white.

"Did you see the thing about Quanah?" Eric asks me.

"Yes," I say.

In May of 1834, the Parker family, all Anglos, moved to central Texas. This was just over a year before the citizens of Texas took up arms against the centralized government in Mexico and formed the Republic of Texas, making Texas essentially its own country before it joined the Union in 1845. The Parker family's home, Fort Parker, is located about 110 miles south-southeast of Dallas as the crow flies, near a town called Elkart.

That May, while most of the Parker men were out working in the fields, a group of Native Americans attacked the fort, killing five and capturing five family members. Among those taken was a ten-year-old girl named Cynthia Ann Parker. The others who were captured were later ransomed for release, but not so Cynthia Ann. Over the years after her capture, there were stories about her, and one Texas Ranger even recounted seeing her, speaking to her, and offering to take her home to her family, but she refused.

Cynthia Ann married the Comanche chief Peta Nocona, who, the museum says, was so happy with his bride that he did not take any other wives, even though it was customary for a chief to do so. Cynthia Ann had three children: her sons, Pecos and Quanah; and a daughter, Topsannah ("Prairie Flower"). In 1860, a group of Texas Rangers happened upon a group of Comanches by the Pease River, a spot located northeast of Crowell and southeast of the town of Quanah. The Rangers surrounded some of the Indians, one of whom was a woman with a small child. The woman was white. It was Cynthia Ann. She was taken, along with her child, back to her natal family—and never saw her husband or sons again.

The Parker family was overjoyed to see her; the narrative at the time was that the Indians were savages, and Cynthia's return symbolized a re-civilizing and righting of a wrong. Even today, I hear white farmers on the plains refer to the Indians as "savages." But Cynthia was unable to readjust to white ways. Her daughter, whom she took with her, died of the flu a few years later, and Cynthia starved herself to death after that. She never stopped trying to return to her Comanche family, and the stories in which she pleads with other returnees to escape with her are heartbreaking to read. In one of the few photos we have of Cynthia

Ann, she stares vacantly at the camera, her hair cut short, as in the Comanche manner of mourning; she had cut her hair, fearing that her sons and husband were dead.

It isn't clear at what point Quanah learned that his mother was white. Peta Nocona and Pecos both died a few years after Cynthia's return, but Quanah lived to become a great Comanche chief, with a notorious reputation for fighting the white man.

In 1873, Quanah and other Comanche were invited to a Sun Dance, which was a Kiowa and not a Comanche tradition. However, all the people of the plains were well aware that their resources—the buffalo— were being diminished by the white men, and that it was now necessary for them to band together if they were going to survive. At the gathering, Quanah recruited men for a raid on the Texas inhabitants of Adobe Walls, near the ghost town of Doan's Crossing. The raid failed, and provoked the US government to engage in a full-scale assault on the Indians of Comancheria. By 1875, the remaining Indians of the Red River Valley were removed and put on a reservation in Oklahoma.

Quanah is often cited as a model Native American who "adjusted well" during this transition. He learned English, made shrewd investments, and became friends with Theodore Roosevelt. He also helped to found the Native American Church movement. He disinterred his mother's remains and had her reburied on his property. In the large black-and-white photo that stands in the Red River Valley Museum, he is dressed in Comanche garb with a pair of braids hanging on his belt; these are said to be his mother's.

Standing there in the museum, I am deeply moved by the story. When I was seven, I went to Japan with my mother for an entire summer. After three months, I found white faces—including my father's—to be sharp and cartoonish, and I was scared of him when we came back to America. I also temporarily forgot the English language. But I have never forgotten how swiftly one culture can simply wipe away another, how elastic the mind of a child is, and how her heart can be turned.

What was it like for this young man to have believed he was from Comanche parents, and then to learn that his mother was one of the enemy, an Anglo, and that she was taken from him and returned "home"? Within the span of his lifetime, his entire way of life was destroyed by his own mother's people. What mental gymnastics did he do in his effort to try to adjust? Did his knowledge of his white blood make it easier for him to accept white society? Did he want to be a part of the people who had reabsorbed his mother?

I think of what Ta-Nehisi Coates wrote of Barack Obama. The former president "sees race through a different lens." And that lens was "born of literally relating to whites, [that] allowed Obama to imagine that he could be the country's first black president." In her essay on biraciality, "Black with (Some) White Privilege," Anna Holmes, who is of mixed race, quotes Erin Cloud, a Bronx public defender: "I am a black woman. I see myself as a black woman, but I also have to be honest. I love my mother. I can't say for many of my black friends that they deeply, intimately, without any bounds love a white person." Did Quanah, in loving his mother, have access to love for the other—the conqueror—that some of his family and friends did not?

I think about my Japanese grandfather, who watched his country being defeated in war, even as his own people committed atrocities in Korea and China, and then, during the occupation of Japan, learned the language of the conquerors, the Americans, to become an English teacher. It was a survival tactic and a smart one, but he hadn't expected to lose his only daughter to the enemy. When my mother took my father to meet her family, my grandfather cast out my mother and disowned her. All her actions from then on were about surviving among the former enemy; the road home was severed. And though my father loved my mother, how many of the illnesses she endured throughout my life were caused by the inability to go home, and by a constant internal pressure to "be good"?

Has my proximity to white people made me blind? Is there something I cannot see because I loved my father and his people so much?

Eric is smiling and looking at the exhibit and looking at me. I both want to know and don't want to know what he is thinking. I assume he cannot be feeling anything close to my own emotions. It makes me feel too exposed to discuss the issue of being mixed—of my being mixed. I came along on this trip to understand our country and to try to see Eric's people more clearly, and I do not want to feel isolated in this moment by highlighting how I, too, am a racial mix. So I do a thing I have learned to do over the years: I try to erase the parts of myself that look out of place so everyone else will feel at ease. I try to match my response to everyone else's response. I say something about how interesting this all is. And then I move on.

—

At dinner we are in the trailer, sitting around the table, eating Emily's spaghetti. We wind yards of pasta around a plastic spork and serve one another and joke, "About five yards of pasta, please."

We are discussing evolution. I am not entirely sure how the subject comes up. Maybe it is Juston who remarks that the hall of dead animals had convinced him that creationism was wrong. Or perhaps we are talking about geologists who have asserted that the red soil of Texas is billions of years old. Or perhaps I bring up the topic. Regardless, at a certain point, Samuel asks Eric: "How old do you think the earth is?"

"Oh," Eric says, a most grave seriousness overtaking his face. "Millions. Millions of years old. Even older than that. Billions."

"Really," someone says. "Why?"

"Been thinking. And reading. And I think the science is correct. We can't just apply the science in one area, like GMOs, and not in another area, like geology." He pauses. "There's some people that believe God just made the earth look old." And the way Eric says this, I know he means that people at the table believe this, that God has intentionally placed rock strata and fossils before us to fool us.

Juston exhales. "And why would God want to trick us?"

"Could be a test," someone says.

"But *why*? It makes no sense. Not if he *loves* us, like he supposedly does," Juston counters.

"How old do you think the earth is?" Eric asks no one in particular.

"'Bout six thousand years," Samuel says. "We're about out of time too." He tells us he was recently in Israel for Bible study with his family and that they had spent a long time on the Revelation. "I think it's definitely right. End of days is coming."

I am flabbergasted.

Sitting there, I do not know anything about the Revelation, except for the occasional Facebook post from friends who grew up in the South and mock the book and swear they know people who believe in the book and in its power.

"What do you mean you think it's right?" I ask.

"There's a lot of signs and we studied them and it's very persuasive. The book says that the tribes of Israel will come together and that there will be a leader from the north, which . . ."

"Putin," Bradford says.

"Yep."

"There's a leader in the north?" I ask.

"Well, the Bible refers to a bear, and there's no bears in Israel. So, must be the north. Like Russia," Samuel says.

Someone has found the passage in the Bible on his cell phone: "It was given power to wage war against God's holy people and to conquer them."

I try not to show any alarm. We are eating dinner together and this is their trailer and their trip and I'm along for the ride. There are many more weeks to go. It's as if I'm standing on the edge of some body of water, and I see only the shore and have no idea how big and deep the lake will be. It might be treacherous in the future—the lake. I should be careful how far out into the lake I wade, and yet it makes me feel nervous, knowing that the lake is there. This feeling is probably compounded by the trip to the museum, and reading about Quanah—and hiding my feelings. Were I at home, or with my parents, we could have talked about Quanah easily. With my parents in particular, who lived a life of racial and cultural mixing, it was always so easy for me to feel at home. But I suddenly feel completely alone. I think about calling my husband, but would he understand how rattled I feel?

After dinner, Eric, Juston, and I go to look at fields. It is still so muddy, I know there are no fields to cut and it is futile to look at them. We are looking just to look. It is also just the three of us, and I wonder if the outing is devised for me, to take me out of the pocket of our group, where Revelation is imminent.

There are animals everywhere. At one point we see eight coyotes and I ask, "Do coyotes normally travel in packs?"

"It's rare," Eric says. "But we're seeing them a lot this summer."

There are pigs, too, and roadrunners and turkeys. Eric falls silent. I ask what both he and Juston think of Revelation, and Eric says nothing. Juston says he read it long ago, and could not make sense of it. He's not sure how anyone can read it and understand it. "If our God is good, and if Revelation tells us what is going to happen, I think it should not be held against me that I could not interpret it," he says with great practicality.

"I don't really think it's accurate" is all Eric says.

"That's why you get along with me and with my dad. We are the rebels." Juston smiles at me.

Rebels? I hadn't realized there were rebels within an evangelical Christian community. But of course there are. There are rebels everywhere. But what are they rebelling against and what are they rebelling for?

Eric continues to say nothing and we keep driving. And this silence is the only answer he has for the time being. I will not be able to talk us—or myself—into a place of coherence tonight with regard to Revelation, or any night in the near future. I am going to live with fractured pieces of a reality I don't completely understand. But I know myself and I know I will try. I will have to wrestle with the Bible. If the Bible is the reason someone like Samuel thinks the world is going to end soon, I am going to have to understand why he thinks this, and if, after reading the Bible, I think it too.

What do I know about the Bible? My knowledge is spotty, pieced together from a childhood at an Episcopal school, work as a church musician, and mandatory readings in high school and college of the Bible as a piece of literature that has given us the foundation of Western literature. I know about Genesis, some lessons from Christ, the Psalms that Emily reads, and Revelation through hearsay. I've been to a lot of museums; I've compared Raphael's Madonnas to the stiffer portraits painted by other Renaissance artists. I've seen the Sistine Chapel.

What I have is an *impression* of the Bible.

Everyone else on harvest *knows* the Bible. It's the one book Bethany and I have in our trailer—and it is her copy. It's like the crew has the Bible on speed dial. When there is a question about scripture, they find the answer instantly on their cell phones.

We drive on. I know we are driving through the usual Texas bramble, past waterlogged fields and wild packs of coyotes and deer. But in my mind's eye, we are driving past a ravine. A giant chasm yawns on the side of the car. In my imagination, Eric and Juston know the abyss is there but don't say anything about it to me. They want me to notice it for myself because that is the only way for anyone to know the abyss is real. As I fall asleep that night, I wonder, lightly, if the abyss was the thing they wanted to share.

Before harvest, Bethany had a part-time job at the local butcher, so she knows a little bit about carving up animals, or at least where the edible parts of the meat are supposed to be on a dead carcass. On Friday, the crew goes hunting and kills a pig, and Bethany butchers it right there in the field where it died. Samuel is delighted and, frankly, I am too. Samuel marinates the meat in Italian dressing overnight, then puts on sweet and spicy barbecue sauce and cooks the pig parts over the grill just outside the boys' trailer in the RV park. We sit outside between the trailers. Emily has a folding table and chairs. We all eat pork that night, along with baked potatoes and steamed mixed vegetables.

"We call this farm-to-table in the city," I say.

"True organic." Samuel smiles at me kindly.

I ask the crew about their hunting. Truth be told, I would like to go again, but I am not invited. A coolness has descended between Bethany and me. It could be anything—that if she is left alone again because the boys are flying a drone to take naked pictures, she does not want to be left with me, a woman who can't drive successfully through the mud. It might partly have to do with my age, or my inability to fix things, like the plugged-up toilet. Maybe it's that I asked if she and Samuel were together, when we all know there isn't supposed to be any dating on harvest. Or maybe it is that I don't believe in creationism. Maybe it's none of these things.

I feel that vague sense of panic I get when a relationship no longer feels quite right, and that something—some judgment—is hidden. Of course, I ask her if something is the matter, and of course she tells me that nothing is. But there is a slight change in the air—a frisson—coupled with minute changes in her body language that tell me something has shifted since the conversation about Revelation.

On Saturday night, Juston stops by my trailer. He is always so formal when he stops by "the girls' trailer." He stands outside and asks to speak with me, and I put on my boots and go out onto the gravel landing.

"I was thinking," he says. "I don't think there's much more you can get out of cowboy church. If you go, it's just going to be the same thing again."

"Okay," I say.

"How would you like to go to Oklahoma City to see a megachurch?"

Another harvester will be arriving at the airport that day, and Juston wants to pick him up; they are close friends. There is also a Barnes & Noble in Oklahoma City. Juston and I have preordered books; this is

mostly how we will get new books to read while on the road this summer. We have no mailbox, and though I can get packages delivered to
general delivery at the town post office, I will mostly opt to have books
waiting at the nearest Barnes & Noble, even if it is hours away. Most of
all, he wants me to see a new church.

"I would love to go," I say. And it is decided.

Life.Church in Oklahoma City originated as the brainchild of a pastor
named Craig Groeschel, who, according to his website bio, established
his church by preaching in a garage to forty people. So successful was
he that his congregation—Life.Church—now "exists" in seven states. I
use the quotes because Life.Church and its services are the same from
location to location, but Pastor Craig, as he is known, can be in only
one place at a time. Because he lives just outside of Oklahoma City, his
weekly messages are recorded, then beamed elsewhere thanks to the
internet, where they can be re-watched. It is a constant question that
morning for Juston and for me: Will Pastor Craig appear in the flesh,
or will we get a recorded message?

It has been weeks since I have been in anything approximating
a city, and my whole body leaps at the sight of the skyline. It's a small
city, but there's no mistaking the rumple of utilitarian shipping facili-
ties and industrial buildings amassed around the central skyscrapers.
I see something else that I haven't seen in days. Graffitti. There isn't a
lot, but I read: "John 3:16." And then a truck passes us on the interstate
and it, too, has a bumper sticker that reads "John 3:16."

Life.Church is in a rectangular industrial building with plentiful parking. Cheerful young men and women in red T-shirts emblazoned with the Life.Church logo are waiting to meet us at the door.
Brochures and paraphernalia line the walls. Life.Church, like other
megachurches, runs a myriad of programs outside of its weekly Sunday
gatherings. For every problem that exists on the secular self-help and
therapy menus, there is, naturally, a corollary for Christians; everyone
has the same problems. I'm immediately drawn to a program titled
"Following Jesus in a Selfie-Centered World." "As you swipe through
your newsfeed, are you exhausted by trying to measure up to the
next person's status update? Counting likes, but at a loss for love? In
#Struggles, Pastor Craig addresses these social media woes and more

through five messages, LifeGroup discussions, a Bible Plan, and more." Well, yes, I think. In fact, I am exhausted by status updates.

I also like the pamphlets on sex. Many of my friends have teased me about spending the summer with twentysomethings who have not had sex and are unlikely to before marriage. To a secular person, this kind of conviction seems ludicrous.

And yet Christians are as plagued by worries about sex as secular people are. Here is an example from a Life.Church seminar: "Just because your expectations aren't being met, that doesn't give you an excuse to quit your marriage. Our vows included the phrase 'for better or for worse, in sickness and in health.' Of course you have no idea what that might mean when you say it, but the vow is still as valid as the day you said it. Just because sex isn't cooperating right now, doesn't mean your marriage is broken." When I point this out to Juston, he tells me that many of the podcasts he listens to are about porn, and how to deal with porn as a Christian, and as a Christian who isn't supposed to have sex until marriage, but is instead supposed to feel guilty if he does indulge—that is, if he even thinks about sex outside of marriage. And porn is everywhere, and it's as easy for a rural Christian to find it as it is for a man living in a city with an office job.

Then there are the programs addressed to men. "What is it about sex, especially connected, meaningful sex shared in marriage, that makes men come alive? Why do we as men want so badly to have the money we need to provide for ourselves and others we love? What is it about being trusted and chosen for a job or a position that feels so empowering? And why is none of this ever completely enough? We always want more sex, money, and power."

We approach the sanctuary, the theater portion of the church. The cavern sucks us in like the event horizon of a black hole. Music blasts through speakers. The pit of my stomach lurches up into my throat in anticipation of an impending high. We choose seats toward the center. Nearby, a man is perched high on a swiveling stool beside a battle-gun-heavy camera, the kind used by network professionals to broadcast games for the NFL.

Juston has taught me that the kind of music we are listening to is called "worship music." This is to be distinguished from "radio songs," which are the pop tunes that have entirely framed my youth and adulthood. All the songs we listened to in the eighties and beyond—the Cure,

U2, Coldplay—and which I assumed were blasted all over the earth, because I would hear them even in the most remote shopping malls in Japan, belong to my secular world and are not a part of Christian culture. Christians, it turns out, have their own music, the way the Japanese have their own pop tunes, except in Japan the biggest pop star of all was always a Western import. I have just assumed this model worked all over the world and in every subculture. But the Christian evangelical is different.

All the songs in Life.Church sound vaguely familiar to me, but I cannot identify them. This is because, Juston tells me, they are derivative. They are written to sound like pop tunes, but they aren't pop tunes. They are like the music version of Mount Rainier coffee shops in Japanese coffee shops: cafés that look like Starbucks but aren't Starbucks, despite the green logo, but meant to be so similar to Starbucks, one doesn't even want Starbucks. These non–pop tunes are supposed to be a total replacement. Who needs Counting Crows when you have Casting Crowns?

Juston has strong feelings about this music. It is the subject of one of his papers. It is the music he grew up with, but it is impossible now for a young person connected to the internet to be disconnected entirely from U2 or from other "radio bands," which Juston prefers, because, as he once explained in a college paper he shared, it is free to dwell in the realm of ambiguity and suffering, whereas worship music must follow a script.

Juston doesn't say that music from my world is "better." He doesn't say it's "more real." He says my music is better and more real *because* people suffer in it and may not be saved at all.

We sing together. Singing is, hands down, my favorite thing about church. Beside me, Juston is nearly expressionless. I find myself nearly crying. My throat constricts like a knot at the end of a balloon intended to retain helium. I am lifted. All around me are men and women lifting their arms, in the open positions of submission. I used to take dance class and I feel like I am in class now, wanting to mirror all the other people as they raise their arms up into the air. The lights on the stage go from red to yellow to blue. This is followed by a video showing pictures of flowing water, and then ice, both of which are accompanied by corresponding audio cues. Our senses are flooded by a full year of all the seasons and colors of Texas in thirty seconds. A new song begins, the lights are turquoise, and we are treated to a medley.

After a series of these worship songs, a junior pastor takes the stage. He's the warm-up act. He struts across the stage and punches at the air with his hands in a way that shows he has mastered the physical vocabulary of urban youth.

I turn and look at Juston. His face is impassive. Had he continued on the path to becoming a pastor, I think, this could be him up here now onstage talking about God.

In all megachurches, the preaching utilizes the tricks of the info-mercial trade. Behind the pastor, a screen flashes images or text to support the main points of the talk. When the junior pastor quotes the Gospel, the PowerPoint highlights the Gospel behind him. If he mentions his kids—and he always mentions his kids—a photo of the kids pops up. Everything is seamlessly produced, showing an ideal life as represented by the pastor: to be married, to be loved, to reproduce, and to know God. That day, our warm-up pastor talks about his child learning the Bible, and the audience coos over a photo that flashes on the screen behind him of a little girl reading a book upside down.

Even as I write this, a voice is chastising me. I find myself feeling superior to all this earnestness, but this is a way of life for people. Perhaps it is I, with my hardened, secular heart, who am overly skeptical. I spend a lot of time with this dual consciousness, and I wonder, with a third voice, if my skepticism is merely a learned thing. At the same time, I keep crying over the music, lights, and ambience.

By noon we learn that we will have the recorded Pastor Craig. Real Pastor Craig was here at 10 and we are here at 11:30. We will have a video.

When he appears, he walks onto a recording of the stage. He is wearing black jeans and skater sneakers. He wears a short-sleeved gray button-up T-shirt and we can see his biceps. He works out. A lot. He works out the way an actor works out. His arms are massive. Arnold massive or The Rock massive, which is to say, unnecessarily so. I think back to the pamphlet in the hallway. "What is it about sex, especially connected, meaningful sex shared in marriage, that makes men come alive? Why do we as men want so badly to have the money we need to provide for ourselves and others we love?"

Usually when a man has worked out this much, there is a kind of self-absorbed cast to his face that registers the amount of time he has devoted to getting his body to this level of beauty. But this egotism is not evident on Pastor Craig's face. His expression is one of open ease and sincerity. "What is it about being trusted and chosen for a job or a position that feels so empowering?" the pamphlet on masculinity asks. Pastor Craig has been chosen for this job. I am crying from the music again and he is here, entrusted with the care of my soul and that of everyone else in the audience. I feel soft and womanly, like the middle-aged female I am who can now relax at last because the Good Shepherd is here.

He begins with a little anecdote, as pastors often do this. Pastor Craig tells us he was relaxing at home one Sunday, watching television, when he was momentarily roused from his repose by news of church fires overseas. And then, he says, he went right back into a state of apathy. He says, "Meh," which he tells us is the sound of apathy. He sounds almost like a cat when he says "Meh," and the incongruity of this large, muscled man meowing "Meh" in reference to the very serious issues he is discussing is so charming, we all giggle. We are supposed to giggle.

"Why did Jesus come? Over and over he says the same thing in different ways. This is what a good leader does." Then he goes on to talk about Jesus's consistent message in having come for the poor and the sick, and then in attracting others to his cause. "Focused passion attracts! . . . I'm pssionate about helping people . . . not just go to church . . . but become the church. . . . That's my passion." He speaks with the punchiness of a football coach explaining the next big play. We are all in this game called life together and he is walking us through the intricacies of the maneuver. Today there are three steps:

1. Focus on something with passion.
2. Embrace what hurts.
3. Become other-centered and move out of the comfort zone.

At the end, when Pastor Craig is done with his rousing message for taking us out of our state of apathy, he does a kind of closer, rapid-fire, intense distillation of the important facets of the message. This large, muscled man—speaking with more authority and confidence and, frankly, more fire than anyone I have seen perhaps since Kenneth Branagh delivered his "St. Crispin's Day" speech at the end of *Henry V*, just before the English defeat the French—believes that we were born fallen and that we have sinned and no one needs to be taught to sin, and that there is a moral standard. God loves us. He loves us so much that he has sent his son to us, and his son died, and we, if we want to be out of hell, can find our salvation in Jesus.

And there it is. The transaction.

I ought to stop crying now, refuse to be manipulated further by anything this man says, since I don't believe in hell. But brain chemistry is persuasive. I am about as loaded with dopamine as I can be, and I cannot access any cynicism to stanch my tears.

"[Jesus] came for the broken [and] the sick. He came for people like you and he came for people like me. And Jesus was the lamb of God who gave his life for the sheep without a shepherd so anyone who calls on his name . . . would be forgiven, saved, and made new!" Pastor Craig entreats someone—some anonymous person out there—to be saved. He knows someone among us will be saved. We will go beyond being good people. We will submit. We will be saved. He calls out for us. There is applause. There is weeping. Again there is the openness, the universal position of human vulnerability, of arms stretched up. He begins to point to those of us in the audience who are submitting now and who will be saved. There is so much crying that I am crying. I'm still crying when it's all over and we file out of the sanctuary.

We spend a little time wandering around the hallways of Life.Church. I am sure that someone will have a T-shirt for sale, though Juston is sure there is no T-shirt for sale. He is patient with my wandering, and says nothing when I am told, finally, by a volunteer wearing a Life.Church T-shirt, that there are no shirts for sale, but that I will receive one if I become a regular volunteer.

Then at last we exit into the heat outside. The asphalt is cooking the air around us as if it is a stove top.

I feel as though I have been put through a factory of emotions: I'm weepy and determined and light-headed all at the same time. I would come every week, too, I think, for a dose of this feeling of goodness and aliveness. And of that big white man caring so much. Even about me.

"This is not going to work forever, for millennials," Juston informs me.

"What?" I sniff.

"Don't you know? We are the generation that is seeking authenticity."

And just like that, my emotions begin to stabilize. It was theater. We had just been to the theater.

"He's a good speaker," Juston says.

"The muscles."

"I was just talking about his presentation skills."

"He brought up hell," I say.

"You noticed."

I think of the Broadway show *The Book of Mormon*. The show spends much of its time making light fun of the Mormon religion and those who believe in it, though at the end, the show suggests that belief can be a powerful force for good, even if one believes in something that isn't true. Like God. This attitude is one I have come to think of as the "kind liberal's" opinion about religion. It is not, I know, a meaningful attitude for Juston.

"He was helpful to me when I was in Germany." Juston says this almost nostalgically.

"What was it about him?"

He has trouble articulating a precise answer that I can understand.

"Is it that you don't believe in hell anymore?" I ask.

"That's not it exactly. And I'm not sure that's exactly true about me." He sighs. "I just wonder now if there is a truth. And if we can know it."

"And if we can know that truth . . . ," I begin.

"We shouldn't have to fear hell in order to know it," he concludes, with equal parts sorrow and practicality.

For the first time in my life, I go to the Christian section of a Barnes & Noble, which, because we are in Oklahoma City, is substantial.

Juston likes Richard Rohr, a Catholic priest and writer; C. S. Lewis; and Mike McHargue, who is known as "Science Mike." McHargue runs a blog and podcast called *The Liturgist*, which Juston frequently listens to in the combine. Like Juston, McHargue was raised in a Christian family, but began to have a crisis of faith about many of the things he was taught, including hell, sex, and evolution. McHargue endeavored to understand his doubt through inquiry, and intellectually, Juston feels he has trod the same path and wants me to read his book too.

I also pick up the Rob Bell book called *What Is the Bible?*, which I have preordered. I try to encourage Juston to read Elaine Pagels, the Princeton scholar who specializes in the Gnostic Gospels, or Karen Armstrong, but I find few books by either in the store.

Also waiting for me is a copy of the Bible identical to the one Emily uses: the New Living Translation. It is my first Bible.

Outside the small Oklahoma City airport, a few people are milling around in boots and hats. Draped on a bench is a young man, looking slightly more casual than the harvesters I have seen. He is wearing a T-shirt and nondescript brown leather shoes that lace up. His arms are long and his legs longer. He looks as though he would rather be up and walking or running or climbing a wall. There is something altogether impatient in this young man's face—the restless expression of some-one curious and intelligent, with a strong and clear sense of direction.

"There he is," Juston says, pulling the car alongside the curb.

The young man looks up and smiles, slightly. He has dark eyes, and just a touch of swarthiness to his complexion. He grins at us without the slightest bit of self-consciousness. He stands up gracefully, like a dancer. He has broad shoulders and wide hands, his entire body seems pegged together with wires and titanium screws, and he moves like a suspended mobile; we are but windup creatures scurrying around, but Michael floats. It is obvious almost immediately that Michael has the wholesome quality of his community. Women walk by, some scantily clad in the heat, but his gaze doesn't linger on their bodies. Is that naivete or decency?

Juston has told me that Michael is one of his best friends, and the three of us share an instant and easy chemistry. I am flattered by how quickly they let me in. They dip inside themselves and then back out again and then back in; they talk school, family, friends, harvest, and sports—and their feelings about each—and weave their inner and outer worlds together seamlessly.

Michael is a Mennonite. He was homeschooled, and now attends com-munity college. He would like to become a police detective. I tell him that before this summer I had assumed that Mennonites were like the Amish except they used more technology, and I had found it confusing where or why or how the technology is permitted. I had assumed that it had something to do with wanting to lead a pure life, whatever that meant, and while their way of life looked quaint from the outside, it made no sense at all the few times I had gone to visit Amish farms.

Eric once took me to see a neighbor in Lancaster County—an Amish farmer friend who worked ten acres of land with his iron plow and mules. We discussed farming techniques, and his methods turned out to be pretty much the same as mine, including his use of the herbicide Roundup. This Amish farmer told me that Roundup was a miracle. He did not see it as a social ill, but as a way to help him raise better food, even as he eschewed the use of a machine run on fossil fuels.

I say all this to Michael and he takes the information in stride, then asks: "Is this what your book is about? I heard you were writing a book."

"Yes."

"So it's a country-versus-city book."

"That's one way to look at it." Very quickly, the conversation escalates in intensity, though not unpleasantly. Juston continues to drive, smiling; he is happy to hear the engaged banter between two people he likes. Michael is fearlessly inquisitive, asking questions, examining and reexamining everything I say.

"The question," I say, "is: Why do some conservative Christians believe in GMOs, but not in evolution? Why is it okay to tamper with the DNA of plants, but not of people?"

"City people don't like GMOs?"

"No."

"Why?"

"They want organic food."

"Costs more. But okay. Well, I can think of two answers for country people and Christians." Michael speaks quickly. He pulls out his cell phone and checks the scripture. Then he tells me that plants are not divine, but that human life is divine. The Bible says this clearly. It is an entirely different thing to tinker with plants than to harvest plants, because God gave us dominion over the natural world. Second, he cites the story of the Tower of Babel, and how man tried to build a tower that could reach heaven. God then punished man for his arrogance by collapsing the tower and forcing humans to speak different languages. Michael does not doubt that should man try to overreach again, God will intervene.

I tell Michael about a book I've read, by the scholar Noreen Herzfeld, called *Technology and Religion*, which investigates the interplay between religion and science. Herzfeld explains that the Old Order religions from Pennsylvania adhere to "the Ordnung," a moral code that dictates how these Anabaptists should live. There are basically three rules that the

Amish and Old Order Mennonites follow when it comes to the adoption of technology, and unsurprisingly, the rules are intended to maintain a connection to God and to one another. "First," the Amish ask, "does the technology provide tangible benefits to the community or individuals within that community? . . . Second, does the technology change the relationship of the individual to the community? . . . Third, does the technology change the nature of the community itself?"

The questions the Ordnung raises are often reflected in similar discussions I read and hear nearly every day in the news and on social media. Consider, for example, the *New York Times* story "Steve Jobs Was a Low-Tech Parent": "We limit how much technology our kids use at home," Jobs is reported to have said. In the same piece, the author, Nick Bilton, quotes Chris Anderson, the former editor of *Wired*, as saying: "We have seen the dangers of technology firsthand. I've seen it in myself. I don't want to see that happen to my kids." A host of ills are associated with the online world and with the technology that delivers virtual reality: bullying, pornography, and addiction. The original *Times* story spawned additional articles on the dangers of the new technology: "Bill Gates and Steve Jobs Raised Their Kids Tech-Free—and It Should've Been a Red Flag," screamed *Business Insider*. "Screen time v. play time: what tech leaders won't let their own kid do," the *Guardian* expounded. Both pieces reported factoids like "Research has found that an eighth-grader's risk for depression jumps 27% when he or she frequently uses social media. Kids who use their phones for at least three hours a day are much more likely to be suicidal. And recent research has found the teen suicide rate in the US now eclipses the homicide rate, with smartphones as the driving force." The Ordnung's caution against technology seems, in this light, to be less old-fashioned than sensibly prescient.

But, as Herzfeld and other writers and scholars have pointed out, technology has been a constant throughout human history. Perhaps ever since the first person realized fire could be portable, we have been shaping and reshaping our environment to suit us through the tools we have created. Each change brings about a loss. Of the written versus the oral tradition, Plato said: "It will introduce forgetfulness into the soul of those who learn it: they will not practice using their memory because they will put their trust in writing, which is external and depends on signs that belong to others."

Pivotal moments at the beginning of the Bible center around the idea of technology—and of creation. Herzfeld cites the same two examples Michael raised. Humans in Genesis are made in God's image. This is not said of any other creature but humans; we alone have an imprint of what constitutes God. And since God created humans, we should assume that part of the human mission is, in turn, to create.

God also gives Adam and Eve dominion over the world; that is, they are to be superior to it. Part of this dominion involves the tools and the technology we build. And in fact, every time I have asked a Christian farmer why he feels it is okay to use technology to farm, he will say to me: "God gave us dominion." The land and animals are subject to us.

When humans build the Tower of Babel, a structure so tall it reaches God, the tower is struck down. When humans worship idols, or false Gods, the idols are destroyed. When God floods the world, it is technology—an ark—that saves Noah and his family. "Dominion without a relationship to God, to one another, and to the rest of creation can produce unforeseen and disastrous results," Herzfeld writes. This is the warning inherent in the Bible, and, as she examines in her book, across traditions. And while the modern era—the era of the atom—might cause some, like Nietzsche—to declare that God is dead, Herzfeld sees the opposite. "In the U.S., three times as many people regularly attend religious services today as compared to when the nation was founded. Technology and religion are growing hand in hand," she writes.

The young men listen to my summary of Herzfeld and all that I have read. Michael is amused. "I don't know, Marie. I know a lot of Amish and Mennonites. And they aren't thinking about the Ordnung."

"I find the way they blend religion and technology so interesting. I mean, the way that you . . ."

"Nah. With farming . . . it's about a lot of other things. Like . . . capitalism."

"Capitalism?"

"Yes, of course. People want to make money. Look. You can't just learn about things from books, Marie. You need actual experience."

After visiting the Oklahoma City National Memorial Museum, we head to Stockyards City, which started as a cattle market in 1910 and bills itself today as "the world's largest stocker and feeder cattle market." This

is where ranchers buy cattle in bulk to take home to their ranches—
that is, to stock their farms.

Juston takes me to a Western gear store called Langston's so I can
buy a proper pair of field boots. Inside the store we are greeted by the
heavy, musky smell of leather from row upon row of cowboy boots and
stacks of cowboy hats the color of pale linen. Juston and Michael linger
over the boot selection, then each chooses a pair for me to try. In the
end, I settle on a pair of Tony Lamas with a red shaft and black foot.
They are state-of-the-art boots, with a spongy sole like a sneaker, and
though they are heavier than most shoes, they will become so comfortable I will wear them all summer. I can slide them on and off easily
when I go in and out of the trailers. They are impenetrable to mud,
barbed wire, and the jaws of a rattlesnake, and they instantly make
anything I wear look stylish.

I buy them steaks. We are at Cattlemen's, a storied steakhouse replete with photos of Republican presidents and rodeo champions on
the walls, and there is too much meat to eat, though it is very good.
Eric calls and asks Juston to order lamb fries, so we do. Juston says that
Eric likes Cattlemen's because they always keep a water glass full, and
this turns out to be true.

"I know who you are," Michael says to me with an unfiltered honesty.
"I've seen you before."

"You have?"

"This is my third harvest. I've been on your farm."

"You have?" I can't believe I don't recognize him.

"You came with your son. Your cousin lost some car keys in a field
and we all tried to find them for you. But you found them on your own.
You were worried because you had left a caterpillar in the car and the
doors were locked and you were afraid the caterpillar would die of heat
if you didn't get the doors open soon."

It's all true.

"The Hoffmeister? Where there was that big storm and we couldn't
finish cutting in time."

"Yes."

"The Colorado. The Alden. And the Gas Plant." He smiles with confidence. He knows all about me. These are all names of our fields. Then
Michael asks me questions, which is something almost no one else in
the crew has done. The questions have the effect of making me feel

seen. I hadn't realized it was a feeling I was missing. He wants to know: What are the big differences between Japan and America? What did I think of church today? He doesn't mind my answers. He is still a boy; it's easy to make him blush. But he has a daring mind that wants to know things, even if what he hears isn't what he expects. He has a quality to him that I've come to understand is what we call "self-assurance." Any answers I give that challenge his assumptions do not change his sense of himself. It is an attractive and reassuring quality, like coming upon a lamppost while wandering around in the fog in the dark.

Juston has warned me ahead of time that Michael is not as open-minded as he is, and that Michael will not approve of my reading the Rob Bell book on hell. This means that on the drive back to Crowell I ask Michael what he thinks of Rob Bell.

He says that he can't approve of Christians who accept only part of the Bible as true. He can't accept Rob Bell, because Rob Bell says that hell is not real. "You can't just take the parts of the Bible that make you feel good and reject the rest," he says. If the Bible is the word of God and is a factual document, as people are taught, then how does one accept only some parts but not others?

"But you haven't read the Rob Bell book," I say.

"But I already know I won't agree with him."

"But you can't know that unless you have the experience of reading it."

He smiles at this. Then he says: "Okay. I'll read it, if you promise to read something I recommend to you."

"Deal."

Juston drives us all the way back to Crowell. Along the way, we pass waterlogged fields. The wild sky is partly shaded by a dark cloud, like a curtain covering part of a stage. The sun casts plum and heather on the clouds and the colors are reflected on the water. The whole thing looks like a purple eye peering out of the sky and boring straight into us. The boys are enthusiastic and we stop by the side of the road for pictures.

I do not know it now, but with Michael's arrival, everything will change. At the moment, I am simply happy to have met someone who wants to exchange the invisible currency of ideas as a way to know each other, as a way to become friends.

FIVE

THE RAIN DOES NOT STOP and there is no work on Monday morning. Still, we rise early. It is dark. To the east, a crescent moon and Venus hang together in a corner of the sky. A blotch of plum stains the blackness, cracking open the night for the sunlight to begin to seep through. The first rays tug open the sky—fingers prying the black moss. The pink spreads across the horizon; you can see it crawling and moving, like a drop of paint in water. Pink soon rings the entire horizon, and we are driving in a broad circle. The sun finally makes its way out from under the horizon, but there is so much atmosphere, and the sun is red; drops of light color the clouds lavender and gold.

It feels as though the sky is lifting off and the earth has just been released from the grip of the dark. The colors of life and the day are now free. We can breathe. We hadn't noticed we weren't breathing, or that the dark was clamped down on top of us. Now the clouds are stretched overhead like dyed netting, as if it was the netting that had kept us trapped overnight. I share this conceit, and people raise their eyebrows. There is work to do. Enough nonsense about clouds.

The pink starts to fade and the light from the now-lemon-yellow sun is squeezed into the bright precision of a laser that sharpens the edges of buildings and windows. Anything with glass is illuminated and turns white. Metal doors glint like knives on the land. The windmills begin to blink. Then the sun rises higher, and the day is ordinary.

Two hundred or so harvesters are grouped around the Great Plains Technology Center in Frederick, Oklahoma, for the annual Case International Harvester kickoff breakfast. To see any group of people who are united by a job is to see variations on a theme. Eric knows many of his fellow harvesters. There is a plain-dressed family, who Eric confides to me are not necessarily the most intelligent crew. A group of wiry, coiled men stand around smoking cigarettes: here are the Brits who work for Jim Deibert again. There is a brutish-looking group watching an action film on a cell phone, an activity that continues into our breakfast of biscuits and gravy, where they sit opposite me.

As we eat, a man speaks to us over a microphone. "The number one distraction for farmers and harvesters is this." He holds up a cell phone. We are not to use our cell phones while operating equipment. "You need to know that there is no more ER in the town of Frederick. You need to remember where you are, so if you call 911, you can tell the dispatcher. You all know how remote your fields are. Most likely you will be an hour or more away from the nearest emergency room."

The room rumbles.

"Remember: 'R' isn't for 'reverse.' It's for 'wreck.'"

Whenever possible, we should drive forward and not backward. There is a series of injury photos, which I decline to watch. Eric has warned me they are old and that the law now prevents newer photos from being used. I've heard enough talk about what happens to men when they engage these machines incorrectly. I've heard how they can be crushed, halved, and bleed to death.

Eric has never lost a man on his crew, but he came close to losing his own life. He was in Wyoming and it was his third time through on a harvest crew. He was twenty-two. He had gone into the bin of his combine, and had left the engine running. He saw that the main auger was dirty, and reached in to clean it out. His hand was in the auger for perhaps just one second.

An auger is basically an oversize screw embedded in a tube. This technology was known to the ancient Greeks and named for the great scientist of antiquity Archimedes. As an auger turns, whatever substance it is in—assuming the substance can hold its form, like water or seeds—will wind around and travel down the length of the screw and fall out the other side. This is how water or wheat can be transported though a shaft.

The combine Eric uses—and most modern combines are like this—have at least four augers. There are two on the bottom of the grain bin of the combine, and these pick up the grain from inside the combine and transfer that grain to another compartment, which also has a large auger. This large auger then transports the grain to yet another auger, which unloads the grain out of the combine and into a waiting receptacle like a wheat truck.

At the same moment that twenty-two-year-old Eric reached into the auger, another harvester got into the combine cab, seeing that the ignition was on in the combine, but unaware that Eric was in the grain bin. This other man started up the motor, and the auger began to whir. Eric yelled and the driver turned off the engine. There had been enough time for only two rotations of the auger at most, but that was enough for Eric's hand to be trapped inside the tube.

The rest of the men on the crew convened around him quickly. They took off the tube that surrounded the screw. He was bleeding, but the blood only dripped; it didn't gush, which is an immediate death sentence with farming equipment.

When the men got the tube off, they saw that his hand was nearly pure white. Someone called an ambulance, then a good thirty-five to forty minutes away, and the ambulance in turn made a call to Flight For Life in Greeley, Colorado, an emergency flight service dedicated to rescuing people in life-threatening situations like this.

Because Eric's hand was white—which meant the blood was not circulating—the men left it inside the machine, packing what was visible with ice. When the ambulance arrived, a nurse prepared to administer morphine. "This nice lady is going to give you morphine," said his boss.

"She's not nice. She's ugly," Eric, ever the truth teller, is reported to have said before the morphine cheered his spirits.

When Juston tells the story, he adds that he asked his father if Eric was sad or scared. "No," Eric told him. "But I was mad."

Eric was flown to the Rose Medical Center in Denver. When the blade was finally removed from his hand, his hand flopped down as though it was already a discarded part of his body. It had remained attached to his arm only by tendons on the front and back; it had been 90 percent severed. Eric was given a nerve block so he could be conscious and try to move his fingers as the doctors reattached his hand to his arm.

He required physical therapy, and a skin graft with tissue taken from his leg. Today he retains 80 percent mobility, though some tasks, like holding loose change in the palm of his hand when paying for a drink at a drive-through, remain impossible.

Nine months later, he was back on harvest. He asked the men who had been on the crew with him to save the combine where he had

had his accident. He wanted to repair it himself, which he did. With the money he collected from workers' comp, he was able to buy a new pickup truck.

"Then I traded the pickup," he said. And before long, he bought his first combine.

One morning I linger after breakfast. Emily confides to me that in the weeks that have passed since our arrival—and that of the other harvesters—at least one crew has opted to leave. The "hogs, hail, and heavy rain" have convinced more than one of the Texas farmers that his crop is a loss, and best left abandoned and unharvested so he can collect insurance. That, at least, is dependable money. The crops have undergone too much of a beating from the animals and the elements. Eric has seen more cattle grazing on fields we had hoped to cut. Around us, the harvest is evaporating, melting like ice in the heat.

Eric has cut 1,500 acres this season. He knows from his conversations with other harvesters that one team cut 150 and another 138 and now those teams are leaving. Usually Eric expects to cut around 5,000 acres in Texas, but that looks impossible now. A few fields do remain, but Eric plans to share this work with Dwayne.

"Most people can't visualize an acre," he says to me patiently. "It's about the size of a football field."

Despite this, he has still cut enough to break even and cover his costs: insurance, the depreciation of the equipment, and his wage and the wages of the crew. But if he had not pushed so hard before the tornado and the hail, we would not have cut enough to meet expenses. "That's an example of how one day can make a significant difference," he says to me. The U.S. Custom Harvesters, Inc., reports that a twenty-year average net for a crew is about two dollars per acre cut. But if the average crew cuts around thirty thousand acres in a year, that would be a rough net of sixty to ninety thousand dollars. In good years—like 2008, when the price of wheat was high—crews netted eight dollars per acre. Other years are a deficit. Eric tends to do better than other harvesters.

"This always happens in Texas," Juston moans.

"Some years," Emily says, "we come just because we said we would."

I think about that word "co-op" emblazoned on nearly every cooperative elevator in every town. Everything operates on trust. The harvesters, the crops, the guns, the hunting, the safety.

That afternoon, the crew is able to put in a half day of work, but not so much work that we eat in the field. Instead, the Brothers and Sisters sit outside in the space between the trailers and have dinner together. Dwayne asks Henry to fix his phone so the photos won't slide around. "You fixed it last year," he informs Henry. "He don't remember because he fell off a silo."

I think I have misheard. It must be the iPhone that fell off the silo.

"Did you drop the iPhone on its head?" I ask.

"I landed on my feet," Henry says.

"Forty feet," Dwayne says.

This is not a joke?

"How did you fall?"

"Just went down. Forty feet."

"Onto grass?"

"Concrete."

"Did you break anything?"

"I have two compressed disks."

"I'll give you a milkshake to try that again," Samuel says.

"Did you hit your head?"

"No."

"Do you remember it in slow motion?"

"No. Just it happened fast. I wanted to get up. My dad wouldn't let me."

"Your dad was there?"

"Yes. He said the hammer fell and then next thing he knew I was there too."

"With the hammer?"

"That's right."

"Were you in the cage?" Eric asks. A cage is an open metal tube that covers part or all of the ladder, so if you climb the silo, you are somewhat encased.

"No."

"Just went over the edge?" Eric asks.

"Could you do that again?" Dwayne asks.

"I bet there isn't two in fifty that fall forty feet and land on concrete on their feet and survive. Did you feel anything supernatural?" Eric asks.

"No."

"Do you ever feel anything supernatural?" I ask Eric.

He looks surprised. "I gotta stop asking questions," he says.

The crew was able to put in another half day of work, and that has shifted the mood. They seem burnished by the work, as though an excess layer of boyish flab has been trimmed away. It is hot, and Michael and Luther wear sleeveless shirts, their biceps lean and taut and tan. The day before, Bradford shot a pig while harvesting. This is a good feeling too.

Juston has become a truck driver. He arrives most mornings with his sweatshirt hood pulled over his head, silent and even a little morose until he has had his coffee. Michael now drives the combine.

The boys eat cereal and I eat a hard-boiled egg Emily has made for me. Bethany, over the last few weeks, has stopped eating Frosted Flakes, but now, like me, eats an egg, or a banana with peanut butter.

"Do your friends spank their kids?" Michael asks out of nowhere. "I think that's more a country thing." Even I am surprised by the question. I don't mind it; it is just that breakfast has always been quiet, with little conversation.

"No," I say. "Were you spanked?"

"Well, yeah. How about you guys?" he asks. No one is accustomed to talking in the morning. But Michael does not seem to care about convention. He nudges the crew one by one. "Come on. Were you spanked?" he asks, until everyone confesses that, yes, they were spanked at some time, except Luther, who may never have needed to be spanked. Samuel nods vigorously and says that yes, he was spanked quite a bit and deserved it, and Bradford wrinkles up his mouth, annoyed that spanking has become an interesting topic of conversation. But yes. He, too, was spanked.

Now that we have all had a small exchange at breakfast, the crew seems more alert. Juston's eyes are shining inside his hoodie, and he asks another question. It is almost as if he and Michael conspired to bring conversation to the breakfast table.

"How about . . . is it true that in the city, when your dog is sick and dying, you have to pay two hundred dollars for a vet to put it to sleep?" Juston asks.

"Unless you have a mobile unit come do it in your home, in which case it costs more," I say.

"I don't know, Marie." Michael grins. "You got two hundred dollars on the one hand, or a buck fifty on the other."

"You mean . . ."

"How much is ammo?" Juston asks. "Is a bullet a buck fifty?"

Michael shrugs. "It's not two hundred dollars."

I look at Bradford, who stays silent. He doesn't chime in.

"Fifty cents," Samuel finally offers.

"My dad says Bambi ruined the American idea about animals. That after Bambi, everyone decided animals have a soul," Juston says.

"I like dogs," Eric offers. "Especially Roscoe."

"Rambo!" Bethany corrects him. They are talking about her dog.

"Would you . . . I mean . . ." I look at Michael.

He shrugs again and gives me the half smile. Then he fidgets. Michael is often restless. His head darts around like a raven on a fence scanning all the forms of life moving around him. "I don't think I could shoot my own dog. I don't really use guns. But the other day, my buddy's dog was basically dying, so . . ." He leaves the sentence unfinished.

"I see."

"I just can't believe city people would really pay someone that much to put a dog down."

I go over this conversation in my mind. Eric talks about the difference between liberals and conservatives. Michael's question again frames our difference as city versus country. I had thought of the big cultural difference as being Christian farmers versus atheist knowledge workers. What, exactly, is it that separates us?

"Juston," I say before he hops out of the trailer. "What's the first city in the Bible?"

"Cain built it," he answers.

So I look up the story of Cain and Abel. In Genesis, God creates the world, then creates Adam and Eve, and then supplies them with the Garden of Eden. Not long after, there is the Fall, in which Adam and Eve are cast out of the garden because they eat the fruit of knowledge. Adam and Eve have two children: Cain, a farmer, and Abel, a shepherd. Both men make sacrifices to God, and we assume that Cain presented

God with wheat and Abel with a slaughtered sheep. We are told that God preferred the sheep. Then Cain kills Abel and lies to God about it. It isn't explicitly stated in the Bible, but most people assume Cain killed Abel out of jealousy.

In retaliation, God sends Cain even farther away from his family, off into the world, where, among other things, he builds the first city mentioned in the Bible: Enoch, named after Cain's son. Some archaeologists think Enoch is the archaeological site Eridu, which is the name of Enoch's son. The remains of the city of Eridu are among the oldest in the world, with some people arguing that it is the oldest city, period. It is located in present-day Iraq, near the mouth of the Euphrates River. Carbon 14 dating places its founding at around 5400 BC.

Modern-day scholars see many meanings in the story of Cain and Abel and the city that Cain founded. Some see Cain's killing of Abel as representative of the shift humans underwent as they transitioned from a hunter-gatherer society to a farming society. Once man could live off of planted crops, he didn't have to roam the earth searching for food and hunting animals to survive. He could stay in one place and build a city. It is instructive, though, that Cain's city comes out of a history of violence; he has let God down and, some would say, needs to build a city to feel safe, because he has moved even farther away from the Garden of Eden than his parents did.

The city doesn't have a very good image. The garden with the tree and the animals is the place to which we are always wanting to return; the city is the place where we have ended up. Then again, even the ancient Greeks wrote their pastorals and their odes to Acadia, that verdant haven outside of the polis, or city. It strikes me how I am spending all my time with farmers, with the occasional dip into the world of men who herd animals, and how neither of these two groups are people I would ever find in the cities to which I am accustomed.

We have been here for a month, and the landscape and the feeling of Texas have worked their way into my blood. I am used to packs of coyotes, to roadrunners and turtles. Everything here is wilder and has unleashed something wilder in me. I've stopped driving with a seat belt, and I am beginning to be able to navigate the roads by the direction of the sun, adjusting as it moves overhead from east to west.

In the evening, I go to see the men cutting a field. As I am driving down the road, I see a coyote hanging on a barbed wire fence. A few feet away is another. And another. I stop the car.

I've seen plenty of dead carcasses by now: deer, hogs, and coyotes. But the purposefulness of this! There are seventeen dead coyotes—I count them several times—and they are hung on a barbed wire fence at regular intervals so there can be no mistake that their lives were taken with intention. Someone then arranged the dead coyotes in a repeated pattern, like a mosaic or a row of bricks making up the foundation of a wall.

This isn't Abel's sacrifice to God. The flagrant killing is meant to convey death, not worship. It is so hot. The air smells of rotten flesh. The coyotes must smell it too. The coyotes must know that this is a message of death intended for them.

The seventeen dead coyotes haven't been here too long, and I think that their death must coincide with our frustration, with the time when the harvest crews began to leave because of the destruction of the crop due to the storm. On the other side of the barbed wire fence, cattle lazily chew and moo and sniff the earth. Each one of these cattle is worth two to three thousand dollars. How many had the coyotes made off with before the rancher decided to hang up the carcasses of the dead to ward off more predators?

No one on the crew has killed a coyote. The tactic we have used to catch pigs—driving on roads and then following the pigs as they run parallel to us—would not work with coyotes, who are much cleverer than pigs, and run away into the mesquite or zigzag across the land to get away from predators. To kill this many coyotes, a person would need something other than a pickup. I realize I have started thinking like a hunter. I am thinking of how much harder and thus how much more rewarding it would be to kill a coyote than a pig. I have turned this thing of hunting into a puzzle and a game and wondered how I might do it well.

I get back into my car and keep driving.

At last we have had a full day of work and now everyone is happy. The long wait for the wheat to dry has ended. Emily drives dinner out into the field. She has everything sorted for us in the back of her Suburban. There are two coolers with spigots: one for water and one for chilled sweet tea. She has made her own hand wipes by dunking a roll of paper towels in soapy water. The food is packed in a series of casseroles or plastic tubs, and there will always be a choice of salad dressings and jams and jellies for the bread. She has a tub on the ground to receive the plastic plates and cutlery, which she will wash and reuse. Nothing is wasted. And there is always a rotation of desserts: brownies, pies, cakes, puddings. In her trailer at the RV park, she has a collection of cookbooks, and I see her sometimes sitting with them, trying to decide what to make based on what she has, and sometimes letting her mind plan what she will buy at Walmart.

That evening the sun sets in a spectacular display of color: everything is bloodred and purple, and I stand on top of the header trailer to get a better view and take photo after photo. Then the lights of the combines far off at the edge of the field come on. In the dark, with only the lights to illuminate them, the combines look lifelike: two bright eyes, and a series of little lights at the rear, like an electronic tail. When it is time to go home, I watch the three shapes driving toward me. Will I know them by how they drive? The first must be Eric, the leader, who moves with intention and makes no mistakes. The second one, bobbing and weaving to get every last inch of wheat, must be Bradford. The third, in a bit of a hurry, must be Michael.

I am right.

The men park the combines in a row. Their spirits are good. It is still hot, though the sun has set, and the morning will be hot. This means the crops will be dry, and even though some farmers are abandoning their fields, there will still be enough work for us.

"Did you see the sunset?" Eric smiles at me.

"Yes."

"I see that, and I think that can't be by accident." He's talking about God. "Just wait till we get to Idaho, Marie."

In the morning, we finish the field and I spend time with Juston in his truck. He wants to know if I've read any of the books I bought. I tell him that I like what Science Mike calls "axioms," or rules devised to help the author reconcile God and science. Two stand out in particular:

> God is AT LEAST the natural forces that created and sustain the
> Universe as experienced via a psychosocial model in human brains

that naturally emerges from innate biases. EVEN IF that is a comprehensive definition for God, the pursuit of this personal, subjective experience can provide meaning, peace, and empathy for others.

I tell Juston that, from a secular perspective, I like and identify with Science Mike's desire to find something transcendent in the world. He does not want the world to be made up of atoms and thus to draw the conclusion that our ability to perceive beauty is accidental.

The afterlife is AT LEAST the persistence of our physical matter in the ongoing life cycle on Earth, the memes we pass on to others with our lives, and the model of our unique neurological signature in the brains of those who knew us. EVEN IF this is all the afterlife is, the consequences of our actions persist beyond our death and our ethical considerations must consider a timeline beyond our death.

"Non-Christians grapple with this too," I say. I am thinking of how our actions affect one another and may reverberate in our cells for generations, according to the latest research in epigenetics.

I tell Juston how I started out unconsciously thinking that out here, where the old-fashioned hobby known as agriculture is maintained, it might be easier to know that old-fashioned thing called God. I am a modern person and can't know the real God, because he doesn't have a place in my world of information and human-controlled experiences. A farmer is conscious of waiting for a seed to sprout and grow, and of being subject to weather, so of *course* he can believe in God and might even need to.

But now that I am on the farm, it is starting to dawn on me that I am not so much engaged in an old-fashioned activity as I am pursuing something essential, which is to say, helping to grow food. Even in the city, people have to eat, and my idea that growing food is an old-fashioned occupation is unrealistic. And when I think this, the idea that God is necessarily old-fashioned also starts to fall apart.

Historians who study science say that we did not always see ourselves at a divide between science and religion. If I—if you—think they are incongruous, this is not because they always were. Before the Enlightenment, the intellectual world would not have been divided into "people who believe in God but not science" and "people who believe in science but not God." There are many reasons for why there has been a schism, including that God and Jesus were *not* about trying to explain the origin and meaning of everything. They weren't even about explaining. They were about being.

In his book *The Territories of Science and Religion,* the scholar Peter Harrison examines the origins of the idea that science and religion must be diametrically opposed. He points to the thirteenth-century religious figure Thomas Aquinas, speculating: "Aquinas . . . may have said something like this: Science is an intellectual habit; religion, like the other virtues, is a moral habit." This position feels lost to me in the way we talk about religion in the marketplace of ideas now. Somehow, the idea that God created the world became more important than our connection to God, and then it became important to discredit God. And in intellectual circles, God became stupid, and science became smart, and the being stupid and smart did not go together.

It is Harrison who points me toward the first thinkers who appeared after Christ's death, and who mused on what had happened. What was it about Jesus and his teachings that so captured people? Jesus was not the only religious figure alive at the time; plenty of scholars have speculated that Mithraism might have become the dominant religion of the day if it had had a better PR plan for widows and orphans.

Here are lines from "the Epistle of Mathetes to Diognetus," a second-century Christian apologist. We don't know who the writer is, only that he was defending and explaining his adherence to Christianity in a letter to another person whose specific identity has been lost to history. "Since I see thee, most excellent Diognetus, exceedingly desirous to learn the mode of worshipping God prevalent among the Christians, and inquiring very carefully and earnestly concerning them, what God they trust in, and what form of religion they observe . . . and why, in fine, this new kind of practice [of piety] has only now entered into the world and not long ago." In other words, to be a Christian was to be a new kind of person and to engage in a new way of life. It was not a checklist of items in which one must believe.

"That is all interesting," Juston says. "But if what the Bible says is true, then Jesus *was* God. On Earth."

"So that is the question. What was Jesus? What was God?" I say. He doesn't answer.

We have finished delivering a load of wheat to the elevator and are now back at the field to get the grain from Bethany, who is now in charge of the grain cart. Only she's not seated in the tractor. She's outside with Samuel, who is standing still, while she walks around him in a circle, their heads nearly touching in orbit.

"That's very close," I say.

"They're dating," he says.

"But they never touch."

"That's what dating looks like for Christians," Juston says. Then he heaves a heavy sigh. "If you date, it's because you are considering marriage."

"I thought there wasn't supposed to be any dating on harvest."

"That's supposed to be the rule."

One last field remains: we call it the Big Field. To reach it, we will need to cross a creek. There has been so much rain that the creek is still swollen. Not even Eric has forded the water to see if the wheat is ripe, or in good enough condition to cut. But this morning, we go out by caravan—two combines, a truck, my car, the grain cart, and Lily—to take a look. We are going on faith.

We drive along Dead Coyote Road, as I have come to think of it, and the dead coyotes are still lined up and wielding their apotropaic powers. We turn off onto a trail that leads us deeper into the wild. I see a herd of cows on the north side of the road running along with us. As we go with our slowly rumbling vehicles—the metal bodies suspended on fat rubber tires crossing the rocks and dirt—beside us, the cows pedal through the air in an excited stampede, all eagerness. An anonymous pickup truck joins our convoy, then diverts off the main dirt road to a side road and begins to blast a siren. I realize that the cows have come to associate the presence of any vehicle with eating; the only time they see a truck is when it is carrying food.

Our dirt road has cattle guards, but in years past, our trucks have bent the metal guards, which are not built to sustain the weight of a semitruck. As a result, all the trucks and combines now go carefully around the guards, through a temporary opening in the barbed wire fence. Trucks are not made for off-roading, but it is the only way to access the field, and it is also part of Eric's work ethic to take jobs that others will not dare try.

This is the third day of a string of very hot days. The boys have cut the sleeves off their shirts. The night before I heard a ripping sound from my bed, and when I looked to see what it was, there was Bethany cutting the sleeves off of her shirt too. Temperatures have reached 102, and early in the morning it is already in the 90s. My body is alarmed. I have come to fear the heat. It is not humid, so the air and the sun sap my body of moisture and I don't sweat much. I could become dehydrated without even knowing it. I park my car by the creek. Because the stream is so full, Eric doesn't think I should try to ford it.

When I jump out of my car—leaving the keys inside, as usual, so anyone can move the car if required—the sandpaper cruelty of the hot air slaps my face immediately. I jump into the oasis of Juston's pickup truck, and he crosses the river.

The Big Field is located on a high plateau, and this dirt road across the creek is the only way to enter and exit. It is the most isolated field I have ever seen.

Once we are over the river, Juston takes over a wheat truck and Eric gets out of his pickup and, after suggesting I ride with him today, gets into a combine. Behind us, the chaos of cows continues to follow the rancher in his pickup truck, with the siren blasting in alarm. "They pronounce it sigh-*reen*," Eric says to me.

The process here will be the same as it is on any field: we need a sample, we need to check moisture, and if the grain is ready, we will cut. Ordinarily Eric would not have brought over so much equipment before being sure the field was ripe, but the combination of the creek and the heat have made him bet we will be working all day today.

Almost immediately, though, Eric finds a problem with the wheel on his combine. The new header has been designed for transport, which means the forward-facing wheels can be rotated so the header can be detached and pulled along lengthwise behind the combine. During transport, a bolt that fastens the rotating wheel has broken. Lily is designed for exactly this kind of situation. It is not possible to carry every single bolt that a man might need, so Lily carries extra-long bolts of all diameters, and Luther, despite the heat, pulls out a torch and begins to customize one of those bolts.

Each field requires a new setting for the sieves and the speed of the rotors on the combines. Eric and Michael confer over the radio. They have to run their machines harder to extract the grain from the wheat than they did on the last field. If the setting remains high, as with canola, harvesters run the risk of mashing everything to a pulp. A good harvester will also periodically get out of his combine and check the patch of stubble over which he has just passed to see if he is losing too much grain. If the combine appears to be leaving too much behind for the ants, then he will need to adjust his settings to keep more grain inside the combine.

The combine sensors tell us that the wheat is ready, and for once Eric does not wait for confirmation from the elevator. At last we are in a field that has not been damaged by the hail, which means the quantity of grain is high. Eric calls in another truck to handle what will be a high-volume day.

On our first pass, we see a group of pigs trotting out of the field to the safety of the trees. When they run, the tops of their ears are visible, flopping up and down in a clownish, inelegant fashion. They are nothing like the wily coyote or the majestic deer. Eric shakes his head. "They are pests. Make sure your city friends understand that the pigs are like the rats of the subway."

We come across a shriveled carcass—just a hide, some teeth, and bones. Nature has sucked all the life and guts and water out of this animal. Eric makes a second pass so we can look at the remains from inside the combine cockpit. He confirms that it was a hog, probably shot, and left so the sun would take care of its body. We keep cutting.

The Big Field is about four hundred acres, a wide sea of the best grain we have seen so far. It is even and thick and there are few weeds; we are rewarded with the feeling of harvesting something that is healthy and was not damaged. It cuts at about twenty-five bushels an acre, and the trucks are barely able to keep up with us that day. They have to work so hard to even get into the field to retrieve the grain, they bobble and whine and grind across the red earth and back out toward the blacktop and then on to the elevator.

There are several hawks in the field that day. Though I have seen hawks flying overhead in days past, it's the first time I have seen them sitting on the ground beside us. I wonder if the hawks are here because it is so hot that the mice are slow. I feel as though the hawks are working alongside us. They are not like the pigs. When I mention this to Eric, he tells me that the hawks are able to work with us *because* of us. If we humans hadn't planted the wheat in which the mice are now hiding, the hawks would not be here waiting for the tiny creatures to emerge.

I have a habit of sending articles to people I like; it runs in my family. For a while, I was sending Eric articles on farming, but realized he didn't exactly like reading a new essay every day. So this morning, I give him a brief summary of an opinion piece by David Brooks that appeared in the *New York Times*. Brooks cites George Packer's proposition that there are four competing narratives about the United States. First is the libertarian point of view, which posits that America is "a land of free individuals responsible for their own fate." Second is the idea that America is globalized, and power concentrates in the hands of a few people. Third is the narrative of multicultural America, where people focus on identity groups and can't find common ground, and fourth is the narrative of "America First," the idea that America has lost its footing due to the contamination of too many other people from the "wrong" parts of the world.

I say that the vision of America that makes me feel most comfortable is the third, because at least in that I feel there is room for my appearance. I say I had never thought diversity would make people feel they could not find common ground; one thing does not cancel out the other.

Eric can see each point of view, but even though he doesn't accept the idea that there are too many "wrong people" in the United States, he does think we ought to unite around a cause. "I think," he says, "let's go to Mars. Even if it's hard. Let's do it."

"Like the pioneers."

"People need to *do* things. You can go and look. But this here is 'see and do.' If we go to Mars, that would be a see and do. It would bring everyone together. It would be good for us."

I am starving when Emily arrives with lunch. I climb out of the combine and immediately begin to eat. Eric tinkers with his combine wheel, and with the new bolt that Luther has made, and Emily chastises him. It is hot, she says. There is no time to waste outside of air conditioning.

And it *is* hot. I burn my hand on the aluminum of the potato chip bag and Eric burns his hand on one of the wrenches sitting on Lily's back. He rinses the wrench with water to try to make the tool cooler. We finish our meal quickly and Emily drives off. Eric continues to work on the wheel of his combine. I am getting hotter and hotter and I feel panic overtaking my body. I am not a hardy person and I know I won't last long in the heat. Then I hear a sound. It is Michael rolling up with his combine. Emily had called him on the CB radio and suggested he pull me out of the heat; she knows her husband and knows he will be fiddling with the bolt and the wheel. Michael opens the door to his combine and I climb into the sanctuary of cold air. It is such a relief.

But we do not even have time to begin a conversation before Michael hears a strange sound coming from his machine. There is a clattering, like a rock is stuck in the header. Eric radios to say that our sickle has broken.

The sickle is the precision part of the header that cuts the wheat. The modern sickle is made up of 140 independent, triangular knives, which are fastened onto a metal slab with bolts. This modular system solves the problem of broken blades by allowing a farmer to take off just one knife and replace it with a new one. Eric had seen the stubble behind Michael's combine, and saw that while it was all cleanly cut, there was a thin stand that had been bent but not broken as the combine swept over it. This happens only when an individual knife in the sickle is broken.

While Eric resumes cutting, Michael and I pull over to Lily again. Bradford is waiting for us.

"Oh, *Bradford.* Bradford will fix the sickle," Michael says.

There seems to be some tension between Michael and Bradford. Maybe the heat is making everyone peevish?

Bradford looks at the sickle in the header. I expect him to bring out his wrench and dislodge the broken knife, but he doesn't. He must see something troublesome beyond one broken knife. He strides over to the side of the header and pounds on a piece of plastic siding, which pops off. There is a compartment behind the plastic.

Michael rolls his eyes good-naturedly and smiles at me.

There is an entirely new spare sickle riding in the compartment behind the broken sickle. It is thirty-five feet long, and as we pull out the old one—I attempt to help—Bradford admonishes me immediately with great ferocity.

"You watch out! That will cut your finger right off!"

"Right off, Marie," Michael echoes.

"I know people who get their fingers cut off. Kids too." Bradford declares this as Fact. His delivery is overly emphatic, like the voice of a kid on the playground you can make fun of for being too serious. I should know; I have been that kid. But at the moment, he looks almost comically tyrannical.

The two men do not make eye contact as they put the replacement sickle on the ground. Then they begin to dislodge the broken sickle. It apparently has so many broken teeth that Bradford has decided, without communicating this decision, to replace the entire thing, in lieu of just putting in a new knife.

The two young men yank at the old sickle and I see how dangerous it is to pull at a thing that can cut off fingers. It takes strength and caution and they dislodge it at last.

"Pick up the end," Michael says to me. He wants me to help. I want to help, even though I am eight years old in farm years. But helping is also clearly not what Bradford wants me to do.

"It's dangerous," Bradford warns. I think about the safety session we all attended, and how hot it is, and how there is no ER nearby, and how an ambulance would need to ford the creek to get here. But I am so tired of being ineffectual. And don't Eric and Michael keep talking about the *importance* of doing things? I grab the end of the sickle. Michael nods at me with a broad smile, and then turns his concentration to the task of carrying the jaws of wheat death away from the combine.

The three of us carry the sickle over to the header trailer and set it down. It will be repaired later. Then the men start to put the new sickle into place. When this new sickle gets stuck due to the heat, Bradford simply hits it with his bare hands until the thing complies. The combine is no match for Bradford, and I recall my father's belief in a man's strength as something that matters. I had always found his attitude sexist. And yet out here, strength does matter. When he's done, Bradford stalks back over to his pickup without a word. Michael smiles at me again and we climb into his combine and continue cutting wheat.

That night I drive out alone for one more look at the country. It is Sunday, but the Deiberts are working. Deep in the countryside, their combines are sending up huge clouds of red dust into the evening light.

Way out in the backcountry, I see the usual coyotes and pigs, and then I see something new: a bobcat jumps in front of me, crossing the road from left to right. And I think how much I will miss this wilderness, even as the hogs, hail, and heavy rain have made for a depressing harvest.

For me, it has been a chance to see something new.

We wake at 5:30 the next morning to drive to Oklahoma. The crew had set up all the trucks the night before, and when I go down to the lot at 6 a.m., every truck has a driver and it is time to roll. We go through Quanah and cross the Red River, and we say goodbye to the land of the Comanche and the places where Cynthia Ann Parker once lived with her husband and children, and where Quanah put up the last brave defense against the white man, before the Comanche gave in to the settling of Texas. For three hours, we make our way north and then west to the town of Thomas, Oklahoma.

By the time we have crossed the Wichita Mountains, the land is changing. The mesquite disappears. The earth is still red, but the environment becomes softer. The roadrunner is gone, though the scissor-tailed flycatcher has followed us and glides through the air everywhere. Ivory egrets land in fields to look for grubs to eat. Eric says much of the farmland now has terraces because a strong storm could wash the land away, and the crops must be buttressed into place. The land, he says, is soft like sugar, and the farms here are beautiful. The softer, smaller fields feel more intimate somehow, and I have an intuition that the land will yield its secrets easily and put up less resistance to my curiosity.

★ ★ ★ ★

PART TWO

★ ★ ★ ★

SIX

THE WIND BLOWS CONSTANTLY. Emily says: "You remember? 'Oklahoma, where the wind comes sweepin' down the plain . . .'"

It was recently Memorial Day and patriotic colors are still blossoming in the cemetery we pass on the way into town. Each tombstone is decorated with a personalized tricolor: there are bouquets of carnations, flags, banners, and corsages, and throughout the town of Thomas, red, white, and blue adorn windows, the eaves of houses, and gardens. We will not be staying at an RV park here but on a quiet, tree-lined street where each home has a garden. On a robin's-egg-blue house, a white tire filled with red, white, and blue pansies hangs from the rafters. Another white cottage is bordered by a white picket fence and the front yard is piled high with bicycles and a plastic wading pool. A few blocks away are a small public park with a swimming pool for children, a grocery store, a coffee shop, and a gas station. Everything signals an assumed safety and quiet for its residents, and joyous patriotism.

The lot where we are parked is next door to a house that belongs to a farmer with whom Eric has a long-standing arrangement. His lawn is thick, fine, and freshly trimmed, and we pull right up onto it. After the gravel-covered RV park of Texas, all this soft green and the surrounding trees and gardens feel lush and luxurious. As soon as we arrive, the crew attaches the trailers to water, sewer, and electricity lines.

When we convene for lunch, Eric thanks God that we have arrived safely. He praises the team for flawlessly moving the machinery across the highway system and for unloading it so quickly and neatly on the large empty lot at the edge of town by the cemetery. Spirits are high. We have escaped the hogs and hail and heavy mud, and the final field in Texas yielded an additional five hundred acres for a total of two thousand; the farmer had given Eric an additional one hundred acres to cut at the last minute. Now the new landscape is filled with the magic of possibility.

There is work to do, and after lunch I go down to the lot where we are parked to see if I can help. We must repair Michael's sickle. We carry it out of the metal compartment on the trailer header where it had been stowed and set it up on the grass. Michael shows me what to do. I am to use a wrench to loosen bolts and then pull off any of the broken knives. Then we will attach new blades. As we work, men from town drive by in their pickup trucks to see what we are doing. They slow down and lean out of the open windows.

"Sickle?" they call out to us.

"Yep."

"Looks like you got women working."

"Yep."

At one point, Bradford comes over and expresses his displeasure that I am helping. "You'll cut your finger right off," he admonishes.

"Right off!" Michael says cheerfully. Then he asks me: "Don't you feel better if you are working? Are you really going to walk around the entire summer with that little notebook?"

"I feel better working," I say.

I can't read Bradford's expression. I can't tell if he is just concerned I will get hurt, or if there is something about me that does not seem capable of work. It can't be that hard to fix a sickle, I think, and if Michael believes I can do this, then I ought to be able to do it. Bradford stalks away, and I am left with Michael, Bethany, and Luther to put the sickle back together.

It turns out that this work is the kind of thing I am good at doing, because it mostly involves eye-hand coordination, which I like. We lay out the long piece of metal that forms the base of the sickle, and then use an impact tool to remove all of the nuts. Then we lift off the sections—the teeth. We replace any knives that are chipped with new knives.

Michael begins to sing "Poker Face" by Lady Gaga. He says he knows the song from the Super Bowl.

"Do you know there are Christians who think that the Super Bowl halftime show is the work of the devil?" Juston says.

I suppose I did know this, but it is hard for me to take it seriously, since I think that if the devil is responsible for anything, it would be something as catastrophic as a wrongful execution or a plague. But I have come to understand that deeply sincere people—people without irony—think that everything in life matters, and that frivolity is not something to be experienced and then forgotten.

While Luther and Bethany listen but do not chime in, Juston, Michael, and I discuss Katy Perry, Britney Spears, Justin Timberlake, and other lapsed Christians. All are former Baptists. They would all be familiar with the kind of church I attended in Oklahoma City. Then I say that one doesn't hear about Anabaptists or other Apostolic Christians becoming pop stars.

"I think," I say, "it's because the Anabaptist tradition is more grounded."

"I agree," Juston says.

Michael doesn't like this line of reasoning. He thinks I am implying that the Anabaptists are a better form of Christians, and he does not at all like that I would draw such a conclusion.

"No," Juston says. "She means that certain conditions yield certain things."

"Dryland won't grow corn unless it is short," I say.

Michael doesn't want to think that one Christian tradition might yield pop stars and another might not. Finally, he isn't too sure about pop stars in general.

"I don't really like Katy Perry," Michael says, "I mean, she started speaking out for gay rights once she became a pop star."

"I support gay rights," Juston says. He feels strongly about this. If Jesus came with a message that we must love one another, then surely he meant we must love gay men and women too. "I think Jesus, if he were alive today, would be for gay marriage too."

"I don't know," Michael says.

"No, I think it's pretty clear."

We circle around these topics for a while as we mend the sickle: the pop stars, the different Christian denominations, and gay rights.

Juston has specific ideas about how faith is supposed to work. We must find God as he is. If God exists, then the burden of discovery is on man. It is not that we must adjust our conception of God to suit ourselves, because God, he says, must be ahead of us. It is we who, with our institutions and limitations, may be making mistakes about how God is to be in our lives.

Michael takes this all in good-naturedly and promises to give Juston's ideas some thought. This is how our conversations will go—from pop song, to God, to Jesus, to basketball, and back to God again. The others rarely participate in these discussions, but I enjoy them. Talking with Michael and Juston reminds me of how I talk with friends—our minds darting around from subject to subject, pulling an idea outside of ourselves to share, then examining it together, then tucking it away and pulling out the next concept. Juston is much happier now that Michael is here. He smiles more often and doesn't just slouch off to his truck to listen to podcasts on his own, but invites his friend to play basketball or do chores together.

We work until Eric zooms by in his pickup truck, looking for Luther. I join them and return to the trailer, where we find Emily standing in the doorway with a tray of chicken patties she cannot broil. The oven is broken. Because Luther is half Eric's size, he can more easily stick his upper body into the oven and assess what is wrong; Eric can fit in only his hand. Luther obliges. He holds up a tiny flashlight that he keeps strapped to his belt, along with the pliers, and looks around inside the oven for a few minutes. Eventually, he emerges. "It needs a new igniter coil," he says in his slightly throaty and husky drawl.

I ask him, "Did the oven tell you: 'Tell the humans I need a new igniter coil'?"

Everyone laughs and Luther blushes and Eric goes off to see about a new part.

We are forever seeing about a new part.

I cannot believe the quality of the wheat in Oklahoma. In Texas, the wheat was often riddled with weeds and damaged, and even a good field like the Big Field was not terribly thick with grain. There, the yield was twenty-eight bushels per acre, while here it is close to fifty. What does the difference look like? Here in Oklahoma, I wade out into the wheat and it rises to my hip; it is so thick, I have to move slowly, as if I am walking through stiff whipped cream. There are no weeds and there is no rye. Each head of wheat is swollen with beads, and the beards—the spiky part of the wheat—stand out sharply, almost proudly, it seems, doing what the head of wheat was designed to do: protect the flesh inside. It is the most beautiful, clean field of wheat I have ever seen. I am grateful. The men will have work. The machines will have work. The farmer will have his crop.

There is a richness and a generosity to this land that are almost palpable. I feel it in how giving the soil is to the wheat it grows, and, in turn, to us. The prickliness of Texas—the cacti, the armadillos and mesquite—is gone, and now we have cottonwoods. Their seeds, coated in a protective padding of downy fluff, drift through the air as if to say that time is copious and the journey from tree to earth is meant to be an amble. We drive through clouds of this floating fluff and it diffuses the light with a warm, fuzzy glow. The cottonwoods themselves grow thickly together, their fleshy leaves nourished by the waters of rivers and streams. All the colors feel more saturated; it is water, I think, that stains the land with brighter greens, blues, golds, and reds.

Of course, the lessons of Texas have impressed upon us that the first order of business must be to get the wheat out of the field as quickly as we can. It is entirely possible for the weather to change and for rain to come through and destroy a crop, or at least to delay the harvest.

Eric takes me around in his combine and we cut a test patch. The machine moves slowly; the heavy heads are like a wall of felt putting up a fight against the knives in the sickle. As we cut, the field is so even and straight that the wind traces the surface of the wheat to form patterns that look like fractals. "I tell the guys," Eric says, "if this doesn't get you sexy and aroused, nothing will."

The field has a different shape to it than any in Texas. Ground in Oklahoma, though beautiful, also rises and falls along soft hills. The earth is granular—like sugar, as Eric says—and so the fields are terraced to prevent water from running off and forming ditches. This is another technique to prevent soil erosion. We must work around these terraces, which appear at regular intervals, like seams in a skirt sewn together out of many pieces of fabric.

Periodically, I see signs with the word "Centennial" placed on the edges of the fields in Oklahoma. I don't think about this too much, but then it dawns on me. Could Oklahoma only recently have turned one hundred? I pull out my iPhone and learn that the centennial signs are part of a program established by the Oklahoma Historical Society and the Oklahoma Department of Agriculture, Food and Forestry to "recognize those families who have continuously occupied their land and carried out farming or ranching operations for at least 100 years." Further searching confirms for me that Oklahoma did indeed enter the

Union in 1907, which is over fifty years later than California, where I am from, and even later than Texas. Why the long delay?

Most Americans have at least heard of the Trail of Tears, when nearly sixteen thousand Cherokee were taken off their land east of the Mississippi and forcibly marched west to present-day Oklahoma. Along the way four thousand of these men, women, and children died from starvation, exposure, and untreated sickness.

The Cherokee, Chickasaw, Choctaw, Creek, and Seminole were known as the "Five Civilized Tribes," a nineteenth-century term with no very clear set of characteristics to bind the people together, but which loosely referred to those nations that had friendly relations with white colonists and had adopted the white man's ways. Many of the Five Civilized Tribes had learned English, had become farmers, and had written their own constitution, as had the Cherokee. In other words, they had done everything "right." In 1830, the US passed the Indian Removal Act to relocate the Five Civilized Tribes from their natal land to the center of the country, on a piece of the large tract of land that had been acquired through the Louisiana Purchase. This land would eventually be known as Oklahoma. It is worth noting that the Cherokee successfully argued for their right to remain on their ancestral land before the Supreme Court, until Andrew Jackson simply threw out the ruling, in 1831. When Native Americans say that the language of the white man is tricky and means nothing, this is partly what they are referring to.

And so the Cherokee and the others marched west to "Indian Territory," with the promise that this land would forever be theirs "as long as grass shall grow and water run, and the reserves shall be their own property like their horses and cattle."

Except that white people decided they wanted this land too. So, with legislation collectively called the Dawes Commission, the government took all the Indians' communal property and divided it up. Each Indian nuclear family was given a homestead to farm, not only shrinking the land given to the tribes, but forcing them to switch from a tribal to a family system. In this arduous process, the Indians were also forced to "prove" they were truly Indian in order to receive a homestead. Freed black slaves and blacks who had escaped to Oklahoma on the Underground Railroad did not qualify for the program. The leftover land that didn't get assigned to an Indian family became "Unassigned

Land." Almost 148 million acres that had exclusively belonged to the Indians were reduced to 38 million for the Native Americans, leaving more than 100 million for white people.

In 1889, Anglo settlers lined up at the edge of the Unassigned Lands. Someone fired a cannon, and the white people ran, rode horses, or rode buggies to claim a homestead. The cannon made a boom when it was fired, and the people who ran after the boom were called "Boomers." People being people, some people ran into the land before the cannon, and they were called "Sooners" because they ran too soon.

Then, in 1907, Oklahoma was "settled" enough to become a state.

Eric and I go to a private grain elevator to test the sample; while there is a cooperative elevator in town, some of the wheat will be delivered to small elevators like this, which buy premium crops to sell for export. There is a man inside dressed like a farmer: the hat, boots, and pliers. He is wearing a long-sleeved chambray shirt and he smells, the odor of putrid, stinking, fetid grain. He has been cleaning out a bin to prepare for the new wheat.

"Everything that lives, smells," Eric mutters to me.

The elevator man has such a heavy accent that I cannot understand everything he says. I can make out that he is praising Eric for being the first to deliver to the elevator—first is the position Eric often seems to be in and the one he likes. The man takes the coffee can with the sample and gives us readings. The moisture comes up at 13.2 percent, which means it is dry enough to cut.

Our sample is so perfect, the man says, there will be no docking, which means there will be no penalty against us. There is no foreign matter mixed in with the kernels: no grasshopper parts, no pebbles, no weeds, and no rye. It is certainly the cleanest sample I have ever seen. There will be only 120 acres total to cut, but the entire job will be a joy for the crew. What one gives up in space and size in Oklahoma, one gets back in these gorgeous, dense samples of wheat. Everything—the wheat, the dirt—is so red and soft and fertile. It's as if flesh itself is bleeding to give us wheat.

The dirt also gets everywhere. In the evening, if there is time, the crew will try to clean the dust from the combines and the trucks. They use either a pressurized-air hose to blow out the dirt, or pressurized water from another hose to spray the equipment clean. The force of the air and the water is so strong, the men wear earplugs and often allergy masks to protect their lungs. Once, Michael took it upon himself to wash my car.

I ask Eric if he has ever tried to buy farmland here. Even I am thinking of buying farmland here. The soil is that beautiful. Land in Lancaster County, and in parts of Iowa, goes for about $10,000 per acre. Land in California, with its Mediterranean climate, is about $13,000 per acre. Here, land is around $2,000 per acre. My farm in Nebraska would go for about $500 per acre. Eric says he has considered it and even bid on land a few times when farms have come up for sale. He likes the area. The nearby town of Clinton has a small fine-arts center, and before Thunder basketball games, the audience prays to God and isn't embarrassed to do so. The nearby town of Weatherford has a university. But the oil-and-gas people are buying the land for themselves, and Eric has always been outbid.

While we are talking, we see a combine go by on the back of a flatbed. Eric is instantly alert, like a dog who smells the scent of another animal. "Johnsons," he says. After a few trucks have passed, a pickup truck goes by hauling a trailer house with a "Johnson Farms" logo on the side. I know, without Eric telling me, that it is another crew just arriving.

But still we are first.

There are good reasons why some land is more valuable than other land; it comes down to soil and what the land can produce. When I mention my home state, farmers will often shake their heads and mutter: "California will grow *anything.*" Not so in Nebraska. Oklahoma, though, can grow more than it used to, and science is a big part of the reason.

Crop breeding has come a long way since the Japanese first created Norin 10. Scientists have bred more dryland varieties of corn and soybeans, which, like wheat, require less moisture than earlier generations of these plants. These new corn and bean types were selected to have shorter stalks, so not as much moisture and not as many nutrients go into the formation of stems and leaves, and this means that corn can now grow farther to the west than it has historically in the United States. On a recent side trip to Kansas, I watched as the fields around me shifted from predominantly wheat to corn. And yet Michael Doane, the farmer I visited there, explained to me that I was still technically in the wheat belt. It was technology that enabled his farm, which had historically grown mostly wheat, to grow additional crops. This greater access to variety allows for what farmers call "rotation," which has numerous benefits.

The gold standard for farmers in the Great Plains is to be able to rotate their fields with at least three crops: soybeans, corn, and wheat. Sometimes farmers will also grow milo, sorghum, or barley.

When crops can be grown in succession on a plot of land like this, it has the effect of naturally controlling weeds. Each crop has unique characteristics. It will grow to a certain height and make its own shade, or it will grow at a certain rate and prefer certain minerals. As a result, each crop has weeds that tend to grow symbiotically. Corn, for example, grows quickly and becomes tall, which means that the notoriously strong pigweed has less of a chance of taking over corn than it does carrots, which are short; as long as the corn canopy can get to a certain height before the pigweed, its shade can prevent the pigweed from growing. But if the pigweed begins to grow soon after the corn sprouts, or if the pigweed outpaces the corn, it may choke a field.

Pigweed versus soybeans, however, is a more difficult match between plants; soybeans are shorter than corn and have a harder time winning the race for access to nutrients. But if the soybeans are rotated with corn, then the year after the corn is harvested, there should be less pigweed mixed in with the soybeans. The farmer has "confused" the weeds, which have suddenly encountered a disruption in what they "thought" was a predictable growing condition.

Science has come up with other tools to trick the weeds. A farmer can plant Roundup Ready corn or Roundup Ready soybeans. These crops have been bred by scientists to contain a gene that prevents their enzymes from binding to glyphosate. When they are sprayed with Roundup, nothing happens, but the glyphosate does kill all the other plants—the surrounding weeds. This revolutionary system has helped farmers to raise clean crops, but over time this seemingly miraculous system has had a cost.

Grains that have been genetically modified not to bind to glyphosate are called GMOs, and a skeptical public does not always want to eat them; they are not grown in Europe, though they are imported. While the technology to make Roundup-resistant wheat exists, it has not been put into production. Wheat is generally so cheap to grow and buy that economics do not favor putting it into production. The liberal use of Roundup has also bred Roundup-resistant weeds, a subject frequently in the news.

In Kansas, Michael Doane showed me a field recently planted with soybeans. He and his brothers and father, with whom he farms, were keeping watch over the soybeans; after six weeks, they would be tall enough to form a canopy that would prevent the pigweed from growing. But if the pigweed outpaced the soybeans, then the field could be in trouble, and this was doubly a worry because, in this part of Kansas, there were now certain strains of pigweed that were immune to Roundup. In that instance, even if the farmer sprayed the field, he could not kill the pigweed, and he would face the possible growth of a superweed, which is all but indestructible.

But there are other tools at a farmer's disposal. If he is lucky enough to own ground with desirable qualities—sufficient water, good soil, a long growing season—he can grow various crops that have different growing cycles and seasons, and thus further "bewilder" the weeds. Whether a wheat crop is planted in the spring or in the winter affects when the crop sprouts, matures, and is harvested, and thus which weeds will develop. A variety of crops is desirable.

The land in Oklahoma, says Eric, has been transformed due to shorter varieties of cotton. Just as scientists bred "dwarf wheat," or the short wheat we have seen on the road, they have made a version of dryland cotton. Twenty years ago, when Eric started coming to Oklahoma, he didn't see much cotton, if any, but now it is in rotation with wheat. And while this has reduced the acreage for Eric to cut, the presence of cotton has allowed farmers to naturally reduce the amount of herbicide they need to spray, because the cotton, which grows in a different season than wheat, helps control the weeds. In the agricultural journal *Farm Progress*, a farmer named Russell Isaacs observed: "The last three to four years, we've really made rotation a priority, getting away from continuous corn. And it's benefitting every crop we raise." And while planting cotton has its challenges, rotation in general has had a positive effect.

A farming technique related to rotation is the use of something called a "cover crop," an intermediary crop planted into the ground but not harvested. Clover and radishes are frequently cited examples.

These cover crops are planted into the soil of a field after a main crop has been reaped. Their presence also confuses weeds because they compete for nutrition, water, and sunlight. On dry land, the cover crop has the added benefit of holding the topsoil in place so it does not blow away. When the cover crop dies, it adds additional organic material to the soil, helping to choke out noxious weeds.

So all good. Who wouldn't want cover crops? Well, the seeds cost money. There is also the ever-present issue of moisture. In a place like Pennsylvania, where the ground receives so much rainfall, there is water to spare for a cover crop; this is not as much the case in Nebraska. And let's not forget that the cover crops must be mostly killed off in preparation for the actual cash crop, and the killer that will get rid of the cover crop needs to be a herbicide like Roundup.

For farmers, all these developments—Roundup, GMOs, dryland varietals—are welcome. This is not to imply that the systems are without problems. Plenty of farmers do not like that a handful of companies have a virtual monopoly on modified seeds, nor do they like it when a company like Monsanto aggressively prosecutes a farmer who has grown his own genetically modified seed for soybeans or corn off of a patented crop. But in aggregate, these new farming techniques have helped to preserve topsoil and prevent erosion, and in some cases have also helped to reduce water usage.

It is often said that farmers are conservative and reluctant to change. There are reasons for this. Thrift—and good farmers are nothing if not thrifty—can go hand in hand with a reluctance to try something new. Farming is often performed with small margins. In 2018, the net cash farm income was projected at $91.9 billion, "down 5.1 percent from 2017 levels. If realized, this would be the lowest level since 2009," according to data supplied by the USDA Economic Research Institute. Breaking down this number further, the average income for a farm household in 2018 was projected at $119,252. However, this income is dependent on money earned both from the farm and from outside sources—a second job. Average on-farm income was projected at $21,130, and off-farm income at $98,122. In other words, most farmers must earn money in some other fashion, and not just off the land.

Let me try to use my own farm as an example. In an average year for which I have data—let's take 2008—we might produce about one hundred thousand bushels of wheat on our combined 3,500 acres of land farmed. (The farm is almost 7,000 acres total, but each plot is farmed in alternating years, in order to give the soil a rest.) If you are a farmer, you probably calculate that this means it yields about twenty-eight bushels an acre, a number that will not strike you as particularly good if you farm in Pennsylvania or Iowa. And this is where I have to point out again that our farm is in dryland, where the average rainfall is fifteen inches per year. Contrast this to Des Moines, Iowa, whose average yearly rainfall is twice that. This means that growing wheat in Nebraska is difficult, unless one irrigates, which we do not.

In 2008, then, if the price of wheat was a conservative $8 per bushel, then the gross profit for our farm would have been $800,000. However, that year we paid out $450,000 in expenses, with $240,000 going to the custom harvesters. Fertilizer came in at $90,000. Subtract the costs and we had a net profit of $350,000 split three ways between family members. That was an unusually good year. Note, however, that as I write this, the price of wheat sits at $4.70 a bushel. Few farmers I have met will say that they farm for money; most tell me they do it because they love the land and the values they can live out by working the soil so we can all eat.

We continue driving. As we pass some farmhouses and barns, Eric asks me if I recognize the configuration of the properties. He is talking about the way the silos stand next to the farmhouses, and about the kind of farmhouses that have been built here; they are two-story, with shuttered windows and a balanced, symmetrical shape. When I fail to say anything, he tells me that the properties are almost like those in Lancaster County. And, in fact, this part of Oklahoma was partly settled by Mennonites.

We pass an old Mennonite church—what is now called an Amish Mennonite church—that has been put into service for the remaining conservative Amish, whose numbers aren't large enough for a church that is separate from the conservative Mennonites; they, the bonnet people, have had to band together. We pass another church that Eric calls "Beachy Mennonite," a conservative group that believes only these Mennonites will be saved when judgment comes. And finally we go look at the state of construction at Dwayne's new church; Dwayne is a more modern Mennonite, similar to the boys in Eric's crew. This new church is a steel structure that to me looks much like a barn. We peer inside; it is a practical facility with community spaces, a kitchen, and offices.

Nearby is a cemetery. Eric explains that I will see the same names over and over on tombstones. Yoder. Miller. Stutzman. Lutz. These are classic Mennonite names. He says that Emily's sister-in-law's grandfather was a Miller, and came from Thomas and is buried here. We find his grave. This is the moment when I realize that Eric started coming to Oklahoma due to a network of churches; he knew someone in Pennsylvania who knew someone in Oklahoma who needed a harvester. And then his harvesting career began.

Living on the coasts, I have grown accustomed to thinking of the middle of the country as a repository for "the old way," a conservative way of thinking that consists of a blur of white people. But I realize that for Eric all the land is a mosaic, and he likes to stop and examine each pebble and marble that the picture comprises. There is even a group of his people here around this church with a cemetery to anchor his roots. It is a piece of his extended family transplanted to this land. He can see himself in it.

"Lutz," I say after we pass yet another Lutz tombstone. "There were Lutzes in my family."

"You were a Mennonite." He beams at me.

"Maybe." Maybe this history is a piece of me too.

It is entirely possible, though not certain, that were it not for the Mennonites, we would not be cutting wheat in Oklahoma. While historians argue over precisely how much credit for the planting and proliferation of hard red winter wheat should go to Mennonite immigrants in Kansas, legend has given them sole credit.

Most of the wheat we have been cutting so far is winter wheat, which means it is planted in the fall, goes dormant in the winter under the snow, then wakes again in the spring to grow tall and ripen for harvest sometime in May, June, July, August, or September, depending on where it was planted. One of the benefits of winter wheat—and we mostly cut hard red winter wheat, which has a ruddy, amber hue—is that it can tolerate low moisture, drawing on whatever water is left in the ground, or the snow that melts in the spring, to sprout and grow and produce kernels.

The Mennonites who brought this wheat to the plains in America stopped first in Kansas, and their story is as much one of adaptation as is the story of wheat. They were, like Eric's forefathers, of German origin, and part of the wave of people who broke from Catholicism in the fifteenth century. But there were many battles in Europe between Catholics and different groups of Protestants, including the Mennonites.

In 1763, the Russian empress Catherine II, known as Catherine the Great, invited Europeans to come and "settle" a region of her expanded country located along the Black Sea. Today this area is known as the Ukraine. In Catherine the Great's time, it was called New Russia and had previously belonged to the Turks as part of the Ottoman Empire. Many of the local inhabitants were Turks or Nogais, an ethnic group descended from Mongols and Turkic tribes. Among those who answered the Empress's offer of free land in exchange for settlement—that is, those who put a European stamp on this part of New Russia—were Mennonites of German origin. By one estimate, the population of Mennonites in this southern region of Russia was about forty thousand by 1869.

The Mennonites thrived as farmers. Among the crops they grew was hard red winter wheat, which did well on the high steppes. The Mennonites were allowed to continue German language instruction and to eschew military service, a privilege that began to seem "unnecessary" by 1870, almost a century later, when rising nationalism and Russia's defeat in the Crimean War led to the proposition that all citizens would soon be eligible for the draft. Since pacifism is a cornerstone of the Mennonite religion, these Russian immigrants began anew the search for a home, turning their sights toward the New World.

In 1873, a group of twelve Mennonite men scouted out land in Canada and the United States. In their report after returning to Russia, the Mennonites shared their observations on available land in the plains, specifically Minnesota, South Dakota, Nebraska, and Kansas. Like the Russian steppes, these High Plains states in the US had little rainfall, but could support a crop like hard red winter wheat.

So it was in 1874 that the first group of around eight hundred Mennonites left Russia. No story can have much magic without a legend, and in the legend of the Mennonites moving to America, it is said that many immigrants packed winter wheat in flasks and burlap bags, gingerly bringing the seeds across the land and sea. In June, they made their way to Odessa, then took the train to Hamburg, and from there sailed by ship to New York City. The transcontinental railroad had just been established, in 1869, which made further movement easier than it had been for earlier immigrants, who had crossed the Americas in wagons and by handcart. Once in America, the seeds that had been gathered in Europe were planted in the new land. Two generations later, the wheat would be crossbred with wheat in Japan, until it produced the fields of today.

When I hear stories of people driving across the country, they often tell me how they found the Great Plains boring and flat. And many pioneers, too, racing through "Indian territory" for the promise of Oregon or California, originally thought the plains were akin to a desert: they had so few trees. They would drive you mad, they said. But to me the plains are uniquely beautiful, with a subtle gradation in topography that suits a ruminating mind. I love the labyrinth of grasses and animals. Today, scientists divide the plains into three categories according to the grass that dominates a given area: short, medium, and high. In the simplest terms, the soil dictates the grass, and the soil is determined by history.

About 70 million years ago, the Farallon slab, in the present-day Pacific Ocean, subducted, or ducked under, the North American plate. Our knowledge of geology is always improving, but the best guess is that the Farallon slab dove at an unusually shallow angle, resulting in a series of startling geographical changes. Usually, when one plate subducts under another, magma begins to bubble up two hundred to three hundred miles from the subduction, leading to the formation of mountains; this is what is happening with the Himalayas, for example. The subduction of the Farallon slab does appear to have caused volcanoes, which would eventually result in the Sierra Nevada Mountains, but it kept moving underneath the North American plate at a shallow angle.

As the Farallon slab moved eastward, it scraped the underbelly of the North American plate for about nine hundred miles. Picture a paint scraper going across a ceiling and removing paint; as the Farallon slab moved, it scratched loose bits off the underbelly of the North American plate, dragging muck along with it. Finally, the Farallon slab began to sink toward the mantle of the earth, and all the accumulated debris burbled up through the crust to eventually form a series of mountain-building events called the Laramide orogeny; the term "orogeny" means "formation of mountains." Over time, the Laramide orogeny gave rise to the Rocky Mountains, one thousand miles east of the California shore. The more the Farallon slab pushed, the more the Rocky Mountains rose. Meanwhile, a net effect of these and other forces was that the Arctic Ocean, to the north, which at that time was not covered with glaciers but with water, poured into the center of North America, east of the Rocky Mountains. This ocean joined with water from the Gulf of Mexico, until they were linked together and made up the Cretaceous Western Interior Seaway. What we today call the Great Plains was once a shallow ocean covered with water. Since this entire landmass was farther south than it is today, the temperatures and climate would have been somewhat tropical.

This ancient sea teemed with life, much of it microscopic—plankton and bacteria. But when these tiny microorganisms died, they fell to the bottom of the sea to break down and contribute to building something new. Most living things comprise carbon, hydrogen, nitrogen, and oxygen. But a small percentage of the material that makes up living organisms does not get remade by this natural recycling process. A tiny bit of this organic material mixes with sediment, remains in the ground, and fossilizes. So you can imagine that, over and over again in this ancient sea, these tiny creatures lived and died and fell, and on top of their bodies, millimeters of sediment accumulated. It takes millions of years for the sediment to pile up in any meaningful way, but it does over time, with that roughly 1 percent of organic material mixed in. This hardened substance is called kerogen.

As the sediment continues to accrue, the whole compilation gets heavier and sinks toward the center of the earth, where the temperature is warmer. In addition, the weight pressing down on the dead organic material and the sediment becomes pressurized, which further raises the temperature, and everything subsequently becomes "cooked," first releasing water and carbon from the kerogen. Geologists, in fact, refer to the strata in which this kerogen is cooked as "the kitchen." As the kerogen continues to heat up, it releases other substances—methane, petroleum, and natural gas.

The more volatile elements then try to escape from the sediment. If the rock is tight, though, it can hold the various escaped elements in place, so you can have strata of rock underground with hundreds of pockets of petroleum and water and gas. But the pressure doesn't stop at these layers of sediment; remember, layers are constantly accumulating above and pressing down. Eventually, the pockets of gas and water that can escape their original home will do so, rising up. Sometimes these transformed substances make it to the earth's surface and evaporate. Other pockets remain trapped underground. Because all of the Great Plains was once an ocean that housed life, throughout the plains there remain pockets of gas and other fossil fuels. Humans often seek to find these substances and get them out.

The Rocky Mountains remained, and continued to rise, and it was this ongoing growth that forced the ocean to recede, beginning around 70 million years ago. At the same time, erosion caused rocks from the Rocky Mountains to wash down into the basin where the ocean had been, and this is why the elevation of the plains is higher to the west than to the east, and this, in turn, is why the short-grass prairie is to the west and the long-grass prairie is to the east; the topsoil is better in the east. Today, there are only traces of the great ocean that once covered the interior; there are fossil beds, chalky deposits of what amount to hundreds of fossilized seashells, and the gas and oil that cover the land.

The Rocky Mountains also help explain why the color of the dirt changes in the plains. In Nebraska it is newer and gray, because the erosion is recent. The heavier sediments from this runoff remain closer to the mountains, while finer sediments—and thus finer soil—traveled toward the east.

The mountains toward the south of the United States are lower in elevation, and this means that much less sediment washed down from their sides into the bottom of the Cretaceous Western Interior Seaway and onto the plain that was left behind. The Pecos River— where Cynthia Ann Parker was recaptured—runs north to south from New Mexico to Texas, and cuts off west-to-east-flowing rivers. This further prevented the runoff of sediment from the Rocky Mountains to the southern part of the Great Plains. As a result, the erosion from wind, glaciers, and rain took away the dirt and sand that had accumulated during the Cretaceous period and sent it down into the Gulf of Mexico. Some 250 to 298 million years ago, erosion exposed the reddish Permian topsoil for which Oklahoma and Texas are famous.

When Eric said the ground in Oklahoma was soft like sugar, he made it sound like a compliment, but softness can also be a vulnerability. The red dirt roads that lead to farming fields are accustomed to sustaining a certain amount of weight from farm equipment repeatedly crossing them. When we arrive, these roads are chewed up from accommodating additional trucks and heavy equipment that is hauled out into the fields to drill and test for precious fossil fuels. Oklahoma is perforated with oil wells.

In Oklahoma, the oilmen practice fracking, which involves boring into the earth, then sending a high-pressure mixture of water, sand, and chemicals into the opening in the rock, producing hundreds of tiny fissures in the rock. The sand goes into the cracks, propping them open. The water mixture is then extracted, along with any gas or oil lingering in the hundreds of tiny perforations that the process has opened. This is how oil companies are able to remove and access petroleum supplies that previously were too scattered and numerous to gather into one place. When fracking is combined with horizontal drilling—in which a drill bores into the ground and then turns at a ninety-degree angle, permitting the fracking to occur over a 5,200-foot stretch of rock instead of a 100-foot stretch of rock—yields can be glorious for a gas company, and for the farmer who owns the mineral rights to the land below the surface.

But once the water is extracted, it must be put somewhere. All around the wheat fields where we work are large vats of water. Here and there we pass mammoth pools, sometimes stored in shoddily built tanks lined with rocks. When Eric sees one of these tanks, he hovers on the edge of the road that goes past the pool. He frowns. "I don't like that road," he will say, his mind reading something in the earth and the soil that I cannot see.

Sometimes I think he is overreacting. Then comes a day when Lily, the grain cart, and a combine all sink into the silky red dirt and cannot move. It is like quicksand. The team springs into action. They say little as they work as quickly as they can.

First, Samuel parks a wheat truck next to the combine; the wheat truck is on a stable patch of road. Bradford extends the combine's auger and dumps the grain he had been carrying, thus taking tens of thousands of pounds of weight off the combine's back. It is enough of a change to free the machine from the soil. Then the tractor dumps its grain into the combine once more, and the combine transfers this grain to the wheat truck, and the tractor, too, is able to move.

Bradford drives the combine over to Lily and turns it around so they are back-to-back. Meanwhile, Bethany, Samuel, and Luther have removed a heavy plastic cable with an eight-inch diameter from the back of the grain cart; the cable is stored there for just such a purpose. The team connects the combine and Lily via this cable.

While Bradford drives the combine, Luther revs Lily's motor. It takes a few tries, but eventually Lily is free. All the vehicles have cleared the field. Eric phones the farmer who owns the land and informs him that the wheat will not be cut. It is not easy to turn down a job; we are a team that will cut for anyone. But in this instance, the risk to the equipment and to the men and women who run the machinery is too great.

In a way, the very qualities that make Oklahoma farmland so valuable are the same ones that also make it so dangerous. This is because the red soil is able to hold moisture that would, in all likelihood, drain away in Texas, and so cultivated plants have more water to drink, and so a greater variety of crops can be planted.

It's partly because now I know how much Oklahoma means to Eric that I go to church on Sunday determined to like the pastor. This church is the same denomination as Eric's back in Pennsylvania, perhaps another reason why he has so much love for this part of the plains. If the Bretheren in Christ Church produced Eric, then I think it will have at its core something of value for me.

The church is down the street from our campsite, and in the middle of a residential neighborhood. It is neither a plain steel Mennonite building of the sort I had seen while roaming the country with Eric, nor one of the stiff, white-steepled buildings of the East Coast. It looks like something you might find in 1960s California. It is brown, with unusual angles, and stands like some kind of butterfly pinned in taxidermy. It has broad windows that send sunlight down into a room decorated with caramel carpet and wall fixtures, so the room glows with amber lighting.

Someone is playing the piano when we enter. We sit in pews and sing worship music, the lyrics projected on a small screen above the pulpit. The one song I recognize is "Amazing Grace." But even this I can't sing along with terribly well, because the melody is not the version I know.

An older pastor gets up and asks the congregation if anyone has specific prayers. One person mentions a family member who has been ill and is healing. Someone else asks for good harvest weather, not just for the farmers but for the custom harvesters now here to cut wheat. There is mention of a youth trip, with young people off to share the Gospel in a very different setting from what they are used to. We pray, and there is an offering. And then the main minister takes the stage.

Pastor Rainwater is tall, smiles broadly, and is definitely heterosexual. I realize now how infrequently I come across this kind of minister in my life in the city. The urban men of cloth I encounter are either some variation of what we would call a metrosexual—a highly sensitive man, attuned to aesthetics and not necessarily at home with a truck and pliers—or a thinker, who approaches religion like a scholar. Alpha males, in my world, run corporations, play golf, become surgeons. Sometimes they are dentists or lawyers. They do not go to church. It is women who lead the spiritual journey in the secular world; but here in evangelical America, it appears to be the men.

Pastor Rainwater speaks of his love for theology. He says he has started to examine the formation of the early Christian church. He is occasionally self-effacing, making sure we understand that he has a sense of humor. He tells a story about how, at the height of the Cold War, Billy Graham went to meet with various religious leaders in Russia. Conservatives criticized him for not taking on a prophetic role. They said: "You set the church back fifty years." I ask Juston what this means, and he explains that conservatives at home were upset that Billy Graham was friendly to the Russians—ingratiating, even—rather than calling them out on the sin that is communism.

"And Billy Graham said: 'I am deeply ashamed I set the church back fifty years. I have been trying to set it back two thousand years!'" Everyone laughs, and he laughs too. It's as if this is the Christian version of going out to dinner with someone for the first time and telling your most disarming joke to set the stage for a great evening.

Once it's clear the joke landed well, Pastor Rainwater becomes serious. He wants us to turn to Acts 2: 41–46. In the Bible, Acts comes after Matthew, Mark, Luke, and John: these four gospels tell the story of Christ and his ministry on Earth. Acts tells the story of the Christian religion and how it spread and how the church was formed after Christ died.

Christians, Pastor Rainwater says, "are called to serve others." The text, by which he means Acts, "explicitly mentions evangelism." God saves people and sends them out to make disciples. This is important. He challenges the congregation to try to have a meal with a nonbeliever, though he knows that most people in the group don't know anyone who isn't a Christian. While everyone chuckles, I think that, as a nonbeliever, I could get a lot of free meals! In fact, I *am* getting a lot of free meals. And a small corner of me suddenly feels guilty. Why am I getting all these free meals?

But then the preaching accelerates. Pastor Rainwater tells us he knows a woman who has set aside her "intellectual pride" and now believes in Christ. Now she is filled with "joy." Twice he equates intellectualism with pride. She has been saved from this pride. She has evaded hell. Suddenly we are in a conversation about hell and about being saved from hell by not being intellectual.

This startles me. He claims to be a theologian who likes reading and sharing theology, but what is that if not intellectualism? Am I being instructed to set aside my mind for joy? If so, what kind of joy? Who is this person I might be without my intellect, and why would I want to be her? He seems to be endorsing stupidity. But this cannot be right. As I look around, everyone is smiling and nodding. None of it makes any sense to me.

At the end of church, we are instructed to greet one another, and the room rustles with people shaking hands and closing Bibles. Though I have been challenged several times by my experiences at church while on the road, this time I feel even more disturbed. I'm distressed by the contrast between what is said in church about hell, and the clearly articulated judgments against people in the sermon, and the feeling of support and acceptance afterward. Which of these two is reality? And how to reconcile these entirely different modes of being? Most of all, what was all this business about giving up the intellect in exchange for joy? What did *that* mean?

A new harvester, Amos, shows up for lunch. Like the others, he is a Mennonite, and he has flown to Oklahoma City this morning to join our crew. He has a broad and fleshy face and squints when he talks, and he moves more slowly than the others. When he speaks, he has the folksiest drawl and accent of anyone except, perhaps, Georgie, and he talks and jokes quite a bit more than the others. Bradford brightens at the sight of Amos. I have rarely seen him smile since Michael arrived.

We all go to lunch at Braum's, an outpost of a fast-food chain that exists only in the heartland, and which is popular with the crew for its cheap prices and burgers. I am miserable about the church sermon, which has left me feeling both confused and deeply alienated. No one else seems the least bit bothered about what was said. The crew happily sits together eating and chatting. It is as though we watched a movie and I saw encoded messages they did not. Or perhaps it is the other way around and they saw what I didn't. Who are these people who will go to a church that advises them to suppress their intellects? Only Juston looks troubled, and I am afraid it is because I have let him down by being so visibly confused.

As we eat, Eric looks around the room. Very quietly, he says to me: "That family there is Beachy Amish. You can tell by the dress. They probably just came from church. Same as us." They are bonnet people, easily distinguished in a crowd. But Eric continues, "That family there . . . they've got to be Baptist. Something like that. But not Anabaptist." I look at the family and something registers in my mind. How can I put this quality into words? They are all white, but they do not have the same stillness of Eric and his crew. Or are they just not farmers?

"That family?" I point to a table where the people look bored. "They don't go to church, do they?"

"Probably not," he agrees.

There is one family sitting together that is just slightly more boisterous than everyone else in the restaurant. "Baptist, probably," Eric says. "I don't know. Could be Mormon, although there aren't many around here."

What would my friends from home say, watching us play this game? Is this a bad thing to do? The truth is I have played many versions of this game before. I have tried to teach friends—white friends—to distinguish between Koreans, Japanese, and Chinese. There are subtle physical cues and mannerisms and a cast to facial expressions that make it easy for Asians to tell the difference between one another. In the early days of our courtship, my husband used to quiz me on the accents employed by BBC commentators; for him, there were obvious distinctions between Scots, Irish, English, and others in the Commonwealth. How is this game with Eric any different?

We continue to scan the room together, and a weird thing happens to me. I am starting to see as Eric does. Another family has what I can only describe as a lush quality. The women have blown out their hair and their makeup is bold but tasteful. "What are they?" I ask.

"Probably Catholic," he says. Ah, yes. The Catholics who did not turn away from embellishment, like the Protestants did.

I was taught—I have trained myself—to look out for anyone who stands in contrast to white people. I have always looked for what I thought of as my people: Asians, brown-skinned people, black people, and Jews. I have looked at white people as a blank canvas on which color appears. It had never occurred to me to wonder or to ask how they were different and if their differences corresponded to how they saw their God. It had never occurred to me to think that they were like crops: "Certain conditions yield certain things." White people, I had always thought, were all the same, anyway.

Michael asks me what I thought of church. We have just gotten out of the pickup trucks and are standing outside the trailers. The rest of the crew gathers around and pauses to hear my response before going back inside their trailer houses.

"I didn't understand it," I say. "If the minister wasn't someone you love so much, I would definitely never go again." I say that underlying the pastor's self-effacement and the joking there was, I suspect, a core of certainty and of self-righteousness. I would not be able to meet the standards of his judgment and I do not see why any adult would want to try. I feel terrible saying this.

But Juston smiles at me. "You are used to a seeker sermon."

"What is that?"

"What we heard in Oklahoma City. Those sermons are designed for people like you. They are written to attract you. This, today, was not."

"What do you mean?" Michael asks.

Juston explains. Embedded in Pastor Craig's sermon were the phrases and the arguments for why we need God and how God could make us *feel* better. Everything from the high that came from the worship music to the videos had been intended to give me an emotional jolt. I was supposed to love that feeling and go back to feast on it on another Sunday, and then do more-intensive Bible study on another day of the week. Life.Church and other churches like it are designed to attract those who are seeking a spiritual home.

The sermon today was for a congregation that was not seeking but already considered the church their home. They simply needed a reminder of how and why their spiritual life existed. "You don't know what each of those phrases Pastor Rainwater said today sounds like to us. You take it at face value. But a seeker sermon is designed to appeal exactly to someone like you," Juston tells me.

"What was so off-putting about today?" Eric asks me, genuinely confused.

I say that the way Christianity was presented—with certain clear absolutes—makes me feel uncomfortable. As an adult, I know I will fail absolutes. And further, since I don't fear hell and eternal damnation—since I honestly don't believe these places and conditions are real—there is no way for me to access what might be good about the church or to find the church necessary to ward off hell. Avoiding damnation just isn't sufficient motivation for me.

I say then that I have had more real and tangible experiences with God when I was sitting in a combine and listening to Eric talk about his faith than I have had at church, where I was warned up front that there are things I can and cannot do if I am to be loved by God.

Juston's face has been tense all day, and now he explodes. "Marie is right," he says. "God never says we have to have church!" he protests. "Why do we have to have church?"

"Oh, Juston." Emily sighs, and I feel for her. This is her son, over whose very soul she worries, and I suddenly feel even worse that I could not appreciate church, because I know how important it is to her. Meanwhile, she is the one giving me the free meals.

"I'm sorry," I say. And I am sorry to have been truthful, because with every day on harvest, I've become more aware that what I think is the opposite of what everyone else thinks. "A lot of the time, I couldn't even understand what he was saying."

"But it's true," Juston replies. "Jesus never mentions church."

"He says we should gather and . . . ," Emily begins.

"He didn't say *church*."

"Juston. You are going to give her the idea that church is a bad thing."

And then I feel awful that we are standing here on a Sunday, arguing about God. If I weren't here, I think, then no one would be discussing the problems of a beloved church. But because *I* am here, Juston is now arguing with his mother, and I take this harder than I should because

I, too, am a mother with a son, though mine is much younger than Juston. So I do what I always do in a situation like this. I start apologizing profusely. "I'm so sorry. I know how excited you were to share your church with me."

"It's better to be honest," Eric says. "You shouldn't lie."

"Don't be sorry," Juston tells me bluntly.

"You definitely shouldn't be sorry," Michael agrees.

No one comes down on me as an unbeliever. This is the thing about Christians. They are always so *nice*. Still, I go into the trailer feeling terrible. I do not like to be different.

I know, rationally, that it is to my benefit to feel God's love for me. I have been reading another book that Juston suggested: *Finding God in the Waves*. The author talks about how knowing that God loves you can protect you by helping to develop the gray matter between the two hemispheres of the brain. When we panic, our neural networks short-circuit this gray matter, and jump straight to the amygdala, which sends adrenaline into our bloodstream. The adrenaline is useful if we are, say, hiding from a pig who is about to gore us with his tusks. It is less useful for daily anxiety, which I, like so many modern people, feel frequently. I would like for the anxiety to stop.

If I could focus on love, or on the principle that some higher power loves me, so my gray matter would develop and short-circuit panic, I would be happy. This would be useful. People who believe in God, it has been demonstrated, have more of that gray matter, which is visible when their brains are scanned by an MRI. But I am having a difficult time understanding how I can engage the transactional model of Christianity—repent, turn to Jesus, who died for me, and avoid hell—in order to build up my gray matter. I am completely unpersuaded by this version of Christianity. Is this truly how Christianity managed to survive and spread in the world for so many centuries?

On Sundays, the crew goes their own way for dinner so that Emily can take a break from cooking. On past Sundays, I have eaten with them. "You are one of us," Bethany had told me warmly—until now, when, maybe, she determined my age, or thought I asked too many questions about God, or realized I failed to drive a tractor. No dinner invitation is forthcoming and the crew has melted into the environment somewhere. I see Juston and Michael saunter off together to play basketball. They seem not at all bothered that the rest of the crew is somewhere else.

I retire to the trailer and do the thing that has always comforted me when I can't quite fit in with group activities. I read. And I write a little. I have this feeling that something is going on outside that I cannot see. There are group interactions and conversations taking place of which I am not a part. And why should I be? I could not understand their church. Then again, I tell myself that just because other people are gathered together does not mean that I might be a topic of conversation.

Maybe an hour later, Emily comes by to ask me if I would like to drive with her to Watonga, twenty-three miles away, to see *Wonder Woman*. No one else, she says, is interested. So we go, and then eat Mexican food afterward.

Our conversations are always pleasant. In the back of my mind I wonder how she finds me, a woman on the road who has left her husband and child at home. She never brings it up with me, and I never feel her judging me. Still, I wonder.

"Did you like the movie?" I ask her afterward. On social media, my friends are abuzz about the film. At last, they all proclaim, an action movie with a heroine.

"More than I expected," she says. "I was a little worried. These days it seems like we want men to be like women and women to be like men. But she was still feminine."

The outing has lifted my spirits, but still I keep reading late into the night. Bethany switches off her light and still I am reading. I hear tapping on the roof of the trailer and the fingers do not stop. It is rain and it grows heavier and it is pounding the trailer now. I look at the radar on my phone and I see an intense pink cloud swelling across the land, clear over into Texas, to the west of us. I know that Monday morning we will not cut.

At breakfast, the mood is low. I assume at first that it is the rain that has quieted everyone. There is almost no conversation, but then Eric turns to Juston and says: "Why don't you go out and see what happened to the roads."

"All right."

"May I go too?" I ask.

Juston nods.

He is quiet in the car; something about the crew seems to have changed and I ascribe it at first to the slow pace of harvest after the initial burst of work we had upon arrival.

In the early morning, the light is gentle and dappled. It had felt sharper in Texas. As we drive along, I note to myself that the wheat here isn't gold. It is amber. A side effect is that at sunrise and at sunset the red wheat and the red earth seem to glow from the inside.

The roads are muddy, and we decide we will need to wait until the afternoon to move the equipment. While out in the field, we have a call from Eric. There is another field to check. I hear only one side of the conversation, but it includes the phrase "Go south at the snake church."

The snake church is a nondescript one-story building made of brick. It does not have windows, but a few frosted-glass slats to let in light. An electrical cable runs from the grid to the building to give it power. It has no sign. Juston isn't sure, but he thinks it is a snake handlers' church.

I have questions, but his silence is so deep, as if it comes from a storm inside his body, and it is this storm pulling down his words and all sounds, so that I know it is futile for me to try to say anything at all. We drive back to the trailers. That afternoon, we do not move the equipment, and we will wait, now, some days to work again, and I will spend my hours reading.

Bethany is mostly silent when I see her in the trailer, and our meals, when we gather, are quiet too. I can feel that *something* is not quite right, but when I ask Juston, he tells me only that the crew is in low spirits due to a lack of work. I try not to let my hyperactive imagination concoct scenarios in which conversations take place about my inability to understand God or church, but I can feel something like a hum in the air, a change in frequency, and I know that the easy camaraderie I experienced in Texas has been replaced by something I cannot yet define. Whatever it is, it is tense.

One evening, Eric comes to talk to me in my trailer. He is distressed. He says he was sitting around with friends who had been making fun of gay people. "Gay bashing, I think it's called?" Eric asks.

"Yes," I say.

The bashing bothered him. He doesn't think that Jesus would have been in favor of any kind of bashing, and he had said so. "I told them gay people had the right to be gay and that I believe God loves them."

In a past conversations, Eric had told me: "I've been reading the Bible. And I've decided there's nothing in there that says there shouldn't be gay marriage. I think that the Bible was against pederasty."

"The Romans," I say.

"Exactly. Jesus never said anything about being against gays. I think those parts people use to attack gays—I think that was about child abuse."

Eric often talks—almost frets—about something he calls "legalism." Most scholars and experts on Christianity define legalism as following the rules of God the way someone might follow a checklist. Legalism means you think you just need to do x and y, and then you get into heaven. In general, legalism is something to avoid because it doesn't connect people to God in a way that is authentic.

Eric's description is a little different. He says that legalism involves "placing human rules above God." Eric likes to quote Jesus, who said in Matthew 5:17: "Don't misunderstand why I have come. I did not come to abolish the law of Moses or the writings of the prophets. No, I came to accomplish their purpose." In other words, whatever Jesus has to teach supersedes any laws or regulations that came before. In fact, he simplifies all the old teachings into two rules. When asked, in Matthew, what the greatest commandment is, Jesus replies: "Love the Lord your God with all your heart, and with all your soul and with all your mind. . . . And the second is like it: 'Love your neighbor as your-self.' All the Law and the Prophets hang on these two commandments."

When people stress the lengths of skirts, and acceptable hairstyles, and the days of the week to avoid meat, they are elevating man-made rules over the simple thing that God wanted, which was to act with love toward everyone.

Appearances can be deceiving, though. A person might look as if they care because of all the acts of charity they make sure others know about, but they might actually be a rotten human being. Gay bashing, Eric says to me, is not what Christ would have wanted. Arguing over the rightness or wrongness of being gay is a form of legalism, and it's not where one's attention should go.

I've started to notice that when Eric talks about his faith, he always talks about Jesus. Every time we consider a difficult question—homosexuality, GMOs, food production—he doesn't tell me what his pastor believes. He always tells me what he understands Jesus to have said. Juston does this, too, to a lesser degree. And when I think about it, this is the story of the Gospels; Jesus preached and taught people and they tried to follow him. This is what Eric is trying to do, and the purity of that action moves me. Remove the artifice of pastors trying to sound funny and approachable and maybe I can see something valuable in being a "Jesus guy," as Juston occasionally tells me he is.

"How did you go from being against homosexuality to being in favor of gay rights?"

"I don't know." Eric shakes his head almost furiously. "Since I was a kid, I just didn't like hearing people make fun of gay people. It bothered me."

His comment makes me wonder how much any of us are capable of change. I could use myself as an example. I was unaware, until college, of the notion of gay rights as a "right." But had I changed? Or had I simply crystalized into a clearer version of myself than I had been before, the person who wanted equality for my friends who were gay. Had Eric actually changed? Or had he simply, when pressed, admitted to himself that he could not tolerate the tormenting of people different from his peers?

The best-known researcher of decision making in the secular world is probably Daniel Kahneman, a Nobel Prize–winning economist and psychologist and the author of *Thinking, Fast and Slow*. According to Kahneman, "Social scientists in the 1970s broadly accepted two ideas about human nature. First, people are generally rational, and their thinking is normally sound. Second, emotions such as fear, affection, and hatred explain most of the occasions on which people depart from rationality." After setting forward this basic premise, Kahneman goes on to undo it, because, he says, it is not true.

People have two systems for making up their minds. The first, which he calls "System 1," makes decisions out of instinct, and works swiftly. When we say we are going with our gut, we are going with

System 1. The second, which he calls "System 2," uses reason and logic and works in a much more lumbering and deliberate way. When you impulsively choose something on a menu, you are employing System 1. When you spend time working out the directions on a map, correlating the map to your location, and then deciding which way to turn to get to the trailer park because you have lost the caravan of big rigs and pickup trucks, that is System 2.

People mainly rely on the output of System 1 in most daily activities. This is in part because we don't have time to deliberate over absolutely everything, every single day. Often, System 1 is just fine for getting ourselves breakfast and dressed for work. But people rely on System 1 because it is easier and speaks "from the gut," drawing on emotions, which just feel good. Kahneman describes numerous psychological tests that System 1 fails. Our instincts don't always just miraculously know what is better. Among other things, System 1 is susceptible to believing that an illusion like the Wonderful Wizard of Oz is correct. System 2 can override System 1, but it requires tremendous effort and time for System 2 to kick in and reveal that, for example, the wizard is just a "man behind a curtain." Quite honestly, when I think of Pastor Rainwater telling me to abandon intellectualism and find joy, it sounds as if he is saying to avoid System 2 and to rely just on System 1.

Many scientists have written at length about what causes the silencing of System 2. Fear, for example, empowers System 1 and prevents System 2 from coming to the rescue. You can think of any number of examples of people suffering from the Stockholm syndrome as being trapped by System 1, obeying their instincts, and who are unable to let System 2 come to the rescue to help them escape.

Other emotions also strengthen System 1's hold over a person. If you grow up influenced by a charismatic figure in your community, then your System 1 might be strongly swayed by that person's worldview, particularly if that charismatic figure inspires fear. You might be afraid to let System 2 convince you that dinosaurs appeared before humans. As Jack Gorman and Sara Gorman say in *Denying to the Grave*: "The more fear a charismatic leader is able to conjure in a potential acolyte, the more powerful is the activation of select brain circuits that will make it difficult for countervailing evidence to have an impact. Charismatic leaders induce brain changes that first heighten the fear centers of the brain, like the amygdala, and then suppress the decision-making areas in the PFC. . . . Dry, pedantic harangues about data will be powerless in the face of these potent effects."

Gorman and Gorman say that the only way to counterbalance the fear that rises up each time you remember whatever it is that has scared you is to feel that you have another safe space to go to, where your contrary opinions are welcome. "Rather, it is critical to make people feel that by using their minds to evaluate scientific claims they are joining a welcoming club of people who trust the scientific method and attempt to get at the truth about what is healthy."

There is also another way in which fear works to keep System 2 at bay. Kahneman and Gorman and Gorman write of the phenomenon known as "confirmation bias." That is, we are biased to accept information that supports what System 1 already believes. We might even throw out information that proves that System 1 is wrong, because we want so much for our "gut" to be right. We reject information—or System 1 rejects accurate information, which means that System 2 never gets to process it—that doesn't adhere to our sense of bias from the start.

This is made even more difficult by the fact that studies show we get a rush of dopamine to the brain when we find information that supports System 1—the same rush we get when we have sex or eat candy. It feels good to find information that we think confirms what we believe; that is, which strengthens our certainty.

But let's say that accurate information makes it through the fear, and through System 1 and into System 2. Then you face the possibility of changing your mind. And if you change your mind about something deeply personal, then you may well go against a group. Gorman and Gorman write that "defying your group is a frightening proposition that must hold the promise of some reward in order to be tenable. In fact, other studies have shown that a decrease in biased thinking is associated with a decrease in amygdala activity. Somehow, we need to reduce the fear that is understandably associated with changing one's mind."

The latest research tells us that we don't often change our minds. Using the issue of gun control as an example, Gorman and Gorman say: "Most important for our understanding of confirmation bias is that beliefs laid down during times of heightened emotion, especially those involving terror and dread, are highly durable and resistant to disconfirmation."

We are all restless that night, and Eric, Juston, and I go for a drive. The land rolls up and down in gentle slopes. It is soothing to drive these roads. It is as if we are being rocked.

We pass the snake church, and Eric says: "Did you notice that there weren't any windows? They hold up a snake, and if the snake bites you, then you don't have the Holy Spirit in you. But if it doesn't bite you, then the Holy Spirit is in you."

"What kind of a church is that? Baptist?"

"No. It's more of what you call a charismatic church."

"As in it depends on a charismatic pastor?"

"No. Like, they speak in tongues. And they talk about the Holy Spirit." From the way Eric says this, I can tell he doesn't think too much of it.

"I wonder how people ever came to believe in that," I say. "I guess it starts early."

"Raised that way," Eric agrees. He chooses his next words carefully. "I don't believe it's the devil that is talking when they speak in tongues. But . . ." He pauses. "I mean, I know they are Christians. But I don't think it's necessarily right."

Then the conversation turns to other subjects—moving the equipment—and I let it drop.

At the top of the next little swell is a cemetery. "Liberty Cemetery," the iron letters on the gate placed over the entrance declare. This is a separate cemetery from the one in town by the lot where the rigs are parked. The sunset seeps through the sheer petals of the bright bouquets sitting on the tombstones so the colors seem almost florid. The dead will have a view of that sunset from this hill. On the horizon are towers with red winking lights. These lights belong to the oil drills and fracking rigs. At night, the towers blink lazily on and off, and if I relax and let myself try to sync with the blinking, it's as if I can feel the earth turning just a fraction of a degree with each blink. I wonder if the dead relax too.

SEVEN

AT LAST THE LAND HAS DRIED and we have taken the equipment out to a field.

Bethany is driving the pickup. I know she has been asked to drive because she is better at reading the road and avoiding the soft spots, and after the incident with the fracking water we are doubly cautious about any of our equipment succumbing to soft soil. Eric tells Bethany to take me down the road to take a look at a plaque marked "Whirlwind." This is the only instruction we are given. But we find the plaque easily. It is raised on a dais and overlooks a meadow. The plaque explains that in 1897 a former prisoner of war and Cheyenne chief named Whirlwind lived here and set up an Episcopal mission to educate young Indian children.

Bethany and I are starting back to the field we plan to cut when I see a sign: "Whirlwind Cemetery."

Nearby, on a promontory overlooking a meadow, there is a cemetery. Far off in the distance is a large river, lined by the heavy green of trees. Waves of white egrets rise out of the riverbed and fly over our heads, their wings lapping at the air and propelling their long bodies through the sky. Someone has been here recently to mow the grass. There are a few bouquets of flowers drying on the tombstones. Here are some of the names:

> Denison Whirlwind: June 4, 1901
> Mrs. Standing Twenty: June 24, 1901
> Infant Turkey Legs: Sept. 12, 1901
> Hookla Turkey Legs: Sept. 20, 1905
> Big Belly Woman: Sept. 13, 1905
> Chancey Sun Maker: Sept. 14, 1905

This is the burial site for Indian children and adults who had been at the mission and who died here. Until now, the only Indians we have seen were in photographs at a museum, and we have talked about them in a theoretical way; they were a people who once lived and now do not and we can contain them behind glass. But now we have come across ground where they once stood and where they now lie. Their actual bodies are beneath our feet. The fact of this upsets me in ways that are hard to define. I had thought I was going on this journey with Eric to understand more about his God and what he calls "the divide" and to learn more about farming. I hadn't expected to encounter the remains of Indians.

We return to the crew.

"Doesn't that look like a spot you would live if you were an Indian?" Eric asks me.

I reflexively say that it does, though I'm not precisely sure what he means. The church would have been located in a lush and shady spot alongside a slender creek that noses through tall grass and low bushes. But wouldn't any place by a river be comforting?

The only time I have ever seen anyone read the land like this was with my father when we went camping. We owned a motor home, and after harvest we would often drive it back to California from Nebraska, taking our time and visiting as many national parks along the way as we could. But my dad didn't like campgrounds. He especially avoided the expensive KOA campgrounds. We skipped showers and went to the bathroom in the woods, and we used the motor home for cooking and sleeping. Because our RV had a refrigerator that needed to be level, my father always looked for a flat space for us to park, favoring deserted roads or pullouts off the highway. Like Eric, he read the land for suitable spots to settle down.

In the *Little House* books, when Pa Ingalls finally finds the land he will claim in South Dakota, he says: "It is just right in every way. It lies south of where the lake joins Big Slough, and the slough curves around to the west of it. There's a rise in the prairie to the south of the slough, that will make a nice place to build. A little hill just west of it crowds the slough back on that side. . . . And it's near the townsite, so the girls can go to school." And this is what it sounds like to me now, when Eric drives me through the countryside and points to places one might want to live, if one lived a different life.

Why do I feel uneasy? I realize that I feel disturbed because Eric sounds like a settler. I know this land was settled by Europeans, so why should it bother me that Eric—my father, anyone—should retain vestiges of a habit that helped to settle the country's interior? The settlement is part of the past, and we are the innocent inheritors of what went before. I am too. I am not to blame for the Indian cemetery on the hill.

Over the radio, I can hear that Amos has a flat tire. The boys joke that Amos will never have a job again due to the flat tire.

"When God is angry," Juston says, "and we need a sacrifice, it'll be you, Amos."

"Ohhh," Amos groans.

"Yeah, Amos can show us an act of faith!" Samuel laughs. "He can walk the auger and if he doesn't fall, then he can stay."

"No!" Michael says. "Amos needs to walk the auger . . . and come back. Then he can stay!"

The boys whoop and laugh.

"And then maybe the rain will stop," Juston says quietly, for it has, indeed, started to rain again.

Early the next morning we wake for breakfast but neither Eric nor Bradford is in the trailer. I understand immediately that this means something important has happened related to work; Eric trusts Bradford implicitly when it comes to work. "He can read the land same as me," Eric says. "He will make the same decision about how to cut a field."

Emily tells us that a new combine has arrived, sent to us by Case, the manufacturer. It is in the lot with the remaining equipment. This new combine is an experimental model that's meant to resemble the other three machines, but it's just the shell that looks the same. The inside has all new equipment, which includes a series of cameras that are supposed to capture images of how and what the wheat is doing by comparing photos of the wheat in the hopper to hundreds of other pictures in a data bank. Based on this information, the combine is supposed to make adjustments to the rotor automatically, so the chaff will be better discarded. Mash too hard and the grain will be ground to a pulp. Mash too lightly and the chaff will not be cast off, and the elevator will dock for MOG (material other than grain).

When I arrive, the combine is sitting on a flatbed. The boys are rolling tires off a forklift and over to the combine, to which they will be attached. It starts to drizzle while the truck driver and Eric are talking to each other.

Eric hurries over to me. "I want you to listen to this guy," he says with great intensity. "Listen to how he sounds like Georgie."

To me, the portly truck driver, with his hat and glasses, looks just like any dude, a fairly well-fed truck driver. But ever since the day in the restaurant when I started to distinguish among the different white families sitting around the tables, I have come to realize how little I know about white people, and how in my mind I am quick to lump them all together.

"Come," Eric says to me, and I follow him. First, Eric makes a show of introducing me—a woman, and a writer at that—to the truck driver. We both say hello, and then Eric asks the driver directly: "Where are you from?"

"You are trying to place my accent," the trucker replies amiably, if a little sadly.

"Well, I guess I am."

And as the driver continues to speak, I hear it—the unmistakable lilt, the way his voice lingers over vowels. He does sound just like Georgie.

"I'm originally from Ohio." He pronounces it "O-*hi*-yuh."

"Where?" Eric presses him.

"Lodi."

"Mennonite?"

"Amish."

"I knew it!" Eric whoops and congratulates himself. "What kind?"

"Schwarzentruber."

Instantly, Eric's demeanor changes. This is no longer purely a game of identification. "Oh my."

"Yes. I left years ago," the trucker says somberly.

"I see."

I look at the men's faces. Eric has in an instant become so remorseful that he is now looking around as though he's hoping to escape the conversation entirely, and the trucker, having been found out, looks sorrowful. What has passed between them is a mystery to me.

The crew calls out to Eric. They are clinging to the tires or to the combine in various acrobatic poses, and they need something—a bolt, a power tool, I don't know what—to make the apparatus come together. Eric strides off toward Lily.

Then the trucker tells me an abbreviated version of his story. He is the youngest of seventeen—the caboose, as he puts it. He was raised in the toughest kind of Amish community that exists, with "tin roofs and outhouses and no electricity and no doctors." He left at eighteen to "sow his wild oats," and came back because he was not prepared to deal with the world outside. His girlfriend, also a member of the community, had remained. But "things got so bad, she wanted to go. And I says to her, if we leave, we're never coming back."

So they left. He found work and they married and now have five children together. He has tried a few Mennonite churches, but they are too close to the Amish church and he doesn't want to ever return to his former home. "I'm at peace with God, though." He smiles at me. Then he taps his chest. "It's the heart that counts." And he walks away.

Later, I look up Lodi, Ohio, and learn about a notoriously tyrannical Amish bishop named Mullet. According to news reports, Mullet's followers would go into a home, forcibly drag out a man, and shear off his beard as a method of demonstrating Mullet's total control over his community—this despite the fact that the Amish do not cut their beards after marriage. Women who tried to leave the community were also caught, and their hair was also forcibly cut. While such a thing can't be classified as a rape in the legal system, for the Amish such haircutting was and is an extreme physical violation that traumatizes its victims.

This man, the truck driver, was a survivor. Eric had heard the accent and placed the man as either Old Order Mennonite or Amish, passing for "English," by which the Anabaptists mean "secular."

"He tell you his story?" Eric asks me later.

"Yes." I repeat the story.

"'Bout what I figured once he said he was from Lodi. Probably goes to a Baptist church now," Eric remarks. I don't know why he thinks this, and since there is no end to my questions, for once I do not press for more information.

We go to the cooperative grain elevator in town. Because of the rain, harvest is slow and men congregate at the elevators as they might at a café or bar in the city. There I am introduced to a farmer named Jimmy, and another man named Rodney, who is the elevator manager. Jimmy is in his sixties, bald, and smiles all the time. Rodney looks to be in his early fifties, handsome and square-jawed. When he's not working the elevator, he flies his cropduster. I saw him earlier in the day in his yellow airplane, zooming over the fields for fun. "That's Rodney," Samuel had said to me.

I show Jimmy my photo of the snake church. "Can you tell me what this is?" I ask.

"Oh! That there . . ." His eyes sparkle. Does he know that his eyes sparkle, and that when he pauses for dramatic effect, his eyes sparkle more? "That there's the snake church."

"What's a snake church?"

Behind Jimmy, Eric gets his half smile, the one that says he is pleased for having recognized something correctly.

"Now, what they do," Jimmy begins, leaning toward me as though I am about to be drawn into a secret, "is they hold up a snake. If it don't bite you, then you have the Holy Spirit. But if it do . . ."

"They don't go to the doctor," Rodney says.

"Eyes and teeth is all."

"Ears?" Eric asks.

"Naw."

"You ain't go to the ear doctor neither," Rodney chides Jimmy.

"Well." *Wahllll.* "That's different."

"I understand," Eric says. "I never do either."

"Are they farmers?" I ask.

"Sure. All of them are. Buried up on that hill."

"I saw that cemetery. That's just for them?"

Jimmy nods. "Been in the news. Quite a few kids died. Won't take the kids to the doctor, and the trouble is . . ." Jimmy's face contorts with pain and sympathy. "They suffer."

The men shake their heads over the suffering of the children and they are quiet. Later, I read about the suffering of the children who later died, untreated, of pneumonia and appendicitis. I read of the terrible pain the children endured as they waited to die, as their parents, because of their so-called faith, would not take them to the doctor.

"What's his name?" Jimmy says abruptly. "Deon?"

"Oh, he died."

"Leg."

There is a pregnant pause, and the sadness Jimmy felt over the loss of the children drains from his mind. His eyes begin to sparkle with mischief again. "He had a tick bite and it got infected."

"Gangrene set in," Rodney says.

"Did they try to cut his leg off?" Jimmy asks.

"I don't know about that."

"I think they tried to cut his leg off. I think that's why he died."

"You exaggerating again. It was the gangrene killed him."

"He had gangrene and that's why they tried to cut off his leg."

"No, I think he had a heart attack."

"Because of the leg."

"Either way, he's dead."

"You know his wife is Gay. Bartender." Jimmy leans forward conspiratorially.

"No, that's just her name. Or was it her mother?"

"Maybe it was his mother."

"Well. She wasn't a bartender. She was . . . a stripper."

The men holler. "That explains why she's so poor!"

The hollering thunders in the elevator. They keep laughing, delighted to have entertained themselves like this on a wet day.

The rest of Eric's crew files in to say hello. They have recently been to Oklahoma City; this is one of our entertainment options, now that we cannot hunt. Rodney asks the boys: "What'd you do in the city?"

The boys mention eating a steak at Cattlemen's.

"There's a great zoo. And the Omniplex," Rodney says.

"Now it's called . . . the Science Museum," Jimmy declares.

"It used to be called the Omniplex, but now they got to use a fancy name. The Science Museum."

"Still. It's great for kids. Exhibits they can play with. And they got magic shows for children."

"That's not magic. That's science," Rodney corrects him.

As happy as Eric has been in Oklahoma, this year has not been the bountiful harvest he had hoped to show me. Less than half the wheat planted last year has been planted this year, 1,500 acres versus 2,000. As in Texas, some wheat here in Oklahoma has been put into pasture for cattle. The dryland versions of cotton have been planted where the wheat was, which makes less work for us. Eric says that harvesters are for the first time undercutting other harvesters in order to compete for the limited number of contracts. We need more work. We

were able to break even in Texas, but we need conditions to improve
in Oklahoma.

One morning, I drive my car out to an oil rig where all the equipment has been parked. There are large metal towers here and some
kind of machinery. Samuel and Michael immediately climb the ladders
to the top of the towers. A moment later, Luther follows. They have no
fear of heights.

"Climbers," I say to Juston. "Your dad has always had climbers on
his crew."

He agrees with me. "Some guys are like that. My dad's a climber. You
kinda have to be if you farm. Have to get up on the bins. My brother,
Winston, is a climber, but I'm not."

A few minutes later, the boys come back down the ladder and jump
into their rigs.

The experimental combine is usually driven by the engineer whom
Case sends to test out the machine. Eric often rides with him and they
discuss how and why the machine is working or the computer is mal-
functioning. Juston drives the truck. Amos, Bradford, and Michael drive
the other combines.

Juston has asked me to ride with Bradford. "You could learn so much,"
he says. And so I ask.

"I was wondering if I could ride with you," I say.

Bradford's dislike of this question is unabashed. I feel the rejection
physically. "Maybe later," he says.

"Okay!" I try to say this brightly.

"Ride with me," Michael says immediately. Instantly, I am relieved.
I ride with Michael until the afternoon, when the engineer goes back
to his motel room to type up his notes from the day's work and Eric
takes over as the driver of the new combine. Then I will ride with Eric.

In cutting a wheat field, much thought is given to the direction
and pattern the combines should make. If they simply go around in
a square, following one after the other, this can cause problems for
the grain cart driver, who is always trying to keep up with the combines, which should keep cutting without having to stop to unload. If
the combines are separated and the grain cart needs to get from one
end of the field to the other in a hurry, it is not helpful if the only way
there is around the perimeter. This is why a combine driver will "break
through" the field: that is, cut through the center of the field to cre-

ate a "new road." Michael is always breaking through. He gets on the radio and says: "I'm going to break through." Occasionally Bradford, too, will break through. But usually Michael gets there first, as he did this morning.

I'm not sure exactly how the conversation turns to evolution, but it does, and Michael tells me he does not believe in it at all. I ask him about carbon 14 dating. I have heard that Michael wants to go into law enforcement and perhaps be a police detective, and this might, I say, require using carbon 14 dating to recover forensic evidence.

"But it's flawed and makes mistakes," he says to me.

"No, it doesn't."

"Sure it does. We all have bias, Marie. Believing that carbon 14 is always right is a form of bias." He tells me that my belief in the fossil record is also a form of bias. "The fossil record is incomplete, and nothing accounts for the leap from hominids to man."

"You think . . ."

". . . that man was around at the time of the dinosaur. Yes. Some species have gone extinct, but God created man to walk alongside the dinosaur."

"Do you believe in Adam and Eve?"

"Yes."

"The earth was created in six days?"

"Yes." He believes in the whole thing. God made Adam from clay and pulled out a rib and made Eve.

Is it possible to be friends with someone who believes the exact opposite of everything I do?

"Are you pro-life?" I ask.

"I am. But I'll tell you something. I get really frustrated with a lot of people who claim to be pro-life, but don't do enough to be fully pro-life. That's something I have to think about. If they are really pro-life, they would help children, not just abandon them. I read this statistic that said that if every church adopted one child, the entire foster care system would collapse."

"Would it?"

"Sure. The numbers add up. So how useful is it really to say I'm pro-life? If I'm pro-life, I have to do more than just say so."

The conversation depresses me, but I tell myself—as I have so often—to remain open. Michael is the one person, aside from Juston and Eric, who asks me questions and who has welcomed me onto the harvesting team. If he is going to remain open to me, I want to remain open to him. If I don't, I will lose the fragile thread that allows me to stay here. And shouldn't I be capable of being in an environment that is different from my own, while still being me? Isn't that one of the great lessons I have learned from international travel and from speaking a foreign language? A person has a self in any environment. Plus, Juston said that everyone else is supposed to learn from me, just as I am to learn from them.

But when I start to share stories of women who might need access to a safe abortion, I find myself stopping short. I think of young women I've known in college, on the cusp of starting their professional lives, who found themselves unexpectedly pregnant. Women whose birth control failed, but who weren't with a "life partner." Women who became pregnant from rape, date rape, any form of sexual coercion. In this highly controlled culture in which I am currently living, none of these examples is relevant.

Just that day, a male friend called from Florida and jokingly suggested I buy a pack of condoms and spread them around the trailers. I chided him. The boys I am with are not, I told him, equipped to handle that kind of joke. I've lived long enough to know that not all highly conservative Christian communities live up to their ideals. But I'm not in one of those hypocritical communities. I'm with people trying hard to actually follow the rules of their patriarchal leaders.

Bradford interrupts our conversation via the radio. "Michael," he says, his voice flat and absent of any emotion. "Can you come back? Bethany can't keep up with you with the grain cart."

During our conversation, Michael has continued to break through the field, then continued to cut wheat farther and farther away from the other combines. The yellow lights on his cab are flashing, signaling that we are three-quarters full.

Michael swings the combine around in a big arc and heads back to the other harvesters. "Are we gonna make it?" He smiles to himself. We are trying to get to the end of a row, which will put us back squarely into formation with the other combines.

"How much more can it take?"

"Li'l bit."

"What happens if it fills up?" I ask. Actually, I know the answer to this question. The grain will splash out onto the cab, and then onto the ground, and will be wasted.

"It won't," he reassures me. Nonetheless, we drive slowly, so the wheat, now piled so high I can't see the top of the stack through the rear window, won't fall. Slowly, slowly, Michael drives the length of the field, and far away I see Bethany driving out with the grain cart to relieve us.

There is wheat already in her cart when she pulls up alongside us, and our load, which is substantial, fills her cart completely.

"Told you we would make it." Michael smiles cheerfully.

Bethany splits apart from us and drives out to where Samuel is waiting in a wheat truck. Michael continues to smile.

That evening, I follow behind the other combines in the pickup. I get stuck in the dirt trying to leave a field, and I ask over the CB if there is perhaps a parking brake preventing me from moving. How could I be stuck in the dirt? Michael suggests that I look to the left for the parking brake, and there it is. It is not on. All the same, I engage the brake and then take it off and try to move the truck. It will not move. I radio for help again.

Out the window, I can see Michael spring back into the combine to answer my call. "Try putting the truck in four-wheel drive," he suggests. So I try that. I press on the gas hard and the truck lurches forward. I am relieved. I turn around and wait for the caravan of machinery to leave the field so I can follow to the next location. Over the radio, I hear Bethany's calm but plaintive voice. She, too, is having problems in the dirt and cannot scale the hill that separates the exit from the rest of the field. The tractor is slipping.

Michael advises her. If she turns to the south, he thinks the path might be less steep and the grain cart can pull the load. Meanwhile, Bradford and Michael continue to switch their combines into transport mode.

Out of my rearview mirror, I can see Bethany slowly scaling the hill. She has made it. Now Bradford is patiently navigating his combine through the open space in the fence, his header trailing behind him. Then it is Michael's turn to pass through the opening, and I follow. We meander along the dirt road.

I watch the sun slip away to the west, the smear of red fading along the cottonwood treetops. A bobcat springs across the road in front of me and I am momentarily startled. Then I glance to the east. A large balloon of orange moon rises as if filled with helium. The crew speaks over the CB about directions to the next field we will cut, but I pick up the radio and suggest they look at the full blood harvest moon. No one answers. So I drive on with the glow of orange to the right, and the moon in echo to the left and I feel happy, if alone; content that nature has aligned these heavenly bodies just so.

Over the CB, Michael reminds me that now that I am on a road, I need to change my four-wheel drive back to two-wheel drive. Then Bradford radios me. "Marie. Park on the oil rig." I look around. It is dark now. Red lights from numerous oil rigs seem to wink at me in choral rounds. There are perhaps seven oil rigs in my immediate vicinity. Where am I supposed to park?

I ask over the radio where I should go, and Bradford repeats his request. "Park on the oil rig." I don't move.

It is Michael who helps me once again.

"Wait," he says, "until I have the header back on the combine and then you can follow me." Only when Michael comes around with his combine assembled and its bright lights illuminate the landscape do I realize that I am back where I was this morning. When Bradford referred to "the oil rig," he meant the same one that I saw in the morning. He meant, *We are on the field where we started this morning and where your car is still located. Park the truck on the oil rig where your car is*, but I needed Michael to translate.

I feel embarrassed that I didn't understand.

I am so focused on my own discomfort that it doesn't occur to me to wonder how it must make Bradford feel that he was not understood and Michael was.

In the trailer that evening, I ask Bethany if she believes in Adam and Eve.

"Everyone believes in Adam and Eve!"

"They do?"

"Well, I don't know." She furrows her brow. "Maybe I believe in Adam and Eve only because everyone around me believes in them. I wonder if I really believe in them, after all."

What was I expecting her to say? Did I think she would be like Michael, or more like Juston? Am I supposed to give her a crash course

in hominids? I tell myself that it isn't ethical for me to disturb her belief system. I act as if I'm on *Star Trek*, enacting the Prime Directive. I
think of her parents, who raised her to believe that the world is a certain way, and that they trust she is on wheat harvest with adults who
will protect her, and that I am one of these adults.

I suggest that Bethany talk to Juston about her doubts. He's part of
her community, and we let the conversation fall. In a way, it's a calcu-
lated decision I make. I like Bethany. I wish that she liked me. If I don't
present myself as a shrill, city-dwelling and evolution-believing person,
perhaps she will like me. This is the bargain I've decided to make.

In the morning, I tell Juston what has happened.

He's incensed. "So it's better that she talks to *me*?"

"I thought I was doing the right thing." I don't want to be accused of
undermining a family's closely held beliefs.

But Juston does not see things this way at all. "If she talked to you
about doubt," he says earnestly, "then she was opening a door. And
she was opening that door with *you*. These are my people, Marie, and
I know how they think. I know what their actions mean, and you don't
necessarily know."

"I was thinking about her parents . . ."

"She's practically an adult. She and Samuel might get *married*. She
wanted to talk to *you*."

But it seems like an enormous thing to take on someone's doubt
and to be an ambassador for the other side. I don't feel that this is something I am supposed to do. I am here to learn. I am here for me. I am
here to understand them. I say this.

"But they are supposed to learn from you too. She was trying to talk
to you," he insists.

Have I been a coward?

Juston presses on. "I don't think you understand that everyone col-
ludes to hold up this structure, which is false, and the harder they work
to insist that the structure is true, the more doubt they secretly have.
I am telling you. I know my kind. I know that this is how it works."

Juston tells me that without outside support Bethany is less likely
to develop her ideas fully and to know that it is okay to have doubt.
She will keep her doubt quiet. It will stay vague and unexplored in her
mind, and she will behave as others do, while still wondering what else
might be out there in the world.

"There are other ways," I say. Aren't there? I feel mildly panicked. For one thing, when Juston talks about "the structure," it's as if he assumes I know what he is talking about, and I am not altogether sure that I do. I know he questions "the structure." Exactly how much "structure" does he see?

"You don't understand." He sighs.

"But the whole world is out there," I insist. "I mean, it's right *there*." He shakes his head.

"Juston. Don't you know any other people who aren't . . . evangelical?" He smiles slowly. "I know *you*."

Usually, when I face a crisis like this, people advise me: just be yourself. But *how* should I just be myself in this wholly foreign environment?

The atheist and scientist Richard Dawkins is unstinting about what it means to believe in evolution: "Much as we might wish to believe otherwise, universal love and the welfare of the species as a whole are concepts that simply do not make evolutionary sense." He also says: "Intelligent life on a planet comes of age when it first works out the reason for its own existence. If superior creatures from space ever visit earth, the first question they will ask, in order to assess the level of our civilization, is: 'Have they discovered evolution yet?'" Everything in the tone here is intended to convey the superiority of the intellect, and the fraternity of intelligence into which a mind enters if allied with the evolutionary way of thinking. Dawkins sounds a bit like Uncle Paul: *Do not,* he implies, *dare to be stupid.*

Even though I find Dawkins arrogant, I know there is something in his message that has infected me and makes me feel cautious about speaking positively of God or of religion when I am in my highly educated, secular circle. The voice of Dawkins, and the desire to be considered "intelligent," make it difficult to talk about God.

So let's consider another approach. Here are the opening lines to Anne Lamott's book *Help, Thanks, Wow:*

I do not know much about God and prayer, but I have come to believe, over the past twenty-five years, that there's something to be said about keeping prayer simple.

Help. Thanks. Wow.

You may in fact be wondering what I even mean when I use the word "prayer." It's certainly not what TV Christians mean. It's not for display purposes, like plastic sushi or neon. Prayer is private, even when we pray with others. It is communication from the heart to that which surpasses understanding. Let's say it is communication from one's heart to God. Or if that is too triggering or ludicrous a concept to you, to the Good . . .

Lamott is a liberal, a writer from the bluest part of the country, which is to say, Marin County, California, and though I do not know her, I cannot help but think she is aware of the voice of Richard Dawkins when she writes. She uses humor, self-deprecation, and a charming modesty to write around people like Dawkins. She knows that God might be "triggering," or even "ludicrous," and yet, she says, she believes in prayer. It is in this delightful, funny, and entertaining voice that Lamott gets away with writing about God for people in the secular sphere.

So these are the voices around which I have unwittingly shaped my thinking: derisive and superior, or self-effacing and funny. If I am self-effacing, I can be spiritual but not stupid. If I'm super-rational, I'm smart, and that matters more than God, anyway.

Neither of these voices or lines of reasoning led Juston to the place he is now. Neither articulated for him what he needed to hear to feel comfortable. Instead, he turned to Rob Bell, the once-popular megachurch pastor turned friend of Oprah, whose mainstream book tackled the subject of damnation. In *Love Wins*, Bell analyzes the twelve times that the New Testament uses the word "hell." If Christianity was built around the teachings of Christ, then it makes sense to focus on how Jesus utilized hell, and if he did indeed define the following transaction: man is fallen, man can reconnect to God through Jesus, and to remain disconnected is to risk going to hell, a place filled with torture and demons and fire. John 3:16: "For God so loved the world that he gave his one and only Son, that whoever believes in him should not perish but have eternal life."

Bell points out that the original Greek, in which the Gospels were written, uses the word *"gehenna"* for hell, which, Bell says, was the location of the city dump when Jesus was alive. In *gehenna*, a fire burned continuously to destroy waste thrown on its grounds. And so, when Jesus says, in Matthew 5: "Anyone who says, 'You fool!' will be in danger of the fire of hell," and "It is better for you to lose one part of your body than for your whole body to be thrown into hell," Bell argues that Jesus is referring specifically to the local dump.

What about the part in a church service when people are told they will burn in hell forever unless they are saved? Bell deconstructs this too: "'Forever' is not really a category the biblical writers used. The closest the Hebrew writers came to a word for 'forever' is the word *olam*. *Olam* can be translated as 'to the vanishing point,' 'in the far distance,' 'a long time,' 'long-lasting,' or 'that which is at or beyond the horizon.'"

Bell concludes that hell is not depicted as the *place* to which all souls will go if they are not saved. Rather for Bell, hell is a state of evil as much as it is one of lovelessness. To not feel the love of the universe—to not feel like a loved being in the world, to not feel the gray matter between the two hemispheres of your brain—is to be in hell. If you do not believe that you as a human are loved—if you cannot feel love from somewhere—then *that* is a hellish existence. When we think of what it means to transcend the ordinary, we are thinking of love and of those who love us. When we are afraid of love—when we are afraid of intimacy—we run the risk of voiding ourselves. To risk love, and to get nothing back, is painful. Faith is the ability to love without such self-erasure.

I think this is one reason why the message of Christ must have seemed so profound—that there *is* some greater love that can change us all to be better and make all people better, and if we tap into this love, everything around us will be transformed.

In Bell's book, it is love, and thus God, that will win the eternal human struggle.

Bell's book has set Juston's mind at ease over hell, Adam and Eve, church, and biblical inerrancy. It is what began to change Juston's worldview; he began not with a desire to be right or a desire to feel smarter than others, or to apologetically declare, "I love God."

He wanted to know what was true, for the truth itself.

"I have a question about your world," Juston says. We are cutting again. I have spent the afternoon with him in his truck, going from field to elevator to field to elevator. Most of the time I go to the elevator to use the bathroom and get water, and then get back into the truck. "Why is sex such a big deal in movies?"

The question comes off to me as similar to Japanese people asking me about America. Only then, I am usually asked something like "Why is tipping? How do we do it?" Or "How do I know which neighborhoods are safe?"

Why *is* sex such a big deal?

I don't think we should be talking about this, but after the incident about Adam and Eve and Bethany, I have strengthened my resolve to be a kind of ambassador from my world.

First, I mumble something about how I'm not an expert. Then I say the only thing I can think of. I say: "It's very powerful. It's a very powerful force, so . . . it gets depicted a lot. And somewhere along the way, the narrative developed that we were supposed to . . . be comfortable with it even if we aren't. Because it's so powerful. And the truth, I think, is that no one knows what to do." I am stumbling.

Juston is unconvinced. "So . . . it's just powerful?" He asks me as if he's saying *Is that seriously all you've got?*

"Isn't it?"

"Well, yeah . . . but the movies make a big deal and then it's not like anything necessarily works out. I don't understand what they are getting at."

"It's really hard to be close to people. Sometimes."

"That's really *it*?" he says indignantly.

"Well, I think at its best, it tells us who we are. Who we can love and who loves us. Maybe there's no more clear explanation about who we are."

"I get that," he says. "And I understand how sex is used in art and how it can be art. But it seems to me—and this is just my opinion—like it gets thrown in there. A lot. And there isn't any meaning and it isn't actually showing anything and I don't know why that is."

I'm intellectualizing. I know I'm intellectualizing and I know I'm falling short of giving him a good answer. "I don't know," I say. We drive on in silence.

It is just after ten at night. Eric is continuing to cut the wheat as long as the moisture level is not too high and the nighttime dew does not settle in and make the wheat stalks too tough to cut. We must work as long as we can. And as a result, there is an unspoken feeling of great satisfaction that at last a day is what it is supposed to be.

Juston and I drive a load of wheat to the elevator in Thomas. I see Rodney with a lollipop in his mouth, standing on the concrete landing outside the office. Kelsey, one of two lovely blond girls working in the office and assisting with paperwork, has parked her car outside the elevator. In years past, she and Samuel have had a flirtatious friendship, but Juston tells me that this year matters are cool between them.

"Bethany?" I ask.

"They're definitely dating," he mutters.

He guides the truck into the dark and narrow tunnel that is the old elevator. I stay in the truck. If I get out, I will always need to get out at the elevator so that the weight of the truck can remain constant, and so we decide I ought to simply stay in the truck. After the truck is weighed, the wheat is dumped, and then the truck—with me still in it—is weighed again, and this is how the elevator knows how much wheat was delivered. I listen to the CB radio, to the voices of the men in the combines and the other trucks. Bradford is mostly in control, guiding who should go where and in what order. I do not hear Eric's voice; Juston assumes his father is out looking for more work to pick up. Somewhere there might be a farmer whose combine quit, or whose intended crew was delayed or didn't show up. We are cutting in two locations, and this means the trucks need to know which field to go to next, and who most needs help receiving wheat. After we are completely done unloading, we get our paperwork from Kelsey, which shows how much wheat was delivered so the farmer has an accurate record of how much wheat he now has in the cooperative elevator. Juston gets on the radio and asks Bradford if he should come back out to the field, and after a moment of consideration, Bradford says bluntly: "No." So we park.

On the way to the lot, we see a fox. As is often the case, I am ecstatic and make a lot of noise over the fox, while Juston doubts what I have seen. My perspective on all things country is suspect, which I suppose is fair enough. But it is a fox. I am sure of it. We sit in the lot in the quiet night waiting for someone to transport us back to the trailers. I am exhausted and suggest walking. But Juston assures me that someone will be coming along soon. Everyone will have heard over the CB that we have parked.

"But we didn't ask for a ride," I say.

"We don't have to," he tells me.

Sure enough, out of the dark come the bright lights of Lily the service truck. Amos is driving. He is in high spirits, he says, and does not want to stop cutting! His twangy voice goes on and on with enthusiasm, and I interrupt and tell him I have seen a fox.

"I want to see a fox!" he declares. A few minutes later, another fox darts through the neighborhood and disappears behind shrubbery. "Fox!" Amos shouts, delighted.

"See!" I am ecstatic. "It *was* a fox!"

Juston chuckles. Then Amos pulls onto the green lawn outside the trailers, and we make our way across the grass to collapse into sleep.

In the morning, Eric takes me to meet two farmers—brothers who, he says, are smart, if eccentric. They remind him a bit of my father and my uncle. When we walk into a barn on one of the farmers' property, a man has crawled on top of a contraption that Eric explains to me is a planter. The man says he is trying to redesign the planter so it will plant sweet potatoes automatically. I don't exactly understand what this means—but I soon will.

We speak briefly to the two brothers. Both men are slim, dusty, and quiet, and in their stillness and cerebral bearing, they do resemble my uncle and father. They tell us that a crew is out planting sweet potatoes and that we are welcome to go and watch. Then they tell me they are trying to figure out the matter of broccoli sprouts. Customers are paying a premium for broccoli sprouts, and if they could figure out how to grow them, then perhaps they could benefit. I am asked: "Are broccoli sprouts an ethnic thing?"

"I don't think so. Maybe a city thing," I say, because I can't think of any "ethnic people" I know whose cuisine revolves around broccoli sprouts.

I am asked again. And again I reassure them that the sprouts must be a city thing. "Maybe it's a Whole Foods thing," I say.

"Ah, Whole Foods." They nod. This answer seems to satisfy them.

Eric and I drive out to the field in search of the sweet potato planters, and I think about how being a couple of hundred miles north like this has significantly changed the possibilities for planting. Now there are cotton, sprouts, sweet potatoes, and watermelons. Crops are rotated. Weeds are controlled.

Eric parks the truck. In the distance I can see a group of people and a variation of the planter we saw not long ago in the farmer's barn. The planter is sitting on top of a slight slope. As Eric and I walk across the field toward the potato planter, we pass piles of ash and what look like wilted stalks that have just been stuck into the ground. In the distance are the workers. I know they will be brown-skinned. In fact, I am looking for brown-skinned people before I even realize this is what I am looking for. My eye is used to seeing migrant workers in California. Memories from past visits to farms overlap; I could be in an artichoke field in California where the workers are also brown.

Finally we reach the planters and they are indeed brown-skinned men and women. After spending so much of the week contemplating the history of white people, I feel strangely divided in front of the brown-skinned workers. I have not seen any brown people for weeks now, except for the time I went to get a manicure in Texas, and that was some time ago. Eric is smiling. He likes to see this new crop. The field is so wide and open and the soil bright red.

"Hey!" a man calls out to me. He has long, almost black hair tied to the nape of his neck. He has on sunglasses and a weathered brown shirt; the cotton is thin and worn from washing and drying and washing. All the men are sweating and dusty. Some wear hats. They are sitting side by side on metal seats, which are spaced at regular intervals on a contraption attached to the back of the tractor. This constitutes the planter. Each of the seats has before it a metal basket, and from a distance it looks as if the men are riding a multiseat bicycle. The workers hold limp green shoots; these are sweet potato shoots and the men are planting them by hand.

"Hey! Are you an Indian? You an Indian?" the man is calling out to me.

The question catches me off guard. It shouldn't. Why shouldn't he talk to me? But in this strange hierarchy in which I have been living, I suppose I had expected to talk to whoever is in charge of the sweet potato planting.

"I see your jewelry. Your earrings! I already seen your bracelets." His voice is so open and friendly, but at the same time I have the feeling that something unintended has happened. It is true I am wearing my Hopi bracelets. I wear them every day.

On a drive back from Oklahoma City recently, I had stopped at an Indian trading post, where I had picked up some Native American earrings made out of porcupine quills and beads. I had also found a necklace made by a Navajo artist depicting "the creator." I feel guilty wearing all this in front of a real Indian, who for a split second wonders if I might be an Indian too.

"No," I say. "I'm Asian."

Beside me, Eric is smiling broadly. He seems unusually pleased to see me having this conversation.

"Oh. You look Indian. We are fifty percent Indian. Cheyenne, Cherokee, and Araphaho. Kiowa and Osage. We come from Tulsa. And everyone else . . . they are Mexican."

"Tulsa," I repeat dumbly.

"Yeah, you know. The reservation there."

"Yes," I say, even though I didn't know there was a reservation there.

How has he come here? I cannot explain it, but tears seep into my eyes. I feel as though he has seen me—seen something in me—that the others cannot, and this side of me he sees in me is abruptly awake. It suddenly wants connection with his story. Did he assume our stories were similar? Did he wonder how I happened to be traveling in the company of white farmers? I have a desperate desire to talk with him further. But the tractor starts, dragging the men up the hill. The workers each put a sweet potato shoot in a tube, which the contraption rolls into the ground, and another part of the planter packs dirt around the shoot so it is firmly seated in place. But the system isn't perfect. As the machinery pulls away, a few men and a woman follow carrying metal poles. Any shoots that did not get stuck into the ground securely are pushed in more firmly. This is how sweet potatoes are planted.

The group rumbles away. Despite all the advances in technology and the men in my crew who work with computers and machinery, it still takes a team of workers to hand-plant something like sweet potatoes. If only, I think, I could have had ten more minutes.

I turn my attention to Eric, who is now talking to Blanca Flores, the owner of the company, White Flower Planting, which is a literal translation of her name. She says she learned to plant from her father, who ran the company initially. When he died, she took it over. The crew is mixed—perhaps more like 60 percent Native American and 40 percent Mexican. She tells us about the potatoes, and how the best ones will be picked and sent to market and all sorted by hand, and how the second tier will be sold separately and turned into sweet potato fries.

The tractor continues to pull away and the men grow smaller. I feel an indescribable sadness.

I think Eric sees the murky sorrow on my face. Gently, he suggests we walk back to the pickup truck. I know now the source of the confusion I have been feeling since our arrival in Oklahoma: it is the intense internal pressure to avoid confronting something I don't wish to see. I would like to believe, as I have on and off for much of my life, that my mixed features are secondary to what is inside of me. It is my interior that is real. But this is impossible to believe in Oklahoma, and certainly not possible in front of the Indian now disappearing over the hill in the tractor. Just as he has seen me, I have seen him, and that exchange brings in his history, or what I can infer of his story, to the land I am standing on now. The Indians do not exist just in museums or in graveyards; they are still here, and the settling of this land and the farming of it are bound up with his people.

In the evening, I replay this moment—the tractor pulling away and disappearing over the hill, and the piles of ash that I now realize were the burned leftovers of the cardboard boxes that had brought the sweet potato shoots out to the field to be planted. The tractor pulls away and the sweet potatoes are planted. The ground has been trammeled, and so what was a crusty, dry surface of red earth becomes disrupted, and dark red earth is now on the surface because the tractor has rolled over the land.

But in my mind's eye this is not what I see. When the tractor pulls away, it is as if I am standing on a vast plain covered by a sheet. The reason the earth turns dark red is because the tractor has peeled back this surface sheet. In my imagination, the tractor turns into a hand turning the covers of bedding. It is as if the tractor had pulled back the top sheet and revealed what was underneath, which is this dark red sheet.

The image plays over and over in my mind. When the sheet is turned back, something slips out. There was a shadow of some kind under that top sheet and it flies out now and has been released and we have seen it, or at least I have seen it. Now it is loose and now nothing will quite be the same again on this voyage. I know what the rules are when a dark thing flies out. You don't run and hide like a child. The rule is that you must go and see what the dark thing is.

It is possible that Whirlwind—the Indian buried by the field we have cut—and Quanah Parker knew each other.

In the north of the Panhandle of Texas, near the Oklahoma border, there is a ghost town known as Adobe Walls; it is about 220 miles north and just slightly west of Crowell, and 250 miles southwest of Oklahoma City. The settlement was established in 1843 as a saloon and trading post for white settlers moving into the area. Settlers blew up Adobe Walls in 1845 and effectively abandoned the structures, because they were repeatedly raided by Indians. But the loss of the buildings did not stop whites from hunting buffalo in Texas, or, for that matter, Indians from attacking and raiding the stagecoaches on the Santa Fe Trail, which ran from present-day New Mexico, through Texas, and on to Missouri.

In 1864, the US government hired Kit Carson to lead a group of some three hundred volunteer soldiers from New Mexico into Texas to quell the Indians. This First Battle of Adobe Walls would be the last time the Indians successfully routed their enemy in any significant way. Outnumbered, Carson retreated to Santa Fe.

Ten years later, merchants from Dodge City built a new trading post a mile from the old Adobe Walls; it was intended to serve the needs of several hundred white buffalo hunters in the area. From 1872 to 1873, so many buffalo to the north had been killed that the buffalo hunters had had to move south, to Texas, to find more game. The remaining Native Americans—Comanche, Cherokee, and Kiowa—understood that these white men would bring about an end to their way of life.

In the spring of 1874, a Comanche medicine man named Isatai'i began to claim that the Great Spirit had imbued him with miraculous powers, and that his people must exterminate the white man. He convinced not only the Comanche that now was the time to fight but many of the Cheyenne and the Kiowa too. They would all perform the sacred Sun Dance, an arduous ritual that involved fasting and, in certain instances, piercing of the skin. Though the Sun Dance was a Kiowa and not a Comanche ritual, Isatai'i explained that completion of the dance would confer complete protection against the white man's bullets, and both Quanah and Whirlwind successfully completed the sacred rite.

We don't know the precise number of Indians who gathered; the best estimates are anywhere from two hundred to seven hundred or more. Led by Quanah and Isatai'i, the Indians attacked the compound at Adobe Walls at 2 a.m. on June 27. Inside the walls were twenty-eight men and one woman. Among the fighters was a young Cheyenne man named O-kuh-ha-tuh, which means "Making Medicine" in the

Cheyenne language. Much later, Making Medicine's name would be Anglicized to the improbable-sounding David Pendleton Oakerhater, and he would also come to be known as Chief Whirlwind.

Like Quanah's, Oakerhater's exact date of birth isn't known, though most guess that he was born around 1848, which would make him twenty-six in the year of the Second Battle of Adobe Walls. He is described as being perhaps the youngest man ever to complete the Sun Dance, and a fierce warrior among his people.

If you've watched any westerns, you know what happened next. The white men had guns and, though vastly outnumbered, were able to shoot at the Indians through the windows of their compounds. More than seventy Indians were killed on June 27, 1874, as they rode their horses in waves against the fort. On the third day, one of the hunters, Billy Dixon, cleanly shot a brave off of his horse. This, plus the wounding of Quanah and the arrival of reinforcements for the white men, swung the battle decisively in favor of the hunters.

The Second Battle of Adobe Walls hastened the US government's plans to entirely defeat the Indians. In less than a year, after a series of skirmishes and battles collectively known as the Red River War—during which the Gatling gun was used for the first time west of the Mississippi—the Indians, including Quanah and Oakerhater, surrendered at what is present-day Fort Sill, Oklahoma. Although, remember: in 1875, Oklahoma didn't yet exist. The entire territory was known as Indian Territory, and had been set aside for the residence of the remaining Native Americans in the United States.

The western part of Oklahoma had traditionally belonged to the Cheyenne, Arapaho, Kiowa, and Comanche, and Quanah helped his people settle in the southwestern part of Indian Territory. In the first few years after his surrender, Quanah grew relatively wealthy. When white ranchers ran cattle too close to the Indian Territory boundary, Quanah would often "get" the cattle that had crossed over and sell them back to the white man who had "lost" them.

Oakerhater, meanwhile, led a very different life. After his surrender at the final Red River Valley battle, in 1875, Oakerhater and seventy-four men were selected to be imprisoned without trial in Fort Marion, Florida, which is near present-day St. Augustine. They were moved on foot, by train, and by wagon back to the east; four men died.

The Indians at Fort Marion fell under the watch of First Lieutenant

Richard Henry Pratt, who believed the Indians could be civilized. His motto was "Kill the Indian and save the man." He put the Indians in Western uniforms, and began to drill them as though they were soldiers. He taught them English and gave them art supplies. Oakerhater appears to have been a model student. He drew pictures of Indian battles in his ledger, which were sold to tourists; today his drawings are worth hundreds of thousands of dollars and many are kept in the Smithsonian Institution. Over time, in a *Bridge on the River Kwai*–type scenario, Oakerhater was appointed first seargent over the other prisoners. He became a Christian and continued his education after prison.

Oakerhater's letters are available online, and one afternoon I read them. In one of them, written in English, he describes his time in Paris Hill, New York, where he went under sponsorship after being released from prison:

"I am very happy. It is very good and I thank you very much. You my dear all Sisters. I love all you. I like you as soon as I saw you. . . . I . . . learn and read and write and sing every day. I study hard pray for we want good heart. We want to love Jesus. We want to learn much. Jesus good to me."

This is a voice I know. This is the voice of someone just learning English, testing their own confidence in a new language and a new faith and a voice that hopes to please another person. The voice both humbles and distresses me. The first time I read these letters, I do not feel joy that someone who had "been a killer" had now found Jesus. I hear my mother's English with all its syntactical errors. I hear myself speaking for her when she goes to the doctor, calls the utility company, or tries to make small talk at a party. I hear my inner voice, furious that after all these years, "a," "an," and "the" are still such a problem for her. Then I am furious with myself for being critical of her, because I hear myself stumbling through Japanese in Japan, hoping no one will be angry with me.

Oakerhater became an Episcopal deacon in 1881 and eventually returned to Oklahoma. He went on to serve as a missionary to his people, and to run the school that had been located here in the field where we had found the cemetery. He was eventually made a saint by the Episcopal Church and, after a window of St. Paul's Cathedral was destroyed during the Oklahoma City bombing, it was replaced by a stained-glass window depicting Oakerhater. By all accounts, Oakerhater truly became a Christian. The letters he writes are sincere. But I want to know how he changed his mind.

After my grandfather died, in 2010, I helped my mother clean out his house in Japan, and I came upon cache after cache of letters written in English. I don't have the letters he wrote to others, but the letters to him tell me something of what my grandfather had to say. He received one from an American who had been stationed in the city of Nagoya during the occupation that read, in part: "From what you have told me in your letter you are a wonderful man and have a great spirit for making your country democratic and a free nation like my own. I was very much pleased to hear that you wanted to start a Sunday School in your home."

I knew my grandfather. Every morning he prayed to his Japanese ancestor gods in his house. He did not go to church and he did not become a Christian and he did not run a Sunday school. He did, however, remain haunted by the war and by his country's transformation and demise. In this letter, I see that he made an effort to appease the occupiers.

So there was Oakerhater, in prison in Florida, certain that he would be executed, and having watched some of his compatriots die. Then he was shown mercy by his captor. I think of my mother, born in a country at war, conquered by the enemy, who then sent her gifts.

Why do we embrace the enemy? Can we and do we truly love them?

Conversation is often the result of emotion, and not careful, rational deliberation. Change comes from crisis. Conspiracy theorists know this. Jack Gorman and Sara Gorman explain: "Conspiracy theorists do not begin addressing their audiences by saying, 'I am going to calmly and systematically take you through a series of scientific facts in order to reach a conclusion.' Rather, they pack emotional appeals into their presentations." It requires emotion to convert, whether one is crossing the bridge into a conspiracy or into a truth. Megachurches use all those lights and music for a reason.

Did Oakerhater embrace Christ, and if he did, what was it about Christ that he was embracing? When he was in prison and the Indian part of him was "killed" so "the man" could emerge, was he fed the transactional model of Christianity, in which he was shown hell, and told that he could be saved from eternal damnation? Was he told he was a "savage" who needed to become a man? Was there a moment in which he learned about Cain and Abel, and noted that Cain was a farmer and Abel a herder, and that God loved Abel more, but left Abel to die? Or was it something else? Something, as Juston would say, that was authentic?

Every cell in my body strains against the image of this brown man and his people, who were beaten and endlessly betrayed, accepting some aspect of what the conqueror believed, and telling the conquered that they had been just to wage war. And yet Oakerhater seems to have accepted all of this. He seems not to have descended into chaos or illness or fury and dispensed with his life but to have been expanded into some other state so elevated that he was eventually seen as a saint and commemorated in a rainbow of stained glass.

I wonder if it is real, this transcendent place he went to, or if it is a figment of his imagination. I wonder if it is a place he learned about by parroting his conquerors, if it is a self he invented for his own survival. Or if it is all true and he learned what I still have not?

EIGHT

SUNDAY COMES FOR US AGAIN and I initially dread going to church. But the moment we set foot in the sanctuary, I know I will love the service today. We are at Pleasant View Mennonite Church, which Dwayne and his family attend. This is the church with the cemetery where Emily's relative is buried. Everything about the decor is self-consciously plain: mossy-green carpet, wooden pews, white walls, and two dark green wall hangings that flank the stage. They read: "Peace be with you" and "Be at peace with each other." The ceiling goes up in a sharp V and a single cross hangs starkly on the back wall. John 3:16 is nowhere. This is all a far cry from the smoke machine and the robotic lights swiveling at the command of a computer at the megachurch.

But what strikes me most are the people, who seem familiar and approachable. These people look like my American grandmother. Everyone appears to me not as if they are presenting their best selves for show but as if they belong to families where the parents are harried and just doing their best.

The Miller family, another combine crew, takes up an entire row in front of us. I count three generations, with a tiny baby perhaps just a few weeks old. We greet one another and ask: "How's it going?"

"All right," they say. "You?"

"Can't complain," we say.

Church begins not with warm-up pastors but with members of the congregation reading passages from the Bible, most of which pertain to the harvest. A tall man in his thirties dressed in a suit leaves the pew where he has been sitting with his wife and children and carries a prayer he has written himself to the front of the podium. He's nervous, but the prayer is beautiful and he grows more confident as he speaks. The prayer begins:

God we come before you this morning with an attitude of Adoration. Amazed that we are able to glimpse your beauty in the morning sunrise, in the changing of the seasons and the ripening of the harvest fields.

We sense your power in the crash of thunder, the shape of the canyons, and the howling of the winds. Creator God, we praise you.

Lord you have blessed us in spite of our flaws. Give us grateful hearts for the many blessings we receive directly from your hands. Lord accept our praise.

Instead of grandiose worship music, we sing hymns that emphasize gratitude: "All I have needed Thy hand hath provided." We sing in four-part harmony, with the men breaking into baritone or bass, and the women into alto and soprano. It is an unexpected intimacy to listen to one another and to shape our voices so they fit together. These hymns take more work than the worship music. A curious side effect of all the effort is that the hymns take on a three-dimensional auditory shape, and the sum of our voices hangs in the air, suspended inside the sanctuary.

There are community updates. A man has been run over by his own tractor when the tractor slipped into reverse, but is expected to survive. Harvest has begun. The Millers all gather in the front of the sanctuary to bless their new baby. We pray for them.

Then the sermon begins. The pastor is blond and boyishly handsome in a John Denver way. But he seems the slightest bit annoyed, and initially it is this irritation that grabs my attention because it, too, feels familiar. It is the impatience of a busy mind that perhaps even just a moment ago was engaged in some other activity. I trust this annoyance more than the glossy smiles of the other pastors I have watched.

Pastor Jeff projects a slide of the Jamaican sprinter Usain Bolt on a portable screen. Then he reads a quote about discipline from Hebrews in the New Testament: "No discipline seems pleasant at the time, but painful. Later on, however, it produces a harvest of righteousness and peace for those who have been trained by it."

Pastor Jeff says: "Usain Bolt . . . is the fastest man on the planet [out of] seven to eight billion strong. He runs the hundred-meter dash in 9.58 seconds. . . . Not only that but he can run the two hundred . . . in 19.19 seconds. . . . What is his recipe for success? Certainly God has gifted him, but . . . he says it is hard work, sweat, and sacrifice. . . . He spends three hours a day, six days a week, training. . . . That's a thousand hours a year for at least the past eight years and probably . . . another four years prior to winning. Twelve thousand hours for the past twelve years so he can be on a track 9.58 seconds.

"We would say it's worth it. Usain Bolt's giving us an understanding of what discipline is. I don't expect us all to go out and start training. But the fact that you've all gathered here today tells me that you have some interest in who God is and who you are in relationship to God. . . . I invite you to start thinking about the time that you spend."

The first thing I think is: This pastor is not going to lie to me and tell me that something is easy when it is not. He is also not trying to scare me into believing the same thing he does.

Pastor Jeff says we must change the way we relate to discipline, which to my Japanese self sounds entirely reasonable. He wants us to train to be like Usain, because someday we will be standing before God, and the pastor will not be there with us. He hopes we will take ownership of our relationship to God. And then he does a curious thing. He starts to talk about the way in which the Bible is written. He brings up Greek words and analyzes them.

"Hebrews is written in a kind of high Greek style. It's unlike most of the New Testament. The only thing that comes close to it is Acts and Luke. . . . We want to pay attention to the translated words." On the projector screen, words begin to appear. It is as if we are in school. "First word at the top there is '*paidaia*.' It's this idea of 'discipline.'

"'*Paidaia*' can also be translated [as] 'education' [and] 'upbringing'. . . . We see this when we read Ephesians. . . . 'Fathers, do not exasperate your children; instead, bring them up in the training and instruction of the Lord.' We see that same Greek word as '*paidaia*' here."

Around and around he goes like this, bringing up the original words from the Bible as he tries to figure out with us—for us—what the words truly mean. He zips neatly around the Bible, putting disparate passages into relation, as though he is organizing a necklace out of beads of Hebrew and Greek that were, until that Sunday, strewn on the floor. But he isn't facile. He isn't trying to be cute, or disarming, or even terribly bossy. He reminds me of an advanced English professor showing his class that he is an expert with a book, and that he knows this book is a complete story whose parts are supposed to work together. Only he's not a PhD drawing correlations between Shakespeare plays; he's a pastor, and the book he's working through, the Bible, is meant to show us how we can be more clearly connected to God.

Another word pops up on the projector screen.

"'*Filios*' literally just means 'son,' [or can mean 'descendant']. It's used liberally throughout the New Testament . . . when it refers to 'human' and not to the divine. . . . [He who has sons cares for them] differently than [he would care for a slave]. We want to pay attention to this 'son' word because there is something different—[a son is] someone that you have a vested interest in. . . . God has a vested interest in you, believer, as a son or daughter.

"'My son, do not make light of the Lord's discipline, and do not lose heart when he rebukes you' [Hebrews 12:5].

"Each one of you has been given the good news, has been given the gospel, has been shown grace and mercy. . . . The author of Hebrews is pointing to an expectation that you're supposed to be doing something with that grace and mercy. . . . We reap what we sow. And so if God is sowing good things into us, should we not be producing good things?"

Pastor Jeff gives us homework. He wants us to memorize a tiny portion of the Bible. "If you memorize the scripture, then it is with you. It changes the way you live because that is what you are thinking about instead of everything else that the world's wanting us to think about." Here is the simple line he wants us to memorize: "Faith is being sure of what we hope for and certain of what we do not see" [Hebrews 11:1]. I like this line. I write it down. I wonder if I am truly certain of what I hope for. I am not at all sure of what I cannot see. But I know what he means: we are the sum of our intentions and actions, and we must, as much as possible, be clear as to what we are doing and why. All my dance teachers used to yell this at me: "Show your intention. Commit to the movement."

When Pastor Jeff has finished speaking, he invites a member of the congregation to stand up and address us. The man who stands up has the slightly uncomfortable, lanky, hands-in-pocket stance of a farmer. His name is David Miller and he wears jeans and a button-up checkered shirt; missing are the pliers. He talks about the wildfires that started in northern Oklahoma on March 6, 2017. Eric has told me about these wildfires, which have devastated the prairie where cattle graze, and while many animals survived the blaze, their food supply has been eradicated and some have starved to death. It is a true tragedy of which the coasts are generally not aware.

Since March, this man has taken thirty-seven loads of hay, a total of 1,063 bales, to the animals so more would not starve. Members of the congregation donated funds for fuel and for hay. He shows us photos he took out the window of his truck in March; there is the scorched prairie, brown and black and dead as the underworld. And then he shows us new photos of the soft green regrowth that signals he can stop delivering hay. The prairie is regenerating.

He breaks down crying when he tells us about taking the last loads of hay to another family. They had thanked him but he had felt the need to thank them. He says: "This is probably the first time that I understood dying on the cross. The point is, you aren't supposed to suffer needlessly. The gospel teaches us how to transcend it." Then he thanks us, the congregation, for the support we gave to him.

Hell is never mentioned that day.

Eric tells me that Pastor Jeff went to Goshen College, which is a liberal Mennonite school. I think he means to imply that Pastor Jeff is a liberal Christian whose theology was reflected in the sermon. And I wonder: Was it liberal because Pastor Jeff tried to tell us how the Bible was constructed and because he sought patterns across the many books to share with us, as an English teacher would? Or was it liberal because we were never told that we were going to go to hell, but that everything we could possibly need was here on Earth and it was up to us to use it?

"I think you liked it because it was more intellectual," Eric says.

I liked it because it made sense to me.

Eric and Emily are happy when I say I want to meet Pastor Jeff in person, and they arrange for this to happen immediately. Pastor Jeff is busy with basketball practice—he works as a coach when he isn't cutting his family's wheat—but he has half an hour on Monday to see me.

We meet at the church and he is wearing shorts and a short-sleeved shirt that shows a farmer's tan. I would not know he is a pastor by looking at him. We exchange pleasantries. We go through the new church, still under construction, and into his office.

"Have you been well treated in Oklahoma?" It is as though he wants to make it clear that he knows we are from different places and recognizes that I might not be well treated. I feel as though a little light has momentarily been focused on me. It isn't an excessively bright light.

I do not feel like a museum exhibit, but more as though I am meeting some second or third cousin who has seen my photo in old family albums and already knows stories about me, but doesn't quite remember how I fit into the family and wants to make sure he's got it right.

"Everyone has been very kind," I assure him.

He is curious to hear what I do. He seems to find it fascinating that Eric was moved to bring me on the road. I tell him that I want to portray this part of the country as human. I say that it must be human, since humans are living here. And he smiles at this, an almost-secret smile, just bordering on indulgence. In an instant, he manages to convey that he knows where I'm from and that he is familiar with the ways of my people. And for just a few moments, his composure breaks. "The one thing I want to know is . . . it seems like whenever we interest the national news media . . . like when there is a tornado . . . they seem to pick the most ignorant hick out there to put on camera. Now, do you know why that is?"

I don't really answer so much as nod. We both know.

I say: "I wish people knew about that man delivering all that hay."

"Do you know," Pastor Jeff says, smiling proudly, "it was his idea to share that in church. He's not really a public speaker. But he wanted people to know who they had helped."

"And that beautiful prayer that man wrote?"

"Also his idea." Then Pastor Jeff draws himself together. We are not here for me to flatter him. He asks: "What are your questions?"

It has been so long since I've been in the company of someone this socially adroit, with this much parry and feint and who doesn't seem to be worried about what I *might* say. This is the thing about questions; they cannot be predicted.

I ask my question.

"Why it is that so many conservative Christians believe in creationism and reject evolution but use GMOs, while my friends in the city don't believe in God, but do believe in evolution and want organic food?"

The question takes its usual while to unpack. We go over some of the beliefs of the people in the crew. We talk about who is a six-dayer—that is, who believes that the world was created in six days—who objects to evolution, who thinks the world will soon end, and how man is divine and how hell is always waiting. It is to his credit that I have no idea where Pastor Jeff stands on any of these issues. His goal seems mostly to understand me, to make me feel comfortable, and for me to know that I can ask questions and that he can understand them.

And then he says: "I'm thinking about that baby we blessed yesterday. There's no way I can look at that beautiful face and believe he is already sinful and going to hell." He shakes his head. "I don't think that's quite right. Let's look instead at how things are supposed to be. We have Genesis one and two, where the world is created and then there is the Fall. In Genesis 3:5, things start to change. We eat animals after the story of Noah and the ark. Do you know that story? Good. Before Noah, we don't eat animals. Genesis chapter nine, verse three. 'Just as I gave you the green plants, I now give you everything.'"

"Before that we were vegetarians?"

That, Pastor Jeff says, is what the Bible implies. But vegetarianism is not the main point he wants to make. There is a term he wants me to know. The word is "shalom." He says he thinks of shalom as "how things are supposed to be," and that the Garden of Eden represents shalom. In that garden, man was friends with and didn't eat animals. The animals also didn't eat one another (like in Disney's *Zootopia*, I think). And in shalom, man took care of the earth too. In shalom, Cain did not kill Abel. Shalom is the place to which we are all always trying to return. All humans, he seems to imply, know this and strive for shalom, and Christians turn to Jesus and his parables to try to work hard to get there. The carrot, to paraphrase Juston, is not hell; it is shalom.

He gives me a bookmark, which at first glance looks like it is printed with hieroglyphics—squiggly lines run from left to right. But he tells me this is a visual representation of the Bible. To the left is a circle: the Garden of Eden. With the Fall, a line juts to the right, out of the circle, and points down. And then that line goes on in different formations as the stories in the Bible advance: here is Moses getting the commandments, here are the prophets, and then Jesus is born. At the end, we return to another circle.

The circle is how things should be. Shalom. And we will return to this.

Eric's son Winston once sent me an email asking if in the city, babies play with cups and bibs emblazoned with taxis and skyscrapers; he had noticed that his soon-to-be-born child had received mostly farm-themed items at the baby shower. No, I wrote back. Even in the city, the early years are partly spent identifying the names and sounds of farm animals, even though most children born in the city aren't going to go to a farm except, perhaps, on a school trip or yearly pilgrimage to pick a pumpkin.

"Oh, well, that's good," he said with genuine surprise. "I'm glad they like farmers."

When my son was born, in 2009, I and the other mothers in my group sang "Old MacDonald" and mooed and neighed and baahed day after day. Many of my son's early-childhood books were about animals, and I took him to the Central Park petting zoo to see the sheep and alpacas, even though these animals had nothing to do with our daily city life—or with elevators, subways, and escalators.

In those days I pureed organic peas and paid extra for eggs from grass-fed "happy chickens." In my mind, purity, childhood, and food were all wrapped up together and set to a soundtrack of songs involving animals. Animals and the barnyard seemed connected with childhood. My son was new to the world, and for a time everything he did would be the first time he had done anything. I wanted each introduction to be gentle. Baby sheep. Soft wool. Chemical-free. Organic and from the farm the way the farm was meant to be, which was something I was sure I knew.

In her book on childhood vaccination, Eula Biss writes: "One of the most powerful tonics alternative medicine offers is the word *natural*. This word implies a medicine untroubled by human limitations, contrived wholly by nature or God or perhaps intelligent design. What *natural* has come to mean to us in the context of medicine is *pure* and *safe* and *benign*. But the use of *natural* as a synonym for *good* is almost certainly a product of our profound alienation from the natural world." We do not live in shalom.

My own parents grew a lot of our food in our garden in California. I couldn't do this in New York. What I could do was control what I bought, and so I did.

As Pastor Jeff talks of shalom and the desire we all have to go there, I wonder if he means that we are always trying to go back to the place where we were friends with animals, where everything was new and nothing terrible had yet happened. All of us are trying to do this. I wonder if this is something we are asking food to do—to take us back to shalom, and if GMOs and famers' use of science strikes us as so unnatural that it disrupts what we want our food to be. Maybe Christians worry about this kind of thing because it is Jesus who will take them to shalom, and not the act of eating.

In reading the literature against GMOs, I come across several standard reactions. There are those who are against anything that has been genetically modified, because we cannot know what the long-term consequences of gene modification might be. The idea is that there may be something harmful lurking in the proteins that will come to bear on our bodies sometime in the future, in the same way that an accumulation of tar in the lungs can turn out to be carcinogenic. A biodynamic farmer once confided in me that he believed there was something "energetically wrong" with modern food, making it sound as though GMOs have the capacity to bestow a voodoo curse on us.

The companies that made cigarettes knew that their products were harmful, but once actively hid their knowledge. What if the same is true of Roundup Ready corn? We are told that it is safe, but what if it is not? Monsanto is getting rich. What if there is something in Roundup's surfactant that is dangerous, and the company is knowingly hiding the data?

I need here to separate Roundup from GMOs, even though they are often linked. Studies have been conducted as to whether or not genetically modified crops are harmful, and there is as yet nothing conclusive that shows any harmful effects. In 2012, the American Association for the Advancement of Science reported: "The science is quite clear: crop improvement by the modern molecular techniques of biotechnology is safe." And: "The World Health Organization, the American Medical Association, the U.S. National Academy of Sciences, the British Royal Society, and every other respected organization that has examined the evidence has come to the same conclusion: consuming foods containing ingredients derived from GM crops is no riskier than consuming the same foods containing ingredients from crop plants modified by conventional plant improvement techniques."

Still I know that some people are afraid of GMOs. No matter how much I read the reports that conventional food is safe, it worries me. Science says my reaction is normal. In the *New Yorker*, the science writer Maria Konnikova explains: "Psychologists have long observed that there is a continuum in what we perceive as natural or unnatural. As the psychologist Robert Sternberg wrote in 1982, the natural is what we find more familiar, while what we consider unnatural tends to be more novel. . . . The natural is seen as inherently positive; the un-natural is not. And anything that involves human manipulation is considered highly unnatural—like, say, G.M.O.s, even though genetically modified food already lines the shelves at grocery stores."

But what about the times I have paused in Whole Foods and wondered if I should buy organic (more expensive) broccoli or conventional (cheaper). Doesn't organic taste better? Konnikova again: "In a 2013 study, a group of Cornell University researchers found that how a food is labelled affects our perception of how it tastes, what its nutritional value is, and our willingness to pay for it." She then goes on to recount how, when a customer was under the impression that a food—a cookie—was labeled "organic," it was deemed to have fewer calories and to taste less artificial than the same product when it was labeled "regular." GMOs, in other words, have a "reverse halo" effect, passing on their perceived negative qualities to food made with nonorganic ingredients. "When it comes to new, unknown technologies," she says, "data always loses out to emotion." I remember Eric's first visit to Whole Foods: "It is *marketing*. Do not fall for it."

A second opinion I often hear about GMOs is that even if GMOs are helpful, the benefits come at the expense of the small farmer. In an essay for the *New York Review of Books*, the critic Verlyn Klinkenborg writes: "Industrial agriculture—shaped by the USDA, by chemical and seed companies, by the vagaries of domestic and export markets—relies on a picture of the family farmer to soften its image. It wants it both ways. It wants to celebrate its technical innovations, like genetically modified crops, computer-driven tractors, and satellite-monitored fields. And yet it also wants to foster our national nostalgia for farming and the men and women who do it. The contradiction is intolerable, especially to farmers." But these are not the men (and few women) I have met out on the plains. While they would certainly like to not have to pay a premium for Roundup Ready corn, and they would like to be able to raise their own seed, complete with the modified protections in place, they also do like that their fields are, as ours have been in Oklahoma, so very clean and productive. They know it is science that has made this possible.

I know that the same people who believe that GMOs are safe also believe that humans are contributing to climate change. I would like to think that I am a thoroughly modern person. I would like to be a person who stands outside of the shadow of superstition, but my System 2 has a hard time overriding my System 1 here. My fuzzy logic kicks in when I'm on my own or talking to a city friend, and I worry about GMOs. This is partly why I'm fascinated by the former anti-GMO activist Mark Lynas. In 2013, Lynas delivered a mea culpa to the Oxford Farming Conference. Lynas used to go out with other anti-GMO activists and chop down Roundup Ready corn in the dead of night, while hiding from the police, who would eventually show up to try to capture the vandals.

"I want to start with some apologies. For the record, here and upfront, I apologise for having spent several years ripping up GM crops. . . . As an environmentalist, and someone who believes that everyone in this world has a right to a healthy and nutritious diet of their choosing, I could not have chosen a more counter-productive path."

In a 2017 editorial for the Cornell Alliance for Science, Lynas penned a piece titled "Europe Still Burns Witches—If They're Named Monsanto." In the essay he examines the fifteen-year extension on a ban of the herbicide Roundup in the UK. "All in all this was a textbook case of how science and reason so easily lose out to hysteria and emotion, especially when you can find a good pantomime villain. This was never about glyphosate as a chemical. It was about glyphosate as a symbol, a symbol for opposition to Monsanto, pesticides, GMOs and a modern farming system which populist factions of different political stripes, led by the Greens, now love to hate."

Both Lynas and Klinkenborg—not to mention the latest issue of the *Farmhouse Movement* magazine for sale at Whole Foods—touch on the reasons we tend to see farmers as either victims of corporations who would like to practice a more "pure" form of agriculture if they were only allowed, or people who should be paragons of natural human virtue, untouched by change and progress. Food, this thing we put into our bodies, is so elemental that we want it to be "pure."

Can it be so simple as feeling that all that work with earth and soil—a concept that even urbanites are introduced to from a young age—appears as a shalom to which we are always longing to return? Has such a deeply held bias in part held us back from a conversation about what food production should be about, which is how to feed everyone? If we are willing to let technology enter so many areas of our lives, and if technology has helped so many farmers and might be a way we are able to preserve the soil on the planet, why can we not embrace the changes science has brought to farming? Soil—the land—ought to be one thing on which we can come together.

I am leaving for the city. I will be on the East Coast for two weeks before I return to the crew. I am finishing a master's degree in a low-residency program that requires my attendance twice a year for classes. The rest of the time we send our work by email to instructors. To reach the residency, I will fly to New York City. I joke with Emily that I won't see John 3:16 the entire time that I am in New York, but she is sure I will.

"I don't think so," I say. "I never saw it until I was in Oklahoma, and I don't think it's because I wasn't looking before."

I can tell from her face that she cannot believe this is true.

When I say goodbye to Juston and Michael, the latter is cheerful, but Juston is sorrowful and more brooding than ever. He's deeply troubled by something. I do not know everything that is weighing on his mind, but I am sure it has something to do with the fact that when the crew is out and about, it is clearly divided. On one side Bradford, Bethany, Amos, and Samuel are all closely allied. On the other side are Juston, Michael, and me. Only Luther—silent Luther—has managed to be neutral. When I mention the split to Juston, he speaks about it with tremendous frustration. "Bradford is a talented farmer. You could learn so much from him if he would just talk to you." But when I have tried to speak to Bradford—or requested to ride in the combine with him—he has continued to be curt. I have stopped asking questions, out of discomfort.

I discuss this tension with Emily. I feel terrible. I'm an adult and ought not to be involved in the social dynamics of a group of young people. What exactly is causing so much trouble? My age? Gender? Questions?

"It's college," Emily says.

"College?"

She cannot describe for me precisely what she means, but I assume she thinks that the extra time we've spent reading and writing has affected Michael, Juston, and me; we are the three who have gone to college. We have been forever altered by books. We will ask questions, and in doing so, we allow an uncharted world to form in our heads. Our world is not so much a place in which problems are fixed, but one in which doors are left open and we live with the uncertainty of what we do not know. We will revisit the open doors day after day, and we share the open doors with one another.

The great educator and philosopher John Dewey hints at this development in his classic book *The School and Society*. The text is taken from talks Dewey gave at the end of the nineteenth century, when he observed: "No number of object-lessons, got up *as* object-lessons for the sake of giving information, can afford even the shadow of a substitute for acquaintance with the plants and animals of the farm and garden, acquired through actual living among them and caring for them. No training of sense-organs in school, introduced for the sake of training, can begin to compete with the alertness and fullness of sense-life that comes through daily intimacy and interest in familiar occupations." In this quote, I hear echoes of Eric insisting that going on harvest is "see and do." I recall Bethany saying how it was a very Lancaster County thing to want to be a "part of the solution." The "fullness of sense-life" captures that quality the crew has when they seem to communicate with each other without the burden of language. And yet, as Dewey argued even at the turn of the last century, this kind of knowledge would be replaced by something else that would be fostered by what has become the modern schooling system. "We must recognize our compensations— the increase in toleration, in breadth of social judgment, the larger acquaintance with human nature, the sharpened alertness in reading signs of character and interpreting social situations, greater accuracy of adaptation to differing personalities." Dewey, I think, could be describing the differences between the members of the crew.

The first thing that captures my eye when I deplane at Newark Liberty International Airport is a "Free Melania" T-shirt, and I duly take a photo and send it to Juston, who does not respond. An hour later, near my hotel, I see an "organic dry cleaner" and I photograph this, too, and send it to Eric.

"Why do they need that?" he writes back to me.

"I guess they like how it sounds," I say.

As I had predicted, the references to John 3:16 are gone. All around me, people are talking nonstop and I think about Pastor Jeff's sermon, in which he said that if we memorize the scripture, it will change the way we live, and that we will be thinking about it instead of what the world wants us to think about. I think of Juston advising me at the start of harvest that my brain will become quiet in the country, and it had. In the city, it is again flooded with sights and sounds.

I'm not unique in thinking that I'm not vulnerable to the messaging of advertisements. And yet now, as I walk through New York City, I'm acutely aware that I'm in a place that wants me to think a certain way. On the subway, sandwich ads cajole me to order my food in a Seamless manner. I am to buy colorful Kate Spade bags and dresses in the company of a mariachi band. I am to have relationship goals and to have confidence in my body through the aid of a gym and in my ability to, at any moment, attract a man through sexual allure.

I feel resistant to what the city wants from me. On the one hand, I am delighted to be around so many ethnic restaurants and to eat with chopsticks and for my eyes to feast on paintings at the Frick Collection. How much I have missed this beauty! On the other hand, the complexity of offerings feels chaotic and manufactured.

Why are there all these words?

Once I am at school, I am startled by how much people complain about the food, and in front of the kitchen staff, at that. No matter how cold Bradford had been to me, neither he nor Bethany would ever have treated waitstaff like this, and the difference in manners surprises me. For me, it feels like a luxury to have a dorm room all to myself, to sleep on a bed, and to eat in a dining hall with a choice of entrées. My mother always taught me not to complain about food; she remembered starving after the war in Japan. From her I know it is entirely possible to run out of food.

In the trailer, I ate what was given to me. The pasta, bagels, sandwiches, and chips—not to mention Emily's un-turn-downable desserts—meant I put on weight quickly. Here the kitchen knows the predilections of sophisticated urbanites. There is always a lean protein entrée and a vegetarian option. The coffee can be flavored with many different kinds of milk, some of which are fat-free.

I did not realize how accustomed I had become to saying grace before a meal. Here I fill my plate with whatever I want, and then sit down and eat. There is no transition from gathering the food to eating it. The informality of it all is familiar, and it is nice to be able to eat whatever

I want and to throw away anything I can't finish. But I also miss the conviviality of the trailer, and the universal appreciation for what Emily puts together for us from Walmart. I miss that no food is ever wasted and that the boys clean their plates without complaint.

The current most frequently cited report on the future of food was published by the UN in 2017, and projects that the world population will grow from 7.3 billion to 9.7 billion by 2050. When this happens, the UN has stated that, at our current rate, we will not produce enough calories to feed everyone. The world's farmers will need to increase their output by 50 percent, and with 37 percent of the earth's surface already dedicated to food production, doubling the output of food seems difficult, without, say, converting more rainforest to farmland, which would raise a host of other environmental issues.

Not everyone has accepted the claims that the UN report makes. Some say that we already produce enough food, but that it is distributed poorly; a 2016 article in the *Guardian* by Suzanne Goldenberg calls attention to one report claiming that Americans throw away half of the produce they grow. Other journalists and science writers point out that population growth is likely to be concentrated in poorer countries, which also have less well-developed infrastructures; better transport and distribution could help eliminate hunger. When I read these articles, I find it hard to know on which side of these speculative arguments to land.

Those in favor of green policies seem to believe we won't run out of food and that we simply need to both eat better and abandon industrial farming; conversely, those who favor the science of agriculture *do* believe the predictions of a food shortage by 2050.

For example, the food journalist Mark Bittman, who has lived in both Berkeley, California, and New York City, writes:

> We can . . . preserve the earth's health, if we recognize that the industrial model of food production is neither inevitable nor desirable.
>
> That is, the kind of farming we can learn from people who still have a real relationship with the land and are focused on quality rather than yield.
>
> The best method of farming for most people is probably traditional

farming boosted by science. The best method of farming for those in highly productive agricultural societies would be farming made more intelligent and less rapacious.

When Bittman writes about people with a "real relationship with the land," I wonder exactly to what and to whom he is referring.

If I think as a city person, I do have a particular image in my head of what the ideal farm looks like. It should mirror the "Old MacDonald" image I was selling to my son, in which a farmer owns a manageable-sized piece of property and rotates crops and raises animals and uses the manure from the animals to fertilize the soil. The surplus food is sold to people in the town nearby, or perhaps carted off to the city. This is, in fact, how a certain percentage of farmers live, if they are in close proximity to a city. I have plenty of friends in both San Francisco and New York who participate in farm shares, wherein they receive a box of seasonal vegetables directly from a local farmer. But, as I've tried to stress elsewhere, this relationship to food cannot, because of the variations in land and weather, be perfectly replicated everywhere.

Sometimes I hear people refer to "monoculture" pejoratively. The implication is that a farmer in Nebraska grows only wheat because he lacks the creativity of the farmer in California who can grow a dwarf strawberry. The negative implications of monoculture always make me a little bit sad because, relatively speaking, this is actually a time of greater diversity for row crops in the Great Plains—thanks to science. But could the monoculture center of the United States become a producer of arugula? Here and there on the plains, farmers do attempt to grow produce, as I saw in Oklahoma. But in general, the growing season— the weather—is so different in the country's interior that it isn't suited for large-scale production of carrots and lettuce. There is a reason why California became the "salad bowl" of the United States.

Still, the idea that monoculture is to be equated with stupidity persists. In his lively and often fascinating book *The Third Plate*, about food and eating, celebrity chef and activist Dan Barber writes: "Cuisines did not develop from what the land offered, as is often said; they developed from what the land demanded. The Green Revolution turned this equation on its head by making diversity expensive. It empowered only a few crops. And in the process, it dumbed down cuisine." The odd thing about this statement to me is that, at least on the Great Plains, the crops *have* become more diverse. Still, I note the use of the term "dumbed down," as though the major grains we grow widely are, like a middle-class sitcom, evidence of poor taste, while spelt and emmer show class.

Note, too, Barber's take on the Green Revolution as forcing everyone—farmers included—into giving up a previous way of farming that was better. Such nostalgia sounds a lot like a yearning for a mythical Eden. And yet none of the farmers I have talked to has wanted to go back to the old yields or the old crops. From the farmer's perspective, farming has *progressed*.

In an email to me, the agronomist and writer Jayson Lusk explains: "Why do we grow so much corn, soy, and wheat in the U.S.? A primary answer is that these plants are incredibly efficient at converting solar energy and soil nutrients into calories (they're the best, really the best). Moreover, these calories are packaged in a form (seeds) that are highly storable and easily transportable—allowing the calories to be relatively easily transported to different times and to different geographic locations." Vegetables like kale or broccoli or even tomatoes are much less calorie-dense, and much more difficult to store and transport. Tomatoes need to be canned or frozen, which takes even more energy than is required to process and transport wheat across land or even oceans.

When I talk to farmers or ranchers on the plains, they say to me: "It's great to have food choice in America." They mean that it is wonderful that a person can choose to eat an all-organic or vegetarian diet if they want to, or choose to eat a conventional diet. They do not see choice of these diets as a moral act but as an expression of freedom particular to America. I am struck, when I hear this argument, by how much it sounds parallel to the way a liberal arts major will insist it is wonderful that a person can choose to believe in whatever faith appeals to them the most in America.

The great British food historian Rachel Laudan is keenly aware of the debate surrounding food and agriculture in the United States. But unlike Bittman and Barber, Laudan uses the lens of history to examine how people develop passion for and dissatisfaction about food. In *Cuisine and Empire*, Laudan demonstrates that food is always an expression of a particular culture, and of its social and religious system. It is partly for this reason that American cuisine evolved to clearly reject the elaborate meals of the English monarchy. But, perhaps more important, Laudan suggests that eating is an expression of existentialism. "Food becomes us as it is assimilated to the human body. If we are dissatisfied with the state of 'us,' then changing eating habits is a way to express that dissatisfaction." And this makes me wonder: When we are dissatisfied with the state of us, what is it exactly about the human being that makes us so unhappy?

I find it interesting that Laudan also agrees with the farmers that this is a time of unprecedented choice and quality for food—and that processing and industrialization are significant tools that have made the richness of choice possible. I tend to agree; for a person who loves eating, it is a wonderful time to eat almost anything, anywhere. It's worth noting that Laudan herself grew up on a wheat and dairy farm in England, so her perspective, even more sharply than mine, is derived from firsthand knowledge of how technology has transformed food production on the land for the better.

While I don't personally know how to reconcile all these issues—locality, variety—into a cohesive worldview, I am fairly certain now of one thing. All discussions of food and agriculture begin with the land. If we do not understand the soil and how it varies from place to place, we cannot truly understand or empathize with the farmer who grows food on that soil and what he contends with. To look only at seeds or cuisines or policies, I am now convinced, is to overintellectualize and to fall prey to biases and ideologies of which one might not even be aware—myself included. Given that so few of us understand the soil, it is not a surprise that we can't understand one another. And as for the 2050 UN report saying that we could soon run out of food, I have come to accept that this *could* happen, because it has in the past.

In his marvelous book *Dirt: The Erosion of Civilizations*, the writer and scholar David R. Montgomery points out that civilizations have repeatedly failed when the farmland—the soil—used to make food for people has eroded and ceased to be productive. "Civilizations . . . don't choose to fail. More often they falter and then decline as their soil disappears over generations. Although historians are prone to credit the end of civilizations to discrete events like climate changes, wars, or natural disasters, the effects of soil erosion on ancient societies were profound. Go look for yourself; the story is out there in the dirt." Montgomery examines the fates of the Greeks, the Sumerians, even the Romans, and points to populations rising and falling around the dirt that grew the crops to feed the people. When the soil fails, the people do too.

Humans have contended with soil erosion for centuries; our own country has battled dust storms and dust bowls, which ended the dreams of many a prospective "yeoman farmer." I have found references to the concept of crop rotation clear back to 1775, in a book titled *Hints to Gentlemen of Landed Property* by Nathaniel Kent. Crop rotation and animal husbandry have helped to restore the soil of the Great Plains, and the practice of these traditional techniques expanded because they have been blended with science through Roundup and no-till farming.

Montgomery tackles the thorny issue of how to preserve and restore soil. He favors "adding organic matter through cover cropping and not disturbing the soil through tillage." I have explored no-till and cover crops. An added element of the issue is grazing.

The standard received opinion about cows is that they overgraze pasture and are bad for the soil, but this, too, is not necessarily the case. After all, the buffalo roamed the prairie and were vital to keeping the grasslands healthy. Montgomery describes how the buffalo were part of the ecosystem. They never grazed in one place too long. After the grass was damaged from grazing, it "grew back . . . with a vengeance. . . . The secret to such resilience lay in the subterranean storehouses of carbon stockpiled in plant roots, soil organic matter, and soil life. . . . The manure and trampled organic matter left in the buffalo's wake recharged the subterranean batteries that powered regrowth."

Montgomery, then, agrees with Bittman's assertion that science combined with tradition is the best way to secure soil health, as long as this farming cocktail incorporates no-till, rotation, cover crops, and grazing. This mix of techniques can go a long way to saving, preserving, and restoring soil health. To make money, though, the farm needs to be large enough to allow for rotation, and to be able to facilitate both animals and crops. There is always the issue of sufficient rainfall to enable a farmer to grow a cover crop that he will later destroy, or put back into the earth. In humid and fertile places like California (which, for the record, irrigates) or Pennsylvania or even upstate New York, the resources are built into the earth. In highly arid areas, like my family farm, rotating is much more difficult, though not impossible. In other words, combining the best of science and tradition may go a long way toward securing soil health and toward making sure we have enough calories to feed a growing population. It may be the best way, for now, that we have to take care of everyone.

By Sunday, I miss my old farming life and want to go to church. I google "Mennonite church Bennington, Vermont." A church pops up with a service starting in twenty minutes. I am not dressed for church, but I put on my sandals, flee to my car, and head out.

As soon as I arrive at the church, I know I have made a mistake. This is not the "liberal" Mennonite church of Pastor Jeff. The girls who stand outside are dressed in plain dresses and wear white caps. Each holds a Bible. A man enters the church dressed in a black suit, and I can see his beard swishing to and fro even though I am behind him. It is as though I have traveled back in time and tintypes have sprung to life. I plan to leave, but the girls have seen me. They are surprised, but smile kindly. "Hello," they say. The boldest of the three strides over and looks me in the eye. "You are welcome," she says to me. "We love to have newcomers join us." I feel tall and bulky, a sensation I have had before, in Japan, among people who have grown up with a different diet and who are accustomed to far more physical labor than I am.

"You're sure?" I ask.

"Please," they say, holding out their hands toward the church. And so I follow.

I sit with the girls on the right-hand side of the church; men and boys are on the left. In most Mennonite churches, I am told later, the sides are reversed, but here the nursing room is on the right-hand side of the church, so this way a mother can attend to a baby in the middle of a sermon if necessary. Church lasts for two hours, and while I have plenty of notes referring to scriptures and quotes from the Bible, I am ashamed to say that nothing of the individual lessons sticks in my mind, except that among this particular group the Ordnung has decided that cell phones can be used for texting, but nothing else, and that at certain points in the service we all drop to our knees and kneel on the floor.

After the service, I am invited to lunch with the Mennonites. I learn that I have just been to a "recruiting church." It is an outpost set up to attract people—even secular people like me—to hear God's word. The couple whose home I visit was not born into the faith, but converted after leaving marketing jobs in Manhattan. The girls who first greeted me are friendly. Most work at a store in Bennington, which is also a "recruiting store." When they learn I have just come from Thomas, Oklahoma, they are delighted.

"There was a girl who used to work here who went there."

"Did you go to the Zion Amish Mennonite Church?" one of the women asks me.

"That's the Beachy Amish," someone says.

I'm surprised that I can now decipher this conversation. "No. Pleasant Hill." Then I say, "You know the names of the churches in Thomas, Oklahoma?"

"There are only so many," one of them says to me.

"We know one another."

It would have been like this during the days of settlement, I think. New Mennonites coming from Russia would have heard about their brethren and would have known who lived where in the same way that Eric started his harvesting career via his church.

At one point after lunch, they sit in a circle on a trampoline, each in a printed dress made with a different floral print but from an identical dress pattern, and laughter rises up between them. There is nary a cell phone or selfie taken. I long to join them. They make it seem so easy to be happy.

I share a car to the airport with my friends Berger and Bea; they are returning to Los Angeles after attending school with me. Bea asks me if I am a Buddhist and I say I am not comfortable with any label. She says that all the Buddhists she knows do not like to say that they are Buddhists. And then she wants to know how I feel about Buddhism versus Christianity. She was born and raised an Episcopalian, but discovered Buddhism as an adult. She insists that Buddhism is a superior religion.

I would probably have agreed with her at one point in my life. Didn't I used to go around saying that Buddhism was a superior religion, precisely because it didn't think it was a religion? It wasn't intent on conversion. But lately I have started to feel uncomfortable with this position, one I held in part because I knew it sounded good. Wasn't this entire framework—that one religion is superior to another—just another version of the Christian argument that one religion has to be right? Wasn't it Christian language?

I start to try to answer by saying that I grew up with Buddhism, so my relationship to it is different from hers. My family in Japan owns and runs a Buddhist temple, and I have spent a lot of time learning about Buddhism from Japanese Buddhists—Zen Buddhism in particular.

"You mean Buddhism to you is like Episcopalianism to me?" Bea says. But, no, this is not what I mean either.

"Let me guess," I say. "You find Christianity old-fashioned and paternalistic and the idea of the sky fairy who sees all to be ridiculous."

This is, in fact, the way she sees Christianity, and I know this because it was how I used to characterize Christianity too.

After a minute I manage to say that what makes Christianity different is that it is the religion of love. Christ made it clear that we are to love our neighbors as ourselves and that we are to feel our connection to the Holy Spirit through our hearts. I say something about how the Romans marveled that Christians would literally die out of love for an idea. But I am thinking now about my friends in Kansas, about how, despite our differences, Eric, Michael, and Juston in particular are capable of holding their hearts open to make room for me. I think of how hard I have tried to do the same.

We are silent. Then Bea says that while she understands this, Buddhism, too, emphasizes love when you get down to it. And I say I know this, but I don't think it is the same. I am not sure that Buddhism motivates people in quite the fervent way that Christianity does. There is for me still something slightly unhinged about Christian fervor. It doesn't emphasize stillness and connection. It is about making true space for others. It knowingly asks us to stretch the heart.

All of a sudden, Berger yelps. There is an ant on the loose in the car. I want to kill it, and Berger says he wants me to kill it because he does not like insects and does not want to look at the ant while he is driving. He is a native New Yorker, relocated to Santa Monica, and nature, he says, is "not my thing."

"That ant is a sentient being," Bea insists. "We should not kill it." Then Berger shouts again and I offer to kill the ant, and Bea implores me not to do so. For an hour or so, Berger screams and Bea asks us not to kill the ant. Finally, it disappears, and we conclude our trip to New

York City. Berger and Bea get off at Newark airport and I drive the car back to Hertz in Manhattan, and later I think that the poor ant is now stuck in Midtown in a rental car, bound for a new destination. But the following night, I see the ant on the twenty-fifth floor of the apartment building where I am staying. It is crawling across the cream-colored carpet, searching for its home in Vermont. And I feel a little sad for it: so close and yet so far.

Then I never see it again.

NINE

IT HAS BEEN DIFFICULT, while I've been away, to get any news from the crew about their time in Kansas. Samuel posted a few photos of a lightning storm on Instagram. I called Emily from New York City, and she told me that when she stands in the middle of the prairie, it is as though she is in an overturned bowl, so flat and vast and still is this land. Eric sounded discouraged. It rained, he said, and there wasn't much wheat to cut. Colorado will be better.

They are now 175 miles northeast of Denver, and only 10 miles from the Kansas border. They have moved from the sugary earth of Oklahoma to the High Plains, a subregion of the Great Plains. The elevation, as the name suggests, is even greater than that of the eastern part of the plains, because they are now closer to the Rocky Mountain range, and the uplift that formed it. The ground is covered with more erosion and runoff and layers of sediment deposited on the surface over time as the mountains shed their skin of rocks and gravel.

The land that would eventually become Colorado, Kansas, Nebraska, and other states was acquired from the French government in 1803, during Thomas Jefferson's presidency, as part of the Louisiana Purchase. The vast tract of mostly prairie land was subdivided into smaller and smaller pieces. Jefferson's dream was that the United States would be populated by farmers. As Jefferson wrote in "Notes on the State of Virginia," "Those who labour in the earth are the chosen people of God, if ever he had a chosen people, whose breasts he has made his peculiar deposit for substantial and genuine virtue."

Then came the transcontinental railroad—the same railroad that would one day pick up my family's wheat and take it off to cities and the coasts. As historian Jill Lepore puts it: "Between Chicago and the Pacific stood the so-called Permanent Indian Territory, the land to which Andrew Jackson had removed eastern Indians, including the Cherokees." Various treaties between 1857 and 1862 further relocated the Arapahoe, Pawnee, and Sioux from their ancestral hunting grounds in the Louisiana Purchase territory onto reservations in what would become Nebraska, Kansas, and Colorado (and other states), and thus further "clearing" the land for settlers.

The Missouri Compromise of 1820 let two states into the Union: Maine and Missouri, one a free state and the other a slave state. But in addition came the Mason-Dixon Line. North of the Mason-Dixon Line states would be free, except for Missouri, which was made an exception—this was the "compromise."

Once Kansas and Nebraska were recognized as territories, their laws allowed for citizens to vote on whether or not they would be free or slave states. Nebraska was clearly north of the Mason-Dixon Line, but Kansas lay directly west of Missouri. Couldn't an exception be made for it, too? pro-slavery activists insisted. Skirmishes broke out. Some settlers moved to Kansas expressly to campaign for or against slavery, or to make their votes and voices count. Campaigning on both sides of the issue was brutal, with reports of voter fraud that led to often-violent and sometimes fatal clashes known collectively as Bleeding Kansas. When I read the paper today, or scroll through social media and hear people insist that they plan to move to red or blue states to make a region more purple, or when people passionately insist on election recounts, I remember that the United States went through such tensions before.

Kansas entered the Union in 1861 as a free state. The South retaliated, withdrawing from the Union and setting off the Civil War. President Lincoln had been trying to pass the Homestead Act for some time, in part to ensure an end to the institution of slavery; individual farmers were not likely to bring slaves with them, but wealthy plantation owners would. Once the Southern states, which had rejected previous incarnations of the Homestead Act, had seceded from the Union and thus could not vote, the Homestead Act passed easily. So it was that the first claim for 160 acres was staked near the town of Beatrice, in eastern Nebraska. The Civil War ended in 1865, and in 1867, Nebraska, and all the states that followed, entered the Union as free states.

Early one morning I fly from New York to Denver to join back up with Eric and his crew. I get a new rental car, a passenger car this time, and drive north to Holyoke, Colorado, which is yet another variation on a theme: a town of about two thousand people, mostly devoted to farming. I pass a blue Wolgemuth truck hauling grain. Luther is driving but he doesn't see me. The crew must be cutting. My heart quickens with gladness.

I cross the railroad tracks to the north of town. There is a sign just outside the trailer park that reads: "Welcome harvesters!" I see them up ahead: two silver trailers and the newer one I have shared with Bethany. There are only a few other trailers in the lot. I don't know if this is because we are early or because the town is overly optimistic about the number of harvesters who will eventually arrive.

I am in time for lunch and the crew is assembling at Emily and Eric's trailer. Eric and Emily greet me warmly, as does Michael, but Juston seems somber. I feel as though there is a pane of glass separating me from everyone. It is as if I'm in one of those science fiction movies in an air lock, pounding on the window and asking to be let in where the oxygen is. I want to say: *But I just defended Christianity and your way of life and the guns and everything from those liberals back east!*

After lunch, I go into the trailer and drop my things. It is tidier than it was before I left. My way, despite my Anabaptist roots, is to live in a "creative mess." I like the movement of books and pieces of papers and projects. Bethany is not like this. Bethany comes in. "Hey," she says.

"Hello!" I say. "How are you?"

"Fine." But her disappointment is entirely unmasked.

Eventually, Juston is forthright, confirming my fears. We are riding in his wheat truck and he tells me that while I was gone, the "girls' trailer" had become a haven for Bethany, Bradford, and Samuel. Bethany and Samuel, he says, sighing, deny that they are dating, but they must be. And not that anything untoward is going on in the trailer, but now that I'm back, it will no longer be their place of privacy. "I hope that with time, everyone will readjust," Juston says.

The wheat here plays with the light in a way it did not in Texas, Oklahoma, and Kansas. It looks so pale, as if the land has been bleached. Eric sees me studying the peculiar color of the fields and tells me that this is white wheat. "We're cutting it for Papa John's," he says.

"You know Papa John's?" Michael asks. I say that I don't, and he nods. Of course I don't.

The men say that they have "added 130 acres to cut," which means the farmer has given them more work. At lunch, Eric and Bradford talk like equals, trying to decide in what order to cut the fields. They speak in the laconic, factual style of pilots. It is the stripped-down language of men. I make a note of this, and when Juston and Michael see me writing, they want to know what I've put in the notebook. So I tell them and they ask me what "laconic" means.

"It means 'using few words,'" I say.

"I don't know, Marie," Michael says. "Just stick to the facts. Don't get too fancy."

"I am writing facts," I say. "But this can't be like some term paper."

Eric is driving the experimental combine, which he finds finicky. To be truly self-driving, the combine will need to adjust to the land and to the density of the crop it is cutting. So far, the camera is unable to identify the difference between wheat and small bits of weeds. This is crucial, because a human operator will adjust the headers and how they grind the material to make sure the hopper gets filled only with wheat, or as much as possible. Corn is big enough for the camera to distinguish it from chaff; wheat is still too fine.

Eric watches the clouds while we eat lunch. "I said they were going to grow and pile," he says. We watch the clouds stack and build and move over us like a shelf.

Eric hurriedly finishes his lunch and says something privately to the Case engineer, which I assume generally conveys his wish to get the grain out of the field as quickly as possible. In other words, he wants to drive the combine and doesn't want to stop to let the engineer tinker with the settings. The engineer nods and retreats to his pickup. Samuel runs to his truck and begins to follow Eric's combine; they are leaving the grain cart out of the process. For a while they continue like this, pushing hard, and the other combine operators, too, head into the field. I sit with Juston in his truck.

But the clouds continue to form. To the west I see strong lightning in vertical lines. They are bright white and it appears there will be no way to avoid the rain. Then the wall fractures and the clouds break up. The wind is blowing the wheat hard. Over the CB radio, Bethany says the elevator reports that hail is coming.

It begins to rain and all the combines race to unload whatever they have into the truck, and then the crew tarps the truck to try to keep the grain dry. Eric moves into a pickup and I follow him. He sits in the driver's seat and reads the clouds, looking for a break. Finally, he texts the farmer to say that we are twenty-five acres short and he doesn't think there will be hail.

"Can you check the radar?" he asks me.

I look. So far nothing appears to be heading for us tomorrow. We linger, hoping for a miracle, but the rain does not stop. We watch bold lightning, and at one point a sharp rainbow arches over the sky. Michael parks just beneath it. The other trucks line up one by one beside him, where the stubble is hard. We go to pick them up.

Michael slides into the pickup and tells me he looked up "laconic." "It says 'few words to the point of rude.'"

I suggest that "laconic" is a poetic word.

Juston starts arguing with me. "I don't think Eric is laconic."

"He doesn't use a lot of words," I say.

"That's 'terse.'"

"'Terse' is 'rude,'" I say.

"It's really important that you don't exaggerate in the book," Michael says.

Bradford has everyone else with him in the other pickup and he drives off, and we drive off too.

Our campsite is by a racetrack and that night there is a stock car race. When we return to the park, the air is already thick with the smell of diesel and the crew tells me it will only get worse. The noise will get worse too.

"You ever been to one?" Eric asks me. "It's a white trash thing."

I haven't, of course.

"It's dusty," Eric says. "And loud."

Emily, Juston, and Michael are not going. "Are you going?" I ask Eric. I am determined to show that I am enthusiastic about everything. It's the only way I can think of for the crew to relax around me.

"I'm thinking about it," Eric says.

We eat dinner in the trailer.

I tell them about the UN report predicting a food shortage by 2050. I bring up the fact that we have cultivated 37 percent of the planet and that unless we deforest the planet, there will not be enough arable land for us to grow all our food. Then I say that we may have to find food from another source. Our forefathers came here, for example, and used this land to develop more food for a growing population. We might need to go to another planet one day! I remind everyone that Eric had brought up Mars, back in Texas. Then I want to know if God could go to Mars and how our concept of God would change once we got there.

Eric furrows his brow and appears to be considering my question.

Bradford tries hard not to laugh.

Michael is the first to speak. "So you want us to manipulate time in order to go to other planets, and if that's true, aren't you trying to be like God, and isn't that wrong? Anyway, man isn't going to be around for too much longer, because the end of the world is coming."

"Why would we manipulate time?" Juston asks, a little irritated. "We could get to Mars."

Then someone mentions *Interstellar*, one of Eric's favorite films, about a group of plucky survivalists trying to address the dust storms and blights that have affected the earth's agricultural supply and hence precipitated a food shortage. Only, in *Interstellar*, the group, under the leadership of Matthew McConaughey's character, doesn't go to Mars, but to a distant yet habitable planet accessed through a wormhole.

"We could go to Mars. We could start there," I say.

"And how long would it take?" Amos asks.

"I always read that the estimated travel time is nine months. We would need to make the planet habitable, but that would be possible. What does the Bible say about other planets?" I ask.

I know that this entire line of questioning is bizarre. I can't stop myself. This is how things go when I know I am not fitting in. I am two people: obsequious me and rebellious me.

Emily remembers something in the Bible about "another flock." She quotes from John: "'I have other sheep, too, that are not in this sheepfold. I must bring them also. They will listen to my voice, and there will be one flock and one shepherd.' Isn't that how the Mormons justify their religion? They—" she breaks off when Eric interrupts.

"That's not other *planets*."

"But that's how they try to justify Jesus showing up in America," she protests.

"Jesus showed up in America?" I ask.

"That's a Mormon thing," Eric says.

"What do you mean?"

Eric purses his lips. He does this when he has to take more time to explain something than he is accustomed to, because there are so many pieces of information to engage and he can't rely on pliers to fix the situation. "The Mormons believe that Jesus was here in the New World. And there's something about how he taught the people who were here . . ."

"The Native Americans," Emily says.

"Well, they say it's the Indians, but I don't know. Anyway, they justify that through this one line of scripture about other sheep in other places. But I don't know that the Gospel was talking about other planets."

Everyone is quiet for a minute. And then Samuel says: "We needed God to get to the New World."

"How could we go without faith?" Eric smiles broadly.

The crew pounces on the topic now. All at the same time, they tell me that the Bible made it clear that God created the heavens and our world. He created everything. It stands to reason that he created all the other planets, too, including the ones we would one day inhabit.

Eric jokes that if we go to Mars, he will be sure to take Luther, because Luther doesn't take up too much room and can communicate with most any machine. The crew laughs.

Then Amos becomes impassioned, and his face is overtaken with emotion and he's ruddy and flushed and his brow is pinched so he almost looks on the brink of pain. And I see that he is there. He is there on Mars with Luther and the farming equipment, trying to raise food for humanity. He announces that God is so much greater than just Mars, so of course God would be with us. He created the universe. People think that man is equal to God and he is not. God would be there with us. "I think people are greedy, and want too much and this is partly why we don't have enough food. If we weren't so greedy, we wouldn't run out of food in the first place!"

"Won't God destroy the planet first?" Michael asks.

"No," I say. "I think that someone like Eric Wolgemuth would want to go wherever he could go next, and that would be outer space."

Eric agrees. "There is no more world to discover. No more West to uncover. We need to go out and up into space next, and our faith will guide us and take us there."

"How will our prayers change?" I ask.

Eric thinks about it. "About the same," he says. "'Give us safe passage. Help us get this part.'"

"Except it'll take the parts longer to get to Mars," Samuel says. "Nine months for delivery."

"If the part's even been manufactured," Amos adds.

For a moment, everyone is deflated.

Then Samuel suggests that a 3-D printer might come in handy, and Amos remembers having seen one that was used to make parts. It would be like that out there on Mars: We would need a new bolt, and Luther would make one with the 3-D printer, and then we wouldn't have to wait for Earth to send replacements. And we wouldn't need engineers. We would need only Luther and Bradford and Samuel, and everything that would break would be fixed.

Then the crew is quiet and we—most of us—sit there for a while and we are not in a trailer in Colorado, waiting for the wheat to dry and looking forward to a white trash car race. We are on Mars, attempting to save humanity.

But not everyone is there. I can see that Michael doesn't find this idea enticing. Nor does Bradford.

Michael catches me outside the trailer when dinner is over. He tells me, "Revelation is coming." He tells me that humans will not last much longer, because God is coming, and there is no reason to go to Mars or anywhere else or to worry about increasing the food supply, because God will come and judge us and Earth will not last.

It is terrible to hear this. I thought we were ready to risk our safety for the chance to save humanity from hunger. I can't believe he means what he says. It must be some other voice that has been planted in him, or some recording he has heard somewhere that he parrots back to me now. *If you memorize the scripture, then it is with you. If you memorize it, it changes the way you live, because that is what you are thinking about instead of what the world wants you to think.*

How can someone so young and full of promise believe in what is essentially a death wish? I wonder how adults could teach this to their children. As a parent, I feel an essential responsibility to leave the world more intact for my child and other young people than it was for me. What Michael says enrages me. Then the rage consumes me and I feel it take over my entire body like a storm and I want to double over from grief because of this lie Michael has been told. *Don't believe this,* I want to say.

But I don't say it. And so, because I am a coward at this moment, I ask instead: "Are you going to the racetrack?"

"No." He grins. "I'm gonna maybe see if Juston wants to play basketball."

"But . . ."

"It's loud, Marie. And it smells terrible. You'll see." He whirls around and walks away then, that wiry, tense frame gliding off toward the boys' trailer. I can't read his mood.

Eric comes out of his trailer and smiles at me. "Wanna go?" He tilts his head toward the stadium, which is already roaring and buzzing with engines. So I follow.

It is terrifically loud in the stadium. We climb the stairs to the bleachers and a sign directs us to go right if we want beer and left if we don't. We sit on the left.

In the combine, Juston is listening to a sermon he gave when he was seventeen. This was before he left for Germany. I remember this period. Back then, Emily glowed when she talked about Juston. She was soft and almost flustered when he played cello and competed in volleyball, as though she couldn't quite believe how her small child had turned into this charismatic, sensitive, and powerful young man.

Juston's sermon is called "Don't Try So Hard." His voice is young and strong, and bears a heavier Lancaster County accent than he has now. I hear it particularly around the letter "o." He sounds approachable, both confident and casual. He begins by talking about hanging out at home and wondering what he will say today in his preaching, just like Pastor Craig talked about hanging out at home when he spoke at Life.Church. And then Juston tells us how God gave him an answer. Juston injects hesitation in just the right places. He says: "As I was eating my peas I prayed to God, 'God, give me something . . . to say.' And as soon as I said that, I got an instant reply in my thoughts . . . God said, 'You don't know what you're going to say, because you're not going to say anything.'" And from there, Juston unpacks that puzzle of a statement, relating it to volleyball and the perils of trying too hard, and how Christians could be divided into those who believe in relying only on themselves and those who believe in relying only on God's help.

"The thing is," Juston tells me as we listen, "even when I was saying all this, I was full of doubt. I just hid my doubt, because I thought doubt was a sin."

The sermon is so articulate, I can see why everyone expected Juston to be a pastor. He is a good and clear writer, and a persuasive speaker. He is handsome, like many of the pastors I have seen in the small churches and megachurches we have attended across the country. He plays sports. He is kind to children and he can read social cues. He even occasionally advises Eric on fashion choices, sending his father back into the trailer to change when a shirt doesn't flatter Eric's complexion. Juston is not, as he often insists to me, a particularly good farmer.

But Juston has turned his back on being a pastor. He doesn't know what to do. In the city, there are many places for lost young men like him. Richard Sennett says: "A city is a human settlement where strangers are likely to meet." Juston would be welcome in the city. I feel sure of this because it was in the city that I, a misfit, found comfort.

Juston tells me: "Doubt used to make me sick. Science used to freak me out because it undermines the scripture."

"Why would that scare you?"

"They teach us that the Bible is inerrant. And if it's inerrant, it directly contradicts what we have learned in science. Then that means the Bible isn't inerrant. And if our entire concept of God is based on what is in the Bible, then nothing is certain. Now I believe science will find what it will."

"Does science still scare you?"

He pauses. "Certainty," he says again. "I am talking about certainty."

"What is certainty?" I ask.

There is a longer pause this time. Then Juston tells me a story about his brother, Winston. Juston says that when Winston was a junior in high school, he was cut from the basketball team. It had been heartbreaking for him, but he stoically went to see the school games. And as he did this, he ended up spending a lot of time sitting in the bleachers and talking to a lovely girl named Amanda.

His senior year, Winston made the varsity team, and by then he had spent enough time with Amanda that the relationship was serious. Winston had come to believe that the reason he had not made the team in his junior year was because God had wanted him to meet Amanda. "That's certainty," Juston says.

Over the CB, Eric's voice interrupts: "I hope the wheat in Nebraska looks this good. If it does, I'll eat my hat."

Juston laughs and nods at the same time, as though to say: *Yes. That's my dad.*

"When did you realize you had doubt?" I ask.

He gives me a tiny smile. It's a weird smile, somewhere between rueful and relieved, as if he's been waiting for me to ask. "You always have doubt, Marie."

"And you don't want to lose God completely." I say this as fact.

"I don't want to lose *certainty*," he says. "Some days I'm not sure about God or the Bible or any of it."

"Maybe the image of God just changes?"

"Some people have written that." He smiles sadly again. "But I don't know. What I hope is that there is a truth. And that the truth is good."

Is the earth the center of the universe? Is the sun the center of the world? Is the earth round? Always there is someone with the niggling suspicion that all is not as we have been taught. Our "progress" as a civilization is bound up with great doubters.

Doubt also appears in the Bible. Abraham doubts that his wife, Sarah, can have children, considering that he is ninety-nine and she is ninety. Jesus gets asked a lot if he is really the son of God. After his crucifixion, all of Jesus's apostles come to believe he has arisen, except for Thomas; hence the term "doubting Thomas." In the New Testament, when Thomas finally sees the newly arisen Christ, he touches the holes in Jesus's hands and says: "My Lord and my God!"

Then Jesus says: "Because you have seen me, you have believed; blessed are those who have not seen and yet have believed."

There is supposed to be a difference between Thomas and the others, because they believed without having to touch the wounds. That is, they believed by faith alone, whereas Thomas needed *proof.* "Faith is confidence in what we hope for and assurance about what we do not see."

But what if John is unnecessarily critical of Thomas? Maybe this little dig at Thomas is intentional, because John wants to cover up something that Thomas might otherwise have tried to tell us if he had been writing the story. The scholar Elaine Pagels, in her groundbreaking work *The Gnostic Gospels,* proposes as much.

In AD 180, a little over a century after Jesus died, the bishop Irenaeus declared that all Gospels but Matthew, Mark, Luke, and John were "heretical." Most people today know of only those Gospels, but there were in fact other documents floating around, purporting to be "Christian," and one of these was said to be written by Thomas. Aside from a few fragments discovered in the eighteenth and nineteenth centuries, the Gospel of Thomas might have remained unknown to us and Thomas himself stuck with the label of "doubting" for all eternity. But in 1945, an Egyptian farmer found a cache of papers inside an urn buried in the Egyptian desert. We call these the Nag Hammadi Library, after the city closest to the site of the recovered documents. There were thirteen scrolls (there were originally many more, but the others were burned for kindling by the farmer's mother), and they have been at the center of biblical scholarship and political struggles ever since they were identified. The Gnostic Gospels make up the majority of the texts in the scrolls, and the remainder are related Christian texts.

"Gnosis" is a cognate of the English verb "to know," and as a school of thought, gnosticism had to do with direct experience, and, more metaphorically, with releasing the spark of the divine that lies inherent in every human being. Because the teachings of gnosticism differ slightly from those of the Old Testament, they have long been considered heretical, and their rediscovery was a cause of alarm for some who remain committed to a more orthodox interpretation of the Bible and of what Jesus taught.

In her accessible account of these Gnostic Gospels, Pagels points out that the Gospel of Thomas may include the earliest sayings of Jesus—even earlier than those of Matthew, Mark, Luke, and John. Perhaps what Thomas has to say should have more authority and not less. Thomas, for example, doesn't claim that salvation will come to us through accepting Jesus's resurrection. While Jesus's life may go on, it is not because his body rose from the dead. He is accessible to his followers through visions and in ecstatic states—precisely the same way he is accessible to us today. He is, in other words, available to us if we turn inward.

Here is one of Pagels's favorite lines from the Gospel of Thomas: "If you bring forth what is within you, what you bring forth will save you. If you do not bring forth what is within you, what you do not bring forth will destroy you." It is a line that to Pagels suggests the perfume of Buddhism, and I find this too. It is what the Buddha might have meant when he said that all beings could become awakened if they followed the sacred teachings of the Buddha on the Eightfold Path.

Some scientists say that our capacity for doubt is hardwired. The biology of doubt is relatively new as a field of study, but certain patterns have been recognized. Our first impulse when we are given information is to believe it. And then we assess it, and it is in this second stage of receiving information—the assessing part—that doubt raises its head; we use doubt to test out System 1. The niggling voice of doubt isn't the devil but a hardwired human tendency to look for a flaw in any kind of architecture. Framed this way, I wonder if another term for "doubt" might not be "intellectual curiosity." Scientists claim to have identified the region of the brain where doubt happens: the prefrontal cortex, the top part of our brain that helps us make decisions, expresses our personality, and guides us through social settings. More specifically, doubt happens in the ventromedial prefrontal cortex, the part of the brain under the brow. It is here that the brain "tags" a suspect idea as false, thus giving rise to doubt.

A writer friend once said to me that in intimacy with another person we build a world. When we lose that person—when they leave us—we lose that beautiful world. This is why breakups can be so devastating and why the death of a beloved is so shattering. It must be like this for someone raised to believe that the house in which they live—the house of God—is stable, only to start to see it as only a mirage. A simulator. How terrifying it is to doubt, to risk losing the entire world.

PART THREE

TEN

WE ARE GOING TO NEBRASKA, and I am hoping that there the tensions in the crew will ease. If it were not for Nebraska and my land there, we would not know one another. It should be the place that brings us all back together.

The colors change as we drive. It's as if the pane of glass through which the sun has been shining has become more clear, and the blue sky pales accordingly and the wheat brightens from amber to light gold. The air smells of sage, and the dry earth is covered with a spread of pebbles. I look at my hands on the steering wheel. They seem to be aging daily. I would lose my vanity if I lived here.

There are windmills up ahead. "Someday maybe we will have windmills on *our* land," my uncle Paul used to say to me. He was forever—and with great enthusiasm—looking for ways to make our land more valuable. Some of the windmills are rotating quickly and give the impression of skinny goosenecks supporting little plastic pinwheels that turn effortlessly in the slightest breeze. Some move slowly, and others, due to the vagaries of the wind, are still.

My parents and I played games to pass the time on the road. We looked for antelope, regional birds, and the Kimball water tower. Antelope are so thin and they utilize their camouflage so well that they can be hard for an untrained eye to see, but I spot a few. I see the yellow-breasted meadowlarks sitting on barbed wire fences. When I see these things, I am filled with joy and longing for the secluded comfort of being with my parents, who loved me. Perhaps going home is the same thing as the search for shalom—for the way things are supposed to be.

Abandoned equipment is everywhere. The carcasses of dozens of combines, plows, and tractors and the occasional midcentury automobile sit rusting and abandoned in fields. They are not even salvaged for scrap metal, an indication of the difficulty involved in getting rid of even one machine, let alone recycling it. It should tell you something about me that when I see all this, I am filled not with sadness but with a nostalgic relief that the objects are still there from the year before. Once we turn off the interstate, we also pass the skeletons of abandoned pioneer homes, the windows broken and the paint chipped.

Somewhere in Nebraska, I spot the first missile silo. Most are set in squat gravel-covered areas bordered by a chain-link fence and labeled with a letter and number, like "E7" or "G4." The Air Force has a base in nearby Cheyenne, Wyoming, partly to maintain the two hundred or so Minuteman missiles interspersed in these fields of wheat. It was a source of great excitement for me as a child whenever we came upon a caravan of armored cars crawling down a country road, or encountered stoic military men in town at the Dairy Queen, lining up to buy ice cream.

Once, my father and I passed an elongated trailer hoisted vertically to deposit a freshly mended missile into its underground silo. But even this did not prepare me for what I saw last fall, when I traveled to the farm to see the planting.

The Knowells family is now in its third generation of farmers who help us work the land. As a child, I often heard the phone ring at 6 a.m., and my father would spring to answer it. "Some farmer," he would say to us at breakfast after my mother and I finally got out of bed, an hour later. That farmer was usually Ray Knowells. His daughter Caroline has become my friend; she met her husband, Caleb, while she was on a harvest crew, as I am, only Caroline knew how to drive a wheat truck. The two of them married and will take over her family's farm once her father passes.

Caroline had texted me directions. I was to drive sixteen miles west from the Knowellses' homestead, then turn south. The county road would do a "correction," a jag in the road that accounts for the curvature of the earth. At the correction, the road would turn west, then south. I was to keep going for a mile. My landmarks were the fertilizer and grain trucks. "Then you'll know you're at the Homeplace," she said. "Where your family had its first homestead. Be sure you set your odometer."

For fifteen miles I was in the country by myself—a lone car. But when I made the correction, I saw an odd shape in the sky. It was a helicopter with something sticking out of the side.

The traffic must be terrible if the helicopter is circling the intersection, I thought.

I slowed down and navigated the remaining turns. My heart had started to thump. This was obviously no traffic helicopter. I pulled my coat over the top of the camera case to hide it. Then I saw the armored cars, the navy blue trucks, and the boys with rifles.

There were men everywhere and I was, as far as I could tell, the only woman for miles. Each intersection on the dirt roads was a checkpoint, flanked by at least six vehicles parked on the corners, with boys in trucks or standing outside. I drove slowly. I tried to do the farmer greeting, lifting up two fingers from the steering wheel and coordinating this casual move with a nod.

I passed a missile silo. By now the helicopter was circling over me, and the scope was examining the inside of my Camry. The missile silo was swamped with military vehicles, too numerous to count, and the surface crawled with men in some kind of orchestrated activity.

I checked my odometer. I had a mile to go, and by my calculations, the Homeplace would not be on a corner or at an intersection. This should mean there would not be extra room on the road for the trucks and tanks and men to park, and I would be on my own. But when I got to where my odometer said I needed to turn, there were, in fact, trucks on both sides of the road. I saw my landmarks—the fertilizer and grain trucks sitting on a field of stubble. The tractor was nowhere to be seen. I turned off the dirt road and onto the field. A boy waved to me—a half-hearted *Do not enter* wave. I smiled as broadly as I could. There had been so much in the news lately about Black Lives Matter. I was not black. But I also knew that the minute I got out of the car and the boys saw my face, it would be clear that I did not belong.

"Hello!" I said when I exited the car.

"Are you supposed to be here?"

"This is my land." At least I thought it was my land. I had followed Caroline's directions correctly, but every plot of land looked exactly the same to me. Perhaps it was not my land. Perhaps this was someone else's fertilizer truck.

"There's no one here," he said to me. I thought perhaps he was saying this because I clearly looked out of place and must have come only to meet someone who did belong.

"Oh, she's probably just over the hill." I laughed. "Planting." I hoped she was over the hill. If I made my way around to the trucks, I would be able to make out the logo of the farm on their sides, and then I would know if this was indeed the Knowellses' equipment and the correct place to be. But there were no names on the trucks. It was possible that these were not the Knowellses' trucks at all. They could, in fact, be any farmer's trucks, abandoned in a field, while the farmer was off in town, or perhaps over the hill. I was filled with doubt.

"You sure you are supposed to be here?"

"Yes."

"There's no one here."

"They will be coming soon."

"We've been here for hours. There's been no one."

"Where you from?" I smiled.

"New York. Upstate."

"It's a little different here, isn't it?"

"I'm telling you." Then he was back on the subject of our conversation. "There's been no one here for hours."

"They'll be coming," I said, feeling ashamed for having tried to flirt with someone half my age, as though this could defuse our situation. If, in fact, I was in a situation. I was not, after all, doing anything wrong. The farmland—if this was my farmland—was mine, I'd been told, and not the property of the US government, though the roads were lined with armored cars and trucks. There were so many men, each with a gun, and then there was me. If this situation escalated, it hardly mattered if I was right.

We went on like this, discussing whether or not I had a right to be on the land, or if anyone was indeed ever going to come over the hill. The boys continued to stand by me, repeating the same line of inquiry, and I hoped that this particular parcel of land was indeed mine and that I had followed Caroline's directions correctly. The helicopter kept circling overhead. And then, when the doubt started to truly infiltrate my body, when I began to tell myself that I was wrong and this was not my land and I was in the wrong place . . . there was a rumble. Over the low hillside, a tractor clawed its way across the earth, rising like a monster out of the vale. The tractor came down the side of the hill and the boys backed away respectfully. As impressive as their machinery might be, they were no match for the mighty John Deere.

The tractor paused. Behind it, two giant wings unfolded and began to stretch out and flatten against the earth. The tractor rolled to the south, then stopped, and the door opened. I had never in my life been so happy to see another human being.

It was Caroline. She was in her forties, and has beautiful, striking features: strong forehead, nose, and full lips. "Sorry!" I heard her yell as loud as she could over the equipment. I bounded to the cab of the tractor and climbed inside.

"Sorry to make you wait. I was planting on the other side of the rise. Did they bother you?" She gestured at the boys with her chin, her hands busy controlling the tractor.

"There's a helicopter," I said lamely. I felt very small and foolish.

"Ridiculous. See they have that scope trained on us? They're just boys."

"They kept asking me if I was supposed to be here."

"Bored, that's all. Take photos if you want. We're not doing anything wrong. There's a hotline we can call if they act up. Plus, they always call us afterward to make sure the boys behaved. We'll file a report if they don't and they all know that."

Off we went to plant the year's wheat on the Homeplace. My land. My home.

Old Highway 71 turns into South Chestnut Street once you reach Kimball and then runs straight through town and right past my grandmother's house. When I was a child and I was bored, I would sit on the stoop and look for the wheat trucks taking our grain down to our bins, located near the railroad tracks on the other side of town. I memorized their marking; trucks were smaller then, and there were many more of them, and I had to pay attention to find our custom crew. But the drivers were often looking for me as they coasted down the hill into town, and they waved or honked when they saw me.

Occasionally I was sent on an errand down "to the bins," where the Quonset hut still stands. The trucks dumped the wheat at the bins, and we stored it there until the price of wheat was high enough for us to sell, or until we simply needed the cash. Then one of the Knowellses would unload the wheat into their own truck and take it to the cooperative elevator a short distance away. When I went to the bins as a child, often it was my father or cousin overseeing the dumping, logging how much wheat we were getting. We knew the amount because the truck was weighed at the elevator before returning to us; the driver had paperwork that showed both his full and empty weights and, given the family love of math, you can imagine the spreadsheets all the data generated. The presence of all these men—including men I did not know—made me shy as a child. Still, it was always an honor to be asked to deliver their lunch, usually a sandwich, very often made with roast beef my grandmother had cooked herself, and a bag of her signature chocolate mint surprise cookies.

My grandmother's house was the grandest in town, with three stories and a basement, French doors, and objects collected from her travels all around the world. It is still the most impressive house in town. Constructed of brick in 1921, the house has heavy eyebrow windows. When I learned the term "eyebrow windows" as a child, I always pictured the attic as a head on a body, looking out at the town through the uppermost windows. It is a house with a grand soul. For years I dreamed of this house—always the same dream: there was a box of letters hidden inside and my grandmother wanted me to find them. She was dead or dying in those dreams, but roused herself to talk to me. I would go into the grand entry hallway and climb the maple staircase to the second floor, where the bedrooms were. In the beginning, she rose from her bed to greet me, but as time went on, I had to go to her room, and I would find her, powdery white, lying on her pale blue comforter, waiting for me.

"Go into your father's room," she always instructed. "There are letters inside his desk. They were forgotten and I want you to have them."

As time went by, the dream changed slightly and I would see only her pale ghost gesturing to my father's childhood room. And then the ghost disappeared and it was a nurse who would greet me. "Your grandmother cannot see you right now," the nurse would say. "But you know you need to retrieve the letters." I always woke with anxiety: we, her family, had forgotten something valuable in Nebraska.

Over the decades, the house in the dream deteriorated. It started sinking into the ground and I had to dig down to reach it. The rooms were still there, but they were moldy. The nurse was gone and I had to go underground to find the entrance to the house before climbing the rotting staircase, alone, to retrieve the papers.

Then one day, very recently, the house was completely restored in my dream. I opened the door and went inside. Instead of climbing the stairs, I went down into the basement, and there was a man there with a pair of pliers attached to his belt.

"Who are you?" I asked.

"I live here now," he said. "And I'll be taking care of the house."

The house is my own self, a therapist told me. I had restored it. Only now it was not my grandmother living inside the house, or even her ghost; it was a farmer.

My grandmother's house was the structure on which everyone in my father's family imprinted, and it taught us what to value and how to live. We would have books, we would travel, and we would collect art, with a particular emphasis on pieces that were made by hand and reflected some aspect of folk religion. At the bottom of the stairwell to the cellar, for instance, were terrifying masks from Indonesia that looked like demons to me. I was scared of the basement as a child. In the foyer, my grandmother had hung a massive teardrop-shaped lattice chandelier that she had carried back with her from Morrocco; the floor was swaddled in a silk rug that smoldered in shades of rust. She arranged tours for visitors, and it was not uncommon for neighborhood children whom I met in the park or at the pool to ask, upon learning who I was, if they might be allowed to come over to see "the things from around the world."

My grandmother's home in Nebraska was an oasis representing all I wanted to be—a grand humanist interested in everything. When people ask me if I experienced racism in my family, I always say no and think of my grandmother. The truth is she favored me and perhaps spoiled me with attention, and postcards from abroad, and the gift of books. She loved that I was bilingual and that my eye would always be turned outward to other countries and cultures to which I would have special access because of my appearance.

When I was twelve, and knew my grandmother was thinking of selling her home, I tried to devise a way to dissuade her. One afternoon, potential buyers were coming for a visit. I threaded a rope from the second floor through the laundry chute down to the basement. At the end of the rope, I hung a bedsheet, and at the opportune moment, when my grandmother was giving her tour of the basement, I began, with one hand, to play a chromatic scale on the small Casio synthesizer a relative had given me in Japan, and with the other, I pulled on the rope to spring my "ghost" to life. Later I was scolded. But she did not sell her home that year, or for many years after. In college, I was given a free ticket to anywhere in the US when I signed up for my first American Express card; I went to see my grandmother. We spent my spring break together discussing the Brontës, eating tangerine sherbet, and driving across the prairie, pretending we were on the Yorkshire moor.

My father had not intended to leave me the farm. He said he hated the farm. He hated going to harvest and being with the family. He hated that he had never found a way to be a successful artist and make money and that he had remained dependent on the farm and the land.

"Not true," Eric told me. "He loved farming."

On the way to harvest, my mother always asked my father to stop for a few minutes so she could collect bouquets of wildflowers. Along with the stops for gasoline or the toilet, the wildflowers were the only reason we ever paused by the rest stop on the otherwise Nebraska-or-bust drive to the farm. My mother always took the wildflowers to the family cemetery, which, as in all prairie towns, is located near the town center. She gave everyone a bouquet, a practice my grandmother admired.

"I don't like store-bought bouquets," she told my mother. "But I like your wildflowers. They are perfect." My mother poured water over the tombstones, as was the custom in Japan. The souls of the dead are thirsty, my mother would say, and my grandmother loved this too—loved that this thoughtful gesture had been transported from Japan to Nebraska.

Uncle Paul wanted my father buried here in Kimball. He wanted to visit my father every harvest, but I would not let my uncle have the ashes. I still remembered my father telling me that he hated the farm and did not intend to leave it to me when he died. I did, however, order a tombstone to be put in the family plot. Because my father had served in the military, we were eligible for a US Army headstone. When I went through the process of filing the papers, I was surprised to see the number of options available for my father's religion. Depending on the religion of the deceased, they got a special little icon: a cross, a crescent, and so forth.

I chose the icon for "humanist" because it showed a human form, arms reaching up as though to embrace the vastness of space and possibility. My father had been an Episcopalian, but I knew he wasn't truly a Christian. We had always talked about everything, including what he believed about God, and I knew he had profoundly intricate spiritual beliefs about the collective unconscious, but what icon could I choose for Jungian psychology?

The headstone never arrived and I have not wanted to investigate what happened to it; I do not want to expend emotional energy tracking down his headstone as if it is a lost UPS package. Still, whenever I visit the graveyard, I pour water over the spot where the tombstone is supposed to be. The rest of them are all buried here, our Mockett and Markley pioneers. All my family and their bones rest here.

Now the caravan rumbles through town, passes the house, then turns east for the RV park. I continue on, past the family bins and bunkhouse, which I will visit later, to the cemetery south of town.

I park the car and tread gingerly over the freshly clipped grass to find my grandmother's tombstone, which reads: "The sun also ariseth." It feels important to do this correctly for my grandmother. Just as I am unscrewing the cap on my water bottle so I can empty the contents onto her stone, I hear a voice: "Well, hello!"

I look up. It is the lawn mower man come to talk to me. He is red-headed and portly and wearing a dirty white T-shirt.

"Yes?"

"I can see you're from out of town and I just wanted to see how you felt about the world. I've been thinking that Trump is like George Bush, with no capacity to apologize or admit fault."

"Is that right."

He keeps talking. "You know, my life hasn't improved under Trump. I still don't have health insurance."

"I'm sorry about that."

"How do *you* feel about things?"

Of all the predicaments that might have interrupted my reverie, my mourning—the very *cinematic* quality of my homecoming—I was not counting on the cemetery lawn mower man.

"I worry," I say.

"I just couldn't vote for Clinton."

"I've heard that a lot."

"What're you doing here anyway?"

What am I doing here? "My family. We're from here."

"Which family?"

"Mockett."

"Oh yeah." He nods. "I heard of them." And then he looks at me with a complete and guileless curiosity. I know what he is wondering. How do I, with my features, fit in here, in Kimball, Nebraska, and how can I possibly be a Mockett? I want to be good-natured about this encounter, but today I don't want to have to explain who I am and why I'm here.

But the lawn mower man wants to talk about Trump so very badly, and I am the conduit through which he wants to process the experience that is bottled up inside of him. He is not moving and he continues to talk about Trump, the tweeting, and his own loss of health care. I feel strangely naked. It's not unlike the first time I went to Japan alone and realized that without my mother's obviously Japanese presence beside me I looked Caucasian to Japanese people. It was as if my features shifted there in the direction of whiteness, and as a result my experiences in Japan changed. I could no longer count on instant insider status. Here I am now with this old pioneer name, and yet it is also very clear that I am "from out of town."

Right now, in the cemetery with my beloved dead grandmother and her carefully chosen admonition that I must, in life, remember to look at the rising sun, is not a moment when I want to be the foil against which the lawn mower man works out his doubts. I excuse myself and get into my car and go back to the trailers to find Eric. I'm sure he will soon be going to the fields, and I want to see them with him.

My grandmother left condensed biographical notes about the family for us; history was a favorite subject. From her, I know that my grandfather Mockett's family came to the United States from England by boat in the early nineteenth century on a voyage that took four months. "The family lived mostly under canvas on the deck—and the ship carried live chicken and sheep for food. They ran out of food and endured some bad storms, but somehow the mother, with five children and no comforts, and pregnant, coped. They settled in Camden, New Jersey," at first, and "they had books and newspapers when they had no food." In one of these books, an illustrated volume of *A History of India*, given to my great-grandfather Percy at age twelve, is inscribed: "Read, mark, learn and inwardly digest." Core Mockett principles by which I find myself living even today.

Percy was diagnosed with tuberculosis, almost a death sentence at the time. The dry air in the High Plains was said to provide relief, so Percy left the humid East Coast for the Oakes Home, a sanatorium in Denver. One of his duties while there was to clean the spittoons. He decided that becoming a doctor was preferable to menial labor, and then went to medical school, graduating in 1901 from the University of Denver. His fiancée, Minnie, joined him shortly thereafter. I have two of her dresses from the twenties: one a gorgeous mauve cut-velvet and silk piece that is partly motheaten, but must once have dripped over her like nectar coating the inside of a glass, and the other with a damask peacock bodice and black lace tulle skirt. When the Union Pacific guaranteed my great-grandfather twenty-five dollars a month if he practiced medicine in the pioneer town of Kimball, he accepted.

"He was proud of the fact that he could find any farmhouse in any kind of weather but once, when he was just learning the country he missed. . . . He became famous during the flu epidemic of 1918 when he kept three drivers going and did not go to bed for three weeks. He slept while they drove."

I know even more about my other great-grandfather, Melvin Markley, because he and my father were close friends. Melvin lived into his nineties, still playing the same violin I learned to play in childhood. He kept a journal from his ninety-first to his ninety-fourth birthdays, and in it are recollections of pioneer life and the days just after the Civil War. His family had been in the United States since the seventeenth century, most likely coming over from Germany to Pennsylvania and settling first in present-day Montgomery County, an area popular with Mennonites and Quakers. In the eighteenth century, they moved to Lancaster County.

Melvin contracted diphtheria when he was sixteen, and it was partly because he sought the possibility of a cure in dry air—as Percy had for his tuberculosis—that Melvin and his family left their Anabaptist enclave and moved to western Nebraska. My grandmother left a typed transcript of the original land deed in which Melvin staked his claim, in 1895, for 160 acres. The government had passed the Timber Culture Act in 1873: people who could grow trees were guaranteed free land, and my great-grandfather evidently was sure he could make some trees grow on the prairie.

An eccentric, Melvin participated in a long-distance correspondence course in fiction writing; recently, my cousin and I found a cache of dozens of his unpublished short stories. Melvin read, drew, traveled, and generally excelled at everything else. His politics were remarkably modern: in his journal he makes it clear he was for emancipation, vociferously in favor of the education of women, though against communism.

So it was that the town doctor and town dentist lived near each other, and that their children met, and that my father and his siblings were eventually born. My grandfather was a year younger than my grandmother, except on November 7: since their birthdays were a day apart, they could claim to be the same age until November 8. My grandmother told me she had detested my grandfather as a child; she'd found him silly and arrogant and had left town as quickly as possible, graduating from college and becoming a newspaper writer and editor in Portland, Oregon. But his love and stubbornness won out.

They married with the promise that they would never move back to Nebraska. My grandmother was living in the Bay Area in 1942, when her short story "Birthday for Lisbeth" was published in *Ladies' Home Journal*, and was broadcast nationally on the radio show *Manhattan at Midnight*. This was the pinnacle of her writing career, though she could not have known it; the letters she and her husband sent back home were breathless with talk of Hollywood and screenplays. But then my grandfather began to entreat his wife to return to Nebraska.

The children—my father and his brother and sister—were told they were going to Nebraska just for the summer and living in a trailer for fun. And then the family stayed. Most of my life I have been told—and believed—that the move was due to idealism. The story goes that my handsome grandfather, a dead ringer for Paul Newman, loved the values of the land and had wanted to pass on his ideals to his children. Additionally, both Percy and Melvin were aging and needed care, so in 1948, the Mocketts left California and returned to Nebraska to look after the farm.

My grandmother never wrote again.

"Want to go look at some fields?" Eric asks when I arrive at the trailers.

We leave the crew to continue unloading equipment in the lot next to the RV park and head for the country.

Eric seems more eager to see this land than any other we have visited.

I think at first this is because we have moved away from the weather and scarcity problems we faced in Texas, Oklahoma, and Kansas. But then I look at the maps of the farmland Emily has given me. The fields are divided into three colors—yellow, orange, and blue—and only in the pickup, examining the maps, do I realize that the lands are color-coded by farm: my cousin Paul's fields, mine, and Eric's. Eric is excited because the majority of this land is his. It is only in my memory that the farm still belongs in its entirety to my family.

But I know all these fields. Each conjures a memory.

"This is where they camped when they moved back from California," I say when we get to a piece of ground called the Tristate.

"I think so." Eric's excitement softens a little. "That pile of rocks there. Your grandfather made the kids collect rocks from the field. That's what your uncle told me."

At another field he says: "My first year I cut with Gleaners and I spilled some wheat right here in front of my father. But he didn't mind and we kept working together."

"I'm sure he noticed you were usually careful."

"Well, I feel bad I spilled it."

It is an idiosyncrasy of farming that people deal in primary colors all day long—the blunt colors of a red truck and a blue hat. And yet the eyes of a farmer are acutely trained to detect the microscopic differences in the shading of wheat. For all that I have heard farmers make fun of the fastidiousness of fashion, there they are—the farmers—picking out one minute detail after another in the landscape.

"See where it's dark there in the draw?" Eric points and I—with my Metropolitan Museum of Art membership—strain to see.

"I guess."

"Still green," he says with finality.

Eric shows me how the wheat is always better on the western side of a strip due to the wind; the mildest winds blow from west to east, and the wind is harsher when it comes in from the east. He steps into the field and asks me to look at the difference between the wheat on the border and the plants in the center. "Caleb did a signature planting move. He put a solid stem around the outside of the field to keep out the sol fly. It starts to chew and can't get through the exterior. Saves the rest of the crop. And," he says, grinning, "no chemicals are required to stop the insects."

Caleb, my father often told me, is an excellent farmer, and uses a variety of farming techniques to help his fields grow. Here and there we pass fields of millet seed, one of the only other crops we can currently grow here, in the most arid part of the Great Plains. Millet has been the crop we use in rotation. It is planted in the late spring in Nebraska and harvested in September, well after wheat. Disrupting planting cycles, remember, is a key way to control weeds. For a long time, we couldn't rotate wheat with any other crop; the lack of moisture gives farmers few options for crops in this region. But now there is an elevator that will accept millet, and with the rising consumer demand for millet, our options as farmers have grown a little bit.

The New Alden is the easternmost field, and this year it was planted first. Very often, harvest begins here. But not always, Eric says. Sometimes a different field can ripen first, depending on the year's wind and accumulation of rain. But this year we will start with the New Alden. I imagine the earth rotating, the sun rising in the east and shining on the New Alden first. Day after day it does this, nurturing that green wheat so it comes up and flowers and sprouts heads, and then the grain bakes. The field goes on turning, turning, turning under the rotisserie that is the sun until the grain in the New Alden ripens first.

At the Petsch, a field my cousin Paul owns, Eric grabs a fistful of wheat and says: "Paul needs to get his butt out here." Paul is still in Seattle at his job with a tech company. Paul is waiting until he is sure that harvest has started before he requests time off from work and launches into the family tradition of driving halfway across the country with a cooler full of snacks. It is hard to coordinate the timing of harvest with an office job. One year recently, I was with Eric on a field we call the Hoffmeister, and Paul was on the phone with me an hour away on Interstate 80, asking me please to wait until he arrived because he wanted to see his field cut. But no, there was a storm coming, Eric said, and we needed to get the grain out of the field. Paul arrived in his family station wagon and pulled into the field just as a massive gray oblong cloud came soaring toward us out of the west. As the air turned cold, the white clouds reached down from the sky in gray tendrils and our scalps cramped from the effect and it hailed. Eric had finished cutting in the nick of time.

"You remember the time on the Hoffmeister . . . ," I begin.

"Yeah, I remember," Eric says.

"So I should call him?"

"I would."

So I do. I call Paul and tell him that the Petsch is almost ready. In fact, all the eastern fields we have looked at so far are ready.

Paul tells me that he checked the weather on his Android. "The weatherman says there is zero chance of rain . . ."

"Eric says . . ."

". . . and I'm going to wait a few days."

"You remember that time on the Hoffmeister . . ."

"Marie," Paul says impatiently, "the weather forecast is *zero* percent chance of rain."

"I know, but . . ."

"I looked at the radar and there is no precipitation anywhere. Nothing growing out in the west."

I glance at Eric, who is tensely examining the field and the sky.

"Okay," I finally say into the phone.

On our way back into town, Eric and I stop at the Knowellses' homestead. The house, which Ray, the patriarch, built himself out of steel, is one-story and rectangular. It sits at the top of a low rise, with wide windows facing both east and west. The home is warm in the winter and traps the air-conditioned air in the summer. It has enough space for an expandable dining room table that can seat twenty. The kitchen is wide, too, with plenty of cupboards and an island in the middle to accommodate casseroles, cakes, and community food. I have stayed in this house as a guest so many times since my father died and have been so comfortable here, watching the sun set from one set of windows and rise from another.

Eric and I pull into the homestead now and he parks the pickup. Caroline, her husband, and her father, Ray, are already in the dirt-covered lot when we arrive, and they stride over—slowly—to greet us. Ray smiles with his lips pressed together and with his hands in his pockets and his pliers by his side. He has an intricately musical way of speaking, at once enunciating every word and caressing it with a lilt.

"Well, hello, Marie." His eyes sparkle when he sees me.

"Hello, Ray," I say.

Caroline ambles over in her dusty boots, and her husband, Caleb, comes over too; he's wearing a cap and mirrored sunglasses. "Hello," he says.

They both walk calmly, almost gently. But I know their movements belie their strength. My family often tells a story about the time Caroline killed a rattlesnake. In the summer, snakes thread through the fields and sun themselves on the roads; the hospital is an hour away if you get bitten. Caroline found a snake on her front lawn and decapitated it immediately with a shovel. Then she buried the head, as is the custom in the country. Birds will eat a dead snake's body but not the head, and God forbid one of her children accidentally stepped on its discarded head and punctured themselves with still-active venom.

After a few moments, Caroline looks up at the sky. "I think it might rain."

"Yep," Eric says. "I think so too."

I look up. The sky is dark gray, but I don't see how this immediately indicates rain. For a moment, I feel small next to the four farmers. They are all so tall and blond.

"Why do you think it might rain?" I ask.

"Just don't feel right." Caroline wrinkles her nose.

"The air is humid and the wind is blowing from the north," Eric says.

"All morning." She smiles at him with understanding and rubs her arms.

"It's Friday," I say.

"If we're gonna cut, we gotta cut today and tomorrow. Paul needs to get here," Eric repeats.

On the way back into town, Eric and I watch a herd of antelope explode into a gallop; he waits patiently while I try, and fail, to photograph the animals. Then we come across a new road in the middle of nowhere. Eric starts down it immediately, despite not knowing what it is for. It is like this in the country; new structures and apparatuses suddenly emerge, with no signage, no warning, and no people. It turns out to be some kind of gas pump; some element is being extracted from the earth. Then we turn around and drive to the trailers.

On Saturday, we cut the New Alden. And then, at dinner, we hear a familiar tapping on the roof of the trailer. It is rain. I know what Eric is thinking: we have missed the chance to cut the Petsch.

On Sunday I want to be with Caroline, whose family meets on the homestead in lieu of a church, and I want Juston and Michael to go with me.

I have been to church in Caroline's home twice before, and I want to share the experience with my two Christian friends.

"Sounds like a house church," Michael says.

"House church," Juston echoes.

"What's house church?" I ask.

Obviously, it's church in a house. This is precisely what Juston says. "It's a church in a house."

But it's also a lot more than that.

After Jesus died, it would be three hundred years before the emperor Constantine legalized Christianity and the government stopped persecuting and killing its citizens for refusing to deny their allegiance to God over the emperor. Until then, the Christian movement was full of martyrs willing to die for Jesus. And because Christianity was an underground, illegal movement, its followers met where illegal meetings are often held: at home.

Once Christianity was legal, meetings did not need to be held in secret, and so began the proper construction of buildings we now think of as churches. In the beginning, synagogues and temples were converted from pagan or Jewish use to Christian use: famous examples are the Pantheon and San Lorenzo, in Rome, both of which were once dedicated to Roman gods. But nowhere in the Bible does it say that people should meet in a building called a church. The closest would be when Jesus says he goes to the synagogue, the Jewish house of worship, to celebrate the Sabbath. While Jesus does ask his followers to remember him and to hold the communion—the breaking and sharing of bread and wine—he does not ask them to hold services in a *church*. There is a moment in the Bible, too, when Peter recognizes Jesus as the son of God, or the Messiah. Jesus replies: "Blessed art thou, Simon Barjona: for flesh and blood hath not revealed it unto thee, but my Father which is in heaven. And I say also unto thee, That thou art Peter, and upon this rock I will build my church; and the gates of hell shall not prevail against it." Scholars have ever after argued over what "my church" means; did he mean "church" in the sense that people would gather together, and their communion was a church? Or did he mean "church" as in a place?

"What denomination are they?" Juston asks me.

"I don't know," I say.

Originally, my family had thought that the Knowellses and Eric were the same denomination, until my uncle had insisted they were not.

"They don't spend Sunday together," my uncle said curtly. "They aren't the same."

"There was a time," said my father, ever the keeper of the exception to the rule, "when Eric's *parents* came and visited the Knowellses."

"They never did it again," said my uncle Paul. "Anyway, they follow something without a name. They don't celebrate Christmas. Something to do with there being nothing in the Bible about the time of year when Jesus was born. We are supposed to be able to relate to Jesus regardless of the season."

"Thanksgiving?" my father asked.

"Oh. They celebrate that," my uncle said. "That's American."

It is decided that Michael will go with me to church. He drives my car out to the homestead, and when Caroline opens the door to the family home, she is smiling and still herself, but more formal. It is the same house and the same people, but also not the same house and the same people. All is quiet. There is no joking. There are no comments about weather or commodities prices.

We sit in a circle around the room. In addition to Caroline's family of six, there are Ray and his wife. It is summer, and so Caroline's sister and brother-in-law are visiting; they come every year to help with the wheat harvest. There is another couple from "a few miles away" and a ranching family with three homeschooled children.

The women all wear their hair up, pinned to the back in buns, or plaited and fastened to the top of their heads. No one wears even a speck of makeup, but there they sit, as though illuminated, each one smiling with enviable contentment. It's the gray matter, I think.

Ray begins with a prayer and thanks God for the day. He thanks Jesus. We sing, and the room breaks out naturally into four-part harmony. There is always something so physical about harmonizing, as though someone has taken your hand when you are walking home and you don't expect it, and there you are in meaningful contact with another person on a little path you have walked alone so many times before.

The service proper begins.

There is no leader. They simply begin speaking one by one. "I was thinking about . . ." is how most of them start. "I was thinking how it is when your gut tells you something is wrong and you shouldn't do it.

And I was thinking about the part in Corinthians where Paul says that his life of faith comes from God's power and not from fancy emotional persuasion or intellectual power, and how important it is for me to not talk myself into faith or into doing things. I can't talk myself into having faith."

"I was thinking about the part in Luke where Jesus says that we can't run from suffering because that might be the way that we have to find ourselves, our true selves. I was thinking that sometimes we have to suffer and how I need to try not to feel sorry for myself when I feel like I'm suffering."

"I was thinking about how in Ecclesiastes it says that crying is better than laughing for the heart. And I was thinking about how we always say we want to have a tender heart so Jesus can live in our hearts."

Their voices are never theatrical. There is nothing performative about the way they talk. The voices simply come from around the room as if they are coordinated, even though there are no cues and no order to how they speak. Even the little children participate. They do not lace their ideas with false modesty, hysteria, or rambling. It is all so unadorned, and I believe, sincerely, that they have all simply been reading the Bible and hit upon a line that has moved them and now they are sharing that line with us.

The accumulation of so many voices, always with this same pattern, makes me want to share. It must be making others want to share. But because the way they share remains the same, they do not become increasingly hysterical, as though they want to outdo one another. Instead, it is as though the sharing only makes us more open, only makes our hearts more open, only makes us let in more and let out more. Everyone means everything. I have never heard anything quite like it. The closest would be a recovery meeting, wherein the accumulation of honest stories makes everyone else more honest and makes them want to try harder to think of ways their behavior has been dysfunctional, and makes them want to share and improve.

Those who have grown up within a Bible study system are perhaps accustomed to others quoting from the Bible and knowing the different parts clearly. I am not. For me, listening to everyone from the age of ten to seventy quote from parts of the Bible I had scarcely read—Corinthians, Acts, and Romans—made me think that there could be no English graduate course anywhere in the United States in which the threading together of parts of the Bible would ever be so insightful. But it isn't solely that they sit there and quote it; they relate the text to the most innocuous parts of their lives.

A recurring theme is the request for their hearts to be softened so Jesus can enter. Sometimes they touch their chests, where their hearts are protected beneath their breastbones, and tap this spot a few times, as though by doing so they can make their hearts more tender so Jesus can enter. The men do this, too, and at first it is alarming to me to see Ray, the patriarch, ask in a quavering voice for a tender heart, and to see tall, barrel-chested Rich do the same. They all ask for tender and soft hearts so Jesus can come inside, and from there, they say, they will act accordingly. It is as if they know that the brain does not matter, but that the heart does, and that if Jesus can enter the heart, the brain will have no choice but to obey its orders.

And I think this too: the accumulation of proud grown men asking to please have a soft heart and for Jesus to enter their heart must, over time, have an effect on everyone. *If you memorize the scripture, then it is with you. If you memorize it, it changes the way you live, because that is what you are thinking about instead of what the world wants you to think.*

At a certain point, Caroline begins to weep. She says she is thinking about the part in the Bible where it says that there is a time for everything, including a time for reaping. She cries and says she knows there must be a time for reaping and for the harvest. And it is harvest now. But how hard it is to be prepared for the reaping of the land, and I realize she is thinking about death; someone somewhere has died.

Now Ray is crying. He is thinking about the part in the Gospel of John where Jesus says he will await us in heaven, and he wonders if he will see God, if he has done well enough to see God, because he knows he is so imperfect. Grown Ray, weeping.

They all continue like this, and I think that if a home has a secret interior where only the most important and perhaps inexpressible things live, it is here, in these uttered phrases. The Bible has led them here to share one by one something from the inside of themselves.

When it is over, everyone files out slowly and I thank Caroline and Ray.

On the ride back into town, I ask Michael what he thinks. He doesn't seem too terribly impressed. "House church," he says. He has seen house church.

"The stuff about the heart . . ." Has he missed the difference between the churches that emphasize fear and this one, which was about love?

"House church." He shrugs.

And so we go back to camp to meet the others.

The rest of the crew seems frosty when Michael and I return. Bethany tells me in passing that she is on her way to Sidney, about forty miles away, to go buy a gun. I try to congratulate her, but even I can hear how hollow I sound. I know nothing about guns. I would like to show that I won't hold gun ownership against her, that I am eager to learn, but all this sounds so obsequious as it spills out of my mouth that I don't blame her when she disappears before I am done with the flattery.

The pickup roars off and the crew is gone, though Juston and Michael remain. I try, again, to talk about my experience at church, but Juston doesn't seem to want to engage in the subject. I assume it has something to do with whatever caused such tension earlier in the day. "Marie," he says. "How about we go to Scotts Bluff to see the Oregon Trail monument?"

"Sure," I say.

The road to Scotts Bluff is flat leaving town, then rises and dips into a shallow valley. Around are white bluffs: the chalky color comes from the calcified remains of millions of seashells left over from the inland sea during the Cretaceous period. Their sculptural shape has been carved by the wind.

The first white travelers documented in Western history who went across the Oregon Trail were captains Meriwether Lewis and William Clark, who walked from Camp Wood, Missouri, near modern-day St. Louis, to Fort Clatsop, near the mouth of the Columbia River, in Oregon. After the Louisiana Purchase, in 1803, President Thomas Jefferson thought it might be a good idea to map his new acquisition, and to figure out how to get from the East to the West Coasts. So he sent Lewis and Clark to scout the way. From 1804 to 1806, in the company of a Shoshone woman known as Sacagawea, Lewis and Clark traversed the new land.

From 1811 to 1840, the route from east to west became essential, though it did not stick to the trail set by Lewis and Clark, which veered to the north and passed through the Rocky and Columbia Mountains via routes that were impassable for wagons and horses. The more formalized 2,170-mile trail cut through the Great Plains farther to the south. This redefined Oregon Trail was initially traversed by fur traders who caught their prey, skinned the pelts, and then sold them to intermediaries, who would resell them until the animal furs could be turned into hats, coats, and stoles for wealthy patrons in eastern cities. Then came the settlers.

When the caravans came across Nebraska to Scotts Bluff, they had faced days of flat plains, grassy prairies, and buffalo. The white cliffs at Scotts Bluff, at the edge of Nebraska, were a signal to them that they were making progress in their journey and that the Rocky Mountains would soon swell up beyond the bluffs.

Eric, Emily, Juston, Michael, and I climb to the top of the bluff that marks the monument and we look west. Our own caravan has been following the wheat belt, which has, in turn, roughly followed the cattle drive. Now we are in Nebraska, and when our harvest is finished here, we will turn west and follow the Oregon Trail, the same way the settlers turned west to venture to Idaho.

I do not know who said what to whom, but that night, Bradford and Eric take me out to show me how to shoot a gun. Eric knows I have never shot a weapon. He comes to my trailer door and knocks, and when I open it, he has his pistol. "Want to learn to shoot?"

"Yes," I say.

It has rained and the fields are wet and there is little to do. But he and Bradford drive me out into the country, a little past the Knowellses' farmstead. We turn off onto a dirt road and park.

Unbeknownst to me, Caleb has set up a shooting range behind his house. He has dug a fairly large pit—at least twenty yards across—the original purpose of which, Bradford informs me, was to dig out gravel to make cement. At the far end of the pit, someone has set up irregularly shaped flat pieces of metal to use as targets. Close to us, a dozen or so empty plastic pallets are arranged to be used as ledges and stabilizers for our arms and for the guns. This is where Bradford's crew comes in the evenings.

I ask Bradford what to do and he tells me to breathe carefully. "Inhale and then shoot on the exhale." His voice is calm and encouraging. Almost warm. His instructions to focus on the breath are the same I have received for archery, yoga, and dance. Before I start, Eric turns my hat around on my head. "You know why snipers always wear their hats backward?" he jokes.

"Why?"

"To keep their hair out of their eyes." My hair is long and has been flapping in front of my face. Now my vision is clear.

I am startled by how the gun jumps. I can't keep my eyes open to see if the bullet hits the target, so the men happily inform me each time I hit my mark. "You hit it. You hit it. Yep." After a while, I start to try to brace the assault rifle on my shoulder better and keep my eyes open to see what I am doing on the other end. It is remarkably straightforward. It also tires me. I'm surprised by how shooting requires the entire body.

I ask Eric how this shooting lesson came about.

"I asked Bradford if he wanted to. I told him he didn't have to. But he told me he wanted to."

A moment later I thank Bradford and he nods stoically, showing no expression. I wish I knew how to talk to him so he would talk back.

After a little while, Eric shows me how to shoot his pistol, and this in many ways is a more elegant weapon than Bradford's AR. It is simpler. I have to work harder to use the sight, and it's as if I must fuse with the gun to hit my target. Then the gun feels like an extension of myself. Hitting a target is a thing my own body can do. It feels good.

Eric asks me if I feel better. He smiles when he asks and he turns his head a little, a slight, cocky twist. He tells me people usually need about ten or fifteen minutes a day and then they feel better. It's the adrenaline rush. Do I feel better? I tell him I do.

Why do I feel better? I have a weakness for anything involving eye-hand coordination. I love eye-hand coordination. I love archery, knitting, threading a needle, and any kind of craft. I like to be on my own. I like to drive.

But also, I'm a predator. Same as any other human being. And this tool in my hand makes me an even better predator. What a wonderful tool, I think. What wonderful tools humans can make.

ELEVEN

THE MEN INDULGE IN A RECURRING FANTASY. They wonder what will happen if the satellites go out. They envision the people in the city rendered helpless without a network connecting their phones to services and money. The city people would not know what to do. They would be left with machines that no one could operate. The city people cannot hunt and they cannot farm, and they would soon go hungry.

"Won't take long for them to show up and take your food, Eric," Amos says one night when we are eating dinner. At Eric's home in Pennsylvania, there is a series of large grain bins filled with corn, wheat, and soybeans. Eric built the bins for himself, so he could store his own crops and opt to sell his harvest when the commodities prices go up; this is cheaper than keeping grain at the local cooperative, which charges a fee for storage.

"We'd feed the people," Eric says. He is eating and chewing, and after a moment, he puts down his fork. "We'd have a soup kitchen. We could do it."

Everyone laughs.

"I'm serious," he thunders. "The church would help. The people would line up . . ."

"They'd try to steal . . ."

"No," Eric insists. "It would work out and it would be fine. We could take care of it."

Usually when this scenario is discussed, the boys use it to frame how in a catastrophe their knowledge would become vital. The fantasy is not a chance to think through how to help people, but a chance to discuss how, at last, the city people would see them and understand that they—drivers of trucks and fixers of igniter coils—are important. Valuable.

In the morning, I have a long ride with Amos. He tells me how he was born to a Mennonite family in Pennsylvania. According to family lore, his mother was pregnant with him when her brother, a farmer, fell from the top of a silo to the bottom and was killed instantly. The family believed that the uncle transferred his desire to farm to Amos, which is another way of saying it is God's will that Amos farm.

Amos's father is a salesman for a satellite company but once owned a motor engine shop. Amos, like Luther, started to work on engines as a young man and liked taking them apart and putting them back together. But Amos wanted the combination of equipment and land. On the first harvest crew he joined as a way to break into the farming world, Amos lost ten pounds because there was never enough to eat. He left that outfit in Montana and tried out Eric's team last year.

Amos feels that corporations are ruining the five-hundred-acre farm, the family farm, and the farmer who loves being the middleman to the food supply and who works his land with joy. "For a farmer who wants to start out, there is no way he can compete. You need at least seven hundred K just to buy land."

"There are small farms," I say. "I see them selling their produce in New York City . . ."

"But that's a niche activity. It's not scalable and not something you can do that makes you feel like you are contributing to a large effort to feed people. Then there's equipment and seed. You don't have to buy seed wheat. Caleb actually grows his seed wheat," he tells me. "All the other grains—corn and soybeans—have to be bought." But not wheat. Wheat is still special and growing it is still the independent way to farm, even if it is not as valuable a commodity.

While GMOs are effective, Amos is afraid that one day soon we will have a weed that a spray cannot handle. Like every other farmer, he is well aware that Roundup is losing its ability to kill everything, and might one day be rendered obsolete.

"But it is not the GMOs or the chemicals that are the problem," he says.

"What do you think *is* the problem?" I ask, without knowing precisely what we are referring to when we speak now about "the problem."

"People don't understand how much heart and soul goes into farming." His voice cracks when he says this. Amos, I have come to understand, is an emotional person. His feelings rise to the surface very quickly, like bubbles floating to the top of boiling water.

"It's often true," I say. People *don't* know.

"Talking about the GMOs doesn't help," he repeats.

And this is when I realize that Amos doesn't think my question is a particularly good question. In fact, he doesn't even think it *is* the question. If, as Eric said so long ago, my question was actually about "the divide," then I ought to stop thinking about GMOs and organics and God.

But the conversation does turn to God. "I don't like snobby Christians who think they know who is going to hell and who is not," says Amos. "I don't believe in predicting the future. But I think God will do something with us to wake us up and show us we had it good. I think he will show us that we are selfish."

I am at once alarmed and struggling to follow his line of thought. "What do you mean?"

"Let me ask you this," Amos says to me. Then he hesitates and takes a breath, and it's as if he needs extra air in his lungs to even ask the question. His manner changes slightly, as if he is about to reveal a secret to me.

"Do you think city people should learn how selfish they are? That maybe they should learn about another way of life?"

I want to point out that I obviously think what farmers do is important or I wouldn't be spending so many weeks on the road with the harvesters. But instead, I say: "I hope I can help with that. With this book."

He takes a breath and tries again. He's like an airplane trying to re-land on the runway. He missed the first time. He's going to take another pass, and now I feel nervous.

He gives me little quick looks out of the corners of his eyes. "Do you think God will deliver a message soon?" He is gripping the steering wheel, with his arms taut and elbows out. Amos is not exactly a guy with excellent posture, so it is alarming to see him so physically engaged with the combine.

"A message?"

"A correction. To show that social media is a deviation from God's message."

"Do *you* think he will?"

He cocks his head and smiles. He won't tell me what kind of a correction. It's almost as if I'm supposed to know what he means, and if I can't figure it out, then he's told me too much. But he is certain there will be a correction and the people in the city will learn about their arrogance. Part of me knows what he means, but part of me, honestly, does not, and the question throws me. That farmers aren't necessarily all that well understood seems obvious to me; they make up only 2 percent of the population in the US, and their numbers are shrinking. Of course they aren't well understood. But what, exactly, is this arrogance in the city that requires such a violent retaliation from God that we should view any message he delivers as "a correction," like one of those "corrections" in the roads I drive out here in the country?

I think of the self-proclaimed agrarian farmer and scholar Victor Davis Lutheron who, in his book *Fields without Dreams*, wrote sneeringly but also with grief: "They [city people] no longer care where or how they get their food, as long as it is firm, fresh, and cheap. They have no interest in preventing the urbanization of their farmland as long as parks, Little League fields, and an occasional bike lane are left amid the concrete, stucco, and asphalt. They have no need of someone who they are not, who reminds them of their past and not their future. Their romanticism for the farmer is just that, an artificial and quite transient appreciation of his rough-cut visage against the horizon the stuff of a wine commercial, cigarette ad, or impromptu rock concert." People in the cities don't see farmers clearly. The farmers are *overlooked*, and instead of being seen as recognizably real, the farmer is romanticized.

Perhaps my connection to this place is some form of romanticism, and I don't truly belong here. I acknowledge this. But I cannot make the leap from ignorance—my own, as a city person—to requiring a rebuke from God himself. The implied threat in that attitude makes me feel this is no place for me at all. My family—I—don't belong here.

So many times I have been advised to sell the farm. My own family—other cousins who long ago got out of farming—tell me: "There is nothing there for you."

I *could* sell the farm.

I could sell the farm, but if I sell the farm, I will lose my connection to this place completely. There will not be any reason to come back at all. And then any knowledge we might share, even if it is the wrong knowledge, would be completely lost and I would sink into the distraction that is the city, with all its billboards and words and books, and the farm would fade completely. We have in my family three times held on to the farm when we intended to let it go. My grandparents went back.

My father went back. And now I am here and I am the least skilled of any of them.

When we go back to the farm, what is it that we have been trying to hold on to?

In the afternoon, I am with Eric in his pickup truck and we are switching fields and heading south to the Nebraska-Colorado border. Ahead of us, Bradford is in another pickup. It stops, and Michael jumps out and strides off, alone, into a field to move the tractor. He doesn't turn and wave and I can see that no one in Bradford's pickup waves to him. Michael is striding almost defiantly, I think, as if he's daring the stubble to stop him from walking. The boys have had a fight. It must have been heated for Michael to stalk off like that without even saying goodbye or giving a gesture of thanks.

The air is humid again. Bits of cloud are dispersed in the sky and the cumulative effect of everything—the unexplained fight, the scattered men, the atmosphere—is of energy atomized and strewn loose. Eric is driving in silence. We go on Highway 71 south of town, and come to the correction line. We make a jag to the right, then to the left, and then the road is straight again until we reach the new field.

There has been a change in these southern fields since we were here on Friday. That slight shade of green in the trough that I had so struggled to see is lighter now and I can see it. Eric gets on the radio and asks some of the crew to come here, to a piece of ground we call the Colorado Section. Eric owns the northern half of the section, and my mother and I own the southern half. A full section is 640 acres, or a square mile. Nearby are the Colorado Quarter, and Paul's land, the Hauserman. These fields are also the farthest from town, and it makes sense to move almost everything here together and to cut these fields at the same time. As the wheat to the north ripens, we can consider dividing the team.

It takes a while to move the machinery, but eventually it comes lumbering down the road, and the men—and Bethany—get to work. I listen to them talk over the radio in Eric's pickup.

"I'm gonna break through now," Michael says at one point, and I watch his combine deviate from the direction everyone else is going, and he begins to bisect the field.

The day passes without a drop of rain. I think of everything turning: turbines, combine blades, and the earth. Now everything is working so well and most of the time we are silent, collecting the grain into the combines, which spew the golden kernels into the grain cart, which then transfers the harvest into the trucks, which then head off into town and return, empty, to repeat the process. My mind slows down, following the rhythm of the work.

I ride with Juston in the grain cart. We talk about my conversation with Amos, and I tell Juston about Michael strutting off to the tractor. I say I know there has been a fight. But Juston won't give me specifics—he says they aren't important.

"Let's just say the crew is divided now. There's a rift between Bradford and his people on one side, and me and Michael on the other."

"But what was the actual fight?"

"It was stupid," Juston says as he drives over the ground to catch up with Bradford, whose combine is flashing its yellow lights, the signal that the grain needs to be emptied.

"Juston. Were you arguing about me?"

"We would be fighting anyway," he says, which isn't exactly a satisfying answer. Then he says: "Well, look. I told the guys that this is an opportunity for them to share what they know about farming with you. It's just so disappointing, because some years you could come and the guys would share stories and you could see how we all come together during harvest. And how we all work together, and everyone would talk to you about organics and GMOs. And you would learn a lot."

"Amos said he doesn't think GMOs are the issue. None of them like my question."

Juston shrugs. "I tell them: Who do you think we grow all this food for? It's the people in the city."

City people are the issue, and I am a city person.

Late in the afternoon I get a text from Paul that he and his family are fifteen minutes away from the bunkhouse, and I drive myself back into town to meet him. We are reunited outside the Quonset. In years past we paid the Knowellses to mow the weeds, but no one has thought to ask them to do so since last summer, and the weeds rise to our knees. There are four of them this summer: Paul; his wife, Barbara; and two of their three children: Amelia, who is in her twenties and works for a consulting firm in New York, and Mark, who is now twenty. One of the last times I saw Mark, he was still a child precociously drawing and designing stadiums on graph paper as a way to entertain himself. Now he is focused on urban planning.

We say hello, then tinker with the keys and the giant padlock that keeps the Quonset doors shut and locked. The doors are heavy and I always have to lean into them to get them to even partially open. It's dusty and quiet inside, and smells vaguely of fertilizer—exactly as it smelled a year ago.

Here is the Quonset, the last of what remains of our family home. Instead of my grandmother's stately 1921 brick house, we have this, a half cylinder steel structure, roughly five thousand square feet total. At the back end is an iron-wheeled wagon, an antiquated testament to transportation, and beside this, a white 1968 Mercedes that belonged to my uncle Bill, who was married to my father's sister. My cousin Paul bought the Mercedes from Uncle Bill, and drove it once from Seattle, where he lives, to Kimball, where it died. Even though lots of people know about cars in Kimball, there isn't a mechanic in town who knows a thing about a European import, let alone one assembled in 1968. There are also two Scout jeeps, which for years were prodded to life by the different men in the family until the Scouts, too, simply died. Neatly arranged around all the vehicles are augers, cables, a picnic table and benches, and tools few of us understand.

The bunkhouse is off to the left. To use it, we have to first turn on the power via a main electricity panel immediately inside the door. This will enable the air conditioning, Wi-Fi, and the refrigerator. Then we open the door.

The first thing I see is my father's battered farm hat hanging on the wall. It was once a pale white, but has become stained over time, as if it was dunked in coffee, the result of exposure to wind, rain, and dirt. We always exhorted him to get a new one, but he considered it his good-luck hat, even after a bad harvest; if he changed the hat after a bad crop, he said, the next year would be worse. In another corner I see his boots. There is no reason for his hat and boots to be gone just because he died, but my insides wince at seeing both articles of clothing standing there, waiting, as if they haven't gotten the news yet that their wearer is gone.

There is a note taped to the wall: my phone number in New York City where I lived in my twenties and thirties. He called it often while at harvest; this was what he did during his downtime. And very often, he called to ask me to please come out to the country. Paul's children came consistently.

One recent year, we averaged forty bushels of wheat per acre. Someone—probably Amelia—gathered a handful of that magical wheat and collected it into a bouquet, where it now stands upright in a coffee can. When I was a child, I remember so many summers when the men lamented how low their yields were: now twenty bushels, now fifteen, now ten. The forty-bushel-per-acre harvest seemed to prove that progress as a concept just needed enough time to be realized.

There is also a box that contains my great-grandfather Percy's tennis trophies. They were rescued from the attic when my grandmother's house was sold, and have lived here ever since; no one is sure what to do with them. On the wall, hanging all on its own, is a large map of Nebraska, covered with a slab of glass. On this, in crayon, someone has traced the contours of each piece of property we own, along with the most expedient route to get there. Even though the US is covered with a hash of country and farm roads, they are not all equally maintained: some are covered with gravel, some are graded, and some are mostly weeds, which means they become roads only in the summer, when trucks and pickups routinely drive over them for harvest. The knowledge of how to get places, then, is precious, and has been documented and handed down to us in this way.

There are notes taped everywhere with instructions, and we follow them as one follows clues in a treasure hunt. We must turn on the water, but expect pressure to come out of a release valve when we do so. The valves on the drains must be open. If there is a problem with the toilet, we should check the pump to the right.

We talk as we work. Paul asks about my trip and I try to tell him lighthearted stories about pig hunting and Oklahoma City. I tell him about Eric standing up to gay bashing and about Michael and Juston and their tireless instructions to me on Christianity.

"It rained, didn't it," Paul finally says.

"Yes."

"And you couldn't cut the Petsch."

"No."

Neither of us bring up that the Android, which had promised 0 percent chance of rain, had failed.

"We need to come up with a better system than driving across country for just a few days," Paul says. It isn't clear whom he is talking to.

"It'll dry," I say.

"I hope it didn't hail."

"We can go look."

"I need to check my email first. I've been driving for twenty-three hours." It is then that I hear them all tapping behind me; the rest of Paul's family are online, checking to see what, if anything, has happened during the drive from Seattle to Nebraska. Their eyes are glued to their screens as they scan, trash, and reply to the many messages that have coursed through the ether to land in their email in-boxes.

The battery-operated key fob that unlocks the door to my rental car has stopped working. I stop at the automotive store and the mechanic there sends me on to the jewelry store to purchase a new battery. A woman named Karen helps me. She knew my grandmother and she knew me when I was a child. She was and is such a good jeweler, my mother used to save all her broken jewelry until we got to Kimball to get it all repaired.

Karen is the kind of woman I used to see everywhere in Kimball—a real lady. She wears her hair pinned up, is always slim, and dresses in low heels and a pencil skirt. As a child, I watched her joyfully help customers find engagement rings, or their first pierced earrings. Then and now her store contains a subtle instruction in the art of practical femininity in a prairie town; a woman should pause for beauty on certain days: birthdays, graduations, and marriage engagements.

Karen remembers me. She remembers my family and my grandmother and the prominence we once had. But our conversation soon veers into regret.

"Isn't it a shame to see Bob and Bernie's house across the street from your grandmother's house? It is in such a state. All those weeds."

"I didn't look closely."

"Did you know that the Catholic school has closed? So many churches have closed."

"My grandmother went to the Episcopal church."

"Yes, that's still open."

"Is there still a garden society? Do people still win prizes for the best garden?"

She smiles. We are talking about beauty, her specialty. "Your family were all gardeners. Your grandmother always went on the garden tours. She loved gardens." Then Karen shakes her head. There are no more garden tours. "So many houses have been abandoned. The town is so full of empty houses."

Is it? "Yes," I say, to agree with her, though I haven't been able to tell just by looking.

"And there are so *many* absentee farmers."

"Yes," I say again.

That's me. I am an absentee farmer. I am pretending to be a farmer, though I live somewhere else.

Karen goes on. She understands why the young people are leaving, but it is such a shame. Is it not a shame? She says this with a pinched, ladylike sadness. I want to resist this portrayal of the town as decaying. This is a place where I have been happy, and after the towns in Texas, which were so acutely drained of people and services, Kimball looks pretty good, with a population of 2,500. But I know the town has changed.

I am taking memories out of my head and planting them everywhere here in front of me, but it's as if locusts or hail or hogs have come, and as quickly as a delicious memory grows, it's wiped away. See now how the stately high school brick building where my father and uncle went— where my uncle forcibly replaced his physics teacher—has closed. The park where the Minuteman missile stood as a testament to American might is filled with weeds, and the missile was knocked over in the wind. There was on the north end of town a historic Wheat Growers Hotel, where harvesters and out-of-towners stayed during the harvest season. I remember when it was full, when the town Laundromat was noisy with men stomping on the floor and trying to get grease out of jeans. I remember all those men in town parading around slowly with their clean and dirty clothes while my grandmother drove her sedan to the post office and the local co-op, which is now closed.

Many of the shops we visited are antiques stores filled with the same random supply of curios that I have seen for sale in every town, beginning in Texas. The dry goods store has a vintage 1950s red cheerleader outfit displayed in its window with a yellow "K" emblazoned on the chest. This is not for sale, though; it's enshrined there as a memory. The Webbs' barn, where I learned to ride, stands empty of horses. The fabric store where my mother and I bought yards of the brown paisley-print cotton that became a dress is long closed. There is no more movie theater and no more drive-in. Look, I say to myself, at what is really here.

Weeds rip through the sidewalk. Houses are boarded up and closed. And still my mind will fix the broken windows and will repopulate the schools and parks and take me back to when my father and grand-mother were alive, and I was here and all was safe and the town was filled with smaller wheat trucks.

The cemetery lawn mower man knew my family's name. Maybe he knew that my grandmother was the grand marshal for the Harvest Days parade in 1983, or that my grandfather temporarily served as the town judge. Or maybe he'd seen our name on the county land deed map in the courthouse. Had he?

Perhaps he had seen our name only in the cemetery.

Once, my grandmother said to me in an offhand way: "You could manage the farm." But when I told this to my father, he was furious.

"I won't die and leave you the farm," he said emphatically. He practically shouted when he said it. But still he died and we kept the farm.

My mother and I did not sell the farm, because it was a tether to my father, who had kept our family whole. It bound us to my grandmother. My mother said she was saving the land for my son and we could keep growing crops, and with help, my son could too. We made him the reason we have kept the land. Long before he could even tell us whether this might be something he would like.

Eric says that we will be in Idaho during the full solar eclipse, and the field we are likely to be cutting will be directly in the path of the totality. This is the first time I've heard Eric predict an exact location for harvest. He has otherwise consistently insisted that it is impossible to know when the wheat will ripen, and thus impossible to determine a schedule. With the eclipse, however, he has visualized a position. Emily has prepared by ordering eclipse-viewing glasses, which have been sent to Pennsylvania. Bethany is going home for a few days for a wedding, and will pick up the glasses and bring them back to us.

Then Eric says: "What if God performs a miracle and the eclipse is not where it is supposed to be?"

Emily mentions how there was a time when some scientists at NASA could not figure out something involving the universe and the sun, then remembered a passage in the Bible about how the sun had once stopped.

"Was this on TBN?" Juston asks.

"What's that?" I ask.

"It's a Christian network."

"It's a slightly fraudulent Christian show," Juston surmises.

"I did *not* see this on TV!" Emily protests.

"It's one of those stories that Christians use to try to prove that the Bible is inerrant. Because if the Bible isn't one hundred percent accurate, the entire concept of God just falls apart," Juston says, spreading out his hands.

"Oh, Juston." Emily sighs.

"Anyway, I think it'll be beautiful." Eric is back to talking about the eclipse. "Maybe I'll just keep cutting. Then we'll go home and people will ask about the eclipse and I'll tell 'em I stayed in the combine."

"It'll be dark," I say.

"How dark? Like midnight?"

"I'm not sure."

"Maybe like early morning," he muses. "Or the evening."

"The sun will be overhead," Juston observes.

"I wonder if I'll be able to see my hand," Eric says.

Late in the afternoon, after the other Mocketts have caught up on their email, they come to the field to see the very last of the Colorado Section cut. They never did make it out to see the Petsch cut, and Eric had simply sent out his crew to cut it without supervision. The matter is not addressed. When Paul and his family show up, Eric cuts the engine of the experimental combine and gets out to say hello to Paul.

After a bit, Eric repeats his line about the eclipse. "Wouldn't it be funny if God made a miracle and the calculations of the scientists were all off by just a little?"

Amelia and Paul immediately say that such a thing isn't possible at all.

"The bodies of the solar system . . . ," Paul begins.

". . . are in motion, and math tells us what is where," Amelia says. "There are objects we don't know about . . ."

". . . but the math won't change," Paul finishes. They say this almost furiously, their heads shaking and their arms crossed. There is something so perfect about their knowledge of science, and their dynamic.

Then Eric laughs and asks who wants to ride in the combine with him. "I do," says Mark, quickly. I watch Mark stride out into the field. He pauses to take a few photos in his dark blue denim jeans, so very clean and sharp. He gets to the combine ladder and turns his chin up and he has that small smile on his face—the same one that his father, Paul, has and that my uncle also had. We joke sometimes that some of the members of our family must be on the spectrum because we are so cerebral. Then Mark climbs the ladder.

That night in the Quonset, my family and I move the picnic table, which used to be at my grandmother's house, to the doorway of the hut, and we hang a lamp from a large metal hook suspended from the roof. We have been tugging this light on the pulley to the doorway of the Quonset for decades, and the simple gesture, coupled with the warm yellow light, fills me with great love.

For Paul, the cutting is all done even though more fields remain for Eric and for me; Paul will head home tomorrow. Amelia will fly back to New York after getting a ride to Denver, and Mark will go with his family on the drive back to Seattle, and the bunkhouse will be left open for me to use.

It is a tradition in my family to celebrate the end of harvest with a big steak dinner, so Paul has cooked steaks for us on the barbecue outside in the weeds, which he's managed to trim by borrowing Caleb's riding mower. This is supposed to be a joyous meal, but it feels slightly hollow. Harvest has ended so soon for Paul.

"I have a question about quantum mechanics," I say. "I understand that we can't predict what a particle will do, and that observation seems to change behavior. Is that because electrons know they are being watched?"

"No." Paul shakes his head immediately. "The behavior changes whether or not the electron is being observed by a human or a machine. What we say now is that our model is incomplete."

"Though we found Higgs," Amelia interjects, "which confirms and completes the Standard Model. I was reading the other day that some physicists think Higgs could be the inflaton."

"No consensus yet, though," Paul says. "Anyway, ha ha, now we don't know what ninety-five percent of the universe is. Thanks, Dad." And from here, for a while, the conversation veers off in a direction I don't fully understand.

When the food—steaks, potato salad, and salad—is on the table, Barbara says to me: "So, tell us about your trip."

"Do we even know how to raise organic wheat?" Paul asks.

I realize I am famished for their company—for company like theirs, which is to say, like mine. The kids—my young cousins—were not there when I asked my uncle, father, and cousin the question about organics and GMOs. So I repeat it, and as we sit there under the lamp and it grows darker outside, we stay in our island of light and toss the ideas back and forth between us like the proverbial football. And the talking and the sharing hearten me.

I tell them about the Rodale Institute, in Kutztown, Pennsylvania, which is twenty miles southwest of Allentown, and not too far from Lancaster County. The institute is named for J. I. Rodale, who was both a farmer and a publisher interested in advocating for organic standards. Rodale died in 1971, but the institute that bears his name carries on his mission of advocating for organic farming and holistic living. To that end, it has developed and championed a "roller-crimper," which is exactly what it sounds like: a device that crimps, or folds, crops the same way a crimper puts a crease in hair. After a field is harvested, a grassy crop like cereal rye is planted into the stubble and left to grow through the winter. The cereal rye grows quickly, knocking out any weeds. In the spring, when the cereal rye has reached the limit of its natural life span, the roller-crimper goes through and bends the grass, killing it, but keeps its root system in place, creating an even bed of mulch. This prevents the soil from being disturbed. Row crops like corn, wheat, and soybeans are then planted directly into the dead cereal rye, though these must be spring plantings, usually in April.

"But you need extra moisture," Paul observes.

"Yes," I say. "Anyone raising organic here just doesn't spray, and deals with weeds."

"What does it even mean for food to be organic?" Paul muses.

"Not synthetic," Amelia says.

"Plastic is synthetic," says Mark.

Except, we all agree, you don't eat plastic. When you eat nonorganic food, you are eating food whose form was influenced by a laboratory. Many decades ago, it was easier to distinguish what we meant by non-organic. We meant food that was brightly colored, like bright M&M's, or green ice cream cones.

My family nods. It is not so easy to define organic food today. We could make water in a laboratory and it would have the same composition as water collecting in a drainpipe after a winter storm. I tell them how as a child, gardening in Northern California, I was appalled when carrots occasionally turned up half-purple, and my mother patiently explained that this was the natural way for carrots to appear until human intervention and breeding favored the orange color that is popular today.

Because we have all lived in a city, we all know, generally, what our peers mean when they talk about the superiority of organic food. We have all heard from friends that organic food does not include pesticides. We are all dimly aware of an article in the *New York Times* that introduced the practice of gene splicing as part of food production. We have read that the tomato might, in fact, contain the DNA of a fish. Such a food is called a "frankenfood."

The problem is the fish DNA in the tomato has never been in the market. A flounder does have a protein in its DNA that enables it to survive the cold, and scientists did try to put this same protein in the DNA of a tomato to see if the tomato could survive frost, or, more practically, long trips in a truck until it reached a grocery store. But the experiment was abandoned because the genetic modification failed to have the desired effect in the tomato and the tomato was not approved for consumption, and not because, as was erroneously reported, the tomato killed anyone. Still, the frankenfood quality of the mythical fish-tomato became the emblem of the anti-GMO movement, and even now we hear people conjure up the image of this mythical Hieronymus Bosch–like fruit in an effort to explain why they adhere to an organic diet.

Still, I say, it was this article—along with a 2001 episode of CBS's *60 Minutes* titled "What Have They Done to Our Food?" in which it was claimed that "up to 70 percent of processed food in the American market contains products of genetic engineering, including soft drinks, catsup, potato chips, cookies, ice cream and corn flakes"—that helped popularize the idea of scary food created by science. I read these articles too. Living in New York City for as many years as I did, I consumed news about my world through the radio, television, and the internet, and during many of those years, I did not go to farms or talk to farmers, and my connection to the land was fragile. And I became convinced that organic food was better, though I could not have articulated what I meant when I said this.

I tell my cousins how, in *The Great Plains in Transition*, the writer Carl Frederick Kraenzel refers to the Great Plains as "semiarid." Other parts of the country are "humid," as in the "humid states," like Pennsylvania and New York. Kraenzel notes how people keep trying to impose humid-area thought patterns onto semiarid areas. There are qualities that people who live on the Great Plains develop that do not mesh with people from humid parts of the country. He talks about the cowboy, whose spirit reflects what the land requires from him. The land where the cowboy lives requires an attitude that is vast and open and not penned into a tiny area because there isn't enough water in a small area for a person to grow on five acres in the Great Plains what one would in the humid areas. The land dictates the crops and the person.

My home state of California has the first and best organic conference on the Monterey Peninsula, where I grew up. I met extraordinary people there: people raising coffee beans between rows of avocado trees and cultivating high-end strawberries flown to restaurants in Las Vegas. I met people who started their organic farms after going to prison in the sixties and realizing they needed to be in control of their own food supply; this translated into going organic. I realized that in California and on the East Coast the wonderful work of organic farmers depends on a few reliable factors, one of which is plentiful water. Anything grows in California because there is always plentiful water— due to irrigation. The East Coast also has plentiful water. The plains do not. Does the land itself dictate what we believe about food and perhaps, by extension, about God?

"Did you know," I say, "that there is no such thing as natural broccoli?"

I tell them a story about how one day I asked Rich, Ray Knowells's son-in-law, my question about food and organics. Rich has a penchant for overalls. He smiles easily and broadly and has large white teeth and a roaming, sparkling gaze. He wears size-fourteen shoes. He sings beautifully.

I asked Rich if he has ever considered planting organic wheat. He gave me an amused smile and recounted a story about hauling some organic oats for a farmer in Iowa. "Never again," Rich said. The organic crop had been full of rat droppings, which stank up the back of his truck so much that he'd had to go to great lengths to clean it. This is the story I often hear about organic crops from conventional farmers—that the food is dirty, difficult to wash, difficult to keep clean, and that science has made farming a cleaner, more efficient way to grow food.

"But do you think we should be trying to farm organic? I mean, wouldn't that be more natural?" I had asked.

"What is natural, Marie?" Rich had replied. And for the first time, this curious, widely smiling man who had always asked me questions about my home and displayed an intense curiosity about the outside world seemed a touch impatient. "Do you know that broccoli is a GMO? There's no such thing as broccoli. It is a created food."

"It is?"

"Organic, all-natural broccoli is impossible," he said. "Doesn't exist. Makes me laugh when I see it for sale."

"But do you think," I had pressed, "that we should be tampering with DNA? Is that not like cracking open the code for life? Is that not playing God?"

"Who is to say what we should or should not do? But, honestly, how could it be bad to make more food for the world? Who is to say that God would not want us to make more food?" The world depends on the science of farming, he said. There was not enough food in the world, and people were starving. Did I not know that even Bill Gates had admitted that were it not for GMOs, there would be 25 percent less food produced in my own country alone? In fact, I had never heard of this at all. "Now, let me ask you, Marie, which twenty-five percent would you like to see starve and not have that food?"

And then I understood that, for Rich, farming is not just an activity that suits the lifestyle of a man who wants to dedicate himself to God, or something that he does as a hobby; it is, in fact, the work of man on behalf of God. To farm is to always be doing something good. It is to create an essential and vital thing. There are good farmers and bad farmers and people who lie and cheat and big corporations that will take away the money from farmers. But to farm, to deal with the uncertainty of weather and rain and rust and pests, is to engage in an activity whose sole benefit is to help mankind.

"It's one reason I wanted to keep the farm," Paul says.

"I know," I say. It feels good to be at the table like this, with my family, discussing everything—God, the food, and the fields—and to feel that together we can come to some consensus. It feels as if this is what knowledge is supposed to do. It is supposed to make us more secure.

It is then, in an offhand way, that my young cousin Mark tells us that he came out to Eric in the combine earlier that afternoon.

"You told him . . . ," I begin.

"That I'm gay. Yes." According to Mark, Eric answered: "Well, I don't understand. But I know my God loves you."

"And what did you say?" I ask.

"I said, 'I agree!'" Mark says cheerfully. His voice is practically singing. It is a hallmark of our family that the most rational members are also the most cheerful. It is as though they don't see the sense in being anything but cheerful. Yes, of course, God loves Mark.

At one point Mark leaves and a few minutes later I hear a thundering on the roof. Paul smiles. He taught Mark how to climb onto the Quonset the same way he was taught by his father and by my father, and they were taught by their father. The Quonset has the best view of the sunset, and with some lingering atmosphere from the storm, Mark is hoping to get a good photograph.

We are all still talking, linking together something about brain structure, religion, and the power of prayer, when a Union Pacific train hoots as it thunders by. It grows darker, and the farthest corners of the Quonset, where the pioneer wagon and the Mercedes-Benz are parked, retreat into the shadows. The Quonset seems to fade altogether. Mark comes off the roof and back into the Quonset. As Paul walks me to my car when I leave, we look up at the stars as we always do. There are so many out in the plains. It was Paul who taught me how to look for satellites, those bright specks of light moving at an even clip all the way across the horizon. And then we say goodbye.

Saturday afternoon, my seven-year-old son, Ewan, arrives for a visit. He and my husband have flown from California to Denver, missing Paul and his family by a few hours. After my husband deposits Ewan with me in a wheat field, he returns to the airport to fly to a conference on the East Coast.

Ewan is delighted to be on the farm. He wears a pair of child's cowboy boots and eats Emily's food—the best, he tells us over and over again. That evening, I mention to Juston that I want to take Ewan to house church again, but Juston suggests something different.

"The church in town is the closest you'll get to hellfire and brimstone. I think you should find out what that's like so you know." And so on Sunday morning, Ewan and I rise in the bunkhouse, now occupied by only the two of us. I put on a fresh pair of jeans and I do my makeup and braid my hair and dress Ewan in clean clothes and we go to town to One Hope Bible Church. It's the first church he has ever been to and I don't prepare him for it; I say that we are going to a place where we will all talk about God for about an hour. He's vaguely familiar with God, because he has seen Eric pray before meals when we have visited.

Ewan's presence has buoyed me, as does the sheer number of people in the church. There must be more than a hundred here in this long, low building made out of stone masonry and notched and stacked logs painted brown so it looks like a log cabin from the pioneer days. Karen, the jewelry store owner, is not here, but the pews are filled with dozens of Karen-like women wearing small sparkly earrings and tightly coiled hair. The women sit with their husbands and the men are dressed in checkered shirts and dark pants, like my father. There are families, too, with children squirming in their seats and the occasional toddler racing around the room. It is exciting to be around so many people, alive with the charge that comes when multiple generations gather.

It is, I realize, the most popular place in town. It is more popular than the bank, the grocery store, and even the Farm Services Agency office.

Pastor Jan retains a boyishness about him, though he is in his early fifties. He has the round face and smooth cheeks and full lips of a man of Dutch descent. His blue eyes are bright in this darkened cabin of a room and radiate clear to the back pew, where I am sitting. Like Pastor Jeff, Pastor Jan looks as if he might have been an actor or a high school sports coach. The men share an impatient alertness, but there is something I cannot initially pinpoint that differentiates them.

Pastor Jan begins speaking on a self-deprecating note. He hopes we will stay after church. "I made you lunch!" Pastor Jan declares. "'Course, it's all leftovers." After everyone chuckles, the tenor of his voice shifts. The leftover food is from a memorial service held the day before. "We are a community in mourning," Pastor Jan informs us. When I was out with Eric, watching the wheat harvest and hoping my family would arrive in time to see their own grain harvested, a young teacher was struck by a car and killed while running on the road by the Kimball cemetery. She has left behind her husband, three children, and the community who loved her.

Pastor Jan's boyish face transforms. He does a thing men do sometimes when they wear glasses. He peers over the top of the frames, so his eyes are at once wider and the space between his pupils and brows grows smaller. He looks severe. He looks professorial. He looks as if he is trying to decide if we are worth the extra effort it takes for him to scrutinize us. He says that in church today we will examine grief through the Book of Job. "The main idea of the book of Job is not the tragedy Job went through. The main idea of the book is that God is sovereign through it all," he says.

Scholars say that Job may well be the oldest book in the Bible, though it is located two-thirds of the way through in a section called "poems." In the story, Job worshipped God and was blessed with a large family and significant wealth. One day, Satan tells God that Job worships God only because Job is blessed; were Job poor and afflicted, he would curse God. But God disagrees and gives Satan permission to kill off Job's family members, take away their wealth, and make Job sick. This is the test of faith.

"The sheriff . . . broke that news, right back there." Pastor Jan points to a corner of the church. "I was not prepared for that news." He is talking about the dead teacher again. He knew he would need to tell the family that the mother had been killed, and he speaks of how difficult this was. In fact, he says, he has just learned about another death from Eric. And then he nods at Eric. The wife of a harvester—one of the Millers who had sat in front of me at Pastor Jeff's church—has also been killed in a car accident.

"How do you handle it?" Pastor Jan asks. "I don't think God ever intended man to handle that kind of stuff well." Job says that just as God has given, God can take away. God makes this decision and Satan is not mentioned. In fact, Satan must ask God for permission to hurt Job. God is the one who tests Job and not Satan. God is in charge of everything. We have a sickness in Christianity in that we blame Satan for everything. Really, God is at the center of it all.

Then Pastor Jan begins to speak with alarming emphasis. It is as if his entire head is on fire, and his blue eyes are the center of a candle's flame. "In the book of Isaiah," he tells us forcefully, "it says that 'I create light and I create darkness'! . . . The God that's formed by our culture is a great big huge old grandpa-looking guy. . . . The God of the Bible is in control of even good and evil and bad!

"We are so sick as Americans that we are so disjointed and disconnected from other people's pain . . . we go home and say things like 'Well, at least it wasn't us.' That's how disconnected we've become to the reality of pain. It doesn't matter if it's you, if it's Job . . . the grace of God is present even in this suffering. . . . Where is God? . . . He's right here. . . . He hasn't left. He hasn't moved. God did not . . . go, 'What's happening?'" he shouts. "He knew exactly what's going on.

"If you believe that God is a grandpa-looking figure who only rains blessings on top of you . . . that is not the God of the Bible. And you have formed a false God in your own heart. We need to be people of theology. We need to be people who know the God of the Bible. Let me tell you how powerful the God of the Bible is!"

What did Job do when he first found out he had lost everything? He went down and tore his clothes, Paster Jan says. Was there anything else that was torn in the Bible? The curtain over the temple was torn in two when Christ died.

"There is a purpose in suffering," Pastor Jan says forcefully. "The reason why God penetrates into the life of people . . . is so he can rescue people from themselves."

I feel as though he is saying that it is foolish to be sad and that to question God is also foolish.

Ewan is terrified. He crawls into my lap and whispers to me, "I'm scared."

"It'll be over soon," I say. And then I add, as an afterthought: "It is okay to be scared." I do not want him to think his fear is wrong. But Ewan has named this thing: it is fear. This is church and this is a sermon of fear and it is everything that Caroline's house church and Pastor Jeff's church were not. I feel fury in church once again. My child is terrified and has crawled into my lap. I put my hands over his ears.

After church, we move into a side room where long tables and folding chairs have been set up to accommodate us for lunch. In an even smaller room off to the side, two long tables are covered with food. The women are unpacking the generous spread, and it is inspiring to see how many casseroles and desserts a community can produce on short notice when asked to do so. There is marshmallow salad, there are pies and cakes, there are vats of pasta and sauce, and chicken casseroles. At the same time, the sermon has so greatly upset me, I want to leave. Eric tells me that while I may certainly leave, he knows the right thing is for him to stay. And so I sit down and urge Ewan to wander off to investigate the cupcakes.

I ask Juston what he thinks of the sermon, and he gives me a momentary smirk. Then he says, calmly: "I like Pastor Jan even if I don't agree with what he said."

And I think, even if he knows how I am feeling, Juston and I can't talk about my distress now. Not here.

This is so far from the small town of Kimball that I knew growing up; I hardly recognize this place at all. The Kimball of my grandmother's house, her occasional Sunday visit to the Episcopal church around the corner, her pot roasts, her book-reading, and her delight in a new scientific discovery are not a part of this place.

Pastor Jan comes up to Eric. He leans over and shakes Eric's hand. It is that thing between men again, where they greet each other in an expansive way.

Eric says: "You must be drained from so much loss and suffering. You'll need to take a break."

Pastor Jan puts his arms on the back of a chair and his upper body droops as he shakes his head. He *has* been suffering. I watch him as he tells Eric how he nearly threw up when he heard that the woman had been killed by a car. She had been struck by a Kimball resident, and the driver, too, was traumatized. There is so much comforting that he has to do, and Eric nods, no stranger to comforting people in the face of death.

I can instinctively feel that I am not supposed to comfort him. It is only Eric who can do this. It is a tête-à-tête between men—protective men—who look after their flock. I would not have known this at the start of my summer journey, but now I feel surely in my body that comforting is not my role.

What is my role? Surely, as a woman, my role is supposed to be to participate in the baking and cooking, which I have not done. My son comes back to me. He has not found a cupcake. He is not hungry. He wants to sit next to me, he says. So I take him by the hand. "It's lunchtime," I say. "And we need to eat now because we can't eat later." We go back, together, to navigate the maze of Midwestern food sitting there in the Tupperware and CorningWare casserole dishes.

As we leave church, I am stopped by an older couple. They know who I am. They were there at the sermon and at lunch and they saw me, and someone said I owned some ground. They looked at my face and determined I must be a Mockett.

The man says he went to school with my father. They remember my grandmother. They ask me what I am doing here and I say something about how I want to write about agriculture, which is true. But I'm also tired and disturbed by the service and I'm hoping my discomfort doesn't show.

I thank them for remembering me. I try to explain why I am here with this harvesting crew and they listen and smile so kindly and they say nice things about my family. And the sheer normalcy of our interaction almost persuades me that the past two hours have not happened. We are being our polite small-town prairie selves, remembering my family as I want them remembered: my brilliant uncle, my cultured and dignified grandmother, and my sensitive father. They know all this about me. But I cannot relax into the homecoming moment this could be.

People are getting into cars, and other people are bringing home desserts consolidated in Tupperware containers, and still other people are going home with empty Tupperware containers (their names written on masking tape stuck to the bottom). The couple continue to stand there, so kind and interested in me. I feel split in two—the manners and the fury. Does no one else see what was so ugly?

My son tugs my arm and I use this as my excuse to go. "I'm so sorry," I say. "It's been a rather long morning." And we go to the bunkhouse to play.

Early the next day, Ewan and I emerge from the bunkhouse, where we have been sleeping. He looks up at the sky and tells me thoughtfully: "God is up there."

"Yes," I say, a little surprised. We don't discuss God at home.

"He is everywhere," Ewan observes. "He sees everything." And then, in his little dramatic fashion, he begins to tell me with great feeling how God controls everything, the dust, the storms, and the wind. He learned this in church. No matter how much I might dislike Pastor Jan, and how much I might have hated the sermon and Ewan might have feared it, the effect has been profound. The awe of watching that grown man speak from the pulpit was enough to convince him that God is real, and I wonder what this dark magic is that has convinced my son that something invisible and unknown to him before Nebraska now exists.

Later, Ewan and I meet Eric and some of the crew and we drive out to inspect the fields. Eric asks Michael what he thought of the sermon.

"I liked it." Michael grins. "I agree with Pastor Jan that God is more powerful than Satan. I agree that God was in control of that lady dying."

"God is in control," Eric agrees. "But I think I detected a hint of predestination talk in the sermon—the idea that God knows who will die and when. And I believe in free will. I believe God gives us a choice. God always allows us to choose to believe him."

"He's a great speaker," Michael says.

"Powerful pastor," Eric agrees.

"Old-school," Juston says.

"Like a young Billy Graham." Michael nods.

Is it because they are men that they saw something of value in this sermon that I can't? Have I perhaps followed them to the edge of some trail, only to lose them, now, because I can't go any farther, because I am a woman and I can't appreciate what it is to be a man in this particular world?

"Did you really like church?" I ask Eric much later, when we are alone in his pickup.

There is a long pause. It is a very, very long pause. Even for Eric this is a long pause. The longest pause yet. "Well," he begins. This is the universal farmers' word of avoidance. "I would say. It was maybe. A little bit shallow." And I decide to let that word—"shallow"—hang there as a point of hope for me.

By afternoon we are cutting and Ewan and I are standing together in a field watching the combines. Juston and I have had numerous conversations about whether or not Ewan and I should try to ride with Bradford or Amos. Two combines come toward us, and I'm unsure who drives which. Ewan puts his hand up as though to hail a cab. Bradford stops and opens his door. And we get on.

"I couldn't tell what you were doing," he chides me.

"Yes, well, we weren't sure either," I say lamely.

Ewan is thrilled. He announces that it is his lucky day because he is riding in a combine. Ewan is delighted by the bumpy ride. He squeals "Whee!" each time Bradford goes over a bump. Before long the combine goes over the bumps faster and faster and harder and harder. Neither Eric nor Michael ever drives this bumpily. Soon Bradford is spinning in circles, ostensibly to cut around a pole, or to turn back and go the way we have come, and each time Bradford does this, Ewan is ecstatic. Bradford has a tiny smile pressed into his face; I've seen the same expression on his father. It is like he is trying not to smile too hard. I remember all the times Juston told me that Bradford teaches Sunday school to little children, and how they adore him back home in Pennsylvania.

Along the way Ewan asks a few boy-like questions. "What happens if a man goes into the grain bin?"

"Nothing," Bradford says, "as long as the combine isn't turned on."

"What if it's turned on?"

"Don't go in the bin."

"What is the yield? What is the moisture?"

"Look here. It says on the computer screen."

"Isn't it funny when the rye goes flying? Isn't the rye cool?"

"It's not that cool." Bradford frowns. "We don't like rye."

Toward the end of the ride we hear Eric's voice come over the radio. "Can anyone hear me?"

"Yes," Samuel says.

"Yes," Bradford says.

Eric wants to know how the cutting is going and Bradford responds, but the message is garbled. Samuel, located at a point between the crews, is able to relay the message that we are finished. Bradford puts on his Bluetooth.

"You look kinda cool with that headset," Ewan says,

"Thanks."

Bradford begins to charge the combine up a steep and rocky cliff.

"You rock climbing?" Amos teases.

"I'm just trying to get a clear signal," Bradford says, and he calls Eric directly to ask if he should send Juston over to Eric's location with the grain cart.

This is the other side of the harvest crew, the side I have been missing. I needed Ewan—a boy—to see it myself.

It is evening, and Ewan and I have driven to the Knowellses' homestead and are waiting now in the dirt parking lot outside the steel building. Caroline pulls up in a semitruck. She is driving to Sidney to take a load of millet to a privatcly owned elevator that specializes in organic grain. Riding with her is the only way we will have a chance for an intimate conversation during harvest.

Ewan climbs up into the sleeper area of the truck. I hear him humming to himself. Then Caroline asks me what I thought of Pastor Jan and I tell her the truth. "I'm afraid something is wrong with me," I say. "I didn't grow up with Jesus. I fear sometimes that I am overly sensitive. Maybe my lack of experience is showing."

I tell her that I feel bad because I would like to believe I have no bias when it comes to church, but that I found Pastor Jan angry and false. I didn't believe him. I did not like that my son had been afraid of him and I did not like that he had made such a great show afterward, in front of us, of needing Eric's comfort.

Right away, Caroline is shaking her head. "No, no," she soothes. "You know what you are talking about." I have a familiar feeling of being rescued by her goodness and friendship.

"I think your lack of experience is better," she says.

Caroline had never been to Pastor Jan's church before and neither had her daughters, but they had all attended the memorial service for the dead teacher. When Jan cried, Caroline didn't believe him either.

I tell her about the sermon and how it focused on God giving Satan permission to bring suffering to Job. The sermon was not designed to bring consolation. We are, he seemed to imply, spoiled and in need of a grand correction when we grieve. "Can that be true?" I ask. Am I soft because I am a mother with a son and I do not wish to see him scared? And because I worry about my son, am I biased and unappreciative of how hard life can and should be, and have I mistakenly transferred these feelings into the grandiose wish that no one should be scared or hurt ever?

We are on the interstate, heading east to Sidney. There is a steady, though sparse, flow of traffic. Mostly we see pickup trucks and large rigs like ours. Caroline drives, pulling levers and switches. The truck is old and the sound from the motor and the road fills the cab at a high volume; we have to yell to hear each other.

She tells me calmly that she agrees that God is in control. She, like Eric, has been taught not to pray for a natural miracle, because rain for her might mean hail for someone else. She can pray for forbearance to deal with any lessons taught, and the ability to persevere. But she must not ask for a specific thing. God is greater than anything we can understand, and our ability to trace causality goes only so far.

She says that she was also taught to look at the Old Testament as predicting what would happen when the Messiah came. Job has to be taken in that context—that Jesus has not come yet, and that when he comes, all the Old Testament rules will be wiped out. No more animal sacrifice, no more of the kind of suffering we endured in the past, because Jesus is here to show us the way to eternity. We have to remember Jesus striding into the temple, effectively telling the priests that their rules and checklists are meaningless.

"You know, people who are wealthy may live and die never being right with God, and people may be right with God but suffer terribly. The point is that he gave us a way to be with him eternally."

I think that the end of days cannot possibly be coming, because people have such a very long way to go to do even a fraction of what Jesus asked us to do. "Do you think the world was created in six days?" I ask.

"I don't question if the world was literally created in six days or more. A day for God could be thousands of years. I just know that Jesus will come back and that humans will be judged. But I try not to worry about when that might be." She pauses. "Sundays are used for honoring Jesus because he arose on a Sunday. We try to think about him and think about phrases in the Bible that relate to Jesus. We don't spend a lot of time trying to scare people into believing in Jesus."

I ask her if her faith has a name, and she says that it doesn't. I ask her if she could recognize others like her, the way that Eric picks out different Christians in restaurants and airports. She says that she has in the past. There is a quality she and others like her can see in one another and they know they are of the same faith. *Certain conditions yield certain things.*

"I think you can tell," she says. "You can see it when people are fo-cused mostly on the words of Jesus."

When my grandmother was alive and I visited Kimball, I saw myself in her house: in the Moroccan chandelier hanging from the ceiling, in her meticulously arranged vinyl records featuring Leonard Bernstein and American musical theater. That is not how Caroline lives. But there are traces of what bound my family to hers in trust and friend-ship. I can sit in her truck and tell her I am not sure I can believe the people who congregate in the largest church in town, and she can tell me that she understands. We are country and city. It feels as though we have found a fragment of the very core of her family and mine that brought us together in the first place. It is, for me, enough to feel trust. It tells me something about the people I came from.

That afternoon I see that the boys are cleaning all the equipment and I know this means we are leaving. I feel at once as if I want to get away from whatever sick and shadowy thing I encountered in church and enormously sad to be leaving this place that was my father's home. I have not returned to the cemetery since we arrived, and I would like to say that I go back there now. I would like to report that I look at my grand-mother's grave and see her command: "The sun also ariseth," and that I feel something of her transcendent love and that this fixes my heart.

"Marie," Eric says. "We need to get permits to drive on Interstate 80 across Wyoming. I was thinking it might go a lot more smoothly at the port if you come. You know. You're a woman."

I send Caroline a text and ask if this is true, expecting her to reply with a humorous comment, but she doesn't. She tells me that it is true. It is a realistic strategy to go to the port of entry to Wyoming with a woman in hopes of making the entry process smoother.

Until now, Eric has chosen routes that generally skirt the main inter-states so he does not have to pay the fee to use those roads. To go to Idaho, however, we are going to have to cross the Rocky Mountains. We are also attempting to drive 576 miles in one day. At that rate, small and scenic roads are a nuisance and we need the interstate; to drive on the interstate, we need permits.

Ewan has stayed behind at the trailer park with Michael. As we drive
to Wyoming for the permits, Eric says: "So, he told me."

"Who?"

"Mark."

Oh, that. "Right," I say.

"You knew?"

"Yes."

"I asked him why he's gay. And he said that it's probably a combination of genetics and environment. But mostly genetics."

"That's right."

No one has ever come out to Eric before; it is a new experience. Mark
had told me, before he left, that one reason he felt safe coming out to
Eric was because he knew of Eric's defense of gay rights, and because
this meant that perhaps one day Mark could return here with his husband and be welcome. And I tell Eric this. But what I don't add is how
precarious all this feels for the moment. All this acceptance relies on the
presence of a handful of us, and I wonder if and when we are gone—
Caroline, Eric, Juston, and I—Mark actually can return here.

I don't know if we can credit my female presence or not, but we do get
our permits at the Wyoming port quite easily. Then we move the equipment to the parking lot of a Peterbilt dealership with which Eric has a
long-standing agreement. Once parked, we get into the pickups, head
back to Nebraska, and stop for dinner at the A&W in Pine Bluffs. There
are two Humvees parked outside. Inside the eatery, Air Force person-
nel are eating burgers and drinking root beer. There are truck drivers,
too, the scrawny, tattooed kind with stringy hair and bodies marinated
in hours and hours of tobacco. At another table, three men and two
little boys all wear caps and jeans; every single one has a set of pliers
attached to his belt. Eric nods at them and looks at me and smiles; he
knows I have recognized our tribe.

"I hate this drive," Amos confides. Ever since our long combine ride
together, he has warmed to me a little: proof, I tell myself, that just listening means people will open up to you.

"Tomorrow you should drive ahead of us and go straight."

"Where are we going, exactly?"

"Pocatello."

"But where in Pocatello?"

No one gives me additional information.

"Just drive straight there," Amos says.

Back in Kimball, I spend a frenzied forty-five minutes cleaning up the bunkhouse and shutting it down; Bradford and others will be back here in a matter of weeks for the millet harvest. Still, I feel sad leaving behind my father's boots and my great-grandfather's tennis trophies.

I wonder how many more times I will come back here. In the last dream I had of my grandmother's house, the old brick family home was inhabited by a farmer who said he would be "taking care of everything." I wonder, too, if I have been coming back to the farm out of some misplaced homing instinct, which has me going through the motions of what it looks like to be a farmer, without any capacity to farm. Have I come here each summer since my father died only to hold the ghost of my family in my arms?

I debate taking the note on the wall in my father's handwriting with my phone number. In the end, I leave it, because I would like to see it there when I come back the following summer.

★ ★ ★ ★

PART FOUR

★ ★ ★ ★

TWELVE

AT 4 A.M., it is still dark when I carry a sleeping Ewan out to the car and deposit him in the booster seat, wrapped in a blanket and nestled with his two stuffed animals, including the intrepid Kitty, who has been to Japan, the UK, and Cambodia, and who will now travel a part of the Oregon Trail.

Emily has given me a walkie-talkie so I can listen to the chatter as we cross the country. When I get to the RV park, the crew is ready to go. The harvesters head off in three pickups, each pulling a trailer. I am the lone passenger car driving in the dark toward Cheyenne.

The only good thing about these extremely early mornings is the sunrise. The sky today is less spectacular than the early dawns in Texas, but it is still a marvel to watch the day appear out of the night. The sun peers over the pink horizon. Darkness and void slowly peel away, yielding to color and shape.

At the Peterbilt dealership, Luther, Samuel, Bradford, and Amos leave their pickups and climb aboard their chosen semis. They test their radios to be sure they will be connected to one another for the long drive. Eric, Luther, and Bethany will each drive a pickup.

Emily circles the parking lot with a basket filled with granola bars and packaged breakfast foods on her arm. She hands them out to the drivers one at a time.

Eric says over the radio: "It's clear to the west." He has been looking at the sky. "I want us to cross before the heat sets in." There is no cloud coverage and there will be no rain and it will be hot today. We begin to pull out of the Peterbilt lot, one driver at a time.

The men are on the radio frequently, advising one another on how they look ("You're looking good, Amos"); who is passing them ("Three motorcycles coming on the left, Luther"); and when a lane is closed ("When you get to the overpass, start shifting left. Lane closed ahead"). We are frequently in the company of packs of motorcycles traveling the interstate on their way to South Dakota. We guess that some of them will go to Sturgis, and then head south to Nebraska to see the full eclipse, which is a week away.

The green part of Wyoming gives way to the rocky western part. Eric doesn't like this landscape as much. There are no more farms and the landscape is rugged—the land of scrawny cattle, refineries, rock formations, and parched earth. This is hard country, devoid of softness and of beauty. There are men on this land, though, and they are drilling for natural gas and oil.

We drive and drive, away from the sun, though still the morning overtakes us, and finally, hours later, it is a bright sky with a hot, high sun, and we make a stop in Sinclair, the eponymous town for which the gasoline company with the dinosaur mascot is named. Ewan wakes up there and I run into the service store to buy a T-shirt and coffee. I ask where we will be stopping next and am told: "Little America for lunch."

We push on.

By the time we reach Little America, I am exhausted. We have been driving for six hours and still have three to go.

In Scotts Bluff the museum displays of the Oregon Trail spoke of the yearning people felt to get to the promised land of Oregon, or even just to Utah, as they set out from Missouri. The display included a special feature on women. At one point Emily and I talked about how, while following their men, the women gave birth and sometimes died on the journey. It wasn't possible to stop men from having sex, we decided. Women got pregnant. The babies grew and were born and the women and the babies either lived or died. We decided we would not have survived the journey. We would have died of heat stroke, thirst, or exhaustion. And here I am now, driving across Wyoming in a car with my son for seven hours, and I am irritated. I do not have the stamina for this much driving, and my fatigue is changing me. But Bethany is in the caravan, driving a pickup truck that pulls a trailer; there are no complaints from her over the radio.

When we turn north, almost immediately the landscape melts from the hardscrabble rock and desiccated brush of western Wyoming and reassembles into something green and wondrous. We are in a subset of the larger Rocky Mountain chain. It rained here recently and everything is emerald. This is not the heavy jade green of the Rockies in Colorado, or even the dark evergreen mountains of the Sierra Nevadas.

These mountains are chartreuse and lime, with wedge-shaped conifers on the summits, pointing upward at a pale blue sky. My eyes cling to the fresh colors with a primal hunger. It is as if a celestial hand has turned up the dial and bleached the colors on a filter covering the land, so all is brightened and heightened. It would have been like this for the people on the Oregon Trail, though this same route would have taken them days rather than hours. Did they, too, cry at the sight of the reinvigorated palette?

The road drops us onto a canvas splashed with green and blue. We fall into a valley and a string of towns. The scenery softens and speaks the language of farming again, but this farming is very different from farming on the plains. Most fields here are tended by robotic sprinkler systems that march along inch by inch, spraying water.

A thin band of silver glitters on the horizon and my mind reflexively translates this into the ocean. But we aren't in California. We are finally entering the Snake River Plain, a four-hundred-mile-long valley in southern Idaho that stretches east to west from the southern border of Wyoming to eastern Oregon. Most of Idaho's major cities are located within this valley, which is curved like a bow, with the southern part sagging down and the ends arcing up. The mountains that border it to the north and east include the enormous dragon's-teeth range, the Grand Tetons, near Yellowstone National Park. And these mountains, in turn, are part of the massive Rocky Mountain range, formed when the Farallon slab subducted under the North American plate 70 million years ago.

The Snake River Plain itself is believed to have been created over millions of years by the Yellowstone supervolcano, a hypothesized hot spot that rests underneath Yellowstone National Park in Wyoming, and which geologists surmise erupts with some regularity every 700,000 to 800,000 years. As the North American plate passed over the stationary Yellowstone hot spot—moving even today at a rate of about one centimeter a year—sometimes lava poured out and sometimes an entire volcano erupted, sending ash all the way to present-day Baja California. As the heated parts shifted to the west, they cooled and compressed and grew heavy and formed a depression; the accumulation of these depressions is the Snake River basin. The remnants of past volcanoes often formed hollowed-out areas, called calderas, on top of the basin, and these calderas appear with regularity, one circle after another, stamping out the Snake River Plain into the deep valley it is today. One of the reasons the Tetons are so high is that the land to their west—the Snake River Plain—is weighed down, thus displacing the mountains farther upward.

Over the radio I hear someone say something about "waiting for escort." Emily calls me and patiently explains that for a portion of Interstate 15 the trucks are required by law to have a pilot car lead them, supposedly so they are "safe." In other words, the law insists on someone looking out for them in exactly the same way they have already been looking out for one another—noticing who is passing and who is not and what might be in the way. The voices grow distant on the radio as I pull farther ahead. Samuel is still looking out for Amos, and Amos is still looking out for Luther. Bradford is still in the lead, looking out for everyone, and Eric is in the rear.

I ask Emily where I should go.

"Go to the Fort Hall Casino."

"A casino?"

"There is an RV park there. That's where we'll be staying. You might see if there is a room in the hotel, since you have Ewan."

"Look at all that wheat," Ewan says from the back seat. "There is a lot to cut. Eric will be happy." Indeed, the fields are heavy—thanks to irrigation. In Idaho, the norm is to refer to farmland as dryland only if it is dry, because most farmland is irrigated. This is in contrast to the part of the High Plains where I have been, where the norm is dryland and irrigation the exception. Both the High Plains and the Snake River Plain have what is called an aquifer—a subterranean supply of water—that can be accessed to nourish crops. Both aquifers are in danger of overuse, and farmers in the part of the wheat belt I have been traveling don't tend to pay the money required to access water; it is expensive and the water is disappearing without recharging quickly enough. But in Idaho most farmers irrigate.

It is not only the heavy presence of water that makes this landscape so alien. There are so many newly constructed buildings painted bright white; gone are the abandoned rain-and-hail-weathered homesteads and one-room schoolhouses of Nebraska. I see a Starbucks. I can buy a good cup of coffee now. There are chain stores of every kind and new churches and malls. I am surrounded by money.

I had thought the drive would take me nine hours, but instead it has taken eleven. I look and feel like an angry, tired single parent with an energetic child in tow. It is an extraordinary relief to park on the asphalt lot of the casino complex. From the outside, the casino is unremarkable: a squat, square building. I can't see even a single slot machine through the windows. The hotel is a much more splendid thing, multistoried, with revolving doors and large glass windows. Discreetly placed posters announce a powwow in about two weeks' time. I walk into the hotel in my boots and my straw hat from Texas. The ceilings are high and the air conditioning is strong and soothing. Ewan runs around in a circle on the tile floor and I stop and try to take in what I see. The signs are bilingual: English and a Native American language.

I am tired and I go to the counter and ask for a room.

There are two women at the hotel help desk. I look at them and they look at me. They are the color of rain-stained earth and their hair is long and black. Their eyes barely betray their curiosity about me, but I register instantly that they are Indians. There are paintings on the wall around me of Indians on the plains. The painted Indians are riding horses and pulling tepees. The logo of the hotel is of the sun, made up of little dots, like mosaic tiles or beads. The Shoshone-Bannock tribes are known for their beadwork; Sacagawea, who accompanied Lewis and Clark, was Shoshone.

What do they see when they see me? I know, as I did in Vernon, Texas, when I had my nails done, that these women *see* me. They have taken in my features, and recognize that I am not white. But they don't ask me any questions. They just assign me a room. Not for the first time, I look at my son, who will always look white to the world, and think: There is so much you will miss. There is so much he will have access to that I do not, because he is white and male. But there is also so much he won't see and so many ways he won't be seen.

We eat in the restaurant and then climb into bed and turn ourselves over to this modern world, where, with cash, all our comforts will be tended to by others. I am in a bed that was made by someone else. The air conditioner whines and my body begins to settle back into its regular shape and I am healing from the drive.

Before we fall asleep, I try to explain to Ewan where we are and how we got here. I try to explain that we have traveled the Oregon Trail in a day.

"And now we are in Idaho," I say.

"I like the logo." He is entranced by the sun symbol.

"That's something to do with the Indians," I say. "Those were Indians downstairs." It did not occur to him in the lobby that he was seeing anything so terribly different from what he might see in San Francisco, or perhaps in Japan. But the fact that these women are Indians is a shock to him and I feel it in his rigid body.

"Why do they speak English?"

"They had to learn it after we took their land away and put them on reservations." Which is where we are now. "Sometimes little kids were taken away from their parents on the reservation and sent to learn English at boarding schools."

"What is a reservation?"

So I try to explain, through a haze of sleepiness, about the white man crossing the plains, and claiming this land and putting the Indians on designated pieces of land called reservations. It feels ridiculous to me to be compressing western history into this tiny conversation, but the questions are natural and deserve an answer.

The seizing of the land is not something he has ever thought about and it upsets him. "It is okay, though, isn't it?" he asks in a small voice. "Because they now have India?"

Oh, dear. "No. India is a very different country with very different people." He curls up next to me, into the crook of my arm, which he has done since he was a baby accompanying me on my research trips to Japan. I pat his forehead and very quickly his breathing becomes even and deep and makes me sleepy too. And like this, we comfort each other, and like this, for a time, I can keep the burden of history away from him and from myself.

A few hours later, the caravan will arrive. After a fourteen-hour drive, the young men will set up camp. The Sisters have been awaiting our arrival, and Carrie has prepared dinner. Had I gone to the camp with everyone else, I would have eaten there too. But there is more that will happen while we are sleeping.

Three of the trailers were left behind on Highway 30 and three drivers will be dispatched to unload the heaviest equipment—the combines—on the lot by the casino, then will turn around to go back for another hour and a half to pick up the trailers, and then turn around to bring back the additional cargo. Eric travels this way because he is so often stopped on Interstate 15 for hauling the extra equipment; his configurations, remember, include a semitruck pulling two large pieces of equipment (a combine and a hopper with headers inside). While Wyoming allows this kind of configuration, Idaho does not, and Eric does not want to weigh his rigs on the scales in Idaho only to pay an additional fine. It simply saves time and hassle to do the final leg in two trips.

What is more, one of the combines—the experimental combine—has been left behind because Eric's entire outfit was set up for only the three machines he brought from Pennsylvania. This means that starting around 8 p.m., after dinner the same day the caravan arrives, Bradford and Samuel leave Idaho to go back to Nebraska. Bradford sleeps from eight till midnight while Samuel drives. They cross the mountains and backtrack through the gray part of Wyoming.

Then Bradford wakes and drives from midnight to 6 a.m. while Samuel sleeps past the A&W at Pine Bluffs, all the way to my family's hometown. They reach Kimball at 6 a.m., load the combine, then turn around and begin the drive back. While I am sleeping off my exhaustion and irritation that we made this long trip in one day, the young men are more than doubling their journey.

Fort Hall was established as a fur-trading outpost in 1834 by Nathaniel Wyeth, who also set up Fort William near present-day Portland, Oregon. Both forts were unable to compete financially with the much larger Hudson's Bay Company, run by the English crown, and were sold to the Hudson's Bay Company in 1837. But Fort Hall's location had been strategic; as settlers crossing the emigrant trails dropped down out of the mountains and into the Snake River Plain, as Ewan and I had done, they needed a place to restock supplies. The fort was perfectly located to greet these new settlers. Not far from Fort Hall, the emigrant trails parted: one could go either west to Oregon or south to California.

A replica of the original Fort Hall, in Pocatello, operates as a museum, displaying photos, animal pelts, and a tepee, and focuses on the 1830s, during which time rugged mountain men trapped animals for furs while looking for new trails through the mountains. Some of the white settlers lived with Native women. The land in these displays is depicted as "new" and uncrowded.

But by the 1850s, the land was much more densely occupied, and the Shoshone were frustrated that so many farmers and homesteads were making it difficult to hunt for buffalo. This led to skirmishes. The Shoshone chief Pocatello periodically led his people in raids against the emigrants in an effort to protect his hunting grounds, and the whites fought back. If this story sounds familiar to you, it should.

In 1863, the US government approved an organized counterattack. Colonel Patrick Edward Connor took his troops out from Fort Douglas, near the Utah-Idaho border, and up into an area near present-day Preston, Idaho, about 110 miles due north of Salt Lake City. More than four hundred Shoshone, including women and children, were slaughtered in the Bear River Massacre, sending the message that attacks against the settlers would not be tolerated. Pocatello, who had undertaken so many past raids against the white man, had heard about this impending attack and sent his people into hiding. He understood that he was witnessing a permanent change to his people and his land. He offered peace in exchange for a new place to live, and in 1868 was granted a residence on a 1.8 million–acre tract of land along the Snake River. This is the Fort Hall Reservation, where the casino and hotel now stand.

As was the case in Oklahoma territory, the size of the Fort Hall Reservation shrank over time. The Dawes Act, which had "opened" Oklahoma for settlement to white people, was also applied to Pocatello's people in 1888. The Shoshone, too, were forced to "prove" that they were members of their tribe in exchange for 160-acre plots per family; the rest was given to white settlers. During World War II, an additional 3,300 acres were seized and developed into an air base, with a promise to return the land once the war ended. Instead, this land was sold to the nearby town—named Pocatello—for one dollar. Conflicts over the land continue today.

In the morning, Ewan and I walk to the RV park, passing heavy construction equipment beeping and barking as it moves across the earth; the tribe is building annexes to expand the casino and the hotel. Behind the construction grounds is the RV park, a shady campsite with regularly spaced asphalt-covered parking spaces, each with a tree and a picnic table. In the middle of the park is a grassy field with a brick building that houses toilets and showers.

It is difficult to read Emily's expression. Is she tired? Frustrated? Is she happy here on the Indian reservation? The one thing Emily always retains, no matter her surroundings, is dignity. When she opens the trailer door to greet me, there she is, immaculate and self-possessed, though we have driven countless hours across the land to set up camp in this RV park, where, not too far away, men and women are smoking and drinking and playing slot machines.

Emily is all business. She makes sure we have slept well, then tells me that Eric has already found fields to cut. He and the Sisters are out in the country. She softens when she sees Ewan.

Emily tells me to drive a pickup truck and not my passenger car. Once I meet up with the crew, I find out why. Ewan and I drive through a newly sprouted, up-to-date *Leave It to Beaver* neighborhood with thick green lawns and houses with lace curtains and shingled roofs. I turn off one of the neighborhood roads, go up another paved road, and then turn onto a dirt road. Outside of town, the roads quickly become unpaved and uneven in quality. In Nebraska, most farm roads can be traversed in a passenger car; many are graded. Not so here. The dirt roads are filled with potholes, and though I drive around the indentations as I was taught to do, the pickup still lurches and bobbles. Juston is waiting in the other pickup; he has been sent to find us. We rejoin the harvest caravan.

We line up to get across a cattle guard. One of the combines bobbled going across and a tire slipped off the rail, causing damage to the underbelly of the combine. Though it still runs, it does not run well. As the other combines cross the cattle guard, the drivers continue to look out for one another, encouraging one another that they cleared well, that their tires are fine.

What follows is a long day of happy cutting. At one point, an elderly man with his wife and their dog in the back of a pickup drive over to see us. The man wears a cowboy hat and has a sly, winking look that reminds me of the cowboys I saw in Texas. His wife—petite, blond, and fully made-up with lipstick—is so perfectly beautiful, like a proverbial porcelain doll plucked from a cabinet and set beside her husband. She must be at least eighty years old. How is it possible that a woman her age can preserve her femininity, and in a pickup truck at that? She is not like the practical women of the plains.

A young blond woman shows up to talk to Eric. She is also stunningly beautiful, only she is in jeans, boots, and a T-shirt. I'm unclear who she is and who is in charge.

We are deployed in two teams: the Sisters cut one field and the Wolgemuth Brothers the other. The fields are located at the base of foothills, and the farmland slopes slightly. Dwayne's silver combines are far away in one corner of the land and we are in another. Then our combines spread even farther apart.

Ewan and I spend much of the day riding with Eric. It is hot and I can see why the Shoshone worshipped the sun; it is so bright outside. At one point, Eric digs into the ground and pulls out a potato. He shows it to Ewan and skins it with his pocketknife and hands it to him to eat. Ewan recoils and Eric laughs and eats the potato raw.

Eric and Amos are dispatched to cut a field that is farther to the south. We will need to take a shortcut across a river, which in turn will require the combines to go under a tall tree that has not been trimmed in years. Eric radios and asks for a chain saw. While we wait, we cut another field, and finally someone drives over in a pickup with the tool we need. Eric clears the hanging branches that might scrape the combines. Then we begin to caravan across the "danger zone," as Ewan refers to the bridge, which is barely wide enough for the tires. In fact, the wheels of Amos's combine puff out on either side of the bridge so it is only the interiors of the tires that keep him centered. He's nervous on the radio, but he makes it across, and we cut yet another field.

"How is it in the hotel?" Eric asks me.

"It's fine," I say. "Surreal."

"Not like the trailer."

"No." And then I tell him how Ewan and I talked about the history of the Native Americans, and how it is that we happen to be staying in a hotel owned by the Shoshone-Bannock tribes.

"Make sure he knows that the white man didn't intend for it to work out that way," Eric says.

I turn this phrase over in my mind.

Eric adds, "They didn't even have the wheel."

This is a new one for me. "Is that like 'the white men had the gun'?" He nods.

It makes no sense to look back and forgive the white man for any of the bad things that happened. This is not a story about forgiveness. The story of the Native Americans losing their land is simply the story of what happened. We had the technology and the weapons and they did not and we took their land. Older empires have come to an end before. Cultures have died before. It is what happens with people.

At least I think this is the story.

Ewan and I visit the town of Montpelier for the "Travelin' West" interpretive exhibit at the Oregon Trail Center. Montpelier, once called Clover Creek, was a campsite used by the settlers on their trek westward. After they came down from the mountains in their covered wagons and with their handcarts they stopped for three days at Clover Creek to rest before going on to Fort Hall. In the exhibit, we can have a small, re-created stroll through what the push west entailed. The trail's years of greatest use were 1846 to 1869, after which the Union Pacific Railroad linked the regions of the country together.

It is 1852, and Ewan and I are leaving the crowded eastern city of Independence, Missouri, for the promise of fresh land in the West. Before we leave, we will go on a shopping trip in a re-created store. We are urged to buy weapons to use against the Indians, who might try to take our horses. We will need a five-month supply of food. We will need a wagon. We will need canvas to cover the top of the wagon, and as we drive through the grass, we will look like ships. People will call our wagons "prairie schooners."

Both England and the United States had a presence in this wild country. To whom would the land finally belong? No one wanted another bloody war like the American Revolution, so the United States encouraged its own people to take this valuable territory one homestead at a time with the hope that eventually it would be too full of Americans to ever be a part of England. In 1846 the US ultimately acquired what would become the Pacific Northwest states, while England took what became Canada. Still settlement continued; there were certain requirements that needed to be met for a territory to become a state, and population of a certain size was one of them. To make the offer more tantalizing, Oregon would be the first place where a woman could own land and have her name on the deed.

The odds are in our favor that Ewan and I will survive the brutal trip, but the statistics are also harsh. Eighteen percent of people who attempt the crossing will die.

Our purchases completed, Ewan and I are ushered onto a re-created covered wagon, which in reality is a small theater that rocks and creaks as though pulled by oxen, while overhead a projector casts shadows of leaves and simulates the rising and falling sun, while prerecorded voices read out letters written on the crossing. When the wagon stops and the curtains part, we are greeted by a woman in period dress who welcomes us to Clover Creek. It is evening and we have stepped back in time to a meticulously re-created campsite. The woman walks us through the campground, explaining that our wagon train moved fifteen to twenty miles each day. She points to a coat made from the skin of a black bear that had tried to take away the last of a pioneer's salted ham. Simulated coals burn over a dying fire, and the sunset glows on the horizon.

When our Oregon Trail experience is over, Ewan and I explore the rest of the exhibits. Downstairs, the museum is full of paraphernalia that chronicles the settling of the town. After the West was won and the Oregon Trail abandoned, the trains came through.

The lady who guided us back in time comes out, like an actor taking a curtain call, and we chat for a bit. I ask the woman if her family had come here on the Oregon Trail.

"Later. On the Mormon Trail. It was terrible, you know. The persecution. Chasing the women and children out in the middle of the night clear into the Mississippi." I realize I do not know my history at all. The Mormon Trail, she explains, started in Nauvoo, Illinois, site of the first Mormon settlement, then headed west, running roughly parallel to the Oregon Trail. The Mormon Trail was taken only by Mormons, who feared being terrorized if they traveled with nonbelievers after incidents of persecution in Nauvoo. And where, she wonders, am I from?

Ewan's standard answer in this case is to explain that he is from New York and I am from California. Then he says: "The farmers are from Pennsylvania."

"Farmers?"

I tell her about our caravan.

"We saw you!" she exclaims. "We came out to look. My husband explained that you come through every year and sell your equipment and go home."

"Are you sure?"

"Five trucks," she says. "Big equipment."

I tell her that the farmers, in fact, do not sell the equipment, but drive it home, albeit along a different route. When it is time to return, they drive record hours in a day and take the interstate back, paying for all the permits to get across in a hurry.

"Well," she says, "you are absolutely beautiful. Just beautiful. Your skin and your eyes and everything. Don't you ever let anyone tell you otherwise."

I thank her, and Ewan and I begin the drive back to the hotel.

Back on the Indian reservation, I play and replay her curious last sentence in my mind: *Don't ever let anyone tell you otherwise.* What history did she see in me that led her to tell me this? It is only when I wake with a start in the middle of the night—Ewan is sound asleep—that I realize I would never have qualified for land in Oregon. It didn't matter that in Oregon women could own property. There would have been neither the Mormon Trail nor the Oregon Trail for me. It was not until 1952 that the Supreme Court defended the right of people of Asian descent to own land in Oregon. Though Oregon was established as a free state, even blacks could not originally own land there. If a settler arrived with slaves, he had three years to set his people free, but the emancipated men and women could not own land themselves and could, in fact, legally be beaten.

The settlers were white.

And now here I am in this skin. A landowner.

On the reservation, the sun logo is emblazoned on mugs and on the signs over the doorways and on the hotel itself. One day, when Ewan has had enough combine rides and history lessons, we stay in the hotel room and make a paper tepee and a paper Fort Hall. I cut colored paper into tiny squares and trace the sun on a paper plate, intending to teach him to make a mosaic. I am exhausted and I want to stay here, in the air-conditioned room in the haven of motherhood, and just let time pass.

In the evening my husband, Gordon, arrives. His meetings are over and he is here to take Ewan back to San Francisco the next morning. We all go swimming in the hotel pool. There are several Native American families there, and soon Gordon is pulling Ewan on a giant floating device while three Native children hold on to the end. The powwow will take place soon on the reservation, and the RV park and hotel are beginning to fill up with people who are here for the celebration.

In the morning, we check out of the hotel. The woman at the counter asks me: "Did you enjoy your stay?"

"Yes," I say. It is the truth.

"Where are you going next?" she asks.

I explain that Ewan and Gordon will go back to San Francisco, but that I will go to the RV park. At this, I see her hesitate ever so slightly.

"Is it OK there?" she asks.

What does she mean? I am used to staying in wilder places with no amenities, and I appreciate that at the RV park at least there is a store and a gas station and even a post office. "Yes," I say, cautiously.

"Are you going to the Sun Dance?" she asks without making eye contact. And there it is. A parting in the air. The staff has been so professional. There has been none of the "Where are you from?" or "Is it your mother of father?" questions that I get in the nail salons. I have been quite sure since I arrived that the Indians see me, and whatever is happening now, I know, is expressly because of how I look. This would not be happening to Ewan if he were here with Gordon.

"Do you mean the powwow?" I ask.

"I mean at Ross Fork," she says.

I have never heard of Ross Fork. "Is it open to the public?"

"Not really. But *you* can go."

My heart quickens. I am at a fork in the road and did not even know it.

I leave the shop and speak to the concierge. "I'm wondering if you can tell me where Ross Fork is."

"You are looking for the Sun Dance?" She smiles.

"Yes," I say.

"It's left out of the parking lot," she says.

I don't explain to her that I am not a tribal member. I don't want her to ask me who my people are, because then she will know that I have no people. I just ask if it's truly okay for me to attend, and she assures me I can go, and that I can even take my son and my husband. It is about ten miles away. I need to drive on something called Simplot Road, which turns into Ross Fork Road, and then I will see it. Another girl comes out from the back of the hotel and the concierge confirms the name of the road I am to take. Simplot Road. Still, I ask again if I may go to the Sun Dance. "Yes," the women say almost in unison.

"You *should* go," one says.

It seems almost biblical to me that if I have been told three times to go somewhere, I ought to go. At least this is what I tell myself.

The three of us have about an hour together before Gordon and Ewan have to leave for the airport, and though neither of them wants to go, they agree to humor me. Simplot Road, a two-lane asphalt road, gives way to Ross Fork Road fairly quickly and we are in the scrubby, barren landscape of Idaho. There is nothing here but the occasional low, rusted tin and tired, pegged-together structure—an Indian home. The road curves and we follow it, passing only one irrigated field of wheat whose plumpness makes it look curiously out of place. Then there is nothing but gray land.

Off to the right, I see some tents and trucks and a curious structure. I say "curious" and "structure," but I'm not altogether clear that's what it is. It almost looks like a mirage, quivering in and out of focus; it might be something made by man, or it might be an accident of nature. "That must be it," I say when we are a little closer. It looks, to my untrained eye, like a distant cousin of a ceremonial structure I might see in Japan, only it isn't made out of bamboo, but out of trees, and in Japan, there is no doubt about ceremonial structures. Even if they are temporary, they are solidly made and clearly marked with a white rope or by a strong color or distinctive details.

A dirt road juts sharply to the right. There is no sign that says: "Sun Dance." But there is a sign in fluorescent handwritten letters on white poster board that reads: "Indian Tacos."

"That must be the turnoff," I say.

We turn off by the taco sign, and continue on another paved road, then turn off onto a dirt road.

There are a dozen or so empty portable chairs outside the structure. Ewan eyes the tree house and the empty chairs with skepticism. He refuses to get out of the car. Whatever is going on, he wants no part of it.

"You have to get out of the car," I say. "You'll overheat in there."

"I'm not going," he says.

My husband is irritated with me. "I can't leave him here alone. So you go," he says. "Go on. Go have a look."

My son looks at me reproachfully.

Nothing much seems to be happening. The Sun Dance is taking place inside a vaguely circular structure fashioned from loosely clustered bushes, branches, and trees. There is an opening on one end, facing east, the direction of the rising sun. Inside the structure is another concentric circle made of trees and branches. In the very center is a tall tree, perhaps fifteen feet high, with a skull hanging near the top. In between the two circles there are branches covering the ground, and lying on the branches are the people.

Outside the structure, other men and women are resting in portable camping chairs where there is shade. Some people hold umbrellas to shield themselves from the sun. I work my way around toward the entrance of the altar. I have been instructed by the women at the hotel not to cross the threshold, and not to go if I am on my menstrual cycle, which I am not. This rule doesn't offend me; it still exists in places in Japan. At the top of the tree is a blue-and-white flag and a buffalo skull. There is a piece of cloth wrapped around the tree too.

I see a friendly-looking lady and I approach her to ask what is happening. Nothing is happening, she says. There will be nothing for a while. Perhaps around five in the evening the dancers will come out for a break and then I will see them. Until then, there is nothing to see.

She has a quality I recognize, or think I recognize. Warm, brown, welcoming, and grounded. Being here reminds me of what it feels like to be in Japan at a *matsuri*—or festival. I am reminded of old Obon festivals in California, where Japanese people share their food and culture with others. Only there are no others here. I am the lightest face, unless you count those of my husband and son, hiding in the car. I go to the taco stand. They tell me there will be no tacos until noon, and for now there are only breakfast burritos.

It is time for Gordon and Ewan to depart for the airport, so we go back to the parking lot of the hotel to say goodbye.

The parting does not go smoothly. At the eleventh hour, Ewan decides he wants to stay with me at the farm and does not want to leave. His little arms are wrapped tight around my torso and he cries over the pain of the goodbye. I cry too. I feel horrible. There is a way for him to stay, and though it is difficult for me to work when he is with me, I could keep him. But it has been decided he will leave, and so Gordon has to pry Ewan off of my body, restrain him, and put him back in the car. Then I disappear from sight and sit in my car, and watch them drive off while Ewan grieves the loss of his mother. Ewan is very sure I should not stay here, and his raw howling sends every nerve in my body into a state of panic and agitation. I should not stay here. This parting is quite possibly the worst grief I have felt, aside from watching someone I love die.

I go back to the trailer to lie down.

Around 4 p.m. I rouse myself after a nap and drive back out to the Sun Dance.

I am not very far out on the road when I hear sirens, and an ambulance and fire truck surge up behind me. I pull over to let them pass and watch them speed ahead to the Sun Dance parking lot. When I arrive, I ask a man if someone is being removed and put in the ambulance and he laughs. "Oh yeah. All day long. They go out. They come back. All day long."

There are many more cars now around the altar, and when I arrive, I see people staggering out from the inside of the hut. I have brought a chair with me and I stand for a long time trying to take in the scene. Around the altar, I see two women limply circling the central tree, caressing it with a feather. Then they come out wrapped in white sheets. Other men—not participants—are going in to change the leaves on the bedding where even now I see bodies lying.

A woman comes out and is greeted calmly by friends. "There is no air in there. No air." Without a word, the friends open up an umbrella and hold it over her head. She asks for a fan. Around me, men and women are carrying small washcloths, and later, when I go to the parking lot, I see that the cloths are being chilled inside ice chests. The men and women are covering the bodies of the dancers with refrigerated cloths. One man is stretched out on a chair, stripped of all his clothes, with cold cloths on his body. Nearly everyone is overweight. If you look at old pictures of Native people doing the Sun Dance, they are lean and fit. These people are not lean and fit.

Some men are carrying sprigs of mint and soon the air smells sweet and fresh. The helpers are trying to cool down the bodies of the men and women who have been fasting and dancing.

I learn the most from the people at the taco stand, who have just enough meat for one more taco. The taco stand is perhaps fifty yards away from the Sun Dance—close enough to walk to, but difficult for the family members resting in chairs to see. Because the dancers are taking breaks, their family members are arriving in groups of two, four, and eight and asking for tacos. We are now waiting for more meat to arrive. There are two smartphones in the taco stand and one plays Native American music while the other blares pop tunes.

The taco stand is a basic kitchen unit: a cooler with pre-chopped vegetables and a hot gas stove. The fry bread is a miraculous thing, a dollop of dough that flowers into a wide receptacle for cooked and seasoned ground meat, lettuce, tomato, and cheese. I eat mine slowly and talk with the cook behind the counter.

The dancers have had no food or water since Friday. They will dance Monday at sunrise and break their fast after. The families are there to provide support.

Three days of fasting. Three nights, two full days, and two partial days.

I once participated in a three-day meditation and fasting retreat in Japan under the tutelage of a Buddhist priest. He told me that in India fasting and meditation take place over a week, but that there is not much reason to go beyond three days. The first three days are the hardest for fasting. After this it becomes easier. The first three days are the ones that produce the most important effects. People have visions after three days. In Japan I was allowed to drink water, but the Native Americans do not.

I finish the taco. And I purchase a bottle of water. It is now quite hot. I don't know what I am staying for—perhaps waiting until the dancers go back into the sacred space. I see a drum set up outside the altar and I think someone might play it and there will be dancing before the participants are folded back into the shrine structure. That is what would happen in Japan. Maybe I will stay for this. I definitely want to come back in the morning when the sun breaks, and the dancers come out and are relieved from the sun and the pain and then finally break their fast.

I walk along slowly, sipping the water, carrying my chair. As I depart, the man who has been chatting with me grins and says: "So, back to brave the sun?"

"Yes." I smile.

Before I go, he asks me where I am from. He never asks me what my nation is, or who my people are, or if I have ever been to the Sun Dance before. From him I learn only tidbits. He has been to a Sun Dance in South Dakota in which the participants go into a sweat lodge in addition to dancing and emerge severely dehydrated. He has never done the

Sun Dance. He is not interested in the upcoming solar eclipse. He has just come back from a powwow in California.

I wander slowly toward the altar. There are many people now, all carrying washcloths, rocks, and branches. I stand there. I wander past the opening, walking back and forth, and then around the periphery.

What goes through my mind is this: I wonder if I can read a book. Would it be a faux pas to read a book? No one is reading a book.

Perhaps twenty feet ahead of me, I see a man waving emphatically in the universal gesture of telling someone to go away.

I have been found out.

I stop. I begin to walk backward, then stop. Is he really signaling to me? He is. I look behind me and see a small child playing with an umbrella. I turn back. He waves even harder. "Put that thing away."

The umbrella?

"Your water."

My water. I am not supposed to drink water here. I can drink water where I had been with the taco, but not here. I apologize and turn around immediately and begin to leave.

Another man intercepts me. He is short, angry, and wears his suspicion sharply all over his face.

"How can you drink water in front of them?" he asks me. "Can't you see they are suffering?" I can. I do. I finally understand that they have been suffering. I have been staring at them suffering for the past two hours and have been lifting myself out of the suffering with intellectualizing about universal religious rituals and Japan and my beliefs on fasting. I have understood only on the surface that the men and women inside the altar are there to dance and fast for three days, chasing a vision. Their families are here to support them and to be a part of the experience, because they are suffering.

And I have committed a grand faux pas. The second man stares at me. I can hear the unspoken question: *How could you do this?* The phrase is in his brain and it is leaping now into his mouth. His lips part and he is about to ask it and he can see on my face that I have heard the question in my head, even though he has not said it.

And my answer is this: *I did this because I didn't know not to.* It is because I am not who they think I am. Because I wanted a story that wasn't mine.

Before he can ask that question, I start to run to my car. I do not want to hear the question and I do not want him to read my face the same way I have read his face, or to hear my answer, even if I don't speak the answer. I know he knows anyway. In the fraction of a second before I start running, I see his face soften, not with kindness but with a mixture of wonder and shock. It is the look a person makes when learning something terrible for the first time, and is stunned to discover that humans are capable of whatever this thing might be.

I apologize as I am running. I tell him he is right and I am completely wrong. I have been drinking water without thinking, which is true. I have forgotten that the bottle is in my hand. *The white man didn't intend for it to work out that way.* He is right. I am wrong. Absolutely. I am not even supposed to be here.

I am afraid I will be found out. I am afraid I will be chastised and exposed as a fraud. I need to leave immediately and so I do.

Even a glance at the Wikipedia entry on the Sun Dance would have made it clear that I was never supposed to be there. My son knew we weren't supposed to be there. Children always know.

My brain begins to flail and make excuses. I was invited. No one asked why I was there. I did not know about the water. I looked like I fit in. In fact, I was enjoying looking like I fit in. I even thought it was a bit of a game, a journalist after a big story. I had been going weeks without fitting in and I was happy to pretend to fit in here. But the rebuke continues in my head. I have made a terrible error. I, who try so hard not to make errors, have made one, and I have contributed to the pain of others. Because of vanity, I have glimpsed suffering that was not meant for me to see.

A ceremonial dance of the Plains Indians, the Sun Dance was outlawed by the US government until the 1970s. Today, completing it is seen as an act of generosity and sacrifice for the community.

But even in writing this, I am committing a transgression, since the dance is closed to outsiders and I am an outsider. My apparent camouflage does not matter.

I have a powerful feeling of wanting to go home. There is no center of belonging. This looked like the Obon festival, which I associate with my mother, but it isn't Obon. It isn't Buddhist meditation and fasting. This isn't a version of home and there isn't another home to go to.

So many of the world's oldest traditions reject words. Language creates a reality whether it is true in the physical world or not. The Native
Americans, the Yazidi, the Shingon Buddhists in Japan all pass on what
they know through action and demonstration and not the written word.
Not everything can be explained through language.

I have committed an act, and it is the wrong act.

I sit in the parking lot of the casino, crying for half an hour. This is
also where I cried after my son left and I am now parched from crying.
Then I call my friends who are people of color and ask questions like
"Where is home?" and "What is a human being?"

They are mostly patient with me, but some are irritated too. Why
don't I know the answer to this question already? When I say I want to
go home, they tell me there is no home. They tell me I don't have a set
of my own people.

My friend Garnette listens to me wail, as he has so often. He doesn't
tell me to stop with the white tears. He just listens and finally tells me:
"Go back. You have to go back to the harvesters and love them. Now
open your heart and go back." He is adamant.

It takes a long time to be calm, though I am more exhausted than
quiet. The conversations have helped. I am sorry to have upset them.
There is only each other, I say to myself. There is only communing with
another. There is only the heart. It is the heart that will allow us to bridge
the gap. I have not used mine as fully and as well as I could have, and I
must try again to do better. But I see no other home than this.

THIRTEEN

I TELL ERIC FIRST. I want the story to be a funny and pathetic anecdote about me and my arrogance in thinking I could go to a Sun Dance and leave with an experience bordering on transcendence. And this, at first, is how I relay the story. Week after week I had been going to Christian churches and leaving frustrated; surely the Sun Dance would be different!

"But it wasn't," I say.

Eric does not laugh.

I tell Amos, who then tells me that he used to walk around the RV park feeling bad for everyone, by which he means the Indians, but he tries now to concentrate primarily on work and not on "the sadness."

Emily wants to know if I found the experience dark. It sounds dark to her, in contrast to church. She, too, used to feel bad once the crew arrived in Idaho, but now she turns to Jesus. She then says she knows she doesn't understand what it is like to be black or Native American, but she wonders: "How long should I feel responsible?"

The question throws me and I can't immediately articulate why it does. No one I know would ever ask a question like this. But the question is not unfamiliar. If I sit with it, which I do, it is a question or a feeling I had many, many years ago. It might even be a conversation I had as a child growing up in my predominantly white town in California. We had only a handful of "people of color" then, a term that did not even exist at the time. We knew almost nothing about black people, though we learned about civil rights. We knew that black people were in America because of slavery and that that had been wrong.

"When I see a black person," I remember a childhood friend saying to me, "I feel bad. I know I don't need to feel bad, but I do." I heard variations of this sentiment growing up, and occasionally someone would say to me: "But you don't make me feel that way, Marie."

Conversations like this stopped when I went to college, because then I was in New York City, and for the first time my features didn't pop against a white background but blended into the diversity of a place. For the first time in my life, I looked at my friends and they were, in fact, from everywhere. Because I do not precisely look as if I am from any one place, I could be from anywhere too. New York was liberating.

But Emily's question makes me search inside myself to see if I have an answer. As the token liberal, I feel I ought to have an answer. I do not. "Do you think you are supposed to feel bad?" I ask.

"I think so," she says.

This seems to be the wrong direction for the conversation to go.

I wonder how many white friends I have who feel this way but don't ask the question because they know it is the "wrong" question to ask, or at least the wrong question to ask *me*. It's pretty easy in the city to hide out in a "Black Lives Matter" T-shirt, do a little yoga, and no one will know that you are wondering, *How long am I supposed to feel responsible?* Maybe this is an example of Eric's dreaded legalism?

Perhaps I should be ashamed to admit that I took the question right to a black friend via text message to see what he would say. Isn't this the classic thing for a white person to do? Go and ask a black friend? But I do ask, because I don't have an answer, and at this point, after so many weeks on the road, I'm past feeling ashamed. His eloquent response went like so: "People are not asking you to show some emotion. What they are asking is that thought be given to their identity, which means coming to terms with their history and treatment in this society. When would you like them to stop mentioning the factors that have shaped them and that still do serious damage to them?"

I spend considerable time reading this message.

In the Christian churches I have been attending, sin has been presented as a personal foible—sin is some way in which we are prideful or insulting. But the churches don't seem to widen the lens to take in how we as a people have behaved: a collective view of sin that considers history carefully. I'm trying to think of what Jesus said about feeling bad. What does Jesus say about feeling responsible? He says the usual things about loving my brother and caring for the weak. I try to psychoanalyze Jesus. What, exactly, did Jesus feel during his time on Earth?

Jesus is not the Buddha asking us to rein in emotion and attachment. He feels everything, and love for people most of all. His feelings spur him into action: he tears down temple walls, or makes sick people well, or gives hungry people something to eat. When people say that

Jesus was God on Earth, I wonder if they mean that Jesus used the full emotional capacity available to a human being, and at the same time each of his actions was consistently an expression of how God truly is, and knows we can be too. The easiest way to sum up Jesus's teachings and acts is in the word "love."

Legalism, as Eric has tried to explain to me, is tricky. People can act out of trickery, so from the outside, if they are following a bunch of rules, they might seem virtuous. What counts is the invisible interior that only God and the self can see. What counts is faith. What counts is the heart.

For all that I am shaken by the Sun Dance and Ewan's departure, I find the beauty of the Idaho wheat—and the joy the crew feels here because they can work hard—is a balm. I begin to feel better over the next few days. Idaho wheat is luxurious. Because the wheat is irrigated, it is dense and thick and stands like a wall of foam. It doesn't shiver or ripple in the wind. I try to wade into the wheat but can't see the ground unless I kick the stalks with my foot and force the shafts apart. When I do, I invariably catch sight of a rodent. Well, no wonder. With 140 bushels of wheat per acre, I would live here, too, if I were a vole. (By way of contrast, recall that there were 28 bushels per acre of wheat in Texas.) There are so many voles and mice, I am nervous about walking into the wheat and stepping on animals. To be a farmer must mean having no fear of stepping on a mouse.

From the high vantage point inside the combine, I can look down on the field and see the fat, bent heads curled on top of the wall; the heads look like tapioca. The combine is reaping white pearls of tapioca out of the field. Gone are the amber waves of grain; this is a spongy, decadent bulwark of iridescent jewels. (*Just stick to the facts. Don't get too fancy.*)

Sometimes there is so much leftover straw that the farmer wants the field cut with the straw tidily assembled into mounds called "windrows," in lieu of the scattered mess the combine usually leaves behind. One can, in fact, change a combine's settings so the discarded straw is scooped together in piles. Later, the straw will be gathered up by a separate machine—a baler—and the clusters of dried straw will be compressed into rectangular bales of hay. Over the course of the weeks, the landscape is transformed: the fields are shorn of their grain and left with streaks of straw, and then the straw is assembled into blocks of hay. Each time this happens, I have to remember my landmarks differently and navigate not by what is growing on the field but by other features: a water tower, a canal, a fork in the road. This is beautiful and generous land. It is no wonder that throughout our trip Eric has reiterated: "Wait till we get to Idaho." It is no wonder he pushed everyone to reach this valley with all the grain and all the work. If the Great Plains were a thin and dusty disappointment, this land is flooded with water and wheat and wealth. If it were a slot machine, the floor of the casino would be covered in gold chips.

But still this is not California, where anything can grow. The first frost comes too early and the last frost comes too late for peas and related crops, like soybeans. And because it gets cold so quickly, other vegetables, like lettuce and carrots, are also out. The weather does allow for potatoes, wheat, and corn, and these crops are grown in rotation.

In Fort Hall—or Pocatello, as we call it—there is so much grain and the combines fill up so quickly that we have to hire additional trucks to get the grain out of the field. The trucks line up—perhaps as many as ten at a time—and the combines unload directly into the hoppers. The elevator here is rudimentary, and the lines for the trucks to unload are long. And the elevator—the actual spot where the grain is dumped—is not like the one in Crowell, or the other elevators with a pit beneath the floor where the wheat can drain quickly and then be whisked up via a series of augers into a tower. In Idaho, the fresh wheat is unloaded onto a conveyer belt, which whisks the grain away and up into an open-air pile. Drivers like Luther and Juston go to one station to be weighed, and then to a different location a good five minutes away to unload. It is an inefficient system. Until now, elevators we've used have had all the parts of the unloading process in one location.

The lack of storage tanks means that the stacks of wheat are exposed to the elements. In fact, a pile of wheat from the previous year is still sitting there, putrid, rotting, and black. All of this seems bizarre. I know that food starts out in nature, which is to say, in the dirt. But it still sometimes surprises me that food starts out *dirty*.

Eric had promised that the sunsets in Idaho would be glorious, and they are. To the west, the land seems to open up to something else—a different color. It is as though we have traveled through colors. If I were wearing those colors as stones, then at the start of the trip I would have had a necklace of coral and jade around my neck. Now the colors have changed dramatically, and I have added fiery opals and moonstones to the mix. The way the colors have shifted ever so slightly as we have moved across the United States makes me feel as if something in me has shifted too—as though the cells that make up my body have slowly been replaced by new cells so I can fit into this brighter, more iridescent environment.

At times the sky appears almost fluorescent. There must be something about the atmosphere in Idaho that affects its sunsets. The alpenglow on the hillsides to the east reflects colored light back onto the white wheat, turning it lavender. Pale dust hangs low over the earth where the combines kick up dirt.

My face here itches from the dust.

There is no wind and everything feels suspended and weightless. It is, I think, a feeling like heaven.

In the mornings, Emily has started reading from the Gospel of Luke. We are reading through the birth and life of Jesus and his teachings. So many of his parables are about the planting of seeds and the reaping of a grain harvest.

After breakfast, we go outside and look at the sky. The sun is rising straight into a dark cloud. Eric predicts rain. By the time we are heading out into the field, there is a double rainbow bent over Simplot Road. "That's rare. We don't usually get rainbows early in the morning," Eric says.

"Why is that?" I ask.

"Direction of the sun to the east and storm coming from the west." He smiles at the rainbow.

The Snake River Plain acts as a funnel for weather patterns. Moisture gathers along the Pacific Coast, and then is conducted through this long valley. Sometimes the moisture gets trapped by the Tetons and dumps snow. Everything here always feels wet. Maybe there have been times when this plain experienced drought, but while I am visiting, I never worry about a lack of water. There is so much water. We often come across pipes in the field that need to be moved by hand before we can cut. The roads are lined by canals and pools, all of which pull water out of the Idaho aquifer and into the fields. Not for the first time, I look at the wheat and recall what Eric often says with admiration: "It is incredible what the Mormons were able to do." And it is. These same canals were hand-dug by the first pioneers and are used today for their descendants to grow potatoes and all this wheat. The land is not thirsty.

I have been reading Revelation. I have learned about the horrible days involving dragons, fires, and deaths. But past the catastrophic portion of Revelation, there is something curious. At the end of time, a city will come down from heaven. The city will be shaped like a square. To me, this descending square-shaped city sounds like a UFO, and numerous conspiracy theorists on YouTube agree. In my research, I also find some new age artwork for sale in which golden, square-shaped cities beam down to Earth to rescue the righteous. But the more important point to me is that this life of bucolic farming doesn't exist in the end of Revelation. People simply live with God in the city.

When I bring this up with Juston, he says to me that most evangelicals would tell me that Revelation is symbolic.

"But they always say we must interpret the Bible literally, so how can the city be a metaphor?"

"These are my people," he explains. "I know how they think. Personally, I love the question."

When I ask Michael about the city at the end of the Bible, he also says the city is a metaphor.

"But you can't pick and choose what is metaphorical, because if you do that, you are creating your own Gospel," I say. It is entirely to his credit that Michael laughs good-naturedly and agrees.

He thinks about it a bit more, and then he says: "Maybe there will be a door. Or a gate."

And so I look at the Bible and discover that the righteous will not go outside the city. Only dogs, sorceresses, and liars will be allowed out. Being outside will not be a good thing. There is no farming in the city, because we will be reunited with the tree of plenty, which hasn't been seen since God slammed the door to the Garden of Eden and put a cherub with a flaming sword in front of it to repel all humans. I joke with Juston that the tree is like the replicator in *Star Trek*, the device that miraculously produces whatever anyone wants to eat and that eradicates the need for farming or for ranchers. We will learn to live inside a city. I say: "We will all live in the exact place so many people do not like."

It stops raining by lunchtime and we all sit outside in the RV park—both crews. Dwayne, like Eric, has a friendly relationship with the dealer who makes his combine of choice, the Gleaner. Dwayne, like Eric, has now been joined by a corporate engineer, Bob, who is testing out a prototype of the Gleaner. Millions of dollars are at stake, and here we are sitting on folding chairs, eating hamburgers in this RV park in a corner of Idaho on an Indian reservation.

The crews both speak highly of Bob, and I take them at their word that he is an expert on the combine. We have barely spoken, and I trust that if I did speak the language of the combine, I would understand how deep Bob's knowledge is of mechanics and engineering. But because I don't speak the language of mechanical parts, all I have access to is this side of him, the side that sits in semicivilized conditions and chitchats at lunch. Bob asks if anyone is going back to college in the fall. Juston is going back and Bradford volunteers that Michael is going back too. No one else is going back to college.

"Someone has to go back to college," Amos says amiably.

Bob wants to know what Juston will study.

"English."

Everyone laughs. I ought to get the joke, but I don't.

"I don't know why I have to study English if I already talk it," says Dwayne.

Juston has a half smile on his face and is nodding. He has been through this so many times before. "Do you like movies, Bob?"

"Sure."

"There's a lot of writing in that. Television too."

I am irritated. This is their world and I am merely an observer. I have been trying—trying—to follow this rule all summer. But the imp of the perverse gets to me and I don't want to be quiet. I look at Michael and ask if this is a good time to ask my new question. He doesn't answer me but smiles his Michael smile, the one he probably uses for his precocious sisters.

I ask: "I am wondering how you all feel about the fact that the Bible ends with a city. It starts with a garden and ends with a city. I finally read Revelation, and it says we are all going to live in a city."

Bradford gets up and leaves. He just gets up and walks away.

"She's right," Samuel says, before he follows Bradford. "Revelation does end in a city."

"I never thought about it," Eric says. "I'll try to think about it."

It is too wet and nothing else is ripe. Michael and Georgie grab the truck; they want to go down to the water. It turns out that the area I imagined to be the ocean is in fact a huge lake—a reservoir, bounded by what is called the American Falls Dam. Fields go right to the edge of the reservoir, and it feels as if we are visiting a wheat field on the brink of the world. It is spectacular the way the grain grows right to the place the land drops down in a sheer cliff. This wheat is chartreuse.

"No, that's barley," Michael corrects me patiently.

There are waterfowl here—ducks and geese. I haven't seen waterfowl since we were in Texas. The boys want to go down to the water's edge. I think they are joking at first. The drop must be at least forty feet and the cliff is muddy and unstable. I see no clear way to get back up.

Michael starts down. I hear rocks crumbling and I imagine him tumbling down into the ravine and cracking his skull. Georgie laughs as Michael goes down. He chastises Michael: "That soil looks pretty weak. I hope you don't die down there." I walk away. I don't want to watch.

A moment later I hear Michael say: "Hey. Aren't you going to help me up?" Then he is back on firm land and just fine. The boys are serious about going down to the water, though, and so they drive along the cliff looking for a suitable path down.

"There," they say at the same time. Water has worn away part of the face of the cliff so it is less steep. In a moment, they are by the water's edge, with Michael suggesting to me, rather sharply, that I ought to be there too. "You've come all this way to the edge of this cliff, not to mention all the way to Idaho with us. What is it all for, Marie, if you aren't going to have the experiences?"

I am midway down the cliff when they start arguing over whether or not they have discovered mountain lion or coyote tracks, and if Michael has startled something out of its natural habitat.

"A mountain lion?" I stop my descent.

"Maybe," Michael says. "But you're halfway down. I think you should come all the way down here."

Then they both laugh and tell me it is most likely a coyote.

Michael was right to insist I come down to the water. I tell him I grew up like this, by the ocean. I could see the water every day if I wanted to. I tell him that it changes a person to see water every single day, and that I think it changes a person not to see water. "I think maybe the colors of the land we grow up with change us too," I say.

Michael is always tolerant of my ideas and moods. He just listens. He never questions what the point is of a woman wondering what the psychological effect of color is, which is a thing about him that I appreciate.

But now he says: "So are you having what they call a midlife crisis?"

A what? I'm taken aback. Am I, in fact, having a midlife crisis? What does he mean, exactly, and why is he asking me? I think about the conversation at lunch about the futility of studying English.

"No. I'm just a writer," I say.

"Well, it's just. You know. You're going around all summer with a bunch of guys. Nah, I'm kidding."

Is he kidding? Is this his question, or did someone from the crew say this must be the case? I feel uneasy.

"You don't know many artists, do you," I say.

"I was kidding . . ."

"This is the kind of thing we do. No, really. *This* is what we are like!"

"Honestly, I was just joking," he says.

But I don't believe him.

Because everyone around me speaks English, it is so easy for me to assume we share the same culture, even though, after four months on the road together, I know our cultures are very different. Time and time again there have been moments that make it clear to me we don't share the same worldview. Michael knows I'm a writer. Maybe a good working definition of an artist is "a person who is perpetually stuck in a midlife crisis."

After a little while, Michael says: "I tried to look up how come the Bible ends with a city. I don't know."

"I feel a little bad that I brought that up at lunch."

"It's an interesting question. I don't know the answer, and I can't find it," he says.

"I think maybe it was a little mean that I asked at lunch," I say again.

Michael shrugs. "The average age of becoming a Christian in this country is eighteen. You have to become a Christian by the time you're eighteen or you probably won't become one. The churches all know this, and it's why they focus on little kids." I think, briefly, of Ewan in Pastor Jan's church. Michael picks up a rock and throws it and it skips three times. But, of course, that is not good enough for Michael, so he finds another rock and this one leaps five times, like a cormorant taking off from the water after successfully catching a fish. Michael is happy. "If you read the Bible, there's a day when Peter converts thousands of people. One day. All adults." Michael squats and looks at the surface of the water, still sending concentric circles out to the center of the lake and back to us, where they break on the shore. "There is something we are doing that isn't right. What was it about Jesus and the people back then that they could convert a thousand people in a day, Marie? Who could do that today? What happened back then?"

The next day we are back to cutting. The heat has dried out the wet grain and everyone is hard at work. There is so much wheat, not a moment can be wasted.

I am in the combine with Eric when Amos radios to say that his combine is making a strange sound. "I was just trying to unload into the truck, and . . . well, I hear thumpin'."

"Can you tell where it's coming from?"

"It sounds like the unloading auger."

Eric and I drive over to Amos. We climb out of our combine and into his, and Amos takes Eric's combine and continues cutting. Eric listens to the machine. It is indeed making a rattling sound.

"I think I know what's wrong," Eric says.

He is going to climb onto the back of the combine and look inside. I am nervous about him dealing with the auger after the story he told me about his hand. And, perhaps as a joke, he turns to me before climbing onto the back of the combine and says: "Don't start anything."

I hear him walking around on the metal machine and then he is back in the cab with me. "Problem's worse than I thought. One of the augers—the unloading auger in the base of the grain bin—is broken. Snapped in two. We need a replacement."

Because we are in Idaho, we hope a dealer will have a spare part, and at one point Eric thinks he has located what he needs in Idaho Falls. I am excited by the prospect of this. I could drive a pickup to go and get a part and bring it back—there will finally be something I can do that is helpful. But then it becomes clear that the auger in Idaho Falls is not a high-speed unloading auger, and that we need the advanced model, which the dealer does not have.

Eric makes a series of phone calls to dealers farther and farther from us. Finally, he finds the part nine hundred miles away. And so Eric sits and thinks of what to do and then his eyes brighten. He has remembered something—someone. He makes a phone call, just out of earshot, and then returns to me. "Let's go to the pickup," he says. He is positively beaming. He looks like Han Solo remembering that he can call on Lando Calrissian to repair the *Millennium Falcon*. I get in the pickup, and we drive to the town of Blackfoot.

The road Eric has been traveling for thirty years is dotted with relationships. For Eric, there are the churches, the fuel stations, and the Peterbilt dealerships. At home, within the network of his friends and his church, he has always been able to find young men who have the skills he needs to go on the road. He mentors them, and they call him from time to time. In Idaho, he remembers that one of his former crewmembers—a guy named Anthony—has settled down with a Mormon girl. She had worked the grain elevator, and Anthony had driven the truck, and they met one summer when he unloaded his haul. They got married and decided to settle in Idaho to be near her family.

Anthony is an expert welder. He also has a job working at a farming equipment dealership and will have access to a torch.

We pull into the dealership, with its shiny Kubota and John Deere equipment parked side by side. Anthony is on the phone via a headset. He's in his late twenties and handsome and wholesome—an older version of the boys on Eric's crew. He is in the middle of cleaning out what looks to me like a concrete parking garage. Eric lifts up his hand in a manner of greeting, then gestures briefly toward himself. Anthony nods, and the next thing I know Eric is sweeping too. The two men work side by side, while Anthony continues his call. And then, the call still in progress, we walk over to Eric's truck. He and I unload the broken auger and set it on the ground, and Anthony finally gets off the phone.

"What happened?"

"Unloading auger," Eric says. "Come loose and I guess this one thumped around for a while before it snapped."

The two men carry the broken auger into the machine shop and lay it gingerly on a table the way actors on those medical shows respectfully place corpses on an ambulance gurney. Anthony snaps on a bright fluorescent light.

They are in their own rhythm, these two men. They are like those turtles in *Finding Nemo*, riding the East Australian Current together, talking or not talking, or stalking around the table, noticing the same thing at the same time, squatting and squinting and lining things up and then nodding at each other, as though half of what they are seeing and saying is communicated by ESP. It is marvelous to watch them.

Anthony whistles. "Snapped in two."

"You got any . . . ?" Eric is whipping his head around.

"Somewhere. I'm sure I got something."

They are talking about how they can weld it so the screw of the auger is symmetrical.

"It'll be heavier," Anthony says.

"Won't matter."

The men nod.

They mean that Anthony will need to weld the broken pieces to another piece of metal, which will make the entire piece of metal heavier than it already is, which will mean more work for the combine, whose rotor will have to turn it.

"Might even work better," Eric says.

Then they stand and stare at it some more. The pause is uncomfortably long for me because I have no idea what is happening.

"Just the parts," Anthony says. "And maybe I can drive it a little?"

"Bring your son. How old is he now?"

"Seven."

Eric shakes his head. "Seven years." And just like that, the imagined nine-hundred-mile drive to get the new part, or the FedEx fee required to get a new part, not to mention its cost, has evaporated. It is a law of farming that the more a man can do himself, the more money he can save. And this, Eric tells me later, when we drive back to the RV park, is what is known as "biblical living." He is referring to the lengths he went to save money and how we were able to call upon an honored friendship for help. "The thing about biblical living," he says to me, a little proudly, "is that it works."

It is Sunday. We are in Mormon country and I have not yet been to a Mormon church. Eric does not want to go, but he strongly suggests that I do. He has arranged for me to go with Veronica, the beautiful twenty-seven-year-old woman whom I have seen driving the white pickup truck. So on Sunday, while everyone else goes to church in Idaho Falls, I wait by the trailer. "You'll know they are Mormons because the guys will be wearing white shirts," Eric says.

He had told me that Veronica would pick me up at 10:30 a.m. sharp, and when she doesn't come, I am nervous. At 10:40 two men in pressed white shirts arrive. Both are young—in their twenties—which makes them around the same age as the crew, but their affect is entirely different. They meet my gaze directly through the window of the car. Maybe they grew up out here and can drive tractors and trucks like Bradford and Samuel, but they also have the impatient and direct gestures of people who have been to the city and, more important, to college.

"Good morning! Are you Marie?" One of the men ducks his head out of the passenger window.

I confirm that I am. "Eric told me to look for guys in white shirts!" I say. "And here you are." They laugh good-naturedly, and we drive to church together. On the way, I learn that one man is Veronica's husband and the other her brother.

Mormons refer to themselves as Latter Day Saints and their churches are called temples. You will know a Mormon temple because it will look like a church but have no cross. This is the first thing I notice. The second thing I notice when I enter this temple is that it is the brightest house of worship I have ever been to. Sun streams through the windows and reflects against the congregation's hair. There are so many women with two-foot-long platinum manes that have been carefully curled, it's as if an entire town from Sweden has been transplanted here. In fact, many of them are descended from Swedes. Everyone is also smiling with unrestrained joy. Their teeth are white and perfect. Pearlescent and pink faces gleam. The congregation does not have the same patient and weathered look I have seen in Texas or Oklahoma; everyone is overjoyed and dressed up. While their clothing is modest— skirts are long and no one is showing off cleavage—this is also not tracksuit-as-formal-wear country. Women wear dresses and heels and have taken the time to extend their eyelashes and coordinate lip- stick and eye shadow. Beauty in this church is not a thing to keep in check, as it has been in Protestant congregations. The sight of all the color and sensuality delights me, and I realize with a pang how much I miss both the ease and the effort that go into an unapologetic devotion to prettiness.

There are so many children and they are noisier even than they were in Nebraska, in part because they are clearly accustomed to interacting with adults. Every family—and they are here together as families—has three or more children, and many of them turn around and smile at me. Often it is hard to hear what the men are saying because of the children laughing, or rustling, or turning around to say hello. And it is only men who speak during the service.

I have grown used to men leading church. However, here the men seem to be even more celebrated. There are ten men sitting together in rising pews facing us, and off to the right there is another cluster of younger men who constitute a group I later learn is the Aaronic Priesthood.

The sermon today is a bit unusual because the featured speaker is a young man just home from his mission. The word "mission" is used by many Christians and usually refers to a young person spending time away from home to help the disadvantaged while also trying to spread the Gospel. The Mormons are famous for their missions; mis- sions are mandatory. They go away for two years and can call home only on Christmas and on Mother's Day and beyond that are allowed to email once a week. The rest of the time they are with their mission leaders and team members, and today a young man has come home with his report, which he delivers to the congregation. He tells us, haltingly, about how good it is to be home from Florida and about the difficulties he faced in trying to spread his faith. Around me, the older people nod every now and then, as though they are remembering their own youthful missions. He says a phrase a few times that strikes me as curious, because I haven't heard it anywhere else. He says: "I know our church is true."

It will not be the first or last time that day that I listen to a Mormon—or Latter Day Saint—tell me that their church is "true" and that their experiences have "proved the church true." I don't initially know what these phrases means, or why they are repeated. I think back to the time in Oklahoma when Juston told me that some of the expressions used by Pastor Rainwater carry layers of meaning that resonate with him in ways they do not with me. It must be like that, I think. "Truth" to a Mormon carries implications I don't yet understand. Later, I read some history to get context.

According to the Mormons, sometime around 2000 BC, a tribe from Israel departed the Middle East and sailed by boat to the United States. These people fragmented into four different tribes, two of which are the Nephites and the Lamanites. Mormons focus on several lines from the Gospel of John: "I have other sheep that are not of this sheep pen. I must bring them also. They, too, will listen to my voice, and there shall be one flock and one shepherd." They believe this is a foreshadowing of Jesus going to the New World, or the Americas. While he was here, Jesus preached and passed on his teachings to the people in this land. They lived well for a time, until the Lamanites became greedy and dark-skinned, and killed off the Nephites, the drama of which was recorded on a set of golden plates by the last of the Nephites, a man named Mormon.

Fast-forward to 1810, Palmyra, New York, when another man, named Joseph Smith, was born. He and his family lived during the Second Great Awakening, a period of Protestant religious revival that lasted roughly from the late eighteenth century to the middle of the nineteenth century, and that contributed to the conversion of many Methodists and Baptists in the United States. Smith's home was smack in the middle of a region so full of fever-pitch revival meetings, it was referred to as the "burned-over" part of New York.

One day the angel Moroni appeared to Smith and instructed him to dig under a tree, where he would find a book made out of golden plates. Smith did as instructed, found the plates, and then "translated" them into English. The manuscript was published in 1830, and the Book of Mormon was revealed.

Central to Smith's concerns was restoration. Any history book about the years following the death of Jesus will trace the difficulties Christians had in establishing themselves while being persecuted and will describe how they were forced to gather secretly in one another's homes—house church. By AD 323, Christianity had become the official religion of Rome, and a bureaucracy supporting the institution was born. But many followers of Jesus remained inspired by Christ the historical figure. When Luther and Calvin both broke from the Catholic Church, in the sixteenth century, they were trying in part to "go back," or restore an earlier form of their faith that focused more on Jesus than on the practices of Rome. When Pastor Rainwater told the joke about Billy Graham trying to set the church back by two thousand years, he was referring to this longing people feel for the actual time of Christ. And Joseph Smith, too, was concerned with restoring the church, or setting its practices back closer to the practices of the time when Jesus was alive. Mormonism should be seen in this context and in this Christian desire to capture something of the past—a shalom, perhaps—even as humans inevitably are also hurtling forward through time.

With the publication of his book, Joseph Smith gained many followers—including, notoriously, at least eleven wives. He moved his fledgling religious movement from New York, to Ohio, then to Missouri, and finally to Nauvoo, Illinois. But in Illinois, he and his followers were taunted for their practice of polygamy, and then he and his brother were assassinated. There was a scramble for power before Brigham Young took over and entreated the Mormons to follow him along the Mormon Trail to the Great Basin, which we refer to today as Utah.

The service I attend lasts for an hour, after which I learn that church has not ended. There will now be another session, which will last for another hour. Then there is another hour after this, and during both of these additional sessions, much is made of the fact that the world will end soon and that Jesus will return. At the conclusion of hour three, the bishop for this particular ward says something I will never forget: "The prophets still speak to us. The gates to heaven are still open."

For many laymen and Christians, it has been nearly two thousand years since Jesus died, and there has been no further signal from God. For Catholics, there have been some inspired saints, and of course there is the pope. But Mormonism puts an end to the longing the faithful have to hear from God through a prophet. Each new

Mormon church leader is considered a prophet who receives divine inspiration.

There is a new holy city and it is here, in the United States.

After church, I go to Veronica's house. Her farm—the Anderson Farm—was started by her grandfather, who is eighty-two years old and still herding cattle even though he is missing a shoulder from when he was shot by a rogue farmworker who tried to steal his horse. The farm was passed on to Veronica's father, who was called away to be a mission leader. Someone had to run the farm while he was gone.

Though there are men in the Anderson family, Veronica's brothers were still too young to take on the responsibility of the farm. So it was that Veronica, who at the time had been working in New York City, volunteered to come home. She had always wanted to farm, she told me. But farming—agriculture school—was not a thing a girl was supposed to do. Fate intervened and now here she was.

It is Veronica, and not her husband or her brothers, who goes to potato seed conventions, who decides when to spray the potatoes with chemicals and whether or not to plant winter or spring wheat. It is Veronica who meets with dealers to try to sell her potatoes at the best price. And it will be Veronica who goes to the tribes to negotiate new leases for the land.

"The tribes?" I ask.

"For the land we rent," she says.

Most of the land the Andersons farm is owned by the tribes who live on the Shoshone-Bannock reservation, but the Indians do not tend to grow the potatoes or the wheat themselves. They lease the land out to farmers and every three years the leases are put up for bid. The tribal council can decide to simply renew the lease or not to put the lease up for bid. To make matters perhaps even more complicated, one of the other large potato growers in the area is ethnically Japanese.

"So all the land we have been cutting . . ."

". . . is tribal land. Most of it. Some of it we own," she says. "My family got here long enough ago that we could buy the land."

Veronica is from a family that arrived on the Mormon Trail, pushing a handcart. The Andersons began with a sheep farm, then bought wheat fields before the reservation laws prevented white men from owning land on reservation property. She is white, she was born on the reservation, and she has grown up with the Native Americans. She has gone to school with the Native Amerians, played with them, and loved them. I stare at her. She is, I think, a version of me, a person who feels trapped in her skin and feels that her essence, and her relationship to the land on which she was born, does not completely show in her face.

I am at the trailers when Juston comes back from wherever it is the crew went after church. I am recovering from a migraine; I have started getting them daily.

Juston stops to talk to me and we go to Panera Bread for lunch. He asks me what I thought of Mormon church. Everything I say comes out jumbled. I say that the way the bishop spoke indicates that society is almost finished. But, I say, it is not finished. How could it possibly be finished? We aren't anywhere near to completing what Jesus said to do.

I say that in the country churches we have been to, there is always so much discussion of the Bible and Christ and how we must find God, but there is never anything in the narrative to suggest that society could be better as a whole. We are forever praying for and blessing some young person who's about to go on a mission to another country. But we almost never—except perhaps at Pastor Jeff's church, with David Miller delivering hay—ask what we can do for our neighbor.

"Well, I agree with you," Juston says. "But it's all churches. The narrative that *we* need to do good for the people right in front of us is *never* mentioned."

"Maybe I'm being too hard on everyone," I say. "Maybe I'm tired." I am tired.

Juston gives me a half smile. "I don't think so, Marie. I mean, you may be tired, but you aren't wrong." There is a weighty pause.

I realize he has been waiting for me to follow this path to be here now. He has been watching me on this trip, watching me interact with all the pastors and waiting for me to see what he sees. He has seen and loved these people all his life and understood them, and feared for them. And he has wanted me to see all this too—to see the broken structure of his world.

Then Juston says an incredible thing. He speaks slowly and carefully, each word beautifully chosen. He tells me that he has been thinking about the troubles within the crew. There has been yet another argument between the factions: Michael and Juston versus Bradford and everyone else. He doesn't give me the details of the fight, only that there was one. And then he says: "Jesus says to love your enemies. I've been thinking that having enemies comes from pain. Having enemies causes pain, and that pain comes from some kind of pain within. We've talked a lot now about the discomfort of seeing Native Americans or blacks, or poor people, or anyone who makes us uncomfortable.

"Jesus said that the only way to end that kind of pain is to love your enemies. Loving ends the cycle of pain and the cycle of having enemies. This was why Jesus emphasized working toward reconciliation. Because if you extend yourself to love others—particularly those who are different—you are ending what for *you* is a cycle of pain. If you do this, then being like Christ is not about *making* people *think* like you, but about loving people as they *are*, wherever they may be."

His words make me cry. I am crying the way you cry when you hear something true. I am crying because the pain I realize we are experiencing is so much more severe than what I knew, hiding out in the city, and I'm thinking about this young person with the strength of vision to see through what has been a simulation of the true thing behind it. I feel terribly alone, and at the same time comforted by this true friendship with a boy half my age.

I tell him: "I haven't yet heard a sermon that tells us to love others. I think it's been only the Knowellses who pray for their hearts to be softened so they can let in Christ, and behave in a way that is Christlike."

Juston is stoic while I am crying. Both Juston and Michael have become accustomed to my teariness, which is humbling for me, since I'm supposed to be the adult when we are together. But at times like this, I feel as if I've gone back in time and my years of adult learning no longer count. I feel myself to be all ages at once. I'm eight on the farm, I'm forty-six in the city, and I'm maybe twenty here talking about God and the structure of the modern evangelical church.

"How did you know . . . why did you decide to talk to me?" I ask him.

"In the beginning," he says, "I just wanted you to see that not all Christians are . . . like that."

"Like . . . what?"

"You know. All the historical baggage."

"And then?"

"I just wanted you to like us. And then I realized we are the same."

FOURTEEN

ON MONDAY, ANTHONY BRINGS THE NEW AUGER. He arrives with it in the back of his pickup truck, with his son at his side. Eric has parked his pickup next to the combine; to put the auger into place, we will slide it in from the outside of the combine, and thus we will need the back of the pickup as a kind of platform from which to both load it into place and fasten it securely. Eric opens one of the combine's outer flaps, like a surgeon removing a layer of flesh from a patient's chest. Then, together, the two men hoist the new auger into the empty chamber. Eric climbs up inside the hopper to finish putting the auger in place. At the end, Anthony climbs around the side of the combine, securing and sealing all the screws. He hangs there like Spider-Man, and sometimes I cannot tell how he manages to stick to the side of the machine. He is like Luther—an amateur acrobat—and I think of how these men love to use the strength in their bodies and never seem happier than when they are engaged in the physical act of fixing.

They give the combine a try. Eric lets Anthony drive, with his child in the training seat, where I usually sit.

There is a small smile on Eric's face as he watches this man and his child go charging through the wheat. This skill—this set of skills that Anthony possesses—is the kind of thing Eric likes to share and pass on to the men he mentors. He likes when they can fix things. He likes when they meet and marry good women and become fathers. I can feel this pride swelling in him as he sits next to me. I can feel his satisfaction in having done well, and his pride in Anthony for having done well too. It is as if this field we are harvesting is a symbol of goodness and we are reaping and harvesting that goodness. All the aphorisms about work and labor bearing fruit have come true, and now Eric is a mentor to men, watching a younger man and his son out in the field, adding to the accumulation of goodness and grain that hard work can bring.

We are only a few days away from the powwow and Eric likes to drive by the site to show me how the Indians are setting up camp. To the east of a large rectangular field is the stadium, where the horse racing and rodeo will take place. A smaller piece of the grounds off to the west is being set up with little tents and sheds that will house craftspeople selling T-shirts, jewelry, and food. All around the perimeter, people have begun to set up tepees and little houses made out of tree branches; the latter are a variation of what I saw at the Sun Dance.

There are several Indian families in the RV park now, and their trailers have license plates from Utah, British Columbia, and Wyoming. One night, after we have finished eating the casseroles and desserts that Emily and Carrie have set out for us, Eric gets up and goes for a walk.

"Where's he going?" I ask Emily.

She gestures at a far corner of the park with her head. "Probably to talk to those Indians. To see if they know any of the same people," she says.

After a while I follow. It is just starting to become dark, which has the effect of ensconcing anyone with a fire, a grill, or a lamp in a little island of light. Up ahead I see three people sitting around a trailer with a canopy. One of the men is turning over some steaks on a portable barbecue grill, while a woman sits in a chair underneath a canvas awning. A third man is sewing beads onto a warbonnet. They are from British Columbia and are here for the powwow. As I approach, the woman reaches up and turns a crank, retracting the canvas roof.

By the time I am standing beside Eric, he is listening patiently as the man doing the barbecuing is lecturing him on the pollution in the rivers in Canada, and how the pesticides and fertilizers have gotten into the water and are killing the salmon. Eric listens as the man talks about the earth, and how we are treating the planet with arrogance and not honoring her spirit. I listen for a while, uncertain how to get out of this conversation now that I am an audience member. Finally, I ask the man with the beads what he is making.

"Headdress. For my grandson," he tells me proudly. He shows me the beadwork, and then begins to attach feathers. "My grandson is six."

"Eagle feathers?" I ask.

"Artificial. He's only six. Real feathers are expensive and there's a waiting list to get access. You have to sign up in Colorado."

And then, while Eric continues to be lectured on the environmental damage being done to the earth, the other man—the one making the warrior headdress—tells me about a secret place in Colorado where the electric pylons are particularly enticing to eagles. "I don't know what it is—maybe it's the elevation or something about the direction of the wind. But the eagles—they land there in the winter, and there is something about the frost . . . sometimes it electrocutes the eagle, and he falls off and dies."

"Oh!"

"And, you know, if you stand there long enough, you can collect him."

"And then you can get feathers," I say.

"You are supposed to turn them in. So the next person on the waiting list can get the feathers. But . . ."

He leaves it at that.

Eric shifts his weight a few times, and at last the lesson on the environment comes to an end. Eric thanks the Indian for his time, and I thank the grandfather for talking to me about the eagle feathers. We make our way back to the trailer.

"I think," Eric says when we are out of earshot, "that they don't like GMOs."

"Nope."

"So what did you learn?"

I tell him about the feathers and he laughs good-naturedly. "I want to go to the powwow with you," he says. "I think it would be different than if I went by myself. What gets me," he continues, his eyes beaming, "is the singing. I love the singing. That's what gets me."

I think about the music at the taco stand at the Sun Dance. I think about my invitation to the Sun Dance, and I realize that Eric knows. He knows there are things that will happen to me because of how I look that won't happen to him.

"I used to hear 'em at night sometimes. When I was a kid," Eric says.

"You did? Where was that?"

"When I lived there. In New Mexico."

I had forgotten completely. His parents had been on a mission for his church starting when he was ten and ending when he was fourteen. He had spent those formative years in New Mexico, going to school with

Native children while his mother taught English, sort of like Veronica's upbringing on the reservation. The details he offers about this period of his life are always slight, but I realize he has what he feels is a connection with the Indians.

"Will we still be here for the powwow?" I ask.

He nods. "I think so," he says. "Can't ever predict." I know how allergic he is to the idea of anticipating where harvest will go next. But this feels relatively certain.

All the combines are working now and we continue to cut the wheat. The evenings go long—the sunsets are a bright magenta, and I feel myself starting to adjust to the new colors. I wake up expecting to see the exact shades of faded beige and green and gold and white that are the dirt and the wheat. I expect the heavy, inky clouds that sometimes press down on us like a layer of celestial squirted squid ink, and the purple colors of the sunset. I spend some time with Veronica and her husband. They teach me to shoot skeet, and to drive a truck—all activities I wanted to do with our crew but was not able to do. They are kind and understand that my skill sets are not their skill sets. But I think because a friendship has formed and because Veronica has lived in the city, she knows how to view her world from the outside and then turn around and translate it for me. I rather like shooting clay pigeons. In fact, I love it. In fact, I'm not half-bad.

One evening, Veronica offers to take me horseback riding. Her husband has gone down to the paddock in an ATV, rounded up the horses, and put bridles on them. He is waiting for us when we arrive in the pickup truck. Everyone, it seems, is in an ATV in Idaho. It is so far from end to end of a field, and often even a pickup cannot manage the roads, and so the farmers go out in ATVs. When we are cutting, I see them out in their ATVs, turning off sprinklers, or programming the walking sprinklers to move out of the way for our combines.

At the paddock, there is a little negotiating. Someone has to drive the ATV and someone else has to drive the pickup. In the end, I am elected to sit on the back of the pickup and hold the reins of the horses while Veronica drives the pickup back to the stable, where we will saddle up.

The horses are as aware as anyone else that I am an imposter. I'm barely strong or heavy enough to hold the horses and convince them to follow as Veronica drives. I end up wedging a foot into the side of the pickup and trying to brace myself with the other foot. Twice, the more stubborn of the horses nearly pulls me out of the pickup, and I scream and the truck stops and I regain control. This goes on until we are back at the ranch, where the saddles are kept in Grandpa's barn.

The light is dying by the time we are ready. I'm not an expert at horseback riding, but I welcome any chance I have to ride a horse. Veronica is patient and we climb up a hill that borders a potato field. The light around us is turning red—the scarlet call to go west—and I am on a horse and I am deliriously happy.

Above us is the Indian cemetery we visited the day before in an ATV. The view from there is glorious. The cemetery is up on a promontory and faces west, so all the tombstones have a view of the setting sun. The stones and crosses are all different shapes and stand and lurch and peak at angles that make the place look alive, as if everything is in a state of leaping. The plots are covered with flowers and toys and beads. There are wild yellow sunflowers mixed in with bouquets of pink carnations and white statues of Jesus with his arms outstretched. The clouds this evening have exploded into white fragments and fly like shattered shards of calcite. The sun is sinking and the clouds are aiming at the sun. The sky is every color: a bright orange where the sun is, yellow above the sunflowers, then blue and indigo behind us.

Veronica looks down and points out the ranch and her home, so small from the top of the hill. "Grandpa always says he can't be buried here," she says.

"Indians only?"

She nods. "You know, he was born here." We watch as the sun slips down and the colors in the sky fade.

Veronica takes me to the powwow. She wants me to see the Indian relay. A Native American rider jumps onto a horse without a saddle and races around the track till he comes back to the point where he started. Then he slides off the horse, and another rider jumps on and races around the track. They do this four times, and the horse and rider who cross the finish line first win.

It is an incredibly exciting event. Riders who look like they are not going to get around the track suddenly overtake other riders. Some riders miss jumping onto the back of the horse. Sometimes a horse misbehaves and shies away. People fall. There is shouting and cheering and a great thundering in the soil.

There are Indians everywhere. They come in pickup trucks and cars and their license plates are from all over the Southwest. Their personalized license plates spell out various iterations of "powwow" and their bumper stickers proclaim that they stood at Standing Rock.

Veronica and I walk through the stalls together. She is the one who actually knows what everything is, even though I am the one who looks as if I might belong. She has been coming here since she was a child, and she loves the stall where the medicine men sell herbs and animal bones. We stop at a stand selling beaded hair clips and purses, and Veronica knows one of the women working there: she is a Mormon. I like the jewelry. Another woman is selling beaded necklaces made by the Hopi in Canyon de Chelly, and I buy one for myself, partly because the display has a propped-up cutout from a magazine article with a photo of Ruth Bader Ginsburg wearing the same design.

The centerpiece of the powwow is the dancing, where Native Americans of all ages and tribes put on festive, brightly colored outfits and dance in a circle inside a pavilion. Veronica has been to see this dancing for years, and she knows that the best way to watch it is either to bring a folding chair and stake out a seat in the front row, or to stand on one of the concrete bases that secure the metal poles holding up the tent. We have no folding chairs, and so we do the latter.

The dancing will go on for several days. On this opening day, everyone will come together in what is called the "grand entry." This procession happens in nearly every powwow, and hearkens back to the early days in the United States, after the complete defeat of the Indians and their removal to reservations. They gathered for powwows and paraded through town to show off their costumes. Over the course of the following days, dancers in different categories will compete with one another. Women will dance in the "jingle dance," so named because of the numerous bells attached to their skirts, which jingle as they move and which were originally made out of curled sardine can lids, but which are now specially made out of metal. There is the "fancy dance," in which mature women wear shawls and dip and bend with a restrained elegance, and the "traditional dance," which is, as it sounds, more rooted in tradition.

Men will also dance a "traditional dance," meant to convey the skills once commonly used in tribal life: some steps resemble battle movements, others mimic hunting or healing. The "grass dance" originates in the stamping motions of the Plains Indians flattening the tall grasses of the prairies before they set up camp. And there is the "fancy feather" dance, which is newer, and full of inspired steps that still keep the contours of the signature fluid movements that mark a Native American dancer. There is such a virtuosic display of beading and embroidery and feathers and tassels that my eye can't rest on just one person to see what she is wearing. So much care has been put into each outfit: the soft white boots on the women, their hair coiled and shaped onto neatly held heads, the eagle feathers affixed at carefully considered angles in their hair.

In the afternoon, I find Eric and the crew cutting yet another of Veronica's fields. Juston is driving truck, waiting for a full load of wheat; some of Dwayne's boys are driving combines, and, as before, Veronica has hired additional trucks to help take the thick wheat out of the field. Everything is running smoothly. I sit with Eric in the pickup for a while. Juston is out playing with a stray dog in the shade. Then Eric turns to me and suggests I drive the pickup, and he will drive Lily to the RV park. And then he says: "Lets go to the powwow."

I follow him through the fields and onto the dirt roads and the pavement, and past the rodeo grounds, where the powwow is in full swing. We drive to the RV park, and he puts Lily in her spot and I keep the pickup in idle. As soon as I see him coming toward me, I move to the passenger seat so he can drive.

We have driven off together before, but it has always been in service of a part, or checking for a ripe field, or to see some aspect of topography or farming he wants me to understand. Eric is *always* working. Eric gets into the pickup and smiles. We go to the powwow.

Eric parks and we slip under a rope, past a tepee, and then we are on the festival grounds. What he really wants, he says, is to watch the dancing and eat some fry bread. He is nostalgic for those flavors. We check the schedule; it will begin in an hour. So we decide first to see what there is for sale. I walk through the stalls and look at the Native American pro-test shirts, the original Diné graphic designs of eagles and Kokopelli, and the hand-beaded bracelets for sale. I buy two T-shirts with portraits of Geronimo and Custer and their respective captions: "Organic" and "GMO."

We come to one of the booths selling jewelry. I look at the woven necklaces for sale; they resemble the one I bought when I was with Veronica, but I don't like these quite as much. A woman catches my eye. "That's a Ray Jack." She nods at my chest. She is referring to the Navajo pendant I purchased in Oklahoma, which depicts "the creator" coming down from the heavens. The pendant is an irregularly shaped teardrop. The piece is inlaid and made from stone. In the center, a square "entity" appears to be coming down through a plain of black sky flecked with gold stars, while turquoise, white, and red beams radiate out of his head. Below him is the earth, which he has just started to form. Back then I thought I would like to have a piece of art depicting an even older crea-tor than the Christian God. And so I had bought the pendant without hesitation, stringing it on a chain made of silver beads.

"Where did you get it?" she asks me.

"Oklahoma," I say. "I saw it and fell in love with it."

"You have good taste. I see your bracelets."

"Thank you." I touch my wrists.

"Who made those?"

"I don't know." I take them off one at a time and hand them to her.

The woman turns the Hopi bracelets over and searches for a signa-ture, which is usually stamped on the back of silver pieces like these. But she doesn't find one. "They are nice, anyway," she says as she hands them back to me.

"Thank you."

Meanwhile, another woman turns her attention to Eric. She asks where he is from, and he tries to explain that he lives in Pennsylvania, but spent his childhood in New Mexico on the reservation. The woman is unsurprised. "You learn to speak our language?"

"Well . . . I don't know. I . . ." I watch with some fascination as Eric blushes. It is unusual to see him so flustered. He is so pleased they are asking him this question and assuming that there is even a possibility he might understand the language of the Navajo. "You know, I *could* understand it."

"It would come back to you," she says. "If you practiced."

Eric is still grinning from ear to ear when we go over to the stall with the feathers and herbs and animal hides. I look at the eagle feathers; all appear to be fake.

We are getting hungry and are on our way to a taco truck, when Eric's phone rings. The reception here is spotty—reception is spotty all over the reservation. But Eric manages to make contact long enough to hear Dwayne's voice over the receiver. Then he hangs up. His mood has shifted completely. "They ran out of fuel." He turns and begins to stride toward the pickup.

We leave the festive environment without speaking. Eric drives back to the RV park, then jumps out of the pickup and hurries over to Lily. This, I assume, is my cue to follow him, so I slide over to the driver's side, this time adjusting the seat for myself. Then I follow Eric out of the parking lot.

"Where were you?" Juston asks me when we return to the field. He is now playing an improvised game of fetch with the gray dog. Eric has taken Lily out into the field to refuel the combine.

"The powwow," I say.

"Oh."

"So . . . someone ran out of fuel?"

Juston snorts. "If you can believe it." He takes the stick from the dog's mouth and throws it out into the stubble. The dog happily runs after the stick. "Did you eat fry bread?" he asks.

"We didn't get that far. We were only there for maybe thirty minutes, and then . . . Do *you* want fry bread?"

Juston purses his lips and nods. "I could eat some fry bread." After a moment he says: "I thought Dad was going to get us some dinner. I thought that was where you were going."

"You haven't had dinner?"

He doesn't answer me, and though he's not upset, exactly, I feel guilty. The entire crew is hungry; there has been no meal delivery that day from Emily, who certainly would have brought food, had she known there would be no food. She must also have thought we were getting dinner. And while we weren't exactly hiding the fact that we were at the powwow, we were hiding the fact that we were at the powwow.

We spend maybe another hour out here in the field, cutting the wheat while the sun goes down. I think that the dances will be starting now.

I have missed the rest of the Indian relay racing. Juston and I watch the combines go around and around while the dog asks us to pet him and play with him, and often, we do.

Maybe two hours later, when it's dark, Eric and the crew return. They are done cutting for the night; the temperature has dropped, and dew has set in to the wheat, making its moisture level too high and the stalks too tough to cut through. We tarp the truck and park all the combines in a row. Then Eric asks who would like to go to the powwow for dinner. Luther, Juston, and I immediately volunteer.

"Get in the pickup," he says. "The rest of you take Lily." Half the crew climbs into Lily, while trying to decide which fast-food restaurant they will go to for dinner. The rest of us get into the pickup with Eric.

And so, for the third time, I return to the festival grounds. There is almost no place to park now; the official parking lot is full, and people have taken to parking on the dirt roads. Even from inside the pickup, we can hear the pounding of the drums and the piercing voices singing. It is nearly eight o'clock and dark and we are starving. I have not eaten for hours. No one has eaten for hours. We find a place to put the pickup; someone is pulling out of a spot. We are all quiet. There is something about the exhaustion, the hunger, and the music from the powwow that has us all moving in a trance as we cut across fields and duck under ropes and slide around tepees to get into the festival.

Eric opens his wallet and hands Juston some cash. "I'm going to watch the dancing. Go get some food and bring me some fry bread." He says this almost sternly. He wants his fry bread.

"Okay," Juston says. I take the crew over to my favorite food truck, and we all order tacos. While I am waiting for my order, I go and get a large tuft of fry bread for Eric to eat. When I return, Juston has my taco, along with his. Luther is diving into a burrito. We move as a team over to the large circled pavilion, which is crowded. Every available spot for folding chairs has been taken up by audience members, but most of the concrete bases are unoccupied.

"You can stand on those," I say to Juston. "Then you can see."

"I'm okay." He scans the crowd. "Do you think we can find my dad?"

"I don't know."

There are so many people. It is dark now, and the darkness highlights the atmosphere of the pavilion. The center of the tent is filled with young men dancing vigorously. The audience comprises mostly

Native faces. The atmosphere is anxious. The dancers are competing with one another, and everyone is watching with tense concentration. But it's more than that. All around the perimeter of the tent, there are teams of men—and a few women—beating large drums made from animal hides, and singing, "Hey ya hey ha," and occasionally chortling.

In the middle of the tent, several dozen men are performing the traditional dance. They wear leather moccasins, beaded tops and belts, feathers on their heads and on their backs. They carry feathered implements, and each has his own style of movement. The motions are fluid but grounded; this is not like ballet, which is always trying to convey a sense of escaping gravity, of the lightness of the human body. In ballet this is known as *ballon*. These steps in the Indian dance feel frictionless and fluid, and are meant to convey men crouching in grass and trees as they hunt for buffalo, or a medicine man removing illness from his people, or a warrior with so much control over his body that he can easily defeat his enemy.

All at once, we see Eric. He stands out, actually. He is the one white person in a sea of brown faces and he is so tall and blond, it is as if a light shines disproportionately on him. He is smiling and looking at the dancing, and bobbing slightly to the drum beating. The three of us watch him watching the Indians. He has a look of joy on his face, the pure, unadulterated, childlike pleasure you see in a young person finding joy in a piece of music he hears for the first time. It is as if he has gone back in time to an earlier version of himself and we are seeing the light of that person shining through this adult exterior.

This is why he wanted to come to the powwow, I think. It has returned him to his childhood. Juston takes the fry bread from me. Luther and I stand on the periphery, watching the dancing, while Juston reaches across the crowd of people separating him from his father. With his long arms, Juston hands the fry bread to Eric, who takes it, dips his head in thanks, and begins to eat. Then the four of us stand there for a while in the brightly lit circle of the pavilion and watch as the Indians cry and sing and dance in a circle.

"He's remembering," Juston says.

"Being a kid?"

"Yeah."

Eric has been generous to me and without judgment. What makes Eric so open and unafraid of me, when some of the others clearly are?

Is it because he lived on the reservation as a child, like Veronica? Because he met Indians when he was so young, he learned early to play with children who didn't look like him at all, but who became, for a time, his friends?

Each night, when the sun sets, I count the days until the eclipse. In the morning, when the sun rises, I think about the moon inching closer to the sun; soon the moon will cover the sun completely. But there is a problem. There are multiple fires burning in the Wyoming wilderness, and the smoke is polluting the sky here in Idaho. Some days the air is so thick with smoke, it rains ash, and though the gray carpeting of the sky means that the sunsets are generally spectacular, we cannot see the mountains to the east. We should be able to see the Tetons by now, Eric frets. If the sky stays dirty like this, we will not even see the eclipse.

Day after day, we rise to find smoke in the air. Day after day, we search the weather forecast for rain, because that would not only put out the fires but would clear out the air. The world has a scrim over it, an additional layer making all things appear uncertain and obscure. Day after day, the crew keeps cutting and working because the heat means the wheat is ripe. I envy their daily connection to usefulness.

There is a day when I am trying to help by moving a pickup, and it is stuck in the dirt, and none of the tricks Michael has taught me are working to get the vehicle moving again. I am so frustrated that I get out of the pickup and begin to walk. This is, in hindsight, ridiculous, as there is nowhere to go without a vehicle, but I am so fed up with the landscape and the potatoes and my general lack of fitting in that I am going to walk. I will walk away in front of the potatoes, and . . .

"Hey, Marie." It's Michael. He has gotten the pickup out of the dirt and is driving alongside me on the dirt road with the window rolled down. He is trying very hard not to laugh.

I know I am supposed to laugh at myself, but if I laugh, it would mean that my stalking off in the middle of a potato field had in fact been ridiculous, when really the problem was just that I could not get the pickup out of the dirt.

"Get in," he says.

"No."

"Come on," he says. "Get in the pickup."

I am so useless and so out of place. "I think I should probably leave," I say to Michael.

"Nah." He shrugs. "You can't leave." My bout of emotion has not impressed him at all. He says, in his very rational way: "First of all, you can't leave until the eclipse." He pronounces it "EE-clips." "And second, you have to stay till the end. You start a thing . . . you finish it," he says very matter-of-factly, as though this is the most obvious thing in the world. As though in the training he received on how to be a Christian and how to be country, this advice about staying till a job was done was a main point of lesson one.

"I can't do anything," I say. "Or, I do everything all wrong."

"Marie," he says. "No one cares."

And so I get into the pickup and we drive back to wherever the crew is next, and sit as they once again harvest the grain from the fields.

The internet and telephone services are so bad on the reservation that I haven't been able to keep up with the news or email very well. When I want to talk to someone, I have to drive off the reservation. My texts often stack up, unsent. Sometimes when I am off the reservation, voice messages and texts will fly into my phone and I will briefly feel connected with the outside world. I call my husband and my son to check in, but the strangeness of what I am experiencing here is so removed from their routine of school and tennis lessons in the city, it is hard for me to convey the depth of what I am feeling. My husband is from Scotland, and his experience of America has been first New York and now San Francisco. My ever-deeper understanding of Christianity in this country—my lived experience—is something my family cannot understand. I am giving myself over to the "see and do" that Eric promised me I would have access to, but this is severing me from my other life.

One day, several messages from my friend Garnette arrive. He is writing to ask me if I know what is so important about the Civil War that someone would want to preserve memorabilia. Well, no, I write back, typing quickly while a satellite is gracing me with connectivity. No one on the harvest crew carries any Confederate gear. Some of the states we have visited were once part of the Confederacy, and here and there I saw the Confederate flag. But no one on the crew indicated excitement or pleasure over the flag.

Garnette has been covering a growing controversy in the city of Charlottesville, Virginia, which is planning to remove certain statues of Confederate war heroes. He wants to talk about the memorials with me, but I have little to offer. I am very far from the culture of statues and memorials, though if I drove a few hours to Salt Lake City, I suppose there I might see statues. Farm fields in general do not have many memorials, unless one comes across a marker for a pioneer trail or an old cemetery.

Then the conversation turns to the subject of the KKK, and then suddenly Garnette, who is black, is telling me that he will be leaving Charlottesville because he does not trust the police to protect people during an upcoming march that neo-Nazis have organized for that weekend. The bars on my phone fade and he is gone and I am left with this strange piece of news that has almost no context.

Over the weekend, the news unfolds, and I follow it when I can get cell phone reception. Mostly, I piece together the news through social media. I am able to gather, by Saturday night, that a young woman in Charlottesville is dead. In the little bubble that is my online world, there is only outrage.

I hope that here in Idaho something will be said in church on Sunday about the violence. It seems impossible for someone not to note that the violence and the hate speech are repugnant and are damaging the country. I mention this to Juston.

"They won't say anything," he tells me.

"What about, like, a prayer?" I ask.

He heaves a sigh. "I know. It's disappointing."

He's right. In church that day we sing a few worship songs about running blameless in front of the Lord. There are messages about living in a fallen world, and turning to God. We pray for missionaries on their way to Guatemala. There follows a long sermon, focused on certain lines in the Gospel of Luke. Not a single word is said about the violence in Charlottesville, about praying for peace, or about the young woman whose life was lost in the middle of this violence. I am despondent.

I pick up the Bible and begin to read it. I have spent four months on the road with the harvesters and have heard or read or looked at something from the Bible nearly every day. And while I am now convinced of the power of the text in this holy book, I feel a deep frustration with everyone sitting here, ostensibly turning to the Lord, with almost no effort made to address the fractions in our country. Then again, maybe the people in this church think it is ridiculous for people in Charlottesville to take down statues of Confederate war heroes. But if we are supposed to love our neighbors as ourselves, shouldn't we be upset that a young woman died as a result of a public protest?

Later, Emily will tell me that Virginia is far away from Idaho, and that most people in church that day are concerned with themselves and with their own problems. Maybe it's because I'm rootless that I invariably end up feeling concerned about events that tie me to others elsewhere.

I have not spent this much time in a purely white environment in many years. I have come to realize that almost all my friends are Jewish, or gay, or black, or Asian, or some combination thereof. My husband, while white, is from a foreign country. My "real" world comprises this patchwork, and it is reflected back to me. I have created my own reality of people, and that reality is not the world I have lived in while "on the farm." But even if I wanted to re-create my familiar world while I am out here, I wouldn't be able to. There aren't any Jews here. There are almost no people of color. I go into the towns to nail salons, and Vietnamese people run these businesses. Beyond this, though, there is no one, except for the few times I am fairly certain I have run into closeted gay men and women.

I fiddle around with the Bible.

On Facebook that morning, I saw a few postings of the quote by Martin Luther King about the complacent middle-class white person. Sitting here in church, I feel I am looking at the complacent middle-class white person who lives in this fallen world with plenty of sin and social injustice but doesn't do much about it. I start to feel that just by being here, I am part of this complacent middle-class white world and I feel my body fill with rage. I have been trying so hard to remain open to this world and to its people, but in doing so, I have kept a part of myself quiet.

This pastor, like others, drones on and on about how special Jesus was and about how we can find redemption and how God loves us and sent us his son. I am both enraged and bored. I look around me. Everyone is listening. So many people are smiling. There is nothing wrong in this church at all. This is, I think, why it is easy to convince the woman in the attic that she is insane, and that Jane Eyre is normal.

I look down the pew at Juston, seated at the end. He is expression-less. It is all exactly as he predicted. He feels me looking at him and he glances over. But his face does not change.

I flip over to the Gospel of John and read some random lines. At the end of a passage, something catches my eye. There are lines about the crucifixion and how the world went dark for three hours, and when it was light again, Jesus was dead.

"It was now about noon, and darkness came over the land until three in the afternoon, for the sun stopped shining. And the curtain of the temple was torn in two. Jesus called out in a loud voice, 'Father, into your hands I commit my spirit!' When he had said this, he breathed his last."

I think, *There is an eclipse coming. Did Christ die during an eclipse?*

After church, we are on our way to a steak house. Eric wants to know how the church made me feel. And I tell him. I'm unable to control my anger. Usually I'm able to express myself thoughtfully, but I can't in this case. They are all so calm. They are all so trained in the words of Jesus and anchored to Jesus that they simply listen to me until I have spilled out all the words and am empty and then we drive to the steak house.

As we pull out of the lot—Juston driving—there is a family standing at the exit. They are Mexican and one of them is carrying a sign asking for food, or money, or help.

"Oh, man. I feel bad," Michael says.

I feel suspicious. I am suspicious of everything. I feel like some overgrown Holden Caulfield who is convinced everyone is a phony. I am sure the church is not a place of sincere worship but a place people go in order to pretend they care about Jesus, and I am sure these people are not starving. I feel I am the only one who knows what is going on, because I have complex feelings and because I am from the city and everyone around me is overly simple. "Who knows if they are starving." I snort.

"I feel bad for them," Michael repeats.

Eric is late meeting us for the steaks. When he finally arrives, about fifteen minutes later, he is vague about where he has been.

Only much later does Juston tell me that Eric had taken a detour to go and buy the Mexican family some food.

I go to Panera Bread with Michael and Juston. It has now been weeks since I have seen a painting, heard jazz, watched dance. I am so starved for the experience of transcendence from human art, I am practically rejoicing inside Panera, which serves whole-grain bread. It's just marketing, I tell myself. Then, I don't care. I want a taste of the city.

We sit in the air conditioning for a while, and while Michael tinkers with his phone, trying to connect it to Wi-Fi, Juston talks to me about church. "I told you they wouldn't say anything."

I've calmed down enough, now, not to respond with anger. Still, I say to him: "I don't even understand the point of church."

"It's true. In a lot of ways, the church is kind of culturally irrelevant now. That's why I, and my friends, loved my urban ministry program at school so much. We saw Christianity that actually meant something to the real world."

Michael's phone finally connects to Wi-Fi, and I change the topic of conversation. I bring up the passage about Jesus and the possible eclipse. Michael tells me to research it.

"But you can't just look up 'eclipse' and 'Bible,'" Michael says. "You'll get a lot of crap. You need to look up what the historical eclipses have been, and then extrapolate from there."

"Part of the problem is that we don't know when Jesus died," Juston points out. "Plus, they've recently had to adjust that he was born in AD 3 and not 0."

"Oh yeah. I heard about that," Michael exclaims.

Ever since I learned that Michael believes the earth is six thousand years old, I am unsure how much science he trusts or does not trust. On the subject of Jesus's birth, and Passover, and the timing of the Resurrection, he seems to be as demanding of historical accuracy as Juston.

My initial search, despite Michael's specific instructions, yields hundreds of references to eclipses in the Bible. In fact, there are plenty of conspiracy theories concerning the impending eclipse, which Dwayne has started to jokingly to call "the apoc-eclipse." And while I already know that these believers in astrology are ascribing great meaning to the event, it hasn't occurred to me that it might also be seen as a sign by evangelical Christians, some of whom wonder if, at last, the end of times is here.

Finally, I find an article in which a writer has, like I have, noted the description of the earth going dark when Jesus died. The article claims that there are certain translations of the Bible that even refer to this darkening as an eclipse.

NASA has charted all previous eclipses. Looking at NASA's data, there does appear to be one eclipse around the time of Jesus's death, even accounting for his new birth date. The only problem is that this eclipse could not have been seen anywhere near the Middle East. What's more, it would not have gone dark for three hours, as the Bible said it did when Jesus died.

I joke to the men that perhaps someone sat there as John was writing his Gospel, admonishing him, "Don't get too fancy. Just the facts. And probably he said: *I needed to write it so people will pay attention and remember. It can't be like a term paper.*" This elicits a few smiles.

It turns out there was a lunar eclipse on April 3, AD 33, that would have been visible from the Middle East, and that lasted two hours and fifty minutes. This excites me. I send the article to Eric. I ask him about it later, but he looks skeptical.

"It could be," he says to me, "that God just performed a miracle."

"The bench" is a geological structure on the eastern side of the valley that slopes down toward the Snake River. It is a caldera, one of the round indentations that formed after the Yellowstone hot spot caused a volcano to erupt thousands of years ago. Eric says that the potatoes on the bench are considered a delicacy; so, too, are the ones grown in the sand in Pocatello on Veronica's farm. He tells me that the wheat up on the bench is now ripe too.

This means that there is now so much wheat, the crews must split up. The Wolgemuths decamp for a farmer's lawn in Hamer, Idaho, which is directly in the path of totality. Eric doesn't say so, but I suspect he wants to get there to make sure we are in their annual camping spot before the crowds begin to arrive. "The news says we are expecting five hundred thousand to one million people just in Idaho!"

I love this new campsite. There is a long line of cottonwoods at one end, and when Emily turns her head to look at them, joy floats right out from the deepest part of her heart and onto her face, so she smiles broadly. The only other time I have seen this expression is when she has looked at a baby. She loves the trees. They have always been here and are a favorite thing for her. She and I walk over to the trees and we hear hooting. Owls? We are like children, looking for them. We find two. They peer down at us, and we gaze up at them. There are no people for miles and it is us two women and the owls.

It is said that an eclipse will make you believe in either God or science. I wonder which it will be for us. What I can say is that it does rain, and the fires do go out, and the air clears.

"Now we just hope there are no clouds," Eric says, his eyes turned up to the sky. The morning of the eclipse, Emily reads the Bible passage where Jesus ascends to heaven.

"Then Jesus led them to Bethany, and lifting his hands to heaven, he blessed them. While he was blessing them, he left them and was taken up to heaven. So they worshiped him and then returned to Jerusalem with great joy. And they spent all of their time in the Temple, praising God."

We are all silent when she finishes. "I didn't plan it that way," she tells us sincerely. "It just worked out like that."

Eric seems almost delighted to find a tent in the potato field behind us. It is only one tent and not the hordes the news had predicted. But it is still a deviation from the norm and he is pleased.

As we drive out to the field we will cut this morning, we see a few more RVs parked on the south side of the road, and men and women emerging from tents after a night of sleep. It is 9 a.m. The eclipse will start at 10:15, but we won't be able to see it happening for at least an hour after that. There is an overpass over the main highway, and there are a few cars already parked there, presumably because it is the highest elevation in the vicinity. Totality—the full eclipse of the sun—will last for only two minutes. For anyone wanting to photograph the event, this is a short period during which to take a picture.

Eric is excited. He asks me frequently how dark it will become. The night before, when we were outside by the trailers, checking to see if the owls were still in the trees (they were), he asked me again if it would be as dark as it was now, and I said I did not know. I have never seen an eclipse before, but still he asks me.

Every now and then a breeze carries the voices of the people gathering on the overpass. Usually it is the high-pitched "Woo-hoo" of a young woman. I wonder if they are drinking. I wonder if they see us cutting wheat in this field. Michael and Eric are each in a combine. The Case engineer is in his pickup. Juston and Luther are driving trucks. When we left the camp that morning, I asked Emily a few times if she will be coming with us, because I do not want her to miss the eclipse. She assured me she would show up eventually. But she is busy in the morning, as she is every morning, cleaning up after breakfast, and hanging the laundry on the clotheslines attached to the fronts of the trailers, and preparing lunch. My maternal instincts lead me to be very adamant—very—that everyone see and enjoy the eclipse. I don't care about sandwiches, but I am insistent that we all have an Experience.

What will it be like, this eclipse? Will the world feel "torn in two," as when Christ died in the Bible? Will any of the crew give up the foolishness that is creationism? Will I feel that God is real and decide I must be part of a fellowship and join a church?

While we wait for the sky to darken, the men go in circles around this wheat field and I fidget. The eclipse is not like any other event I've been to. If this were the ballet or the theater, I would know in which seat I wanted to sit. If this were a stationary natural wonder, I, too, would have found something to stand on to try to get the best photo possible. But I have no idea what to expect.

Because I am an impatient person, I start putting on my eclipse glasses early. I can't see a thing. I have been warned so often not to look directly at the sun that I feel a certain amount of trepidation when I start turning my head up to where the sun is supposed to be. But there it is: a bright spot in a sea of darkness and in the upper right-hand corner is a bite mark. The eclipse has begun. I text Michael immediately. "You can see it starting," I say.

He doesn't stop his combine, but he texts me back a moment later: "That is pretty cool!"

Juston gets out of his truck and puts his glasses on and looks at the sky. "Whoa."

God is not performing a miracle. Or maybe he is performing a miracle. We hear cheering coming from over by the highway overpass.

It gets colder. I check my phone and see that the temperature has dropped by a degree. Time passes and it gets even cooler. After a while, I put on a second T-shirt that is tied around my waist. And then it is even colder. After 11 a.m., I have put on my button-up shirt.

The sky is growing darker, but it is not like any dimming of the sun I have ever experienced before. It is not like a cloud passing over the sun so the world is more gray, and it is not like the setting sun, when a part of your heart reaches for the sun and yearns for it to come back from behind the mountains. It is like a dense slab of violet glass has been placed over the sun; it reminds me of the ultraviolet lights my mother used when I was a child to urge her African violet collection to bloom. The air has a chilled, indigo quality. I think about a study that claimed it was only recently that people both had a term for blue and were able to see the color. As a child in Japan, I was irritated that my mother used the same word, "*ao*," for both blue and green. I would correct her and say she must say "*midori*" if she meant green. She would scold me back.

"We didn't distinguish between green and blue until recently," she would say to me.

With the eclipse, it is the dawning of a new color, and this color is covering us. My hands are a shade I have never seen before—like something only a filter on a computer screen might conjure. It grows colder and I put on my sweater and the air is heavier now. Only it isn't heavier. It is the same weight it has always been, but the addition of the lavender makes everything feel heavier. By now, Michael has stopped his combine and is standing with me. He is cold, too, and he runs to get the sweatshirt he had brought along with him. We both thought we could withstand the cold; the eclipse would be just a passing thing.

One by one, the men bring their rigs over to where we are standing and turn off the engines. They park neatly, as though it is the end of the day and we are getting ready to go to dinner. Finally, Emily arrives, too, in the pickup. She has an early lunch with her but no one is ready to eat yet. Only when Emily is finally here does Eric bring his combine to a halt.

The eclipse is unstoppable. I put my glasses on and look at the black slab of nothing that is nearly covering the sun and then I take off my glasses and I am in an ever-darkening world. It is as if I am losing my eyesight. It is getting darker and more blue now and the entire horizon seems ringed by orange. I look back at the crew one more time, and they all have their glasses on, as if we are in a 3-D movie theater. Eric puts his arm around Emily and she leans back against him and they both crane their necks. The moon slips tightly over the sun, sealing it shut, and the sky goes dark, ringed only by a fiery halo of white light. It is as if a dark disk has been tossed on a febrile, alabaster sea.

It is so dark we see stars. There is cheering coming from the highway overpass. I can see the combine, Eric in his hat, and Juston in his hat, all in silhouette. Their heads stick up out of the earth into the part of the sky that is still bruised with light.

Eric is whooping approval. He is in a delighted state of awe when he suddenly shouts: "Look at the Tetons! Look at the Tetons!" In the dark, I see him pointing to the east, like an usher in a darkened movie theater gesturing toward an exit. I look.

Three triangular giants of granite puncture the ground. Their feet are invisible, but the tips of their raw teeth are illuminated in rose light. They are like objects behind a scrim, performers who were invisible until now, when this fragile time between day and non-day is spread thinly enough over the horizon that we can see the jaws of the Grand Tetons yawn open. How many times has Eric lamented that I have not seen the Tetons?

"Wow!"

"Whoa!"

The sky has revealed to us what we could not see before. It is a moment I want to hold. I would like to fly under totality as the band of darkness creeps along the United States, moving to the southeast. For some, the eclipse is still impending, and for others it has already passed. Totality will glide across the United States, giving those in its seventy-mile-wide path a view of darkness for just over two minutes. To keep up with totality, you would need to be able to travel at 2,955 miles per hour in Oregon, slow to 1,462 miles per hour over Kentucky, then accelerate again to 1,502 miles per hour as the band of darkness reaches Charleston, South Carolina. The shadow would then fall off the planet and into the meaningless darkness of space.

It begins to brighten slowly. The Tetons start to fade, like spirits returning to their world beyond the veil. Their rosy heads go out like matches losing their spark. They melt into the horizon. The sky becomes a child's version of blue: cobalt. After a while, we take off a layer of clothing and the day warms. If I put on my glasses and look up, the moon is still eating the sun, or perhaps the sun is spitting out the moon, but on the earth, the eclipse has ended. The world roars back to life and people start their engines and begin to drive off to wherever they will go next. In our corner of what was once the path of totality, the men get back into their combines and semitrucks and continue harvesting wheat.

We move camp again. Eric wants to show me the bench, the farthest we will go on harvest to cut wheat. The leftover caldera—the lava flows—make this land slightly elevated. It is like a storybook, with little lanes that dip and dive over rounded hills covered with potatoes, wheat, and sprinklers. We are very close to the mountains here, and they border the farm fields. They are so close that at one point Eric takes me into some of the foothills, and it doesn't take long for the wheat to go away and the aspens to appear. It is like time traveling, this traversing from fields into mountains.

He asks: "So do people from your world think that people from my world are stupid? You know, that the boys wait to have sex until they are married?"

It is sometimes hard not to idealize this Christian way of life. There are Emily and Eric, supporting each other so harmoniously in this endeavor, and crossing the country every year to harvest wheat and turn young boys into men. They are utterly devoted to each other and to their family. He has built her a home and installed a beautiful kitchen within the home. He feeds poor families and rescues people whose cars have broken down by the side of the road.

"Yes," I tell him. "They think you are stupid."

He nods. "That's about what I figured. So is everyone in the city promiscuous? I mean, I could see how that would happen."

"Not everyone," I say. "And even if they are, I'm not sure they are necessarily happier."

Back at the trailer, I say goodbye to Juston. He is leaving early to go back to college. I feel so sad about this, but he is determined to go and he is tired of harvest. It has not gone the way he had hoped. He wanted it to be a chance for me to learn about the fellowship of farmers.

We are standing by the trailers while the laundry flaps on a clothes-line, waiting for Emily to take him to the airport. "One thing I've learned," he says, "is it's all true. The Fall. Cain and Abel. The whole thing. The story is true. Not the facts. But the message."

I don't want him to leave thinking this, and I start to protest that it is my presence—my alien presence and all my questions—that has con-tributed to the chaos. I really want in this moment for all the problems to be mine, so he can keep the harvest for himself and his family. But Juston is unyielding. He is adamant that it has nothing to do with me, the city, or my language skills, or with the fact that in farm years I am only eight years old. He gives me a quick hug and gets into the white Suburban with his mother, and leaves to fly back to Pennsylvania.

I go out to the fields with Michael, who stoically announces, as he al-ways does: "I'm gonna break through." He drives the combine out into the center of the field and charges off on his own. In his mind, I know, he is putting in a pathway to make it easier for everyone to get around. But this time we go out so far that by the time we turn around and come back, the grain bin on the back of the combine is very full, and the yel-low lights have long been flashing. We need to get out of this field, but the only way to do so is to either cut a path ahead of us, run over the wheat and drive out, or backtrack, which would be a waste of fuel and a long way to go to reach Bethany to dump our load. And so we forge ahead slowly, hoping to get out of the field before the bin is overflowing.

"We gonna make it?" I ask.

"I think so." Michael smiles. He's not the least bit worried about the grain bin on the back of the combine. He likes this tension of the unknown.

All of a sudden, there is an unexpected dip in the ground and the com-bine lurches. "Aaah!" Michael groans. It starts to rain wheat. It sounds as though someone is on the roof of the cab slowly releasing a fistful of ball bearings over our heads. The wheat sprinkles to the ground, where it is lost, and a few kernels settle on the window ledge outside. We have only a few yards left to go, and Michael drives even more slowly.

Bethany, who has been hovering on the horizon, realizes that we cannot get out of the field. She has seen the spillage, and she drives over to us. Michael cuts the engine and waits.

"Michael." It is Bradford's voice over the radio.

"Yeah."

"You need to come back. It's a waste of fuel for Bethany to go so far out for you."

I watch Michael's face. It is awash in good humor and passionate annoyance. "All right!" he says with forced cheerfulness into the radio.

Juston told me there was tension between these two men. When he said he had defended Michael, was it just over combine-cutting habits? All the same, I feel uncomfortable with tension, and so when Veronica invites me back to her ranch, I accept immediately.

That night we go out to the potato field right outside her home, and she digs up fresh potatoes for us to eat. They are ready; potato harvest will begin in a matter of days. She shows me how the skins are tough and thick now, and in the kitchen, she makes twice-baked potatoes. After we pray, we begin to eat, and the potatoes are delicious. I have forgotten how good a truly excellent potato can be. Veronica asks us all to reflect on what we have learned as a result of farming. For her it is how varied the decisions are that she needs to make. For her husband, who did not grow up on a farm, it is the number of decisions. I say I am astonished to realize how much I live in a world created by language.

"What do you mean?" Veronica asks. "I think I know what you mean. But can you elaborate?"

I tell her about a time I was standing around Lincoln Center in New York City at Christmas, and how I was struck by a pang of sadness. I was sad because I was staring at an enormous poster of a Tiffany & Co. ad on a bus stop, and I was thinking that I had never had a Tiffany moment. I had never had the robin's-egg-blue box presented to me, with a token inside that advertising promised me was a symbol of how much I meant as a woman.

"I told myself I shouldn't care whether or not I had ever received a Tiffany box. I am not the type to care about a Tiffany box. I'm a writer. I'm supposed to care about small, handmade works of art. Nothing corporate," I tell her. But I was sad that I did not have one. It should have been a warning to me that my cravings are affected by advertising. Even when I think I do not care about money or status or objects—or beauty—I do. And this is part of living in the city, which swirls with advertising and its messages. Not so on the farm. There is an absence of ads, of psychological manipulation—beyond, perhaps, the Bible.

In *Sources of the Self: The Making of the Modern Identity*, Charles Taylor discusses what it is to be a modern person. "The invocation of meaning also comes from our awareness of how much the search involves articulation. We find the sense of life through articulating it. And moderns have become acutely aware of how much sense being there for us depends on our own powers of expression." Over and over he makes this point: that to be modern is partly about being able to articulate one's being.

Contrast this, Taylor says, with Martin Luther, who "in his intense anguish and distress before his liberating moment of insight about salvation through faith, his sense of inescapable condemnation, irretrievab[ly damned] himself through the very instruments of salvation, the sacraments." It wasn't articulation that got Luther through; it was faith.

Over and over again, Taylor stresses the importance of narrative for a modern person. It is the way a modern person works, and by "modern," I know he means what the harvesters refer to as "city" and "college." A modern person is able to tell the story of himself as an individual. It's an idea, argues Taylor, that developed in the Romantic period and has carried beyond it. "With the development of the post-Romantic notion of individual difference, this expands to the demand that we give people the freedom to develop their personality in their own way, however repugnant to ourselves and even to our moral sense." And while we need one another, we need to be able to express what makes us individuals. This is what the modern world demands. Our own personal narrative.

Other thinkers see a weakness in all this constant talking about oneself. Richard Sennett, for example, is certain that our continuous turn inward has created an extreme culture of narcissism, which he says has replaced anxiety as the primary source of mental illness. "Masses of people are concerned with their single life-histories and particular emotions as never before: this concern has proved to be a trap rather than a liberation."

I am so relaxed in Veronica's home. She is, I decide, what Juston and I would call a Jesus person; she is someone who focuses on the actual words and deeds of Jesus. She is also a city person and she understands me. That night, I stay in her basement, surrounded by a wall of books. There are some children's books I recognize. Many more are about God and are published by Deseret Book Company, which, Eric has explained to me, is a Mormon publishing house. Still, the very fact that I can sleep with books is an enormous comfort to me, and I climb into bed feeling that I am in a version of reality that feels familiar.

In the morning, Veronica takes me to the "potato shed," a building where Idaho potato growers meet regularly. She is the only woman. The men are discussing how they need to prepare for the coming harvest season. She shows me the potato sorting facility. Potatoes come in on conveyer belts and are photographed by a row of cameras, which measure the size of the potatoes and then automatically know which conveyer belt to flip the potato onto. Depending on where the potatoes are sent, they are boxed, bagged, or processed. We have a quick lunch, after a visit to the Idaho Potato Museum, and then my phone abruptly has service and is flooded with text messages. I even have a note from Michael asking if I have left, which strikes me as mildly alarming.

I am thinking about returning to the crew when Veronica says: "I'm going to have a home teaching. Would you like to come?" Two women from her church, one of whom is Native American and grew up on the reservation, will stop by. I could meet them. And so I stay.

Sally is fair-skinned for an Indian; I learn later that she is mixed, like me. She speaks with excitement about her daughter's upcoming wedding and the ongoing decisions over whether or not the wedding will take place in the temple or in another location.

Sally smiles a lot when she talks. She drops details about her life like bread crumbs meant to lead an attentive listener on a trail. She was at the festival, she says, and I realize she means the powwow. She laughs as she tells me that her father always said: "You been to one festival, you been to them all." She hadn't agreed as a child, and now she did. Her husband is Navajo.

We speak about the festival and I mention the beaded necklace I purchased and she's happy. "Those necklaces were a good price and you chose meaningful designs. I tried to go back to get a necklace but the lady was gone."

I mention that there had been another stall where I had seen a necklace I liked. This was the stall that Eric and I had visited together. "Oh, that was Terry, my friend. Her prices were high," says Sally.

She tells us about her life on the reservation. She describes an elderly family member who turned off the water in the house, and who was encouraged to turn the water back on so the sewage didn't simply sit in the pipes but was flushed out the way the design was intended. I think about how this older person is one of the last living links to a time before America was America as it is today, and how we take for granted modern plumbing even though it is relatively new. I tell her about Japan, and about how, over the course of my life, I have watched modern sewage systems implemented there too.

Occasionally, she cracks a joke about having "lost the land." She talks about her "Jojo," who I guess is her great-grandmother, born in 1884, and who remembers seeing her very first covered wagon cross the plain. Jojo was so scared, she ran and hid in her tepee.

The conversation goes on like this. She says she is a devout Mormon who loves her family, loves her people, and knows her land was lost. Her soprano voice is round and almost girlish, though she must be in her forties.

She wants to know about my project and so I tell her about the conundrum I have faced regarding organics and GMOs, science and God. She laughs in a trill and says that the Indians didn't like the crossbreed of buffalo and beef, called beefalo. The original Indians farmed organically, she says. They were a resourceful and talented people living on the plains.

I wonder if the Indians have strong feelings about organic food now.

"Maybe city Indians," she says, still laughing. "The rest of us are worried about diabetes. Trying to avoid McDonald's because the doctor told us to."

I mention that according to the Bible people were vegetarians until the Flood. But she challenges me. Cain and Abel both offered God sacrifices, but Cain gave only plants; Abel gave a goat. For what purpose had Abel sacrificed the goat if it was not for eating?

There is now a strange dynamic between us that I cannot name. It's as if we have established an electric cable between us and we are both conducting across it, though for what purpose I don't know. On the surface we are having a pleasant conversation, but we are also not having a pleasant conversation. The electricity in the cable makes me feel that at any moment it will overheat, and I don't know why this is happening or why we have this cord between us, but we do.

I ask her where fry bread comes from. I don't know why I ask. I guess we are talking about food, and we have moved from the Indians and the buffalo, to McDonald's, to the Bible, and I just wonder where fry bread, which everyone treats as a Native food, actually originates.

She tells me it comes from the Navajo, who also walked the Trail of Tears. This was not the history that I knew. She said that they were huddled together in Oklahoma with bags of coffee, flour, sugar, and salt given to them by the US government, and were eating out of these bags, but still dying by the dozens. They had dysentery. They were undergoing a holocaust. A Union soldier finally took pity on the Indians and showed them how to turn the flour into dough. And thus fry bread was born.

"My people eat it too. We all eat it," Sally says. She laughs and she trills again. "We were farmers once, you know. You hear about the Navajo. They were farmers and they were organic. They grew corn and you hear these stories that they tell, about how high the corn was! Up to the roof." She shakes her head.

"It's a legend?" I ask.

"No, no. It was really that high! The old-timers will tell you it was as high as the roof of a house! Taller than a man! That's what they say. And now it's so short. It's only three feet high and they can't make it any taller."

I am thinking there must be something wrong now with the soil, or moisture, or fertilizer. I say this. "Maybe it's a new kind of varietal . . ."

"It was the firewater," she says to me sharply, her voice catching a little. "'Don't drink the firewater,' the elders said." Her voice abruptly deepens. "But my people drank the firewater that the white man brought. *My people*," she repeats, as though one of us has said this phrase to her and she is echoing it back. And then she looks at Veronica. "Your father said to me: 'What is this? *My people*. Your people are my people. I was born on this reservation too.'" She laughs lightly, referring to Veronica's father, now off serving his mission. "And in those days, I was so bitter, so bitter about my people and the loss of my land. And your father told me to seek a testimony from the Book of Mormon. And I thought, Okay. He's right. And the word 'land' had come to me. Into my head. And I started to read."

I do not know which way this story is going to go. The electrical cord between us has grown hot and I am holding it with burning hands. I am listening to her speak and I can sense there are different threads in her life and the cable is made up of these different threads and they are not all in alignment. I think she has decided that I know this about her, and all the threads are activated and all are giving voice to themselves and she is speaking them all at once. Does she always use all her voices at once? Or does it depend on the audience? And as I am sitting on the edge of the sofa, feeling very uncertain, I see her grow emotional, and watch as a storm comes over her. I see this tempest just as clearly as the storms I have watched cross over the plains. Her voice quavers. It is unsteady and it is breaking and it isn't holding her words well anymore. The girlish voice is faltering. She sobs: "I saw that each place in the Book of Mormon where it says 'land,' it says 'righteous people.' 'Righteous people.'"

The room loses its air. Usually I have a sense, like a radar, of what will happen a split second before it does, but I have no idea what will happen now. She says: "And I realized God allowed the land to be taken because we were no longer a righteous people. We used to have corn that grew as high as the window, but we drank the firewater and now the corn is only three feet high and we are fighting diabetes."

She finishes. This is how she has worked through her bitterness. This is what she found in the Book of Mormon. My brain is caught in a stunned loop. I have now traveled so far from everything I have ever been taught, and from every intimacy I have ever shared with another person. I lack the language to know how to begin to answer.

"Isn't it interesting how God allows things to happen through wicked people," Veronica says quickly.

"Yes," Sally agrees.

A hundred dollars and I would not have known that this is the sentence I am supposed to say. I see that my thinking is all wrong. I have just heard this story about the corn and the firewater and it did not occur to my mind to generate a sentence about God and "wicked people." I am eating sentences like "I'm sure your people were righteous," or "But you didn't have guns. Or the wheel," or "The white men made so many promises, but they lied."

And though I try to keep up with the thread of the conversation that is now continuing, I lose it. The electrified cable between us is now cold. I am in a small storm of my own. Are we really going to sit here and accept a version of events in which God has taken away the land because the people—her people, all of those people—were not righteous? This is not the version of Christianity that I have come to respect. It cannot be correct. But of course I see why this is the version of Christianity that some people would *like* to be correct.

Over the following days, when I share this story with a few people, they either react with shock and silence or they try to take the story one step further. The Indians had "not always been nice." The Native Americans were primitive and had never managed to develop the wheel (again), and in this version of events, I am told it is a shame that the Native people have said nothing about the gratitude they should feel that their lives now could progress. "They have been allowed to pro*gress*."

Veronica knows my horror in having heard this story. She knows, far better than I do, the complicated history of this land. She can see that, for me, hearing Sally's story is like touching a wound. It is as if Sally let me touch her wound and then I knew at last I had a wound too. My brain feels raw. Veronica says to me: "Our relationship with God puts us in a centered place and makes us more open to personal revelation." And personal revelation is not the same as general revelation.

If I have a personal revelation in this moment, it is not that God has deemed Native Americans an unrighteous people and thus taken their land intentionally to give to the Mormons, who are more righteous. My thought is: I am unprepared for the level of emotion and thought that has gone into the architecture of a world that enabled the taking of the land. They have taken the land right down to the pockets of kerogen. The architecture of this world feels to me like a psychological prison. They have thought of everything, these people who have created this world. I have no idea how to begin to dismantle it. And in my skin, I cannot pass through unnoticed.

Over and over again, I start to see that these conversations about race rest on a simple concept: to be white is to not know what it is to be a person of color. Sometimes to be white is to think one knows what it is like to be a person of color. And to be a person of color is to be like anyone else. This means that if a person of color points out that his people were victimized, then he is trying to make himself and his history sound "special." If we are all the same, as Christ said, then no one is special. To accept Christ, therefore, means that one does not embrace a victim mentality or emphasize the parts of one's personal history that are unpleasant. One should simply have faith. If one cannot find solace in faith, if one does not know that God is looking out for oneself, and if one thus embraces a victim mentality, then all is not well.

"But it is a fact," I say to Eric, "that you are not coming from the same starting point as a person of color. You simply aren't."

But though I can argue this—though I can point to the disproportionate deaths of minorities in custody, or the still disproportionate lower number of people of color in university or serving as heads of corporations, not to mention the blinding whiteness of corporate boards, or elite men's clubs, or the Mormon Quorum—though I can point to all of this, I can still be met with an insistence that whatever the white person sees as reality—particularly if he or she is armed with the love of Jesus—must be right.

Why is the distress I see—that any person of color sees—not understood as both subjective and real, but is instead dismissed as a symptom of a lack of faith in the other side? Why must it come down to a leap of faith?

All this is revealed and I stare at it. Once you see a thing, you cannot unsee it. Just because it isn't in front of you at a particular moment doesn't mean it is not there. I think of the new color during the eclipse—the violet scrim—and the rose-colored mountains jutting out of the horizon, which had, until that moment, been invisible. The mountains were still there. They are still there now.

The new camp is set up right off a dirt road in a remote area on the bench. There is a potato field to the west. Before us, the land swoops down into more potato fields and then wheat fields, and then rushes over another foothill to the east.

Carrie and Emily are in Emily's trailer. Carrie is on her way to deliver a thermos of sweet tea to Dwayne, and she offers to drive me out to the crew. She has a no-nonsense quality that I love. "She's city," Juston and Michael have said to me. Is this what I recognize in her?

"There has been drama," she informs me as we drive.

"What happened?"

She tells me that the tension between the boys has become so charged that Michael and Amos were out-and-out screaming at each other. It had something to do with Michael once again breaking through the field, and Bethany not being able to keep up with the grain cart, and Bradford being angry at how Michael was cutting, and then somehow things went from this tension to yelling in plain view of everyone. Mennonites don't yell. Emily and Carrie had gotten involved and phoned Eric, who'd then had to take matters into his own hands.

It had not been my imagination, then, that Michael's phone text had seemed strange. He had wanted to talk to me after the fight.

Carrie drops me off by the trucks, which are waiting for their load of wheat, and I send Michael a message to tell him I am here. The crew is moving fields and Michael is on his way back to the trucks. He asks me to wait for him and he will drive me to the next location. Not too long after, I watch his large red combine roll into view, like an oversize crustacean. He opens the door for me, and I clamber up the metal steps and slide in.

Combines, like tanks, can cover every kind of terrain, but the ride is neither fast nor smooth. As we move single file to a new field, Michael tells his version of the events of the day and I listen. There is so much tension now, he says, though he tries to analyze where he might have been at fault in it all.

"I thought maybe if I left, it would get better," I say.

Michael is silent. So silent I can feel the vacuum where there is something he wants to say, but doesn't.

"What is it?" I say this very quietly.

He nods a bunch of times—little bobs—as though he is agreeing with the voice inside his head that is willing him to speak. "Do you think . . . nah. I don't want to say it."

"It's okay. Whatever it is."

"I mean, it's not your fault," Michael says. "The crew split into teams and Bradford's side doesn't want to talk to you."

"They don't, do they?"

"Nah. They don't understand what you are doing. Amos just keeps saying, 'I hope she tells the truth!' And I keep asking them how you are supposed to tell the truth if they don't talk to you. So you know. You can't ride with them. You can't drive a tractor. There's me. Now Juston is gone. And so you end up with Eric. I mean, it makes sense."

"Yes," I say. "Yes." I can feel that some code of conduct has been violated.

"I should go," I say.

"I think maybe it's time."

"Okay."

"I hate to put it like that, Marie, but I think it's a good idea. I know I said you should stay to the end. But harvest is almost done. Give them a week without anything else to think about. A week when it's only them and they don't have to worry about you and the book."

Michael drops me off by the trucks. We have moved to a new field and it is so dark I wonder if we are really going to cut. For a few moments all is still. A mother moose and her calf saunter by, and I stand with the crew, stunned, as the long-legged animals melt into the gray shadows on the horizon. All of a sudden Eric is beside me, with Lily. "There was a moose," I say.

"You saw one? Good." Then "Come," he says to me. I follow him and get into the service truck.

Eric picks up the radio and speaks to the crew. "I'm with Marie. We're going to move pickups." Then he looks over. "So tell me. What did you learn?"

I push past the emotions conjured up in my body by my conversation with Michael, and the moose sighting, and tell him about Sally and about the story of the corn and the firewater and the Book of Mormon. And he listens all the way through, eager, as always, to apprehend something new about the world and how it works. And when I am done with the story, he shakes his head and says, "That doesn't sound right."

Neither of us can say anything else for a while.

"Some people say that's why the Holocaust happened. The Jews were no longer a righteous people," he finally tells me.

"Do you think . . ."

"That doesn't sound right to me either. You look at Jesus. He did *not* go around killing people." He shakes his head. "Like I say. I believe in free will." I think: *He's a Jesus guy.*

It is very dark when we get to the abandoned pickup. I climb out of Lily and into the pickup and follow Eric back to the site where the trucks and the combines have been left by the crew. Luther and Michael are still there—the others have gone back to the main camp. And so we pick up the extra boys and drive back to the trailers, where Emily has supper waiting.

I don't give much warning that I am leaving.

Because I am in Idaho, it is easy to find services that will ship my books and paraphernalia home to San Francisco. Had we still been on the Great Plains, it would have required considerable planning to get to a town that had boxes and tape for sale.

It's so quiet when it is time for me to leave. The crew has long been gone from the campsite; they are out in the field, working. But I say goodbye to Emily and I try to make it quick because it is emotional for me. She calls after me: "I will pray for you and pray that you find Jesus!" There is an unrestrained and incautious quality to her voice that I have never heard before, as if she's singing at a register I didn't know her voice could reach.

This is the real Emily, I think, the one who is worried that I haven't found Jesus, and that I am in particular need of him. I tell her, "Thank you," and get into my car and drive.

★ ★ ★ ★

PART FIVE

FIFTEEN

I WAIT TO FEEL MY OLD SELF REAPPEAR, but it doesn't. When I talk, it is as if my speech has been affected, and I can't carry on conversations the way I used to. I try, for example, to tell my friends who are people of color that there are in fact other people in the heartland who do not want Trump as president, and who I believe are good people, but who do not know any people of color. In some instances, I am told that this is not true, and that people in the heartland do know all about people of color but choose to ignore them. And I say that the only times I ever saw people of color in harvest were when I drove—sometimes for an hour—to a nail salon, or when I was on an Indian reservation. But still they are sure that in the country there are people of color and it is not possible to escape people of color.

If my friends who are people of color had seen me talking to white people in the heartland, would I have seemed excessively acquiescent, and to be enabling prejudice against my own people? Would I have seemed weak? Have I, in trying so hard to build a bridge, simply erased myself? I need to be angrier to speak to the people in the heartland. There is no being righteous without being angry. I think about this, and I think of the last few days on harvest, and I set both of these experiences inside my head, as if my brain is a little scale, and the scales swing wildly back and forth.

I wander around the city that is my home. There are so many words everywhere, and because this is San Francisco, someone is always trying to get me to pay attention to an app for my phone that is going to make my life easier. I can simply live here in the city with all these people, and the diversity of goods will flood into the city, and as long as I retain my ability to look at all the words and pick all the ones I want, I can adorn my life the way that I want, as though every transaction that takes place is a Starbucks order. At the end, someone will call my name and hand me my cup of coffee made precisely the way I want, with all of my customized, individual decisions implemented by a team of other people, and in this cup, I am drinking my own individual self, to be distinguished from everyone else.

I can fool myself into thinking that everything that disturbed me in the country is not in the city. Because, of course, all the things that are in the country are in the city too. How did we even get the land on which we built the buildings? And doesn't the city still need the food that comes from the country? We still require that land. We are still thinking the way we must think in order to settle the land. If we had not settled the land the way we have, then we would not have the farms. We would not need to restore the soil. We would not need to control the weeds. The prairies would be intact and the animals would still have their home.

It doesn't take too long after I'm home for me to pause in the grocery store. Should I buy organic? Maybe I am completely wrong to defend the modern system of farming in any way. Maybe if I didn't own land, then my own confirmation bias would not seek the science that defends how we farm. Maybe I would become a consumer of organic food only. And this feeling of being split—a feeling I know so well—annoys me. I feel as if I am not quite any one person and that I am always trying to appease someone else—a representation of a human that is more whole than I can ever be.

But I do own land. I own land because my great-grandfather Melvin decided he could plant trees on 160 acres of land, which the government gave him for free, after clearing the land for settlement. The government gave Melvin the land for free, after removing the Native population that had been there onto reservations, so the land looked empty when he arrived. Our family prospered. We farmed and my father went and served in the military, and on to college, and his siblings, too, became educated and traveled citizens of the world. And then I was born, and, were it not for the sentimental streak in our family that made us hold on to the land, I would not have gone and asked the questions I have asked so the land would speak back and tell me its history, which I would hold with me when I returned to the city.

Why does the Bible end with a city?

Revelation was not a slam-dunk canonical text, and much ink has been spilled on the history of its inclusion, and near exclusion. Luther didn't want Revelation in his newly reorganized Bible at all. People continue to argue about the author, known as John of Patmos, Patmos being a small island in Greece with a cave where a Christian mystic had been sent into exile. But was this the John who wrote the Gospel of John, or someone else entirely?

Most people do agree, however, that Revelation should be seen as wartime literature, as it was most likely written during the first century, when Christians were being persecuted and the second temple in Jerusalem had been destroyed, and the Jews and followers of Christ scattered. Christ had said his second coming would be very soon, and this was the hope and the message with which his followers had been left. It was now a hundred years after he died, and still he had not come back. Conventional wisdom says that John of Patmos was trying to comfort Christians who were being persecuted by the Roman emperor. A more modern view of Revelation is that the author was trying to both comfort and inspire local Christians in Asia Minor, where John of Patmos lived, who were thinking of modifying their Christian beliefs in order to live more harmoniously with the majority of locals, most of whom practiced the religion of the occupying Roman Empire. They were trying to fit in. John was trying to scare them into holding the line. Daniel Kahneman and the Gormans say that when our confirmation bias is affirmed, it feels good. Revelation confirmed a lot of preexisting bias.

For most modern evangelicals, Revelation is a book to be taken literally, and where, literally, does the Bible say all the good people go to start over once Christ finally returns? To a city.

The Bible is replete with images of the city, beginning with Cain. But if we focus on the few key texts referencing both the "New Jerusalem" and the "New Earth," as Revelation does, there are two citations to examine. The Book of Isaiah contains a reference to the new earth, or the new world, which will be created when man is finally redeemed from sin: "See, I will create new heavens and a new earth. The former things will not be remembered, nor will they come to mind. But be glad and rejoice forever in what I will create, for I will create Jerusalem to be a delight, and its people a joy." Isaiah says that when this new Jerusalem is created, everyone will forget the old world; we will all start over with no memory of the past. Isaiah is from the Old Testament, which means that Christ with his message of brotherly love has not yet shown up.

Ezekiel, also in the Old Testament, foresees a new earth and a new Jerusalem, though his prophecy is so elusive and complicated, it is occasionally referred to as one of the most difficult Bible texts to understand. All the same, he took the time to lay out clear dimensions of the city of new Jerusalem. This city of 4,500 cubits on each side is about 1.5 miles on each side. Note that the land outside this city is intended for other purposes, including food production and farming, with traditional tilling.

John of Patmos would have been aware of Ezekiel's vision when he wrote—or was inspired to write—Revelation. But there are some big differences between Revelation's new Jerusalem and Ezekiel's. John of Patmos is not describing a rebuilt Jerusalem put back on its hill so the temple of David stands once more. His new Jerusalem is a new city that comes down to the new earth from the sky, like a spaceship, after the old earth has been destroyed. "I saw the Holy City, the new Jerusalem, coming down out of heaven from God, prepared as a bride beautifully dressed for her husband. And I heard a loud voice from the throne saying, 'Look! God's dwelling place is now among the people, and he will dwell with them. They will be his people, and God himself will be with them and will be their God.'"

We are given the actual dimensions of this new city in the Bible. In the New Living Translation, we are told: "The angel who talked to me held in his hand a gold measuring stick to measure the city, its gates, and its wall. When he measured it, he found it was a square, as wide as it was long. In fact, its length and width and height were each 1,400 miles. Then he measured the walls and found them to be 216 feet thick (according to the human standard used by the angel). The wall was made of jasper and the city was pure gold, as clear as glass. The wall of the city was built on foundation stones inlaid with twelve precious stones."

Other translations of the Bible claim that the city will be 12,000 furlongs on each side. The King James Bible refers to 12,000 stadia. Depending on whether you take the "stadia" or the "furlong" position, the city will be either 1,400 or 1,500 miles on each side. If each side of the city is 1,500 miles long, then each side of the city would be about the distance from San Francisco to Denver. The top of the city would penetrate the earth's atmosphere. Most of the illustrations I find online seem to envision the city as a giant cube, though some artists interpret the vagueness of "height" to mean that the city could be a giant pyramid.

This new city is "gold, as clear as glass." There are twelve gates, and the foundation is covered with every single jewel, which means it gleams like a rainbow. The city will include a tree of life—not spotted since man was exiled from the Garden of Eden—on either side of a river that flows through the center of the city, and which will every month produce fruits for everyone to eat. This is the end of farming. Everyone will live in the city except for "dogs, those who practice magic arts, the sexually immoral, the murderers, the idolaters, and everyone who loves and practices falsehood." The city is now the place to be; there are no bucolic estates out in the country.

The "gold, as clear as glass" line was confusing to me until I spent several days online, lost in the many renderings of new Jerusalem that artists have attempted over the years. In addition to the practically minded blog posts for which people have folded yellow paper into a cube, then plunked the cube down on a globe to demonstrate exactly how big the new city will be, many artists have drawn what the new earth and the new city might look like. Some of the cities cannot escape the lure of MGM's Emerald City in *The Wizard of Oz*, and are depicted with turrets and spires, even though John of Patmos is pretty clear that the new city will be flat and shiny. Of the many images I saw, the one that most intrigued me depicted the city as made out of a material that looked like an LCD screen that was gold but clear; on the inside were the trees of life, the jewels, and the rivers.

So this new Jerusalem is not the same as Ezekiel's new Jerusalem, and the rabbit hole that is the internet will provide you with many explanations of why this is.

Some will say that the two cities contradict each other completely. The believers in inerrancy say either that John's vision cancels out Ezekiel's or that the cities are a metaphor for something going on inside of us or on Earth. One of the other explanations I have read postulates that Ezekiel's vision of new Jerusalem is here with us now, and that John of Patmos was very clearly describing the future. Regardless, most Christians who believe in the prophetic value of Revelation are certain that it foreshadows what is to come.

Because there is no mistake: Revelation is the end. We are nearing the end. The problem for me as a reader is that the book does not end with "the end." The end is a city. This, evangelicals say, is metaphorical. Either way, why are we not paying more attention to what's inside that city? Why do we not talk about the renewed tree of life?

I had joked with Juston that the tree sounded like the *Star Trek* replicator, but in fact, this idea is not so far-fetched. If there are no more farms in new Jerusalem, this means we will have found some other way to make food; the Bible does not imply that we will have stopped eating. As if by magic, the tree of life will give us something to eat. What is technology but a kind of magic?

It takes a while, but eventually I hear from Juston. He is back in school—back in his world of books and classes. He's still upset at how badly the summer went, and I'm still convinced I can see what he can't, which is that the crew isn't used to difference, by which I mean me, and that I caused all the tension. If there could be three versions of this story—me, the white me, and the purely Asian me—we could compare them, and then we would have proof of what really happened. We would have data points. Instead, what we have is my own subjective interpretation. And in my interpretation, the land saw me and responded to me because of my face.

I am perplexed by Juston's insistence on staying at his Christian university. If he has figured out how his world works, and if he sees all its flaws, why would he continue to stay there, studying everything through the lens of the Bible? Why won't he come to the secular world? At the same time, there is something not quite right about my longing for him to come over to "my side." It speaks of conversion, as if all he or any of us has to do is pick a team. It means I am trying to turn him into something else, and this is not what I want to do to him, or to anyone else. So what is he hanging on to?

I ask him. And he tells me that his life in college has been fundamentally changed by two teachers he has had and that he would like me to meet them.

I go to visit Juston at school.

The teachers have heard of me. One whom I will call Thomas teaches Bible studies and theology and on the surface reminds me of many of the scholarly men I have met in my life. He is white, married, in his late fifties, and physically fit from walks and biking. He has short white hair, and a smile floats easily across his face.

Our early conversation is in a Starbucks. We talk in circles, revisiting points as we get to know each other, before breaking off into anecdotes about biking trails, or Juston's farm, or wisdom I have gleaned from the Bible. I want to demonstrate that I am open to whatever he might say, that I have not shown up with an encrusted shell of urban, secular skepticism, and that my reflex is not to treat his faith as a joke. And he wants, very clearly, for me to know that it is not his place to judge me.

We speak around topics in the Bible. The subject of shalom comes up—that perfection encapsulated in Genesis 1 and represented by the reappearance of the tree of life in the city at the end of the Bible. "Is that a city or a metaphor?" I ask.

"Oh, it's a city," he assures me.

We spend quite a bit of time talking about the nature of faith and certainty. And then he says: "I see my job as saving kids from fundamentalism."

He is a Christian who has lived among Christians, searching for students who want to know God—Jesus—but who want relief from the world of lies in which they have been raised. It seems like a gargantuan task. "How do you do that?" I ask

"It takes time. It is a long game. Every now and then I toss out a line and see who catches it and who is ready. And they reveal themselves."

"What do you say?"

"I might ask a class: 'What is the opposite of faith?' And invariably, because of the way they have been raised and taught, some of them will say: 'Doubt.' And then I reply, 'Wrong! The opposite of faith is certainty.' To doubt is natural." He shifts his weight in his seat and his eyes ignite. "And then, inevitably, there will be one or two who come up to me afterward and say: 'That thing about faith. Can we talk about that?' And then from there we can start to deconstruct the cultural, messed-up things that have been tied up in what's actually essential to the Christian faith."

There is a narrative we follow in the secular world about how someone goes from being an evangelical Christian to a member of the "modern" world. In that narrative, the Christian realizes that the Bible is full of inaccuracies, and realizes that many of its treasured beliefs are false. I am thinking of when my cousin Brian and I recently went to see an exhibit on the Dead Sea Scrolls. After my year with the Bible and all my churchgoing, I had found it deeply moving to see fragments of these old texts that humans had lived and died to protect and pass down to us, now living in a future world they could not have imagined. Brian looked at me and said: "Well, that was sort of like an exhibit on *The Lord of the Rings* for me, and why people believe in fantasy." And I had understood this too.

It was in fact the exact question—"What is the opposite of faith?"—that had prompted Juston to take note of Thomas. Juston had been so filled with doubt, he had felt almost unable to contain it. And yet doubt is invisible. You cannot know as you walk down the street who is filled with doubt and who is not. Particularly if people smile. You can look at faces and bodies and try to scan for expressions of doubt, but the human is a remarkable creature, capable of deception.

When I ask my friend who studies evolutionary biology why we doubt, he says, with complete and sincere rationality: "Every model needs a testing mechanism." It must be part of our design to doubt. So doubt is not the enemy of God. Rather, doubt is losing faith altogether that there exists something in us that wants transcendence and that we can find it.

I ask Thomas how long he has been finding these students and he tells me it has been thirty years. Three decades of patiently looking for anyone who is a seeker. There are students who, for whatever reason, must go to Christian colleges, but who are suspicious of the stricter elements of evangelical thinking. Once in school they do not know where to turn. The world of the city—my world—feels like too abrupt of a transition and isn't always supportive of or sensitive to their desire to maintain a connection to Jesus. And these students are not looking to "get out." They are looking for a true communion with God. This is his work; he waits, and year after year he looks for the students who need him.

Because he is fluent in the language of Evangelicalism, Thomas can deliver an entire sermon the way the architects of the institution expect but that reflects things he believes. He can find students like Juston and ease their pain, pointing them to the books and the thinkers and the ways of being that allow them to be Christians, but perhaps closer to what Christ actually intended. Because, he says, this search and these conflicts about what is true are ancient.

Juston takes me to see another teacher. We meet in a small window-less office. This teacher, named Bruce, runs an urban ministries pro-gram in which young people go into the city once a week and volunteer at a multipurpose facility that provides immunizations, AIDS medica-tion, and primary health care in a poor neighborhood.

He has only twenty-five minutes for me. "So," he says breezily when we sit down, "what are your questions?"

I explain that, during the summer, I ran into so many instances of being told that some behavior or attitude was "city." And at the same time, I saw that there were certain tensions that revolved around the issue of race. "When they are upset," I say, "what are they upset about? Is it city? Or is it race?"

He nods in the way people do when they are trying to suppress a laugh, and he says: "It's race. Okay? It's very simple. This country was founded on the principle that landownership is for white men. Everyone else was either cleared out, put on a reservation, hired to work, or en-slaved. It is a history that this country has not yet come to terms with. And when you go into the city and you see the faces of black people, you must deal with it. You might reread Martin Luther King Jr. He was our last great prophet."

"And Revelation ends with a city," I say. "Is the city metaphorical, or is it real?"

"It's a city." His eyes gleam.

"My understanding is that evangelicals often say that it's a metaphor . . ."

"Convenient, isn't it." He's from Australia and has the kind of deep baritone voice members of the Commonwealth have when their child-hoods knew no nasal, coastal American twang. "They make it meta-phorical when it suits them and literal when it suits them."

"Then how do you know it's literal?"

His answer, when he gives it, is so pure and so straightforward, I won-der why I did not think of it myself. He says: "Because. God loves people. And the people are in the city."

★ ★ ★ ★

EPILOGUE

★ ★ ★ ★

IT IS ONE YEAR LATER and I am in Kimball for harvest.

A storm is approaching and I am sitting in the entry to the Quonset, alone, watching as the first raindrops fall. My back is to the west, my face to the east. The water falls on the back of the Quonset first, moving over me in a sheet. The water starts to stain the ground. I think, *Why is it that certain parts of the concrete retain their gray color and do not become wet?* If the water is falling randomly, why is there a pattern to the dryness? Juston texts me from the field and asks where I am and I tell him. "I'm sitting in the doorway to the Quonset," I say.

My cousin Paul has returned from photocopying documents at the courthouse and he finds me sitting on the ground. I took a time-lapse movie of the pattern the rain made when it fell, and we talk about the pattern, and wonder why some parts of the concrete seem to stay dry longer, as though they can resist the raindrops. When Eric and Juston arrive, they find us discussing the video.

"That sounds like something the Mocketts would talk about," Eric says.

Paul goes inside, and for a time, it is Eric, Juston, and me, watching the rain.

"It's about over," Eric finally says. Then, "There will be a rainbow soon."

"That way?" I point west.

He smiles. "That way." He points east.

We stand in the doorway and gaze eastward. After a while, Eric goes to the back of the Quonset and comes back carrying the picnic bench. He sets it down with a thump in the entrance and the three of us sit and stare at the sky. It is as if we are sitting in a theater, waiting for a performance to begin. The rain fades. And then to the left, I see a faint pattern, a two-inch spread of color: red, orange, yellow, green, blue, indigo, violet. It is as if someone is painting. The colors are faint, and it is as though someone is painting them over and over, brightening the colors and stretching them wider until they bend into an arch.

"There it is!" I stand up. I look at Eric, and he doesn't say anything, but he is smiling.

The rainbow smiles too. It widens into a full arch from end to end. One side merges into the new pickup truck that Eric is driving, and over the top of the abandoned buildings across the street, and then leans down over a tree and into the ground. It is so low.

"There must be a double," Eric says. "Usually there are two, if one is low like that."

And so we look, and sure enough, above this first rainbow is a second one.

I know that Eric has said this about the rainbows only because he knows the sky and the rainbows and storms. I know that it is years of observing clouds and water and the sun that led him to know that the rainbow would appear here, but it is still a magical thing to me that he could see what was coming.

It feels as if we are the only people in the world watching the rainbow. As the storm continues east and the sun emerges from the cloud cover, the colors intensify. Eric smiles harder.

"Do you like your work?" he asks me about the book.

"Yes," I say. "It will be hard to let go."

He nods. "What surprised you about it?" he asks.

So I tell him that the thing that most surprised me was how terrible people could be. I am talking about our country's history. I should know, I say, that people are cruel to one another. But I had not realized how cruel. And at the same time, I said, I had not expected to have a meaningful experience of the Gospels and of Jesus.

"I felt like I was being cut in half," I say. "On the one hand, I was learning again how terrible man is to man. And on the other hand, I was learning why Christ's message matters. Half of me was being lifted up. And the other half was so terribly hurt."

"The hurt is why we have Jesus," Juston says.

"You can't have one without the other?" I ask.

The men nod. "Maybe you're a Christian." Eric smiles his private Eric smile, the slightly self-satisfied one.

"Maybe," I say. "I do think that everything he said was true."

"If everything he said is true, then do you think he was the son of God?" Juston asks me.

"Does it matter? He told us what God is. Everything he said we should do is what God is."

My cousin Paul comes out for a moment to look at the rainbow. "Is that my imagination, or is there an extra streak of violet in between the rainbows?"

"Looks like it," Eric says. "Take a photo. Camera won't lie." Paul takes a picture and goes back inside the bunkhouse.

We sit and talk a little more. Luther is working on the farm for Eric; so is Samuel, and both have returned for harvest. Everyone else is new. There are no women on the crew this year. Bethany and Samuel are dating. The dynamic between the crew, Juston says, is harmonious.

Lately, Eric has been wondering if, had he been alive during the colonial days, he would have killed Indians. He would like to think he would not have killed anyone. But he is not sure. In Scott City, Kansas, they had, as a family, gone to the El Quartelejo Museum, which is housed in a reconstruction of an Indian pueblo and recounts the history, archeology, and geology of western Kansas. He had passed that museum for thirty years, Eric says. Finally, this year, they had all gone inside together.

Eric nods at the rainbow. "That'll be the peak about now. If you want your picture without the telephone wires in the way, now would be a good time."

There are still a few clouds in the sky, but they are white now and the color of the sky is blue. The second rainbow has dimmed but the first one has brightened in intensity. I run out to take some pictures, and then go back to the picnic bench to watch the rainbow fade. It holds its shape for us for a long time. Whoever is painting the colors is not going to let go easily. The right side disappears first, and the original left side remains. Then it is just the upper left corner, with the red most prominent. And then the red, too, slips away, and the day is bright and hot and yellow again.

ACKNOWLEDGMENTS

I am grateful to my agent, Ellen Levine, for her enthusiasm for and belief in this kernel of an idea. Thank you to Ethan Nosowsky at Graywolf Press for his trust, care, and guidance. Without the Wolgemuth family, there would be no harvest and there would be no adventure and I am indebted to the entire family and to the crew. Thank you to all the people in the Great Plains who appear in these pages and shared their world with me. I am particularly grateful for Pastor Jeff, Cos Cosgrove, Mark Jalovick, the Lovelands, and the Slagells.

I am glad to be home with Graywolf Press, and the fabulous Fiona McCrae. Thank you to Katie Dublinski, Marisa Atkinson, Steve Woodward, and Jeff Shotts. Thank you to Emily Fox-Penner and Yana Makuwa for vital last-minute assistance and to Caitlin Van Dusen for thorough editing. Thank you to Angela Bagetta for expertise in publicity and Caroline Nitz for the support from home base. Thank you to Martha Wydysh at Trident Media for all her help.

A special thank you to Garnette Cadogan and to Annie Dillard. The Birkhofers and Yung families were generous with their knowledge and time; thank you for sharing your hearts and teaching me to open mine. Thank you again to Juston Wolgemuth for teaching me to see the world anew.

I am grateful for my creative community. In no particular order, thank you to Mark Sarvas, Jennifer Carson, Benjamin Anastas, Craig Teicher, Sean Patrick Muldowney, Kaytie Lee, Michael Smith, Idra Novey, Sunil Yapa, Jeffrey Lependorf, Rick Barot, Porochista Khakpour, Matthew McKelway, Christa Paravanni, Alia Volz, Allison Devers, Deborah Green, Scott Janssens, Jennie Livingston, Alan Heathcock, Rebecca Loveland, Mark Wunderlich, Dave Moses, Greg Pliska, Eurydice

Kamvyselli, Rigoberto Gonzales, Ken Chen, Jessica Mendels, Oliver de la Paz, April Ayers Lawson, Geffrey Davis, Karissa Sanbonmatsu, Jenny Johnson, Barrie Jean Borich, Tomas Morin, Hasanthika Sirisena, Todd Alexander, Steven LeComber, Liz Mandel, Stephen Sparks, Rachel Malina, Vu Tran, Claire Dederer, Kurt Kurasaki, Scott Killdall, Marlon James, Susan Cheever, Julian McNamara, Kate Farrell, a few anonymous people, and Doug Bauer.

Thank you, Sumaya Agha, for a friendship that began in high school and for your gorgeous photographs. The Bennington writers workshop gave me solid support, and structure; thank you, Sven Birkerts and Mark Wunderlich. Thank you to the UCross Foundation for a safe haven to do numerous revisions. The Dora Maar House in Menerbes, France, was the most beautiful place to do final edits. Victoria Chang and Ed Skoog invited me to Idyllwild Writers Week, where I was lucky to finish copy edits at Sky Rock.

Thank you, Orlando White, for asking me who my people are, and starting a conversation that continues. Jean Paul Courtens, Kent Lundberg, and Grant Lundberg were very generous in demonstrating how they farm organically. Thank you to the MOSES Organic Conference and Eco-Farm Organic Conference for not only teaching me so much about farming but for the work they do to help educate and train current and future farmers. Thank you, Jayson Lusk, for taking time with our correspondence. Michael Doane and his family taught me about the wheat belt and the importance of soil health. Matt Friederichs understood my story before I did. Steve Casner was so generous with his friends and contacts. Patrick McConigley walked me through eons of geological history; thank you to Nina McConigley for helping me to more accurately portray our heartland.

Thank you to the Mockett, Markley, and Quinette families and to Brian in particular for housing me and feeding me through so many drafts and to Jane who was there from the start. My mother, Kazuko, has always been a force for good. My husband, Gordon Drummond, made my absences from the family possible and has always shouldered numerous responsibilities with so much grace, patience, and care. I can't work without you. Thank you to Ewan Mockett Drummond for assistance with the bibliography, and for his sure moral compass.

BIBLIOGRAPHICAL NOTES

I could not have written *American Harvest* without these books and the many others that I list below. There are many books about the theological and historical roots of evangelical Christianity, but I was especially grateful for those that attempt to represent or explain the lived experience of Christians. The authors that Juston recommended to me—Rob Bell, Mike McHargue, and Richard Rohr—were particularly helpful in that regard. I am also deeply grateful for the scholarship of Karen Armstrong and Elaine Pagels.

Wilfred M. McClay's *Land of Hope: An Invitation to the Great American Story* offers a comprehensive, if conservative, account of the formation of the United States, while Jill Lepore's *These Truths: A History of the United States* covers a broader canvas by incorporating the voices of characters such as George Washington's former slave Harry Washington. I learned a lot from books by historians David Brion Davis and Albert J. Raboteau, who explore the role Christianity played in the institution of slavery and within slave communities.

Mark A. Noll's *The Civil War as a Theological Crisis* and David L. Chappell's *A Stone of Hope: Prophetic Religion and the Death of Jim Crow* do a beautiful and grounded job of tracing Christianity's impact on the great struggle for civil rights; separately, I was convinced by Jill Lepore's argument that historians have not done enough to study religion as a face of the human story.

While writing *American Harvest*, I tried to understand my own biases; if I could do that, then perhaps I could better understand those of other people. I am indebted to Daniel Kahneman's *Thinking, Fast and Slow* for its analysis of how and why we make decisions. It turns out that our gut isn't always wiser than our rational mind; it also turns out that our rationality isn't always equipped to convince us of what is true. Sara E. Gorman and Jack M. Gorman's *Denying to the Grave: Why We Ignore the Facts That Will Save Us* is a wonderful companion read.

I have always loved cities, and after I wrote this book, they have taken on greater meaning than I had ever expected. The wonderfully rich scholarship of Jane Jacobs and, in particular, Richard Sennett has transformed my sense of the complex significance of cities and the ways in which they can shape and change the human experience.

When quoting the Bible, I have defaulted to the New International Version. Because Emily uses the New Living Translation, when she speaks, she quotes that version of the Bible. In a few instances, characters read from the King James Bible.

Abbott, E. C. "Teddy Blue" and Helena Huntington Smith. *We Pointed Them North: Recollections of a Cowpuncher.* Norman: University of Oklahoma Press, 1955.

Armstrong, Karen. *The Bible: A Biography.* New York: Grove Press, 2007.

———. *The Great Transformation: The Beginning of Our Religious Traditions.* New York: Alfred A. Knopf, 2006.

———. *A History of God: The 4,000-Year Quest of Judaism, Christianity and Islam.* New York: Ballantine Books, 1994.

Barber, Dan. *The Third Plate: Field Notes on the Future of Food.* New York: Penguin Books, 2014.

Bell, Rob. *Love Wins: A Book about Heaven, Hell, and the Fate of Every Person Who Ever Lived.* New York: HarperOne, 2011.

———. *What Is the Bible? How an Ancient Library of Poems, Letters, and Stories Can Transform the Way You Think and Feel about Everything.* New York: HarperOne, 2017.

Bender, Thomas. *Toward an Urban Vision: Ideas and Institutions in Nineteenth-Century America.* Lexington: University of Kentucky Press, 1975.

Berry, Wendell. *The Art of Loading Brush: New Agrarian Writings.* Berkeley, CA: Counterpoint, 2017.

———. *Citizenship Papers.* Washington, DC: Shoemaker & Hoard, 2003.

———. *The Hidden Wound.* Berkeley, CA: Counterpoint, 2010.

———. *The Unsettling of America: Culture and Agriculture.* San Francisco: Sierra Club Books, 1977.

Biss, Eula. *On Immunity: An Inoculation.* Minneapolis: Graywolf Press, 2014.

Bloom, Harold, interpreter. *The Book of J.* Translated by David Rosenberg. New York: Grove Weidenfeld, 1990.

Bogard, Paul. *The Ground Beneath Us: From the Oldest Cities to the Last Wilderness, What Dirt Tells Us about Who We Are.* New York: Little, Brown, 2017.

Bordewich, Fergus M. *Bound for Canaan: The Underground Railroad and the War for the Soul of America.* New York: Amistad, 2005.

Borg, Marcus J. *Evolution of the Word: The New Testament in the Order the Books Were Written.* New York: HarperOne, 2012.

Boynton, Robert S. *The New New Journalism: Conversations with America's Best Nonfiction Writers on Their Craft.* New York: Vintage Books, 2005.

Brown, Dee. *Bury My Heart at Wounded Knee: An Indian History of the American West.* New York: Holt, Rinehart and Winston, 1971.

Brown, Gabe. *Dirt to Soil: One Family's Journey into Regenerative Agriculture.* White River Junction, VT: Chelsea Green Publishing, 2018.

Cameron, David Kerr. *The Ballad and the Plough: A Portrait of the Life of the Old Scottish Farmtouns.* Edinburgh: Victor Gollancz, 1978.

Carson, Rachel. *Silent Spring.* Boston: Houghton Mifflin, 1962.

Carter, Kent. *The Dawes Commission and the Allotment of the Five Civilized Tribes, 1893–1914.* Orem, UT: Ancestry.com, 1999.

Chan, Francis and Preston Sprinkle. *Erasing Hell: What God Said about Eternity, and the Things We've Made Up.* Colorado Springs: David C Cook, 2011.

Chappell, David L. *A Stone of Hope: Prophetic Religion and the Death of Jim Crow.* Chapel Hill: University of North Carolina Press, 2004.

Claiborne, Shane and Jonathan Wilson-Hartgrove. *Becoming the Answer to Our Prayers: Prayer for Ordinary Radicals.* Downers Grove, IL: InterVarsity Press, 2008.

Crosscombe, Coz and Bill Krispin. *Place Matters: The Church for the Community.* Fort Washington, PA: CLC Publications, 2017.

Davis, David Brion. *Inhuman Bondage: The Rise and Fall of Slavery in the New World.* New York: Oxford University Press, 2006.

Davis, Ellen F. *Scripture, Culture, and Agriculture: An Agrarian Reading of the Bible.* New York: Cambridge University Press, 2009.

———. *And Still the Waters Run: The Betrayal of the Five Civilized Tribes.* Norman: University of Oklahoma Press, 1940.

Dawkins, Richard. *The God Delusion.* New York: Mariner Books, 2008.

———. *The Selfish Gene.* Oxford: Oxford University Press, 2016.

Debo, Angie. *A History of the Indians of the United States.* Norman: University of Oklahoma Press, 1970.

Dewey, John. *The School and Society*. Chicago: University of Chicago Press, 1967.

———and Evelyn Dewey. *Schools of Tomorrow*. New York: Dutton, 1962.

Diffendal, R. F., Jr. *Great Plains Geology*. Discover the Great Plains, edited by Richard Edwards. Lincoln: University of Nebraska Press, 2017.

Douglas, Mary. *Purity and Danger: An Analysis of Concepts of Pollution and Taboo*. London: Routledge & Kegan Paul, 1966.

Dunkelman, Marc. J. "Next-Door Strangers: The Crisis of Urban Anonymity." *Hedgehog Review* 19, no. 2 (Summer 2017): 44–57.

Edwards, Andrés R. *The Sustainability Revolution: Portrait of a Paradigm Shift*. Gabriola Island, BC: New Society Publishers, 2005.

Ekblad, Bob. *Reading the Bible with the Damned*. Louisville, KY: Westminster John Knox Press, 2005.

Emerson, Michael O. and Christian Smith. *Divided by Faith: Evangelical Religion and the Problem of Race in America*. New York: Oxford University Press, 2000.

Emerson, Ralph Waldo. *A Year with Emerson: A Daybook*. Edited by Richard Grossman. Jaffrey, NH: David R. Godine, 2003.

Fea, John. *Believe Me: The Evangelical Road to Donald Trump*. Grand Rapids, MI: Wm. B. Eerdmans, 2018.

Federal Writers' Project of the Works Progress Administration for the State of Nebraska. *Nebraska: A Guide to the Cornhusker State*. New York: Viking Press, 1939.

FitzGerald, Frances. *The Evangelicals: The Struggle to Shape America*. New York: Simon & Schuster, 2017.

Foer, Franklin. *World without Mind: The Existential Threat of Big Tech*. New York: Penguin Press, 2017.

Frank, Thomas. *What's the Matter with Kansas? How Conservatives Won the Heart of America*. New York: Metropolitan Books, 2004.

Fraser, Caroline. *Prairie Fires: The American Dreams of Laura Ingalls Wilder*. New York: Metropolitan Books, 2017.

Frazier, Ian. *Great Plains*. New York: Farrar, Straus and Giroux, 1989.

Fukuoka, Masanobu. *Sowing Seeds in the Desert: Natural Farming, Global Restoration, and Ultimate Food Security*. White River Junction, VT: Chelsea Green Publishing, 2012.

Genoways, Ted. *This Blessed Earth: A Year in the Life of an American Family Farm*. New York: W. W. Norton, 2017.

Gittinger, Roy. *The Formation of the State of Oklahoma, 1803–1906.*
Norman: University of Oklahoma Press, 1939.

Gleick, Peter H. *Bottled and Sold: The Story behind Our Obsession with
Bottled Water.* Washington, DC: Island Press, 2010.

Gorman, Sara E. and Jack M. Gorman. *Denying to the Grave: Why We
Ignore the Facts That Will Save Us.* New York: Oxford University
Press, 2017.

Greenblatt, Stephen. *The Rise and Fall of Adam and Eve.* New York:
W. W. Norton, 2017.

Grove, Noel and James Sugar. "North with the Wheat Cutters." *National
Geographic* 142, no. 2 (August 1, 1972): 194–217.

Gwynne, S. C. *Empire of the Summer Moon: Quanah Parker and the Rise
and Fall of the Comanches, the Most Powerful Indian Tribe in American
History.* New York: Scribner, 2010.

Hanson, Victor Davis. *Fields without Dreams: Defending the Agrarian Idea.*
New York: Free Press, 1996.

———. *The Land Was Everything: Letters from an American Farmer.*
New York: Free Press, 2000.

Harrison, Jim. *Dalva.* New York: Washington Square Press, 1988.

———. *The Road Home.* New York: Washington Square Press, 1998.

Harrison, Peter. *The Bible, Protestantism, and the Rise of Natural Science.*
Cambridge: Cambridge University Press, 1998.

———. *The Fall of Man and the Foundations of Science.* Cambridge:
Cambridge University Press, 2007.

———. *The Territories of Science and Religion.* Chicago: University of
Chicago Press, 2015.

Hawgood, John A. *America's Western Frontiers: The Story of the Explorers
and Settlers Who Opened Up the Trans-Mississippi West.* New York:
Alfred A. Knopf, 1967.

Hecht, Jennifer Michael. *Doubt: A History: The Great Doubters and Their
Legacy of Innovation from Socrates and Jesus to Thomas Jefferson and
Emily Dickinson.* New York: HarperCollins, 2003.

Herzfeld, Noreen. *Technology and Religion: Remaining Human in a
Co-created World.* West Conshohocken, PA: Templeton Press, 2009.

Hoagland, Edward. *Hoagland on Nature: Essays.* Guilford, CT: Lyons
Press, 2003.

Hoganson, Kristin L. *The Heartland: An American History.* New York:
Penguin Press, 2019.

Horn, Miriam. *Rancher, Farmer, Fisherman: Conservation Heroes of the American Heartland*. New York: W. W. Norton, 2016.

Howe, Daniel Walker. *Making the American Self: Jonathan Edwards to Abraham Lincoln*. New York: Oxford University Press, 1997.

Hunter, James Davison. *To Change the World: The Irony, Tragedy, and Possibility of Christianity in the Late Modern World*. New York: Oxford University Press, 2010.

Isenberg, Nancy and Andrew Burstein. "Cosmopolitanism vs. Provincialism: How the Politics of Place Hurts America." *Hedgehog Review* 19, no. 2 (Summer 2017): 58–69.

Isern, Thomas. *Custom Combining on the Great Plains: A History*. Norman: University of Oklahoma Press, 1981.

Jackson, Helen Hunt. *A Century of Dishonor: The Classic Exposé of the Plight of the Native Americans*. Overland Park, KS: Digireads, 2012.

Jackson, Kenneth T. *Crabgrass Frontier: The Suburbanization of the United States*. New York: Oxford University Press, 1985.

Jacobs, Jane. *The Death and Life of Great American Cities*. New York: Vintage Books, 1992.

James, William. *The Varieties of Religious Experience: A Study in Human Nature*. San Bernardino, CA: Renaissance Classics, 2012.

Jones, Robert P. *The End of White Christian America*. New York: Simon & Schuster, 2016.

Kahneman, Daniel. *Thinking, Fast and Slow*. New York: Farrar, Straus and Giroux, 2011.

Kamp, David. *The United States of Arugula: How We Became a Gourmet Nation*. New York: Broadway Books, 2006.

Kent, Nathaniel. *Hints to Gentlemen of Landed Property*. London: J. Dodsley in Pall-Mall, 1775.

Kermode, Frank. *The Genesis of Secrecy: On the Interpretation of Narrative*. Cambridge, MA: Harvard University Press, 1979.

———. *The Sense of an Ending: Studies in the Theory of Fiction (with a New Epilogue)*. New York: Oxford University Press, 2000.

Kidd, Thomas S. *God of Liberty: A Religious History of the American Revolution*. New York: Basic Books, 2010.

Kingsnorth, Paul. *Confessions of a Recovering Environmentalist and Other Essays*. Minneapolis: Graywolf Press, 2017.

Kraenzel, Carl Frederick. *The Great Plains in Transition*. Norman: University of Oklahoma Press, 1955.

Kugel, James L. *The Great Shift: Encountering God in Biblical Times.* New York: Houghton Mifflin Harcourt, 2017.

Lamott, Anne. *Help, Thanks, Wow: The Three Essential Prayers.* New York: Riverhead Books, 2012.

Laudan, Rachel. *Cuisine and Empire: Cooking in World History.* Berkeley: University of California Press, 2013.

Lazor, Jack. *The Organic Grain Grower: Small-Scale, Holistic Grain Production for the Home and Market Producer.* White River Junction, VT: Chelsea Green Publishing, 2013.

Lepore, Jill. *These Truths: A History of the United States.* New York: W. W. Norton, 2018.

Lewis, C. S. *Mere Christianity.* New York: HarperCollins, 2001.

———. *The Problem of Pain.* New York: Macmillan, 1944.

Logsdon, Gene. *Letter to a Young Farmer: How to Live Richly without Wealth on the New Garden Farm.* With a foreword by Wendell Berry. White River Junction, VT: Chelsea Green Publishing, 2017.

Lüdemann, Gerd. *Heretics: The Other Side of Early Christianity.* Louisville, KY: Westminster John Knox Press, 1996.

Lusk, Jayson. *The Food Police: A Well-Fed Manifesto about the Politics of Your Plate.* New York: Crown Forum, 2013.

———. *Unnaturally Delicious: How Science and Technology Are Serving Up Super Foods to Save the World.* New York: St. Martin's Press, 2016.

Lynas, Mark. *Seeds of Science: Why We Got It So Wrong on GMOs.* New York: Bloomsbury Sigma, 2018.

Maher, Harmon D., Jr., George F. Engelmann, and Robert D. Shuster. *Roadside Geology of Nebraska.* Missoula, MT: Mountain Press Publishing, 2003.

Markofski, Wes. *New Monasticism and the Transformation of American Evangelicalism.* New York: Oxford University Press, 2015.

McAlister, Melani. *The Kingdom of God Has No Borders: A Global History of American Evangelicals.* New York: Oxford University Press, 2018.

McClay, Wilfred M. *The Masterless: Self and Society in Modern America.* Chapel Hill: University of North Carolina Press, 1994

———. *Land of Hope: An Invitation to the Great American Story.* New York: Encounter Books, 2019.

———. *A Student's Guide to U.S. History.* ISI Guides to the Major Disciplines, edited by Jeffrey O. Nelson. Wilmington, DE: Intercollegiate Studies Institute, 2014.

McGrath, Alister. *Christianity's Dangerous Idea: The Protestant Revolution—a History from the Sixteenth Century to the Twenty-First.* New York: HarperOne, 2007.

McHargue, Mike. *Finding God in the Waves: How I Lost My Faith and Found It Again Through Science.* New York: Convergent Books, 2016.

McMurtry, Larry. *The Last Picture Show.* New York: Dial Press, 1966.

———. *Lonesome Dove.* New York: Simon & Schuster, 1985.

———. *Rhino Ranch.* New York: Simon & Schuster, 2009.

McPhee, John. *Rising from the Plains.* New York: Farrar, Straus and Giroux, 1986.

Mercier, Hugo and Dan Sperber. *The Enigma of Reason.* Cambridge, MA: Harvard University Press, 2017.

Merritt, Jonathan. *Learning to Speak God from Scratch: Why Sacred Words Are Vanishing—and How We Can Revive Them.* New York: Convergent Books, 2018.

Montgomery, David R. *Dirt: The Erosion of Civilizations.* Berkeley: University of California Press, 2007.

———. *Growing a Revolution: Bringing Our Soil Back to Life.* New York: W. W. Norton, 2017.

Morgan, Dan. *Merchants of Grain: The Power and Profits of the Five Giant Companies at the Center of the World's Food Supply.* Lincoln, NE: iUniverse, 2000.

Nestle, Marion. *Food Politics: How the Food Industry Influences Nutrition and Health.* Berkeley: University of California Press, 2007.

Newberg, Andrew and Mark Robert Waldman. *How God Changes Your Brain: Breakthrough Findings from a Leading Neuroscientist.* New York: Ballantine Books, 2009.

Nichols, Alice. *Bleeding Kansas.* New York: Oxford University Press, 1954.

Noll, Mark A. *America's God: From Jonathan Edwards to Abraham Lincoln.* New York: Oxford University Press, 2002.

———. *The Civil War as a Theological Crisis.* Chapel Hill: University of North Carolina Press, 2006.

———. *The New Shape of World Christianity: How American Experience Reflects Global Faith.* Downers Grove, IL: InterVarsity Press, 2009.

———. *The Rise of Evangelicalism: The Age of Edwards, Whitefield and the Wesleys.* Downers Grove, IL: InterVarsity Press, 2003.

———. *The Scandal of the Evangelical Mind.* Grand Rapids, MI: Wm. B. Eerdmans, 1994.

Oakerhater, David Pendleton. Letter to Mrs. Mary Burnham. http://
digital.library.okstate.edu/Oakerhater/Letters/DPO06141878.html.
June, 1878.

Otto, Rudolf. *The Idea of the Holy: An Inquiry into the Non-Rational
Factor in the Idea of the Divine and Its Relation to the Rational.* London:
Oxford University Press, 1950.

Pagels, Elaine. *Adam, Eve, and the Serpent.* New York: Vintage Books, 1988.

———. *The Gnostic Gospels.* New York: Vintage Books, 1979.

———. *Revelations: Visions, Prophecy, and Politics in the Book of Revelation.*
New York: Viking, 2012.

Pearcey, Nancy. *Total Truth: Liberating Christianity from Its Cultural
Captivity.* Wheaton, IL: Crossway Books, 2005.

Peterson, Eugene H. *The Message: The Bible in Contemporary Language.*
Colorado Springs: NavPress, 2002.

Pollan, Michael. *In Defense of Food: An Eater's Manifesto.* New York:
Penguin Press, 2008.

———. *The Omnivore's Dilemma: A Natural History of Four Meals.* New
York: Penguin Press, 2006.

Porterfield, Jason. *The Homestead Act of 1862: A Primary Source History
of the Settlement of the American Heartland in the Late 19th Century.*
Primary Sources in American History. New York: Rosen Publishing
Group, 2005.

Raboteau, Albert J. *Slave Religion: The "Invisible Institution" in the
Antebellum South.* New York: Oxford University Press, 2004.

Rah, Soong-Chan. *The Next Evangelicalism: Freeing the Church from
Western Cultural Captivity.* Downers Grove, IL: InterVarsity Press,
2009.

Ratner-Rosenhagen, Jennifer. *The Ideas That Made America: A Brief
History.* New York: Oxford University Press, 2019.

Richter, Sandra L. *The Epic of Eden: A Christian Entry into the Old
Testament.* Downers Grove, IL: InterVarsity Press, 2008.

Robin, Marie-Monique. *The World According to Monsanto: Pollution,
Corruption, and the Control of the World's Food Supply.* New York: New
Press, 2010.

Robinson, Jo. *Eating on the Wild Side: The Missing Link to Optimum
Health.* New York: Little, Brown, 2013.

Rohr, Richard. *Falling Upward: A Spirituality for the Two Halves of Life.*
San Francisco: Jossey-Bass, 2011.

Rosenberg, Alexander. *How History Gets Things Wrong: The Neuroscience of Our Addiction to Stories.* Cambridge, MA: MIT Press, 2018.

Rubenstein, Richard E. *When Jesus Became God: The Epic Fight over Christ's Divinity in the Last Days of Rome.* New York: Harcourt Brace, 1999.

Sagan, Carl. *The Demon-Haunted World: Science as a Candle in the Dark.* New York: Ballantine Books, 1996.

Sandoz, Mari. *The Cattlemen: From the Rio Grande across the Far Marias.* Lincoln: University of Nebraska Press, 2010.

——. *Crazy Horse: The Strange Man of the Oglalas.* New York: Alfred A. Knopf, 1942.

——. *Love Song to the Plains.* New York: Harper & Brothers, 1961.

——. *Sandhill Sundays and Other Recollections.* Lincoln: University of Nebraska Press, 1970.

——. *Slogum House.* Boston: Little, Brown, 1937.

Schniedewind, William M. *How the Bible Became a Book: The Textualization of Ancient Israel.* Cambridge: Cambridge University Press, 2004.

Scott, Eugenie C. *Evolution vs. Creationism: An Introduction.* Berkeley: University of California Press, 2005.

Scott, James C. *Against the Grain: A Deep History of the Earliest States.* New Haven, CT: Yale University Press, 2017.

Sennett, Richard. *Building and Dwelling: Ethics for the City.* New York: Farrar, Straus and Giroux, 2018.

——. *The Craftsman.* New York: Yale University Press, 2008.

——. *The Fall of Public Man.* New York: W. W. Norton, 2017.

——. *Flesh and Stone: The Body and the City in Western Civilization.* New York: W. W. Norton, 1994.

Sernett, Milton C., ed. *Afro-American Religious History: A Documentary Witness.* Durham, NC: Duke University Press, 1985.

Shannon, Fred A. *The Farmer's Last Frontier: Agriculture, 1860–1897.* Vol. 5 of *The Economic History of the United States.* New York: Farrar & Rinehart, 1945.

Sloman, Steven A. and Philip Fernbach. *The Knowledge Illusion: Why We Never Think Alone.* New York: Riverhead, 2017.

Smarsh, Sarah. *Heartland: A Memoir of Working Hard and Being Broke in the Richest Country on Earth.* New York. Scribner, 2018.

Smoley, Richard. *Inner Christianity: A Guide to the Esoteric Tradition.* Boston: Shambhala, 2002.

Stilgebouer, F. G. *Nebraska Pioneers: The Story of Sixty-Five Years of Pioneering in Southwest Nebraska 1875–1940.* Grand Rapids, MI: Wm. B. Eerdmans, 1944.

Stone Barns Center for Food and Agriculture. *Letters to a Young Farmer: On Food, Farming, and Our Future.* Edited by Martha Hogkins. New York: Princeton Architectural Press, 2017.

Taylor, Charles. *Sources of the Self: The Making of the Modern Identity.* Cambridge, MA: Harvard University Press, 1989.

Thoreau, Henry David: *The Illustrated Walden: Thoreau Bicentennial Edition.* New York: TarcherPerigee, 2016.

Toly, Noah. "The New Urban Agenda and the Limits of Cities." *Hedgehog Review* 19, no. 2 (Summer 2017): 36–43.

Trimble, Donald E. *The Geologic Story of the Great Plains: A Nontechnical Description of the Origin and Evolution of the Landscape of the Great Plains.* Medora, ND: Theodore Roosevelt Nature and History Association, 1990.

White, Morton and Lucia White. *The Intellectual versus the City, from Thomas Jefferson to Frank Lloyd Wright.* New York: New American Library, 1962.

Wilde, Parke. *Food Policy in the United States: An Introduction.* New York: Routledge, 2013.

Wilder, Laura Ingalls. *By the Shores of Silver Lake.* New York: Harper Trophy, 1971.

———. *Little House on the Prairie.* New York: Harper Trophy, 1971.

Wilson, Edward O. *The Creation: An Appeal to Save Life on Earth.* New York: W. W. Norton, 2006.

Wirzba, Norman. *Food and Faith: A Theology of Eating.* New York: Cambridge University Press, 2011.

Woodward, C. Vann. *The Old World's New World.* New York: Oxford University Press, 1991.

Worthen, Molly. *Apostles of Reason: The Crisis of Authority in American Evangelicalism.* New York: Oxford University Press, 2014.

Wright, N. T. *The Day the Revolution Began: Reconsidering the Meaning of Jesus's Crucifixion.* New York: HarperOne, 2016.

———. *Surprised by Hope: Rethinking Heaven, the Resurrection, and the Mission of the Church.* New York: HarperOne, 2008.

Yates, Joshua. "Saving the Soul of the Smart City." *Hedgehog Review* 19, no. 2 (Summer 2017): 18–35.

Zahnd, Brian. *A Farewell to Mars: An Evangelical Pastor's Journey toward the Biblical Gospel of Peace.* Colorado Springs: David C Cook, 2014.

———. *Sinners in the Hands of a Loving God: The Scandalous Truth of the Very Good News.* New York: WaterBrook, 2017.

MARIE MUTSUKI MOCKETT is the author of a novel, *Picking Bones from Ash*, and a memoir, *Where the Dead Pause, and the Japanese Say Goodbye*, which was a finalist for the PEN Open Book Award. She lives in San Francisco.

The text of *American Harvest* is set in Scala Pro. Book design by Ann Sudmeier. Composition by Bookmobile Design & Digital Publisher Services, Minneapolis, Minnesota. Manufactured by Sheridan on acid-free, 30 percent postconsumer wastepaper.

This book is made possible through a partnership with the College of Saint Benedict, and honors the legacy of S. Mariella Gable, a distinguished teacher at the College.

Previous titles in this series include:

Loverboy by Victoria Redel

The House on Eccles Road by Judith Kitchen

One Vacant Chair by Joe Coomer

The Weatherman by Clint McCown

Collected Poems by Jane Kenyon

Variations on the Theme of an African Dictatorship by Nuruddin Farah:
  Sweet and Sour Milk
  Sardines
  Close Sesame

Duende by Tracy K. Smith

All of It Singing: New and Selected Poems by Linda Gregg

The Art of Syntax: Rhythm of Thought, Rhythm of Song by Ellen Bryant Voigt

How to Escape from a Leper Colony by Tiphanie Yanique

One Day I Will Write About This Place by Binyavanga Wainaina

The Convert: A Tale of Exile and Extremism by Deborah Baker

On Sal Mal Lane by Ru Freeman

Citizen: An American Lyric by Claudia Rankine

On Immunity: An Inoculation by Eula Biss

Cinder: New and Selected Poems by Susan Stewart

The Art of Death: Writing the Final Story by Edwidge Danticat

A Lucky Man by Jamel Brinkley

Oculus by Sally Wen Mao

Support for this series has been provided by the Manitou Fund as part of the Warner Reading Program.